Louis Nedelec

The History Of The Early Cambro-British Christians

Louis Nedelec

The History Of The Early Cambro-British Christians

ISBN/EAN: 9783741138225

Manufactured in Europe, USA, Canada, Australia, Japa

Cover: Foto ©ninafisch / pixelio.de

Manufactured and distributed by brebook publishing software (www.brebook.com)

Louis Nedelec

The History Of The Early Cambro-British Christians

CAMBRIA SACRA;

OR,

THE HISTORY OF THE EARLY CAMBRO-BRITISH CHRISTIANS.

BY THE
Rev. LOUIS NÉDÉLEC, O.C.

"Memento dierum antiquorum, cogita generationes singulas; interroga patrem tuum et annuntiabit tibi, majores tuos et dicent tibi.

Remember the days of old, think upon every generation; ask thy father, and he will declare to thee; thy elders, and they will tell thee."—DEUT., xxxii 7.

DANIEL OWEN AND CO., CARDIFF.

DEDICATED

(BY KIND PERMISSION)

TO THE MOST HONOURABLE

JOHN PATRICK CRICHTON STUART,

MARQUESS OF BUTE.

zed by Google

CONTENTS.

CHAPTER I.

SUMMARY OF THE HISTORY OF RELIGION IN BRITAIN, FROM THE INTRODUCTION OF CHRISTIANITY, DOWN TO THE ARRIVAL OF ST. GERMANUS, AS THE CHAMPION OF TRUTH AGAINST PELAGIANISM.

Britain described first by the pen of a Roman General—Customs and civilisation of the Britons—Bold horsemen—Religion represented by Druidism—Its organisation—The oak tree and the mistletoe—Duration of the Roman occupation—Its influence on the natives—Introduction of Christianity—Contrast between the military conqueror and the peaceful messenger of the Gospel—St. Peter and St. Paul, St. Joseph of Arimathea, Bran, Claudia, and Pomponia Græcina—Intercourse of nations created by the wide-spread Roman Empire a means in the hands of Divine Providence for the propagation of the Gospel—Second and third centuries—King Lucius—His family—Sends Ambassadors to Pope Eleutherius—His conversion, and that of his subjects—A Hierarchy established—The names of Churches built in Britain under Lucius—His death and burial in Gloucester—St. Mellon—First Bishop of Rouen—The first nine persecutions against the Church not carried out in Britain—Publication of the tenth persecution—Constantius puts his household to the test—St. Alban, the first British martyr—SS. Aaron and Julius, martyrs at Caerleon, on the river Usk—Constantius on his death-bed, at York, foretells better days for the Christians—Constantine Emperor—St. Helena—British Bishops assist at various Catholic Councils on the Continent—St. Ursula and her companions Martyrs—Pelagius, or Morgan—Palladius in Ireland and Scotland—St. Patrick—St. Germanus and Lupus—A few observations on the fall of the Roman Empire.

(Page 1 to 49.)

CHAPTER II.

THE CAMBRO-BRITONS AND THE PAPACY.

The history of the British Church, confined to the western part of the island, from the days of Germanus down to St. Augustine—In the fifth and sixth centuries Britain, and Cambria in particular, produced a legion of saints, whose history is not generally known—Dubricius, Cadoc, Illtyd, and others at the head of this glorious epoch—A visit to Llandaff Cathedral—Its history by the Verger—Wrong notions of the public at large respecting the early Cambrian Church—The Britons and the Papacy—Pope Eleutherius—British Bishops at the Council of Arles, in 314, at the end of which a Synodical Letter was sent to Pope Sylvester, requesting him, as he had universal jurisdiction, to extend the decrees of Arles to the whole Church—The first Bishops of Llandaff gave an account of the state of their diocese to the Holy See—Councils of Brefi and Caerleon approved by Rome—Howell Dda, the Justinian of Wales, goes with his Code to Pope Anastasius—St. Kentigern lays his scruples concerning his consecration before St. Gregory—Pilgrimages to Rome frequent—St. Cadoc—Gildas's present of a bell to the Pope—Extraordinary privileges granted to the Pope by the Welsh laws—St. Augustine and the British Bishops—The British Church, although disobedient, never ceased to acknowledge the supremacy of Rome—A similar misunderstanding between St. Patrick and the Church in the South of Ireland—Wilfrid and Coleman—Urban, Bishop of Llandaff in the twelfth century, writes to Pope Calixtus II. that his See ever acknowledged the supremacy of Rome—Catholic Brittany converted to the Catholic faith by British bishops and monks—Unity of faith and religion an idle dream without the Papacy—As a citizen, the modern Briton respects authority ; as a Christian, he acknowledges none—The ancient Cambrian *belle* and the Pope. (Page 50 to 90.)

CHAPTER III.

THE HOLY EUCHARIST.—CONFESSION.

Belief of the Cambrians in the Holy Eucharist both as a Sacrament and as a Sacrifice—In their eyes the most exalted dignity on earth was that of the Priesthood—Gildas rebukes some of the clergy for not celebrating Mass often enough—The Britons and the Altar cannot be disconnected—St. Samson, when leading the life of a hermit, joined his brethren every Sunday for the celebration of the Mass—St. Cadoc of

Llancarvan killed by the Saxons whilst celebrating Mass—St. Winefred slain on the threshold of a church whilst the Holy Sacrifice was being celebrated—Welsh Princes on their knees before the Altar—The Altar of Sacrifice stripped and the Church closed—Its effect upon the people—The Judges, on their appointment, required to take the oath during Mass—A woman bringing a suit as to the paternity of a child has to swear before the Blessed Sacrament—The informer taken to the church by a priest, and there cautioned against perjury—The Indian's respect for the Catholic Altar—Legal punishment of sacrilege—Communion at the hour of death a general custom amongst the Welsh—Geraint and St. Teilo—The priest, whilst travelling to a sick call, cannot by law be a trespasser—To be deprived of Communion considered a great punishment—According to the Code of Howell Dda, a child is to go to Confession at seven years of age—A bishop, by privilege, the confessor of a king—Maelgon's instructions to his soldiers concerning St. Cadoc, his confessor—Unreasonable objections against this admirable institution of our Lord—Revival of Confession in the Church of England in our days.

(Page 91 to 121.)

CHAPTER IV.
PIETY TO THE DEAD.

Piety to the dead a sacred and general custom in Britain—The Welsh anxious to be buried by the walls of a church or a monastery—The devotion for the dead exemplified in Brittany, which received its customs from Britain—St. Cadoc made pilgrimages for the souls of his departed relations—Prayers for the dead constantly mentioned in Charters—The Kings of Glamorgan very particular on this point—The murderer praying at the grave of his victim—Charter of Gwerock, Duke of Brittany, to St. Ninnoc, a Welsh nun—Piety to the faithful departed an act of gratitude and justice—Piety to the departed reflected in the Celtic tales—St. Augustine, the great African Bishop, in his book entitled "Confessions," requests the reader to pray for his relations—The writer makes a similar request.

(Page 122 to 146.)

CHAPTER V.
SAINTS HONOURED AND INVOKED IN THE BRITISH CHURCH.

Doctrine of the Council of Trent on the subject—The lives of saints written and read for public edification—Beautiful and original sentiments emanating from the pen of the Biographer of St. David, in concluding the life of that saint—The names of saints bestowed on towns, villages, valleys, and mountains, both in the land of their birth and that of their labours—Pilgrimages to churches dedicated to saints—Custom of settling differences at their tombs—King Arthur, at the battle of Badon, invokes the blessed Virgin—Popular tales convey the same custom—The names of Saints invariably mentioned in Charters—Pope Honorious II., in his rescript to Urban, Bishop of Llandaff, uses the same form of expression—St. Gunstan, patron of Armorican mariners, in his youth a poor sailor boy, invoked by the mariner—The confidence of our forefathers in the intercession of saints was often a deduction from miracles witnessed in their lifetime—Ancient British Hymns to St. Curig and St. Julitta, republished by the Welsh MSS. Society—A double hope is entertained by the writer that in course of time the Festivals of the British Saints will be revived in our Missal and Breviary, and that converts to the Church, in their acts of donation for religious purposes, will again make use of the old phraseology, so touching and Catholic. (Page 147 to 170.)

CHAPTER VI.

MONASTIC LIFE.

Christian perfection consists in the love of God and of our neighbour—The practice of the Evangelical Counsels pointed out by our Lord as the surest road to arrive at that love—Religious communities in the Church from the earliest ages of Christianity, in the East and West—Monasticism in Britain, and especially in Cambria—Monasteries numerous—The cloister finds recruits in every class of society—Number of monks in three princely families of South Wales in the fifth century, as an illustration of public opinion in those days—Numerical strength of some monasteries in Wales—Some enter the cloister when young, others in their old age—St. Ninnoc—Her family and birth—Her intended marriage—Stratagem she used to obtain the consent of her parents to become a nun—Her departure for Brittany—Tewdrig, King of Glamorgan, becomes a hermit at Tintern—The Cambrians force him out of his cell to lead them to battle against the Saxons—His death—St. Suliau—Runs away from home—His speech to his father's messengers—trials from his sister-in-law for refusing to marry her—Legend of St. Efflam and Honora—Like St. Alexius, Efflam leaves his wife on the night of their marriage—Honora follows her husband to Brittany, and there becomes a nun—St. Patern, a mere boy, wishes to follow his father to the cloister—Sent to Cardiganshire—The family of Hoel, the first Armorican King, enter religion whilst residing in Cambria—The hermit and the Cenobite—Diary of the various exercises in a cloister—Continual public prayers in the great British monasteries—Extraordinary devotion in Lent—Revival of Monasticism in Britain—It cannot be uprooted.

(Page 171 to 220.)

CHAPTER VII.

THE SAINTS AND SUPERNATURAL EVENTS.

The saints endowed with supernatural power in the East as well as in the West—Difference of opinion as to the authenticity of this or that particular miracle—St. Dubricius is favoured in a vision with the designs of Almighty God on St. Samson—Visions of St. Patrick in relation to Ireland—Tugdual commanded by an angel to cross over to Brittany—The same command given to St. Samson—Apparition of the dove as a mark of the presence of the Holy Ghost—The angel at the hour of death—Vision of St. Keyna—Death of Paulus Aurelianus—St. David warned of the exact day of his death—St. Kentigern sees the soul of David taken up to heaven—Prophecy of St. Kentigern concerning the Anglo-Saxon race—Advice of St. Gildas for the obtaining of the gift of prophecy to the Bards of Britain—The saints cured various infirmities, enumerated in the hymn to St. Armel—Privatus' wife and daughter cured by St. Samson—St. Maglorious' reply to a Breton Prince—The miracles of St. Ninianus, in Scotland—The saints in connection with wild beasts and the dragon—The saints and the devil—St. Gunstan and the devil—Sacred Wells—Sacred springs spoken of in Holy Writ and in early traditions—St. Meen—St. Tailo's well.—St. Winefride's well.

(Page 221 to 261.)

CHAPTER VIII.

A FEW OBSERVATIONS ON THE SERVICES RENDERED TO SOCIETY BY THE EARLY BRITISH MONKS.

Unfairness of modern opinion in reference to Religious Orders—Spiritual and corporeal works of mercy—Superiority of the former over the latter—Missionary works of the Cambro-British monks—St. Patrick and St. Brieuc disturbed even in the cloister by their zeal for the salvation of souls—The voyage undertaken by St. Malo in search of the Fortunate Islands, in order to convert their inhabitants to the faith of Christ—Pedrog's journey, for the same purpose, to far-distant India—St. Cadoc's travels to Scotland and Brittany—St. Maglorius in his old age wavers between the solitary and the active life—Bishops, in the early Celtic Churches, generally chosen from monasteries—Provisions by which monasteries secured attention to the spiritual welfare of the districts surrounding their houses—Poetry and numbers made use of

by British missionaries in the instruction of the people—
Example of this system of teaching by numbers—The
monastery a place of refuge in time of distress—Extraordinary
privileges granted to St. David by his countrymen—Minute
description of the same in the "Liber Landavensis"—St.
Meen, the prince, and the prisoner—Light-houses built and
maintained by monks—All necessaries of material life produced within the monastery—Perfection and energy of
monastic farming operations. (Page 262 to 288.)

CHAPTER IX.

DUBRICIUS, FIRST BISHOP OF LLANDAFF.

Dubricius at the head of a great period in the history of
Britain—His birth—State of Britain at the time—Dubricius
consecrated Archbishop of Llandaff by St. Germanus—
Antiquity of Llandaff—Generosity of the Cambrians to
religion—King Meurig, of Glamorgan—A few remarks on the
leading characteristics of British Charters—Promulgation of
the Charter of Meurig—Procession along the banks of the
rivers Taff and Ely—Work of Dubricius in South Wales—
Education his speciality—In his days a great number of
women entered the cloister—Solemnity of taking the veil—
Dubricius transfers his See to Caerleon—Coronation of King
Arthur in that city by the Archbishop—Speech of Dubricius
at the battle of Badon—The Council of Brefi—Dies at Bardsey
Island—The relics of St. Dubricius removed from Bardsey
Island to Llandaff—The writer's appeal to the public for help
to build a church between the rivers Taff and Ely.
(Page 289 to 323.)

CHAPTER X.

ST. TEILO, SECOND BISHOP OF LLANDAFF.

How the biographer commences the Life of St. Teilo—His
birth and education—Teilo, David, and Paderu at Ty-gwyn ar
Taf—Trial of their virtue—Pilgrimage to Jerusalem—Teilo
elected to the See of Llandaff—The yellow plague—Emigration
to Brittany—On his way through Cornwall, Teilo receives the
confession of Geraint, a Prince of the province—Remains in
Armorica for seven years, during the greater part of which
time he leads the life of a religious—Returns to Llandaff—
Fulfils a promise made to Geraint, by visiting Cornwall and
preparing him for death.—Teilo reorganises his diocese—
During a battle he prays, like Moses, that his countrymen
may obtain a victory—Miracles performed by St. Teilo—His
death at an advanced age—Dispute about his place of burial—

The name of Teilo given to localities both in Wales and Brittany—"The Liber Landavensis" called "The Book of Teilo." (Page 324 to 350.)

CHAPTER XI.

SAINT OUDOCEUS, THIRD BISHOP OF LLANDAFF.

St. Oudoceus a Breton by birth—On the death of St. Teilo he is elected by the people as his successor in the See of Llandaff—His administration—Councils held under his Episcopacy—State of the country—Oudoceus and the three Chieftains—Measures taken by Oudoceus before pronouncing sentence of excommunication—Meurig resists for two years—Morgan submits at once—Gwardnaeth sent to Brittany—Oudoceus undertakes a journey to Rome—Towards the end of his days he retires into solitude—Comparison between him and St. Ambrose of Milan. (Page 351 to 375.)

CHAPTER XII.

ST. CADOC, FOUNDER OF LLANCARWAN.

Family of St. Cadoc—Baptised and educated by Tathai, at Caer-went—Contrast between the monastery and the home of the chieftain—Cadoc departs from home—The Swine-herd and Cadoc—The uncle and the nephew—Foundation of Llancarvan Monastery—Travels of Cadoc—Induces his father and mother to leave the world—Cadoc and the princes—Maelgwyn and the Abbot—King Arthur and Cadoc—Life of the founder of Llancarvan during Lent—Leaves Llancarvan—Departing advice to his brethren—His death—Cadoc as a Fabulist—The man who killed his greyhound—The old woman and the yarn, a lesson on unity amongst brethren—The Cambrian maiden who allowed herself to be painted—Religion painted to suit interests and prejudices—A visit to Llancarvan in 1878.
(Page 376 to 416.)

CHAPTER XIII.

ST. ILLTYD THE KNIGHT.

Illtyd a name held in veneration by the Celtic traditions—Birth and early life—Came over to Britain as a soldier—Casual meeting of Cadoc and Illtyd at Llancarvan—The latter resolves to leave the world—The step rendered difficult by the fact that he was married—His wife consents to his dedicating himself to the religious life—Illtyd a hermit—Protects a stag against Merchion and his huntsmen—Impression made by the hermit on the Cambrian chieftain, who grants a large tract of land to the recluse—Dubricius and Illtyd—Antiquity of Lantwit-Major—University of Illtyd in that locality becomes the greatest seat of learning in Britain—The system of education at Lantwit made manual labour obligatory—Illtyd visited by his wife, Trynihid—Refuses to see the lady—Persecutions from the agents of his benefactor, Merchion—Illtyd secretly leaves his brethren—His retreat being discovered, he is forced to come back to Lantwit—The latter end of his life veiled in obscurity. (Page 417 to 445.)

CHAPTER XIV.
ST. DAVID, THE PATRON OF WALES.

David the popular name in Cambria—King Arthur and David contemporaries—Birth of the saint attended by extraordinary phenomena—Foretold to St. Patrick in a vision—David at Lantwit-Major—His mother retires to a convent in Brittany—David restores sight to his old Principal—Pilgrimage to Jerusalem—St. David at Glastonbury—Restores the first church built in Britain—Burial of King Arthur in that locality—Monastic life of David—The rule of St. David—The Council of Brefi—David absent in the beginning—On his way to Brefi restores to life a youth, who becomes his acolyte during the Council—St. Dubricius resigns—David chosen to be his successor—Puts into canonical form the decrees of Brefi—Another Council at Caerleon—Both sent to Rome for approval—Spirit of that legislation reflected in the subsequent customs of Wales—The Archiepiscopal See removed from Caerleon to St. David—The Patron of Wales and miraculous wells—His death—Great confidence of his countrymen in his powerful intercession in heaven—The three first days of March kept holy in Wales—The finest church in the Principality erected to the memory of David. (Page 446 to 479.)

CHAPTER XV.
ST. SAMSON, ARCHBISHOP OF DÔL, BRITTANY.

Samson's parents twice before the altar, once on their marriage day, after, on their taking the monastic habit—Samson a child of prayer—Education entrusted to Illtyd, who prophecied his future career—Strong faith of Samson—Power of the sign of the Cross—Embraces religious life—Father and mother at first rather reluctant—His exemplary life—Hatred borne to Samson by two nephews of Illtyd—His residence at Barry Island, near Cardiff—Visits his sick father—The result of this visit—The entrance of father, mother, uncle, and aunt into the cloister—Becomes Abbot of the convent at Barry Island—Visit to Ireland—Retires into solitude—Ordered by a Synod to give up this kind of life—Consecrated Bishop—Circumstances connected with the event—Samson's departure for Brittany—Delayed in his voyage—A Pagan feast and the Missionary—Leaves his father, Amon, behind—Meeting of Privatus and Samson on the shores of Brittany—Samson and the Frank King—Dôl and Tours—Episcopal work of Samson—His death—Heavenly melody heard at his funeral—*Résumé* of his wonderful career—Extraordinary supernatural assistance he received from his guardian angel. (Page 480 to 516.)

CHAPTER XVI.
St. Paulus Aurelianus, or Paul de Leon.

Early tendency of young Aurelianus to asceticism—Leaves Lantwit-Major, with the consent of Illtyd, at sixteen—The British saints models of temperance—Beginning of missionary life—First appearance of the angel bidding Paul to leave his country—His arrival at Ouessant, an island off the coast of France—Strange ideas about this island in Pagan times—Landing on the shores of Armorica—Aurelianus and the wild beasts—Arrival of the British colonists at Batz—A local Prince becomes their benefactor—The people want Paul to be consecrated Bishop—Stratagem resorted to on the occasion—Paul at the court of the Frank King—Return to Armorica—Episcopal career—The Bishop and the hermit—Paul and Tanguy, guilty of the murder of a beloved sister—The uncle and his nephew, Jovin—Paulus Aurelianus in his old age—His death—Contention concerning the place of his burial—Occismor, the cradle of the British race in Armorica, forgotten—Replaced by the small town of St. Paul de Leon—Beautiful cathedral erected to his memory—Chapel built in the locality by Mary Stuart, Queen of Scotland, in thanksgiving for her safety from a storm. (Page 517 to 558.)

CHAPTER XVII.
St. Gildas the Historian.

Early Life—Surnamed the "Aquarius," or "Water Drinker," by the students of Lantwit-Major—Visits Ireland—Missionary life throughout Britain—Gildas sails across to Brittany—Gildas and the Lady Tripbinia—Various monasteries built by Gildas—Warned by an angel of the day of his death—Orders his body to be thrown into the sea—Gildas as a writer—Motives which induced him to take the pen—Some extracts from his writings—Constantine rebuked—Maelgwyn—Certain resemblance between St. Jerome and Gildas as writers—Britain is described by Gildas—Although not more corrupt than other nations of the period, still deserved the severe reproaches of the saint—A priest's duty not to connive at the crimes of nations or individuals. (Page 559 to 584.)

PREFACE.

ON Thursday, the 17th of August, 1876, I visited Llandewi Brefi, Cardiganshire, with the determination of not passing through that county without making a pilgrimage to the valley within which had been held the most important ecclesiastical Council ever assembled in Cambria.

<small>Visit to Llandewi Brefi.</small>

After walking eight or nine miles from Lampeter, along the river Teifi, under a tropical sun, I reached the village about mid-day.* Vehicles standing at the doors of public-houses, a number of people strolling about in holiday dress, whilst others pic-nic'd on the banks of the stream, now nearly dried up, indicated that some festivity was being held. I was informed that the annual meeting of the members of the Church of England, honoured by the presence of the neighbouring Protestant clergy, was the cause of this unusual week-day gathering. The Church people mustered in fair strength, and, as far as I could judge from those whom I addressed, Welsh was the language of the district, for many could neither speak nor understand any other.

I proceeded, in the first instance, to examine as closely as possible the spot on which the Church stands; for the legend, as told in the "Lives of the Cambro-British Saints," distinctly states that the ground on which the sacred temple was afterwards built had risen under the feet of St. David, so as to form an improvised platform, from which he could address the thousands eager to listen to his eloquent teaching.

<small>* There is a railway station about a mile from Llandewi Brefi.</small>

The place itself seemed to testify the truth of the legend. I saw before me a mound of earth, rising gradually to a height of twenty or twenty-five feet, comprising an area of about an acre, on the summit of which stands the church, having the tower in the centre, as usually found in Cambrian ecclesiastical buildings.

After looking into the church, half of which has been neatly restored, I sat down amongst the graves, to survey the neighbouring mountains. With the aid of a powerful field-glass, I examined a picturesque gorge, which is also spoken of in the Welsh legends as having been cleft by Divine power. Some of the peasantry made a free use of the glass, and pronounced it to be the most ingenious invention ever made. No doubt it was to them a novelty.

Whilst thus occupied, I was accosted by the vicar, who kindly offered to become my guide, and directed my attention to the Staff of St. David, as a stone of some height planted before the door of the church is called. But when I drew his attention to the fact that the mound whereon we stood tallied exactly, in its formation, with the statement in the legend which asserts that it rose miraculously under the feet of St. David, the reverend gentleman remained silent.

Indeed, it is difficult to call in question that the power of God is displayed at suitable times, and unwise to ridicule the faith of our forefathers, who deemed it a duty they owed to truth to hand down to posterity accounts of miraculous events.

I presented my card to the vicar, and in the course of the day observed that I had become an object of interest, which I attributed to the following circumstance:—

Several lectures on the first three Bishops of Llandaff and on SS. Cadoc and Illtyd had been reported by the *Western Mail*, and read in Cardiganshire as well as in the southern counties of Wales.

The memory of ancient Welsh bishops and monks being revived in a Catholic church, and their lives set forth before a Catholic congregation as models for imitation, and that by a Catholic priest, had sharpened public curiosity and attracted attention to the lectures; so, when it was perceived that the name on the card corresponded with that of the lecturer on the Welsh saints, in St. Peter's Church, Cardiff, the discovery, instead of estranging the reverend gentlemen from me, had the effect of drawing us closer together.

In the evening I took tea in the Board-school, and, amongst other queries from some of the gentlemen, I noted the following :—

" Was I a Jesuit ?"

" What could be my purpose in reviving the ecclesiastical history of Wales ?" etc., etc.

" Had I the honour to be a member of a society formed *ad hoc ?*"

" Who supplied the funds ?" etc., etc.

To the first question, I replied that I trusted I was a disciple of Christ, but felt bound to state distinctly that I had not the honour of being a member of that great society, so worthy of praise, yet so much misunderstood and abused.

On the second point, I frankly informed my inquisitors that in studying the religion of ancient Cambria, the object I had in view was my own edification and that of my fellow-men. Breton by birth, the history of Cambria offered me particular attractions. We were first cousins. For years our forefathers had stood together in politics and in religion. In the battlefield they fought side by side, and in the church they worshipped together round the same altar. The Catholic faith had been planted on the shores of Brittany by Welsh bishops, priests, and monks, and this the Bretons never forgot.

I was happy to certify by personal observation, that the old Celtic tongue, spoken by Dubricius, Paulinus, and David at the Council of Brefi, was still, after so many centuries, the language of Welshmen; but I begged to express my heartfelt regret that the same old tongue from the lips of their present spiritual teachers no longer instilled the same one and unchanging faith. In my tour through Wales, I saw temples opposed to temples, creeds to creeds, and found religious dissension everywhere. Not a hamlet but was under the bane of two or three different religions, sometimes even more. (General assent.) The grocer and the baker were dogmatising against the minister of the Church of England—(assent)—and they themselves are divided on ritualism, on the relations of Church and State, and other serious subjects.

I had remarked that intelligent Welshmen throughout the country bewailed the total disorganisation of the city of God in the land, and yearned for the future day which would sweep away religious anarchy and once more bring back peace and union to Welsh homes. For myself, I fully shared this feeling, and prayed to Almighty God to restore to a nation which had lost it, unity of faith. Influenced by this wish, I had resolved on disinterring the ancient Cambrian saints from their graves, in the hope that the history of their saintly lives, and of the religion they had taught, might help the work of restoring the faith in Cambria.

<small>Love of the Cambrians for the history of their ancestors.</small>

There are very few people on earth more anxious to study the records of their ancestors than Welshmen, or who listen with a deeper interest to the recital of the teachings or doings of their forefathers.

In the prospectus of the great Eisteddfod held at Wrexham, in 1876, amongst the subjects on which papers were invited I find the following, so characteristic of the Welsh mind :—

"Best compilation of historical facts connected with the early British Church :—

"I. A compilation of the best evidences of proof of the existence of a Christian Church in Britain within the first century after its invasion by the Romans, during their stay, and at the time when Augustine with his fellow-missionaries arrived in Britain, in 597.

"II. What information can be obtained of the places where Christianity was established, whether by occasional congregational assemblies, the building of churches, or the foundation of monastic institutions—more particularly in Wales ?

"III. By whom and by what means was the first earliest introduction of Christianity effected ? £15 15s., given by

T. T. Griffiths, Esq., Wrexham, and a gold medal by the committee (English).

Dr. Newman, whilst yet connected with the Church of England, had planned out the hagiography of the ancient British saints. The chronological arrangements are to be found in his "History of my Religious Opinions." What a pity that such a well-stored mind should not have enriched English literature with a work on a subject of so much importance!

Protestant writers who have dealt with this subject have not done justice to the ancient British Church or to her saints. Holding a different creed from our forefathers, they have misrepresented their faith and ridiculed their religious customs, or maintained a contemptuous silence in their regard.

These historians seem to have ignored that there is such a thing as the *science* of the *saints*—clearly treated, defined, divided and sub-divided, with as much method and order as zoology, botany, and astronomy, medicine, and other sciences expounded by our best professors. Perhaps in their lives they never read St. Basil, St. Augustine, St. Theresa, Schram, Görres, and a host of other spiritual writers who, from St. Denis the Areopagite, in the first century, down to Father Faber, have told us what a saint is, and how Divine grace operates wonderfully in his soul.

I. A *saint* is a man who, whilst in the flesh, kept to perfection the law of God, loved, according to His word, the Lord with his whole heart, his whole soul, his whole mind, and his whole strength, and his neighbour as himself!!! The saint practised, to an heroic degree, the theological virtues—faith, hope, and charity; and also the cardinal virtues—justice, prudence, temperance, and fortitude. The science of holiness.

It is not the power of performing miracles, or the gift of prophecy, or extraordinary visions which constitute sanctity, but the practice of the Gospel precepts and the following of the law of God.

The tests by which we may know a saint are as follows:—Did he believe in God, trust in Him and love Him above all things, and love his fellow-men as himself, as commanded by Jesus Christ? Can we trace in his life a ready will to give to every man his due, a horror of any injustice whatever? for this is included in the virtue of justice.

A saint should be endowed with prudence—a science which consists, as St. Basil tells us, in *the true knowledge of what we should do* in the various circumstances of life.

Did he, by temperance, guide his natural appetites and keep them within the boundaries of the law of God?

Did the virtue of fortitude strengthen his will in following the right path through trials and dangers; nay, instil into it a certain instinct which would lead it to rush nobly to encounter difficulties?

We all know that *dogmatic and moral theology* fully treat these subjects in all their details.

II. The saints, as a rule, practised the *Evangelical Counsels*, as the best means to advance in the love of God and man, which constitutes real sanctity. Obedience, poverty, and chastity have been and are now the rules of monastic life, and sum up the Evangelical Counsels. No sooner was Britain converted to the religion of Christ than a large proportion of her children embraced with enthusiasm the practice of these counsels of the Gospel. This will be evidenced in these pages. In point of fact, all the early British saints were monks.

For the information of such readers as may wish to study this branch of divinity, I beg to refer them to "Ascetic Theology, a Science which Explains the Practice of the Evangelical Counsels." * Hundreds of divines, from the first to the nineteenth century, have treated this matter. The learned Benedictine, Schram, is perhaps one of the best and most methodical writers on the subject.

III. God is wonderful in His saints. These holy souls, pure as crystal, powerfully reflected the light of the Holy Ghost. The grace of God lifted them to the supernatural regions, in which they saw and heard things it is impossible to describe,

* Migne's 'Dictionnaire d'Ascétisme.'

as St. Paul said when he was caught up to the third heaven. This branch of the science of the saints is called *Mystic Theology*, and treats of visions, ecstacies, miracles, conflicts with the devil, supernatural apparitions of our Lord in the holy Eucharist and on the Cross, of the blessed Virgin, the angels, or the saints, and other phenomena, such as walking on the sea, like St. Peter, standing on fire without being burnt, etc.

Various works may be consulted on the matter, dating from the earliest times of Christianity down to our own days. Amongst these, Görres, a German writer, may be read with interest. The French translation of this book is entitled "La Mystique Divine, Naturelle et Diabolique."

This branch of saintly science is, I beg to observe, a science of observation, consisting of facts, authentic, visible, and most carefully examined.

As a rule, the servants of God made little of these extraordinary heavenly gifts; for their existence does not constitute sanctity. Judas performed miracles, and yet betrayed his Lord. Holiness, they all knew, consisted in keeping the law of God. However, their Divine Master favoured them with these supernatural graces for their own spiritual benefit and for that of their fellow-men, and thus glorified His name.

The servants of God should, as a matter of course, reproduce in their thoughts and in their actions the teaching of dogmatic and moral theology, as well as the rules of ascetic divinity, and also share in the extraordinary gifts which come under the head of mystical theology. We cannot understand or meet with a saint of Jesus Christ disconnected with these sciences, for he is a saint because he kept the laws of God and the counsels of the Gospel, as far as possible. And the friendship which he enjoyed with his Divine Master was often revealed by miracles or other wonderful signs.

Writers who should ignore these principles are not qualified for the great work of recording the actions and thoughts of the noblest children in the Church of Jesus Christ; they are utterly unable to do justice to the subject; an illiterate man might as well attempt to write on astronomy.

In point of fact, we expect to find everything supernatural in a saint. The end he aims at with energy and perseverance is supernatural, and the help he relies on for success is the heavenly grace of his Redeemer.

For the conquest of heaven, for the service of God and of his neighbours, he waged war against irrational passions, against the devil and the world.

A worldly-minded man pursues a *temporal* end, the saint an *everlasting* one. To him every other aim is blindness and folly. In all his undertakings he asks himself the question, *Quid hoc ad vitam æternam?*—"In the other world, how far will this or that action benefit my soul?" He fully understands, with the author of the imitation of Christ, that an humble peasant who serves his Maker is wiser than the greatest philosopher.

The present age has witnessed the existence of men of prodigious intellectual talents; they opened our railways, laid our telegraphs, both on land and under the ocean. Materially, they deserve the title of benefactors of their fellow-men. They are now dead and gone to another world, and enjoy not in *this one* the benefit of their inventions. If they neglected the salvation of their immortal souls and the service of God, they trifled away the few days of their existence on earth.

The saints applied their minds to the study of the only needful science, and threw the whole energy of their souls into securing everlasting bliss.

If in the worldly man we admire persevering efforts, continued labours, self-sacrifice, say, in winning victories on the battle-field, realising a fortune, etc.; let us not wonder at finding the saints extraordinary in their labours and exertions in the acquirement of Divine love. For the sake of their Master they subdued their passions, devoted a whole life, in suffering, in mortification, and in self-abnegation, to benefit their fellow-men.

Enlightened by the Holy Ghost and strengthened by His grace, they became perfect masters in the science of holiness and practised it with unwonted zeal. This explains the parting from father and mother, brothers and sisters, their mode of living—so severe and painful to flesh and blood, and at times incomprehensible to a material man.

The task of recording the memory of the Cambro-British saints has been taken in hand by two classes of writers— monks, in the first place, and, later on, modern authors have devoted their talents to the subject. The former, as a matter of course, were better qualified to depict in their true colours servants of God, who, like themselves, had embraced the religious state. A soldier is the fittest exponent of war, and the best to teach us how battles are won and lost. An engineer will be able to explain the mechanical arts with greater clearness than any other man. To a chemist we look for the best work on chemistry. By the same rule, any person who wishes to understand what a saint is, must refer to those who have studied and practised what holiness consists in, through the writings of men who valued the spiritual life. *Two classes of writers. Their respective capacity.*

In monasteries great care was taken to keep alive the memory of those who had rendered themselves illustrious in the service of God and religion. Their lives were set forth as an example. Such of the brethren as possessed talent as historians were directed to carefully note down their actions, and these records were read to the community on particular occasions, such as their anniversaries.

The monks were eminently men of faith, and lived in an age when society at large could boast of being untainted by the infidelity and materialism which at present prevail. Thus, men of faith, of hope, and of charity are reproduced in their writings; men who, moulded in the spirit of the Gospel, were poor in spirit and meek; who lamented the days of their banishment in this world, because they looked forward to a country where they would become ennobled in the company of Jesus Christ. Men who saw God because of their purity of heart—who, with courage and patience, suffered persecution for justice sake.

At times, however, the monastic hagiographers have fallen into exaggerations on the subject of miraculous events. It must be admitted that in several instances those recorded were not well authenticated. Popular opinion in those days of faith was easily deceived, through the fact of spurious or imaginary supernatural events being mixed up with *real* miracles, which were or could not be denied as having been performed by the saints. Some hagiographers have, no doubt, overstepped discretion in stating as facts events which could not be proved to have taken place. Perhaps such writers would have acted more judiciously in bringing out the virtues of the servants of God.

In reference to supernatural occurrences, some Protestant historians exhibit an utter, and we may say deplorable, scepticism. They even brand hagiographers with the stigma of ignorance and superstition, terms which they constantly apply to the monks, simply because they record miracles, apparitions of angels, celestial visions, etc.

These gentlemen must have read the Bible, and, no doubt, believe in Holy Writ. Now, the Old and the New Testament abound in narratives of supernatural intercourse between heaven and earth. In both Testaments the angels are continually spoken of as descending from heaven on special errands to Moses, to the Prophets, and to the Apostles. The devil tempted our Redeemer in the desert, and an angel appeared to Him on the eve of His death. They delivered St. Peter from gaol, and visited St. Paul. The Prophets of old performed miracles, so did the Apostles. Are we, in order to gratify our views or indulge our prejudices, to fix a limit to the power and bounty of God?

Supernatural events can stand the test of examination; they are facts, often witnessed by thousands of spectators, both friends and foes, and all are constrained to admit their truth. The circumstances, places, and persons concerned in them are named in detail, and the events are frequently commemorated by building churches and granting charters, and are handed down to posterity by hymns, traditions, or local religious festivals. In a word, such events bear within themselves the evidence of their having taken place. Are monks, then, superstitious or ignorant because they have recorded them?

Perversity or prejudice, unfortunately, often veils truth. The Jews could not deny the miracles of our Lord, yet they resorted to any subterfuge rather than acknowledge His divinity.

These somewhat severe but truthful strictures cannot be applied to the Welsh Archæological Society. These gentlemen have published the MSS. as they found them, leaving everyone to form his own opinion on the subject.

The Rev. Professor Rees, M.A., Oxford, in his "Essay on the Welsh Saints," dedicated to the Marquis of Bute, 1836, may be taken as a fair specimen of this class of writers. A great deal of information is to be gleaned from his work by the student of history, who will find in its pages many useful notes on the illustrious champions of Christ in Britain.

This book may be compared to the official registers preserved in the sacristies of our churches, which duly record, day by day, the birth, parentage, death, and, it may be, marriage of the inhabitants of the parish. This is the characteristic of the "Essay on the Welsh Saints," and in the capacity of a registrar its author has rendered service to history.

But any person who may wish to derive edification from the religion, faith, and spiritual life of the early British saints, will but waste his time by reading the essay. The science of the saints is not familiar to the author, who even professes to lay it aside as superstitious and monkish.

One might have expected more religious reverence and a deeper instinct of faith in a clergyman of the Church of England and a distinguished professor of St. David's College, Lampeter. The fact of a minister of religion being unable to appreciate, instinctively, nobility of soul in men who reproduced in their lives the eight beatitudes, and practised every precept and counsel of the New Testament of our Lord, reveals, unfortunately, a degraded state of Christianity.

The learned Professor of Lampeter allows himself to be drawn away from historical truth by his religious prejudices. If there be anything historically true, it is the fact that the early Christians in Britain were Catholics to the back bone.

Yet, this the Rev. Professor Rees repeatedly denies, without bringing any telling argument to support his assertions. The following is amongst the strongest he adduces: that Britain received the faith from the East; from this he draws the broad conclusion that the Britons had no connection with the Papacy of Rome. What does all this come to? Nothing. Italy, France, and Spain received the Christian religion from the East. Our Lord Himself and all His apostles belonged to the East; St. James, of Spain, came from Judea; St. Peter, of Rome, from Gallilee; St. Denis, of Paris, from Athens; yet all these were Catholics, like St. Joseph of Arimathea, the founder, it is believed, of Glastonbury Abbey, in England. The same professor advances other erroneous assertions on the Real Presence and the Invocation of Saints—doctrines of the Gospel which formed a part of the religion of ancient Britain. These subjects are dealt with in Chapters III., IV., and V., to which I beg to refer the reader.

The study of the ancient Hagiography of Britain presents a great many difficulties to overcome. The old manuscripts are to a certain extent lost, or not yet published in such a form as to make them accessible to the public. The Welsh Archæological Society has rendered a great service to history in this respect, and spared no trouble or expense in bringing to light the ancient records of the servants of God in the island of Britain.

The society will, no doubt, do more in future. Where, for instance, are the hundreds of Welsh saints whose names are mentioned by Professor Rees? the history of their lives must exist somewhere—on the shelves of public libraries or in the possession of private families.

In Brittany, Albert le Grand, a Dominican monk, and Lobineau, a Benedictine, have brought to light the MSS. of the British saints who laboured and died in Armorica, and given the names of the places where the MSS. are to be found. In Ireland, the Rev. John O'Hanlon has undertaken a similar work. Even when we have the original of the ancient records on our desks, all difficulties do not disappear. These lives, in the course of centuries, have so often been re-copied or compiled, that chronological errors, defacement of names, and inaccuracies of circumstances have crept in. The *amanuenses* were not infallible, and seem at times to have paid more attention to calligraphy than to accuracy. There is sometimes a difference of date, and circumstances connected with the life of one saint are introduced into that of another. This kind of study requires a great store of comparative judgment, and a spirit of fair and loyal criticism. In the MSS. we find truth, but it is covered with the dust of ages, which must be swept away before it shines forth to us in all its brightness. The patience and skill of an artist who has to re-colour an ancient picture are required in such a work.

The following plan has been adopted in the classification of matters contained in this book:—

Plan followed hr the "Cambria Sacra."

The primary object I had in view was to revive the memory of the illustrious servants of God, the pride of the British Church in the fifth and sixth centuries. Before handling the subject, I thought myself bound to place before the reader a summary of the history of the Christian religion in Britain up to that period.

The fifth and sixth centuries formed the brightest era of the faith amongst the pure British race. The bishops, abbots, professors, and, we may add, many of the princes of that period, by their holy lives and high cultivation, exercised a wonderful influence over their fellow-men in their lifetime, and after death commanded the veneration of succeeding generations.

At the head of that period we find Dubricius, Cadoc, and Illtyd, who left at their departure from this world a multitude of servants of God as eminent as themselves, such as David, Teilo, Samson, and others. Thus, a natural plan is already traced out to any biographer or historian. I have somewhat departed from chronological order by placing the lives of St. Teilo and Oudoceus after that of Dubricius. I thought I could not separate the three first Bishops of Llandaff, invariably placed side by side in the charters of their cathedral.

Whilst perusing the ancient documents which contain the lives of these eminent servants of God, I noted down as I proceeded some striking features of their religion and faith, such as their ideas with regard to the organisation of the city of God on earth, their firm belief in the doctrines of transubstantiation, practice of confession, piety towards the souls in purgatory, invocation of saints, etc.

My attention was drawn to these subjects by the repeated assertions of modern historians, who persist in stating that these doctrines never formed a part of the religion of the ancient British Church. Three or four chapters are devoted to the enlightenment of the reader on this point. Those following deal with monastic life in Wales, and then come the lives of the first three Bishops of Llandaff, those of St. Cadoc, Illtyd, St. David, and Samson, their disciples, and others.

I must apologise to the reader for all short-comings in style, and strongly appeal to his indulgence. I have handled in my days too many languages to be master of any.

My mother tongue was *Breton* ; it carried my first prayer to my Maker. My classical education was conducted in French. At twenty, I acquired my first knowledge of English, on English soil, and for about fourteen years expressed my thoughts in that language.

Ordered to the island of Mauritius, although under the English flag, French became once more the medium through which I had to discharge the duties of missionary life—not to mention the *Creole* language, a mixture of all the idioms of the East, such as Tamul, Chinese, Malay, and African dialects, condensed together in a French patois, enabling the various nationalities of which this beautiful little island is the centre to understand each other.

In this Hagiography particular attention is given to place before the reader a truthful and honest narrative, grounded on facts and gleaned from ancient British and Armorican documents. Imagination and rhetoric are discarded. Sometimes, however, the writer cannot help giving scope to his feelings, as he dwells in admiration on those olden times ; for the coldest heart, when visiting Babylon, Carthage, Athens, or places sanctified by religion, such as the Holy Land or Rome, cannot remain insensible.

My task is simple; it is that of a spectator who looks dispassionately on olden times and bygone events, as they roll on before his gaze.

Perhaps this unpretending and short narrative may induce a more refined pen to supply a much-needed want—the revival of the ecclesiastical history of the British race on a larger scale.

I beg to express my most sincere thanks to all those who have encouraged me in this work—some by sympathy and kind letters, others by co-operation.

I cannot forget the help I received from the Cardiff Press, particularly from the *Western Mail*. This paper published in its wide-spread columns the substance of twelve lectures on the Welsh saints given at St. Peter's Catholic Church. The *South Wales Daily News* reproduced those on the first three Bishops of Llandaff, and sent one of its reporters to St. Peter's.

As far as I could learn, these lectures, given to test public opinion, were favourably received and extensively read.

In a town in the west of Wales, a desire was expressed that what had appeared in the *Western Mail* should be reprinted in the form of a small pamphlet; I discouraged the idea, by stating that a work on the subject was about being published.

Clergymen of the Church of England, and gentlemen from Swansea and other places, have expressed a similar desire.

Writers of periodicals, Government surveyors, whose instructions are to collect, as far as they can, the historical facts connected with the places they are surveying, have at times called on me.

Several of my brethren in the priesthood, wishing to lecture on the ancient British Church in the winter season, wrote for information.

The Catholic authorities, Dr. Brown and Dr. Hedley, have written encouraging letters, and some Cardiff gentlemen have been so kind as to read over some of my manuscripts.

The writer concludes this preface by declaring that he is an admirer of the old axiom, "*Errare humanim est, perseverare diabolicum.*" It is easy to commit an error, although the greatest care be taken to secure historical exactitude. This observation applies not so much to leading facts as to matters of detail.

It is the duty of any right-minded recorder to be ready to acknowledge *proved* inexactitudes; for it is not unlikely that, although he has made a particular study of the subject he handles, there may be others who possess a more extensive knowledge on the same question. One who is not open to conviction, shows evident signs of pride and obstinacy.

CANTON, CARDIFF, *January* 16*th*, 1879.

ERRATA.

On page 15, for legions and auxiliaries were constantly *been*, read *being*.

Page 49: Senate *of the* Roman people, read Senate *and* Roman people.

Page 94: For *nunquam*, read *nunquam*.

Page 235: On the first of *May*, read *March*.

Page 315: The history of *Bangs*, read *Bangor*.

Google

CHAPTER I.

SUMMARY OF THE HISTORY OF RELIGION IN BRITAIN, FROM THE INTRODUCTION OF CHRISTIANITY, DOWN TO THE ARRIVAL OF GERMANUS AS THE CHAMPION OF TRUTH AGAINST PELAGIANISM.

HISTORY fails to dispel the clouds that hang over the infancy of Britain. Who were the first settlers in the Island? How long after the Deluge did the tide of emigration, constantly flowing from the plains of Babylon, the cradle of mankind, take to reach the British Islands, is uncertain.

What route did it follow? Was it along the coast of the Mediterranean on the African shore, and then through Spain and France? Or, did it slowly advance along the banks of the Danube and the Rhine till it reached Britain? Or, was the country invaded by two different columns, one coming through the south, the other through the centre or north of Europe? Ancient records do not make this clear; nor does it come within the plan of these pages to discuss the various opinions on the subject.

2   CAMBRIA SACRA.

Britain first described by the pen of a Roman general.

The first description of the country, its customs and laws (religious and civil), is due to the pen of a Roman general, Julius Cæsar.

When the first conqueror of Britain and his legions took possession of the island, they found it inhabited, from the shores of Kent to the Mountains of Caledonia. The South Coast, fronting Gaul, was even densely populated.

The inhabitants were a hardy, bold, and warlike race, ruled by several petty kings independent of one another, a circumstance which rendered the task of Cæsar and his soldiers rather an easy one. In the scale of civilization they stood rather low; and their dwellings, clothing, and diet indicated a society in its infancy. As the Romans made their way inland, they found the dwelling-houses very primitive and rude. A low stone wall supported a conical roof with an opening at the top for the exit of smoke and the admission of light. Near their huts, palisades planted in the ground formed an enclosure to protect their cattle from marauders and wolves. The people, as a rule, lived chiefly on the produce of the chase, as well as on fruit and milk; however, they cultivated some narrow plots of ground round their habitation.

On the South Coast cultivation was in a more advanced state. Here the Romans met with some sumptuous mansions, groves, and orchards; and marl was used as a fertilizing agent in agriculture. The science of extracting minerals from the ground and working them was known and cultivated; though not to the same extent as in our days, when the iron and coal of England replenish all the markets of the world.

The dress of the natives was in keeping with an infant state of society. Untanned skins and cloth of their own manufacture covered their bodies; in the North, however, they were more scantily clad. As with the present Aborigines in the many islands of the PacificO cean, tattooing was a general and favourite custom.

Early trained to arms and hardships, the British adults were fond of excitement, and spent most of their time in campaigning or in hunting. On horseback they could not be excelled; for their feats of horsemanship astonished even the Roman legionaries. Rushing at full gallop on the declivity of steep hills, the Britons had such command over their horses as to be able to stop them almost in full career.[1] In battle they made use of chariots drawn by two, four, and even six horses; and could fight standing on the poles of these chariots or on the bare backs of their foaming steeds, with much the same assurance as our modern circus riders.

Bold horsemen.

Women followed their fathers or husbands to the battle field, and by their gestures and shrieks animated the combatants. This practice seems to have been common to all Celtic races; for we read in the life of St. Patrick that he

(1) Sammes Britannia Antiqua.

succeeded, although with difficulty, in persuading the martial ladies of Erin that the excitements and dangers of the battle field were not in harmony with their gentle sex, and that Almighty God had designed them to bring forth and rear children for society, rather than to countenance their slaughter.

<small>Religion represented by Druidism</small>
The religion of the Britons was Druidism, and their god and goddesses, with Celtic names, were not dissimilar to the divinities in the mythology of Pagan Rome. Traces of the primitive revelations could be discerned in their theology. Thus, they acknowledged the immortality of the soul, and taught that beyond the grave rewards or penalties awaited the departed spirits, according as their lives on earth had been spent. In their creed we also find that they believed that sins and guilt were atoned for by the shedding of blood; and animals and even human beings were sacrificed on their altars. When the country was in great danger, the favourite victims chosen to avert the evil genius were the assassins, public malefactors, prisoners of war, or even some relations.[1]

The Druids were the ministers of this religion, and formed a numerous and most influential body. To keep up a certain hierarchical unity in this privileged class, one of them was elected Archdruid or High Pontiff, and resided either in the Island of Man or that of Anglesey.

<small>(1) Sammes, Britannia Antiqua.</small>

Once a year they met in public assemblies to discuss scientific questions, or give their advice on social or political matters; for their influence and authority were great and extensive. In critical and grave circumstances their opinion was asked for and invariably followed, for in the opinion of their countrymen they possessed two indisputable titles to respect; they were the ministers of the gods; and, as a body, in learning and the sciences had not equals amongst the Britons. This good reputation had even crossed the sea; in Europe the British Druid ranked foremost in medicine, in natural science, and magical arts; hence their schools were not only frequented by native students, but also by foreigners from Gaul. Long was the course of studies, extending over 15 or 20 years. At a time when the art of writing was little known and less practised, verses and numbers, to a great extent, were the usual medium of communicating knowledge, and of stamping it upon the memory.

The Celtic *Dero* (oak tree) was invariably the natural temple, under whose wide-spreading shade the Druids met for Divine worship, sacrifice, and public deliberations. Hence majestic long avenues of oak groves were common throughout the country. The mistletoe, a parasite growing on apple as well as on oak trees, was held sacred, and used not only as a medical agent, but as an antidote against poison and preserver from witchcraft and malice. On

The mistletoe

its discovery in a forest the circumstance was followed by a religious ceremony. The most honourable of the surrounding Druids, clad in a white robe, ascended the tree, and cut off the mistletoe with a golden knife. The sacred branch was not allowed to touch the ground, but was received in the whitest of cloths by a minister who stood under the tree. The ceremony ended by the sacrifice of two heifers.

Such is the substance of what has been handed down to us by Cæsar and other historians of ancient Britain's religious and social condition.

The Roman rule in Britain lasted about 500 years, that is to say, from the 55th year before Christ to A.D. 411.[*]

Although naturally conservative and tenacious of their own customs and language, the Britons, no doubt, felt the effects of foreign influence. The more polished manners of the conquerors, their superiority in science and art, produced no slight changes amongst these barbarians; whilst their laws checked deeds and customs peculiar to savage tribes. In this, the remotest part of the empire, emperors and proconsuls failed not to encourage and enforce, wherever they could, the study of their national language. Of course, Latin was to be used in all official transactions and spoken by the invaders. If the mass of the people tenaciously adhered to their own idioms, the nobility, as a rule, learned Latin,

[*] Lingard, History of England.

and prided themselves in speaking it with the purest accent.

The civil and military administration of the country was framed on the Roman model. The island was divided into three parts, Britannia Prima, Britannia Secunda, and Flavia Cæsaris. High roads, opened throughout the length and breadth of the conquered land, placed it in communication with the seat of government.

Along these high roads, fortresses constructed from distance to distance, and garrisoned by veterans or auxiliaries, insured the submission of the Britons.

In her numerous colonies and stations, it was the policy of Rome to allow her rule to be shared by native potentates; thus the Herods in the East, as we read in Holy Scripture, retained the title of king. In Britain many of the old chieftains, or petty kings, were left in possession of rank and title as long as they did homage to the supremacy of Rome, and brought the annual tribute into her exchequer; just the same as the sovereignty of England is recognised in our days by the Rajahs of India.

However, during the foreign occupation, a remarkable change was effected in the island, by the introduction of Christianity. Before the last Roman soldier had embarked for Gaul, another and more lasting rule had been established in Britain, gradually, it is true, but striking deep root in the minds of the people.

Introduction of Christianity.

The Master of that new empire was Jesus Christ of Nazareth, Son of the living God. In the fifth century, as we shall see later on, Druidism had faded away before the zealous and more enlightened Disciples of the heavenly Creed, and had lost its influence over the Britons. The men of Christ, as the monks were called, occupied the Roman fortresses, and took in hand the education of the British youths. The Druids, forsaken by the people, retired to the mountains or lonesome islands; and their order, unable to recruit fresh subjects to replace those who died, insensibly disappeared.

The old Celtic tongue, rich in figures, terse and energetic in utterance remained; but it conveyed new ideas on the Diety; its unity, and the form of worship.

Contrast between the military conqueror and the peaceful Messenger of the Gospel.

"God is wonderful in His Saints," as the Psalmist observes; by them he converted the world. Pagan Rome was at one time the Empress of the Universe, and, by the force of her arms, ruled from the river Euphrates to the Clyde in Caledonia; her fleets held undisputed sovereignty of the ocean, and, by her wealth, she commanded supremacy in all the markets of the world.† The humble and peaceful apostles of Christ, without armies and fleets, but solely by the persuasion of revealed truth, their edifying lives, and untiring zeal, assisted by Divine grace, brought all the nations of the world to bow

† Godwin de Præsulibus.

INTRODUCTION OF CHRISTIANITY.

down their knees to Jesus of Nazareth, crucified on Mount Calvary. Cæsar took possession of Britain at the head of 30,000 infantry and 2,000 horse. Eight hundred ships conveyed his legions from the shores of France to the coasts of England. Some humble but intrepid missionaries unassisted, except by the grace of God, planted the standard of the Cross in this land, and gained its inhabitants to the religion of Jesus Christ.

Cæsar and his legions have long since disappeared; they only exist in the pages of history; but the teaching and work of the Messengers of the Son of God still remain alike in crowded cities and remote villages.

As regards the introduction of Christianity into insular Britian, the first questions naturally enquired into are:—Who were the first Apostles that taught the religion of their Divine Master in the land? Who were their first converts, and at what period were they gained over to Christ? *First century or Apostolic age.*

The first century of the Christian era is surrounded by dense clouds, and not much information can be arrived at respecting it. In the second, the horizon becomes clearer and documents more abundant. As we descend the stream of time the dead come forth from their graves.

It is asserted by many ecclesiastical writers, of no small repute, that St. Peter, the first Pope, and St. Paul, the Apostle of the Gentiles, preached the Gospel in Britain. On one side, there is nothing to prevent us from believing it; on the other, we find no arguments strong enough to prove, as certain, their presence in this land. Both may have visited England, but it cannot be satisfactorily ascertained. Peter and Paul (especially the latter) were zealous, active, and intrepid travellers; when there was a question of forwarding the interests of their Divine Master, nothing could deter them. After all, there were no insuperable barriers to check their aspirations; even in those days of slow locomotion, a journey from Italy to Britain could not occupy more than a month, for Dr. Lingard observes that heavy goods, such as metals (especially tin), were conveyed from Cornwall to Marseilles in about thirty days.[1]

<small>Joseph of Arimathea.</small> It is also asserted, by ancient monastical historians, that Joseph of Arimathea, who waited on Pontius Pilate and claimed the honour of burying, in his own family vault, the body of his crucified Master, preached the Gospel in this country. Godwin, Protestant Bishop of Llandaff, gives us an interesting dissertation on the subject.[2]

Amongst other details he informs us that in an old manuscript, preserved at the Vatican, it is stated that Joseph of Arimathea was shipped by the Jews in a decayed and leaky vessel, along with Lazarus, Mary Magdalen, and Martha, and sent adrift on the ocean. However, these victims

---

(1) Lingard, History of England, vol. 1.

(2) Godwin de Præsulibus.

of Jewish bigotry and hatred were not deserted by Divine Providence, which steered their frail bark safe into the port of Marseilles in the south of France. Thence Joseph came over to Britain, under the following circumstances. A certain disciple, named Philip, had often come in contact with the Druids in Gaul, and from them had learned that their Chief High Priest dwelt in the great island in the north-west. He thought it advisable to bring the light of the Gospel into the very sanctuary of Druidism, and carry on the work of conversion at headquarters. Joseph of Arimathea and twelve others were chosen for this important undertaking. The missionaries, on landing in Britain, settled at Glastonbury (the Isle of Apples), which was kindly bestowed on them by a chieftain.

The earliest traditions of Britain fully coincide on this point, and call this interesting spot in Somersetshire the *first ground* of God; the first *ground of the saints* in England; the *rise and fountain of religion* in England; the *burying place of the saints;* the *mother of the saints;* they *also say that it was* built by the *very disciples of our* Lord.[1]

Roman officers, whether military or civil, did not disdain to intermarry with the races whom, by the sword, they had conquered and made subject to the senate and Roman people; nor

---

(1) Camden Britannia.

do we read of any regulations issued by their Governments forbidding such unions;, on the contrary, they tended to cement friendship and foster attachment to the new rulers. In the East, Felix the Proconsul, to whom Paul appealed for protection, was married to Drusilla, daughter of Agrippa; and in Britain, Constantius Chlorus shared his destiny with Helena, the mother of Constantine the Great.

British historians record with pride the conversion of two ladies of British race, who *thus* married—one a Patrician, the other a Roman general. Their names are Claudia and Pomponia Græcina.

Claudia

Of Claudia little positive is known beyond her nationality and her conversion to the Christian Faith. This, however, is surmised:—That she was daughter of Caractacus[1] (Caradoc), who for nine years kept the invaders of his country at bay, until at last, defeated and taken captive, he was led in chains to Rome to adorn the triumph of the conqueror on his march to the capitol. He had thus to appear before Claudius and Agrippina, with his wife, his daughters, and his aged father, Bran. The Emperor behaved generously to his prisoner, and gave him his liberty. However, Bran and the rest of the family were kept as hostages to answer for the fidelity of the pardoned British patriot. In the course of time, Bran became acqainted with the religion of Christ,

(1) Nicholl's Antiquity of Wales.

was baptised, and, when allowed to return to his native island, landed in Britain a sincere Christian.[1]

As for Claudia, his granddaughter, after receiving the best education that could be imparted to a patrician lady, she married into the senatorial family of Pudens. Her beauty, talents, and the distant land from which she came, made her such a favourite in Roman society, that even poets deemed it their duty to celebrate, in their verses, this much admired British lady. Martial speaks of her thus:—

> Though Claudia doth descend of British race,
> Yet her behaviour's full of grace ;
> Her beauty far the Italian dames surpass,
> And for her wit she may for Grecian pass.

However, it is not this worldly tribute of praise which renders her memory interesting to the Christian enquirer so much as her immediate connection with the head of the Church.

The names of Peter and Pudens are inseparable. Cornelius the centurion, who was the first Gentile officer converted by St. Peter to the religion of his Divine Master, belonged to this family, and introduced his Apostolic teacher into the patrician household of Pudens, whose guest he became in

---

[1] The Iolo manuscripts contains the following short notice in reference to this point: Bran, the son of Llyr, was the first to bring the Christian faith to this Island from Rome ; and is, therefore, called Bran the Blessed. With him came Ilid, an Israelite, who converted many to the Religion of Christ. Eigen, the daughter of Caradoc (Caractacus), son of Bran, married a chieftain named Sarllog. She was the first female Saint of the Island of Britain. Iolo MSS., page 514.

Rome. The prince of the Apostles repaid his hospitality, by winning to the faith of Christ crucified, Pudens and his wife Claudia. The holy sacrifice of the mass was offered under their roof, and thus, in history, this senatorial mansion is looked upon as the most ancient church in Rome. The Cathedra Petri, or the chair of St. Peter, in Rome, as it still exists, was the gift of Pudens and his British consort Claudia.[1]

Pomponia Græcina. Aulus Plautius, left by Claudius at the head of the Roman forces in Britain, married Pomponia Græcina, believed to be also of British extraction. On the return of her husband to Rome, where he received a petty triumph, she followed him. In this new Babylon, to her great sorrow, she soon became acquainted with the vices, intrigues, and scandal of the Palace, and of Roman society at large. Disgusted with this degraded state of society at court, she turned to the religion of Christ, which was then beginning to attract public attention in the capitol. This step was the signal for trials and persecutions. Her reputation was attacked on all sides, and to such an extent, that the family considered it their duty to call her to account for her conduct before a tribunal composed of her nearest relations; according to Roman custom, her own husband presided at the examination. Amongst many heads of accusations, the only one proved to be true was the fact of her having embraced

(1) Cardinal Wiseman, Fabiola.

a false superstition (the Christian faith), and thus bringing disgrace upon the family.

However, her husband, Aulus Plautius, declared her innocent, inasmuch as she was entitled to liberty of conscience, and therefore free to follow the religion she liked best.[1]

Such are the scanty materials and somewhat uncertain records handed down to us relative to the introduction of Christianity into Britain, its first propagators and followers. It is not likely that such an interesting country as Britain, one which held so high a position in the estimation of Rome, should have been overlooked by such zealous men as the Apostles.

The administration of the immense Roman Empire required a well-organized system of locomotion. Legions and auxiliaries were constantly been moved from the East to the West, and *vice versa*. The same may be said of the almost innumerable civil staff employed by the Imperial Government. A mass of men was thus on the constant move, from one end of the world to the other, as the exigencies of public service required; and fleets, day and night, crossed the ocean, bearing to their respective stations the servants of the immense Empire. To find a parallel in our own days, we must visit the Colonial and Indian Offices of Great Britain, in London, and study its connection with the British Colonies scattered all over the world.

---

(1) Henrion Histoire Ecclesiastique,, Tome xi., page 862.

The great extent of Roman rule helps the propagation of the Gospels

Christianity had already many followers in this army of Pagan Rome; and, wherever they went, they propagated the name of Jesus of Nazareth and His Divine religion. For the early Christians were in earnest, and spared no pains in forwarding the interests of their heavenly Master.

Thus, the intercourse between various nationalities created by Roman ambition was a providential means, made use of by the Church of God, for disseminating the Gospel. The Christians in a Roman legion, whether quartered on the river Usk in Wales, in a fortress in Yorkshire, or in any other part of the globe, would erect a Catholic altar for the holy sacrifice of the Body and Blood of Jesus Christ.

However, through lack of trustworthy documents, we are unable to state precisely the extent of the Gospel's propagation, or the proximate numerical strength of the faithful amongst the Britons, in the first century of the Christian era.

Second and third Centuries

Let us now place before the reader a synopsis of the work of the Christian Religion in Britain, its progress, trials, and final triumph, down to the days when Germanus and Lupus came over as champions of Catholic truth against Pelagianism.

In the second century, the Ecclesiastical History of Britain becomes more diffuse and precise. The country feels a certain pride in announcing to the world that the first crowned

INTRODUCTION OF CHRISTIANITY.

head who embraced Christianity and propagated its doctrines amongst his countrymen, was by birth a Briton.

The name of this king was Lucius in Latin, Lewfer Mawr (the Great Brightness) in his native language. He was the son of Coyle, a British Chieftain, who, unlike most of his compeers, had willingly accepted the Roman yoke. Coyle in his youth had been sent to Rome to be educated, and on his return, had succeeded to his father's kingdom. During a long reign he won the affection of his subjects and the respect of the Roman rulers, to whom he did homage, and paid the usual tribute, with the greatest regularity.[1]

When Lucius ascended the throne, his subjects could boast that their young Prince was superior to most of the native chieftains, for his father had bestowed on him all the advantages of education which he had himself acquired in Rome.

Not only from the Romans, but also from such of his own subjects as had travelled abroad, either as students or soldiers, Lucius heard narratives of the wonderful miracles wrought by Christians—their heroic attachment to their faith, even through the greatest trials—and of the rapid progress of their religion in every class of society. This led him to take a great interest in the study of Christianity. In a short time the impression produced on his mind by the history

King Lucius becomes a Christian

(1) Sammes, Britannia Antiqua, p. 256.

of the birth, life, death, and resurrection of our Lord excited in his heart a desire to become a Christian. On being informed that Eleutherius, the chief Pontiff of this heavenly religion, resided in Rome, he determined to send ambassadors to this Vicar of Jesus Christ. Two envoys, duly accredited, set out for Rome, to petition the Pope to send missionaries to Britain for the purpose of instructing their master—King Lucius—and his people in the faith of Christ.[1]

Eleutherius received the embassy with the greatest kindness, and on learning the object of their mission raised up his hands with emotion, and thanked Almighty God for having thus visited with His grace the remote land of Britain. The envoys seem to have received baptism in Rome, and returned to their sovereign accompanied by two missionaries, Fugatius and Damianus—or, in the Celtic tongue, Fagan and Damian.[2]

<small>St. Fagans and Merthyrdovan hamlets in Glamorganshire are named after these two Apostles.</small>

The Britons were, no doubt, ripe for conversion. The missionaries met with a people ready to receive the Gospel. We read of no desecration or bloodshed in connection with its propagation; and, wonderful to relate, the Imperial Government—the declared enemy of Christianity in every other part of the globe—remained indifferent to its introduction and progress in Britain.

(1) Nennius places the event in the year of Our Lord 187.
(2) Geoffrey of Monmouth calls them Faganus and Duvanus, and these are the names by which they are still known in South Wales.

Shortly after their arrival the two missionaries entered on the work, and baptized King Lucius, many of his officers, and a multitude of his subjects.

The Protestant Bishop, Godwin, observes that the truth spread with rapidity through the length and breadth of the land. The zealous teachers, Fagan and Damian, unable to attend to the spiritual wants of so many thousands who were desirous of instruction, thought it best to return to Rome to plead the cause of the British neophytes, and urge on the Pope the necessity of sending them further assistance.

He granted their request, and they returned to Britain with additional labourers. The propagation of the Gospel then progressed with even greater rapidity.

In accordance with orders to that effect received from the Holy See, a Hierarchy, similar to that established in other parts of the world, was constituted in Britain.

It corresponded with the civil divisions of the country, and comprised three dioceses, or archdioceses—namely, London, York, and Caerleon. York had jurisdiction over the North of England; to Caerleon, on the river Usk, Wales was subjected; and London exercised jurisdiction over the rest of the country.[1]

The conversion of Lucius and of a large proportion of the Britons is not a pious fiction, as some modern writers endeavour to maintain. It

(1) Godwin, Geoffrey and others.

is based on facts difficult to deny. The archives of the most ancient churches throughout Britain afford proof beyond doubt that this Christian Prince was connected with their foundation. Godwin, the Protestant Bishop, elucidates this fact with great erudition.

<small>Churches erected in the days of Lucius.</small>
The first church ever built in London was that of St. Peter, Cornhill, which was erected by Bishop Heanus, or Theanus. He was greatly assisted in his work by the cup-bearer of Lucius. Elvanus, the second Bishop, built a library in connection with the same Church, and gained over many Druids to the Christian faith.

The See of York owes its origin to the zeal and liberality of the same saintly king, and its first Bishop seems to have been a missionary named Samson.

The first Church erected in Llandaff, near Cardiff, Glamorganshire, was also in a great measure the work of Lucius. St. Fagan preached the Gospel in this part of the island; and a Parish Church within a mile or two of Llandaff was named after him, and has handed down to posterity the appreciation with which his zeal and Apostolic labours were regarded by past generations.

The Church of Winchester, dedicated to our Saviour, was opened for Divine worship in October, 189, by Fagan and Damian, under the auspices of Lucius. For about a hundred years religion flourished in that part of the country.

Under the persecution of Diocletian the Churches were levelled to the ground, but on the accession of Constantine to the dominion of the Roman Empire, the Church of Winchester was re-built, and dedicated to Amphilobus, the Priest sheltered by St. Alban, but later on put to death through hatred of Christ.

The writer of these pages regrets his inability to supply fuller or more graphic details in connection with this first Royal convert received into the Church as a Sovereign; we do not find his name associated with any daring exploits on the battle-field, but he may be justly styled the protector and even the propagator of the Christian faith in his native land.

The very fact of his embracing Christianity despite Druidical prejudice and Roman opposition, and of his zealous and open exertions to further its extension, shows beyond doubt that he possessed a noble mind, and was endowed with an energetic will; for many there are, even in our own times, who, having been inspired with the knowledge of the truth, are yet so weak-hearted as to shrink away from it, through pusillanimity and human respect.

It is not unlikely that the conquerors of Britain, though not openly persecuting the Christians by endeavouring to force them to offer incense to idols, and on their refusal condemning them to torture or death, yet caused them in many ways to suffer for the faith, through withholding the full measure of justice from them at their tribunals, and depriving them of many rights and privileges. They may thus have suffered from the action of many petty penal laws.

It is stated that Lucius bestowed both constitutional and civic freedom upon the Christians, and granted them special privileges in regard to law and land. Coyle, his father, had gone to Rome to study profane science at the seat of Empire. He, from the same city, brought the faith to his countrymen. He led a life of celibacy after his conversion, and was the first Prince in Britain to practise continency, which so many thousands followed him in adopting, in accordance with the counsels of perfection taught by the Gospel.

King Lucius buried at Glo'ster.

Some annalists contend that Lucius, in his latter days, retired to Germany, where he preached the Christian faith and received the crown of martyrdom. But this Lucius of the Teutons must not be confounded with the British Prince of the same name, who, according to the more probable opinion of grave historians, gave up his soul to his Maker in Gloucester, and was there buried, Anno Domino 201. His feast was celebrated on the 3rd of December, the day of his death, and on the anniversary of his baptism, May 28th.[1]

---

1. Mathew of Westminster has handed down the following notice in reference to this:—

Anno Gratia CCI., Inclytus Brittanorum, Rex Lucius, in bonis actibus assumtus Claudio cestria ab nac vita migrovit ad Christum et in Ecc'esia prima sedis honorifice sepultus en. (Sammes, Biitt. Ant., p. 266).

INTRODUCTION OF CHRISTIANITY. 23

The records of Church history, handed down to us from the death of Lucius to the tenth persecution under Diocletian, are very scanty.

During this period, however, the British Church was fruitful, not only in native clergy, fitted to supply its own spiritual wants, but also in missionaries to foreign countries.

I may here cite St. Mellon, first Bishop of Rouen, Normandy. Mellon, probably a member of the British aristocracy, was led by curiosity to visit Rome, the capital of the conquerors of his native land, which, whilst yet a Pagan, he had heard extolled for its beauty, refinement, and population. In the Holy City, however, he became a Christian, receiving baptism from the Pope St. Stephen, Anno Domino 257, who sent him to preach the Gospel in Gaul. *St. Mellon first Bishop of Rouen.*

Mellon laboured with zeal amongst the Neustrians, and when consecrated Bishop fixed his See at Rouen, about the year 260. His Episcopal administration lasted fifty years, and during this long period he built several Churches, and laid

---

In the Iolo MSS. we find the following passage in connection with King Lucius:—

St. Lleirug, King of the Island of Britain, the son of Coel . . . . sent to Rome for a Bishop to return with him, in order to baptise such of the Cymry as embraced the faith of Christ. Pope Eleutherius granted him as Bishops, Elvan, Medwy, Dyvan, and Fagan.

St. Fagan was Bishop of Llansanfagan, where a Church was dedicated to him.

St. Medwy occupied the See of Llanmedwy, which also possesses a Church dedicated in his name.

The Church and College of Glastonbury were dedicated to St. Elvan, the first Bishop of that See, (Iolo MSS., p. 514).

It may not be out of place here to remind the reader that the two last-named Saints—Medwy and Elvan—are supposed to be the two Ambassadors sent to Pope Eleutherius. In the City of Rome they received baptism, and later on ordination, and were thus enabled to preach the Gospel to their countrymen.

as it were the foundation of the Cathedral of that city on the very spot it now occupies. The noble Gothic building which in our days is the glory of the capital of Normandy of course traces its origin to a more modern date.

St. Mellon died at an advanced age, and rich in noble deeds, at the beginning of the fourth century. A beautiful village near Cardiff still bears his name.

<small>The first nine persecutions against the Christians not carried out.</small>
The Britons were spared all the horrors of the first nine general persecutions. If the edicts of the Roman Emperors were officially proclaimed throughout the land, they turned out dead letters, as no Proconsul or Magistrate had either the will or could spare the time to carry them into execution.

In France, Spain, and Italy, as in the East, Christian blood was shed in torrents. The Amphitheatres became the scene of the protracted struggles and final victory of thousands of martyrs. But in Britain, the followers of Christ were allowed to remain undisturbed, although perhaps some minor penal laws may have been put in force against them.

This leniency on the part of local authorities proved beneficial to the Church. The Christians when persecuted elsewhere fled for shelter to this island, where, the moment they landed, they felt safe. Thousands of the faithful children of the Church who were marked for destruction in Gaul and Spain crossed over to Britain, and thus added to the strength of the Christian community.

However, on the 27th of February, 303,[1] a first edict of persecution was issued, with orders that it should not only be published, but also rigorously carried out throughout the Empire.

This edict enacted that all Christian Churches should be levelled to the ground, all copies of the Holy Scriptures should be confiscated and burnt, and the followers of Christ should be tortured, without any distinction of rank, age, or sex.

Christians were debarred from honours and dignities, and were deprived of their possessions. Any one could sue them before the Magistrates, but they were to have no power of appeal to the Judges. They were pronounced incompetent to claim redress in any civil court, either for robbery, violence, or any injustice whatever that might be committed against them. In a word, they were declared outlaws, in the fullest sense of the term.

Shortly after the first a second and third edict, referring particularly to the Clergy, were proclaimed. By order of these, the ministers of the Christian religion were at once to be arrested and tortured, unless they offered incense to the idols.

Explicit orders were at the same time sent to Britain to enforce these penal laws in the strictest manner.

---

(1) Henrion, Histoire Eccles. Tome 13, p. 54-55.

Constantius Chlorus was then the Cæsar of the West. In religion he was a Philosopher. As a ruler, history gives him the credit of being a just man, and of possessing a discerning mind, and a heart inclining to mercy.

He was aware that the Christians, as citizens, were as loyal, if not more so, than their persecutors, and that they had as much right to believe and follow the religion of Christ as the Romans had to worship Jupiter or Mars; therefore the cruel and impolitic edicts which ordered the extermination of the Christians were enacted without his approval.

However, for the moment he had no choice but to publish the decrees, being assured that if *he* individually was reluctant to carry them out, no such scruple would be felt by many of his Lieutenants and Magistrates.

Constantius puts his household to test.
A considerable portion of his own household belonged to the Christian faith. Summoning these together, he read to them the Imperial orders, and told them that under such circumstances it would be necessary for them either to offer sacrifice to the national gods or resign their respective offices. He would allow them time for reflection.

On the day appointed for receiving their decision, a great number declared that they would rather forfeit their position than become renegades, whilst others pusillanimously professed themselves ready to offer sacrifice to the national deities. Having listened to the noble refusal of the Christians to barter faith for worldly advantage, and to the cowardly subservience of the Apostates, Constantius gave his own opinion as to their respective conduct.[1] In no measured terms he condemned the base acquiescence and the cowardice of the renegades, telling them that he never henceforward could place any confidence in them, for they could not be true to the Cæsars who had proved traitors to their God, and deserters from their religion. He then informed them that he would for the future dispense with their services, and dismissed them. The faithful Christians on the contrary he retained near his person, and, convinced of their loyalty, entrusted to them the most important affairs. Moreover, it was from amongst them he selected his own body-guard, and during his whole life he placed the greatest confidence in their loyalty.

This policy does credit to the discernment of Constantius, and is a strong proof of his common sense.

It is a time-honoured axiom that he is not to be depended upon who abjures what is, by a right-minded man, deemed most sacred—his conscientious belief.

Had the officers employed by Constantius in Britain been endowed with a similar nobility of nature, the tenth general persecution would not have been carried out there, any more than the

---

(1) Henrion, Hist. Eccl. Tome XI., p. 66. Lingard, Hist. of England.

nine preceding ones. However, such was not the case.

St. Alban
In the persecution of Diocletian, Christian blood was shed all over Britain. St. Alban, who is looked upon as the proto-martyr of England, suffered at Verulum. A priest named Amphibolus—later on the patron saint of Winchester—was pursued by the lictors of Diocletian. St. Alban, whilst yet a Pagan, offered refuge to the fugitive, and concealed him in his own house. Struck by the demeanour of his guest, and by his pious life (for Amphibolus spent most of his time in prayer), Alban enquired into his religion, and soon became instructed in the doctrine of Christ. On the Governor being informed that he gave shelter to a priest a band of soldiers was dispatched to arrest the servant of God. To defeat this intention Alban induced Amphibolus to exchange garments with him, and fly beyond the reach of his persecutors. Then, taking his place, he presented himself before the Roman soldiers in the caracalla, or long robe, worn by the priesthood. He was brought before the Governor at an hour when the latter was offering sacrifice to his gods. Hearing how his satellites had been deceived, he flew into a great passion, and exclaimed—" Since the priest Amphibolus has escaped through your exchanging clothes with him, you shall now die in his place, unless you offer sacrifice to the immortal gods." Alban, who had already declared himself a Christian to

the soldiers, said, with determination, that he would never obey the Governor in offering incense to dumb idols. "But who are you," replied the Governor, "who dare to resist my command? What family do you claim kindred with?" "It matters little from what family I spring. If you desire to know my religion, I am a Christian." "But," repeated the Governor, "what is your name?" "I am called Alban; I adore the only true God, Creator of heaven and earth." The Governor—"Either sacrifice to the idol, or die a miserable death by the hand of the public executioner." Alban—"You, Governor, sacrifice to your idols; I will not so debase myself. They can neither hear the prayers of their worshippers nor come to their assistance. Those who sacrifice to them have nothing but eternal punishment in store."

The Governor, exasperated, ordered him to be scourged till his bones were laid bare, and a pool of blood covered the ground under his feet; but Alban remaining steadfast, the angry judge commanded the executioner to strike off his head. It was at Verulum, then a flourishing city, that Alban suffered for his Saviour. On their way to the place of execution they came to a bridge built across the river Cole. This bridge was crowded by thousands of spectators, and all the efforts of the soldiers to clear a passage proved fruitless. Alban, longing to die gloriously for his Divine Master, besought them to open a way across, when, behold! the bed of the river became dry, and more than a thousand persons passed safely to the other side—the water, says Gildas, standing like walls on both sides.

The commanding *officer* was so struck by this miracle that he threw himself at the feet of Alban, and begged either to die in his place, or, at least, in his company. On his refusal to cut off the head of Alban, he was condemned to die with him, and thus shared his martyrdom. St. Alban gained his crown on the 22nd of June. Verulum has fallen to ruin, but a more modern town erected on the same spot commemorates, by its name of St. Albans, the first martyr of Britain.

<small>Martyrs of Caerleon</small> Many other saints of both sexes were slain in the cause of their Divine Master throughout the country. It is said they numbered thousands. South Wales participated in the glorious roll of martyrs. Caerleon—its seat of government—was the scene of not a few executions. History has transmitted the names of but two of these Christian heroes—Aaron and Julius, or Jules. Both these saints were Britons, and both seem to have gone to Rome in their youth to pursue their ecclesiastical studies, and in that city to have been admitted to Holy orders. The martyrs had probably been the priests of Caerleon, Usk, and the country adjoining. If we rely on the traditions which exist in South Wales, even at the present day, we will find that the persecution in this part of Britain was carried on with extreme

severity. Ten thousand martyrs, it is asserted, shed their blood at Caerleon, on the river Usk. The authorities of this district must have intensely hated the very name of Christianity, and waged a religious war à outrance against the followers of the Saviour, who were here very numerous and deeply devoted to their faith. It is again to be regretted that no detailed narrative of the noble struggles of these heroic souls, as also no list of their names, should have been preserved for our edification.

As Aaron and Julius were eminent amongst the Confessors, two Churches were erected by their countrymen on the spots crimsoned by their blood—one on the east, the other on the west side of the river. London also possesses the record of the martyrdom of Augulus—a priest who, it is believed, was a bishop. Lichfield, or the City of Carcasses, witnessed the noble death of hundreds of the followers of Christ.

Constantius Chlorus had taken more a passive than an active part in the persecution, and, as far as he was himself concerned, had only levelled the Churches, sparing the living temples of God. Therefore, as soon as he felt himself independent of his colleagues in Rome, he ordered their edicts to be altogether annulled in Britain.[1]

To his son Constantine, however, was reserved the glory of putting a stop for ever to the cruel and iniquitous war waged by the Roman Empire

---

(1) Gildas.

against the Church. This young Prince, on hearing of his father's illness, hastened to York to attend his death-bed, and received from him his last will. Constantius, presenting the future champion of the Church to the assembled councillors, thus addressed them:—

<small>Constantine Emperor.</small>
"I leave you my son as my successor in this Empire. With God's assistance he shall wipe away the tears of the Christians, and avenge the tyranny practised against them. In this, above all, do I place my hopes of felicity."[1]

This address gained general approval. and was heartily applauded by all the Legions, for public opinion already held in execration the long persecution so cruelly carried on against the Christians. If such were the wishes of Constantius—one of the few Cæsars who favoured the followers of Christ—they were fully realised.

It may here be interesting to relate the incident connected with the conversion of Constantine before his entry into Italy. He was favoured by beholding the apparition of a cross in the air, on which appeared the words, in Greek characters, "In hoc signo vince"—through this sign shalt thou conquer.

After the overthrow of Maxentius, the victor emancipated his Christian subjects, and became their benefactor throughout the Empire.

His mother, St. Helena—who, according to the generally received opinion, was British by birth—

(1) Sammes, Britannia Antiqua, p. 314.

followed the example of her son, and embraced the religion of Jesus Christ.

Her latter days were entirely devoted to good works, particularly those of restoring the Holy Places connected with the birth, life, and death of the Redeemer, both within and without Jerusalem. It was she who discovered the true cross on which the Saviour had died, and built Churches both over His sepulchre and the manger in Bethlehem, which was His first resting-place on earth.

<small>St. Helena</small>

When this Imperial matron departed from earth, the Church bestowed upon her the title "Venerabilis et Piissima Augusta"—an august and most pious Princess. Never was a title more correct.

The great revolution in religious matters effected by Constantine changed the entire face of the world. Not only was liberty of conscience granted to the Christians, but decrees were enacted by which the ministers of that religion, through force of circumstances, were obliged to assume the same position, both socially and politically, as that held by the Hierophants of the Paganism which was fading away.

Under the auspices of Constantine the Christian Priesthood became the Clergy of the Empire.

In Britain the Church rapidly recovered from her sufferings. The Christians returned from the forests and the mountains and re-built their[1]

---

(1) Gildas.

temples, having a particular regard, in several instances, to dedicate them to such of their brethren as had nobly given their lives for Christ. Accordingly, the new Church at Verulum was named after St. Alban, whilst that of Winchester was dedicated to Amphibolus, the martyr, who had been the priest of the district when the persecution overwhelmed it. At Caerleon the same rule was followed in perpetuation of the noble sacrifice made by Aaron and Julius.

<small>British Bishops at the Council of Arles and Rimini.</small> So flourishing did religion become at that time, that the British Church sent three of her most distinguished Bishops to represent her at the Council of Arles, in 314. These Prelates filled the Sees of York, London, and probably that of Caerleon.

In the middle of the same century we again find British Bishops on their way to join the assembly of their Episcopal brethren, convened against Arianism. This time their destination was not to the South of France, but carried them beyond the Alps to Rimini (Ariminum) in the Romagna.

Constantius, the son of Constantine, had ordered that all the travelling expenses on this occasion should be defrayed out of the public purse. The Bishops of Aquitaine, Gaul, and Britain preferred living at their own expense, in order to show the world that they were independent of the Emperor. Three of the English Prelates, however, having no means of their own, and being unwilling to burthen their Episcopal brethren, availed themselves of the Imperial offer, remarking that their maintainance would fall lighter on the public purse than on that of individuals.

In closing this short notice of the tenth persecution, and its noble victims, it may be well to call the attention of the reader to the glorious martyrdom of St. Ursula and her companions, which took place towards the latter end of the fourth century. These daughters of Christ were not amongst those who fell victims to the deliberately issued Penal Edicts of the Emperors—they met their death through the ferocity of the Huns. The circumstances connected with this event may be thus briefly summed up. *(St. Ursula and her Companions Martyred)*

The Emperor, Gratian Flavius Clemens Maximus, came to Britain and caused himself to be proclaimed Cæsar.[1] Having consolidated his power in the island, he then turned his thoughts to the conquest of Gaul, and for this purpose collected a large army, with which he sailed for the Continent. He first attacked the Armoricans, upon whose shores he landed. So desolated did this province become through the war, that but few of its inhabitants remained on its soil, those who were not slain in battle retiring to the interior of Gaul.

Maximus, anxious to re-people the country, published a decree, by which he invited a hundred thousand of the peasants of Britain to come to

---

(1) Geoffrey of Monmouth, Roman Breviary, Supplementair.

Armorica and settle there. An army of thirty thousand soldiers was allotted to protect this colony from hostile attacks. These forced immigrants, on their arrival in Armorica, were distributed throughout the province, and thus Maximus created a new Britain on the western coast of France, which, in course of time, became known as Brittany.

Having arranged all to his satisfaction, Maximus bestowed the new province on Conan Meriadec, and proceeded to complete the final conquest of Gaul.

Conan Meriadec was not long in possession of his dominion when he discovered a drawback. So great was the numerical disparity between the men and the women, that it was impossible for his subjects to procure British wives, and he was unwilling that they should intermarry with Gauls.

In this dilemma he looked to his native land for the future mothers of his people, and dispatched messengers to Britain to place before Dianotus, King of Cornwall, the special difficulty he laboured under in Armorica in this respect, asking at the same time the King to bestow on him in marriage the hand of his daughter Ursula.

Dianotus acceded to the wishes of Conan, and issued a summons to the daughters of the nobility, and also to a great number of young women of inferior rank, requiring them, whether willing or unwilling, to assemble at a given date in London, where he was collecting a fleet to transport them to Armorica.

INTRODUCTION OF CHRISTIANITY. 37

This arbitrary measure may have pleased some, particularly those who had husbands in Brittany, and perhaps others who were not unwilling to marry there.

But a great number naturally felt aggreived at being forced to leave their native land and their relatives and friends. A few, like St. Ursula, had vowed virginity, devoting themselves to heavenly espousals. To these the commands of the King were especially obnoxious.

The fleet, with its living freight, sailed down the Thames, but in the channel encountered a violent storm, and was dispersed. Many of the ships foundered, and those which weathered the tempest were driven by the westerly gale towards Holland and Belgium, on whose shores the crews and passengers landed, in a most forlorn condition.

The brutal soldiers who had been appointed to guard the unfortunate women, finding them thus at their mercy, and having no respect either for chastity or liberty of conscience, required their victims to sacrifice their virtue, and also to offer incense to Pagan deities.

Ursula, in the name of all, pleaded their cause, and appealed to the honour of the soldiers for protection and respect towards defenceless women. *St. Ursula and her Companions.* She said that their destination was Armorica, to which place it was their intention to proceed, to join their relatives, friends, or husbands. They therefore hoped to be allowed to travel unharmed to the camp of Maximus, who would provide them with the means of making their way to Armorica. They belonged to the Catholic faith, which ordained chastity, not only to the virgin, but to the married woman and widow.

Being commanded by their captors to renounce their faith, these virtuous women declared that they would die rather than abandon the religion of the Redeemer of the world; and they also sternly refused to forfeit their chastity. This so exasperated the soldiers that they rushed on the defenceless victims, and put them to death. One only, named Cordula, contrived to escape; but, struck by the determination of her companions, and the spectacle of the turf reddened with their blood, she hastened back, proclaimed to the barbarians that she also was a Christian, and claimed, like them, the privilege of dying for her Divine Master, and following the souls of her friends to the throne of God. On this the soldiers, in their fury, at once slew her.

The martyrdom of these Christian heroines took place on the 21st of October, in the year of our Lord 383, and their memory is held in great veneration. The Emperor Theodosius was in the habit of invoking St. Ursula and her companions when in danger, and at the commencement of his battles. It is rather difficult to indicate exactly the number included in this martyr band, but some assert that it amounted to eleven thousand.

INTRODUCTION OF CHRISTIANITY. 39

Conan Meriadec could hardly be consoled on learning the fate of his promised wife, Ursula.

Breton historians relate that later on he married Darerea, sister of St. Patrick, who, they state, was born at Pondaven, a village in the Diocese of Quimper, Finisterre, and thus neither Scotland nor Wales can claim this Saint amongst their noblest sons.

If Arianism found place in the minds of some Christians in Britain, the number was so trifling that this erroneous doctrine can scarcely be said to have taken root in the island.

The same assertion cannot, unfortunately, be made in regard to Pelagianism.

Morgan, a Briton by birth, as his name clearly indicates, was a lay Monk of Bangor, North Wales, near Chester. Nature had not favoured him physically, as he was blind of one eye, and otherwise disfigured. However, he was endowed with great intellectual powers, and possessed a strong will. Going on pilgrimage to Rome, he became attached to that city and its inhabitants, and determined to make it his place of abode. There he improved his education, and became known amongst the Roman literati as a good Greek and Latin scholar. Later on he proceeded to the East, where he changed his Celtic name into its Greek equivalent—Pelagius. He adopted the errors of Theodorus of Mopsuestia, about the year 400.[1]

Pelagius or Morgan.

---

(1) Henrion Hist. Eccles. Tomo xiii., p. 584.

Pelagius denied the doctrine of original sin and its consequences. According to his opinion there was no necessity for divine grace for the enlightenment of our mind and the strengthening of our will. Such a doctrine, according to his theory, upset the whole scheme of redemption, because, if mankind was not guilty, there was no need for a Redeemer, and the seven sacraments instituted by our Lord, as seven channels of grace, were useless. As a modern writer[1] has observed, Pelagianism is the eldest sister of the rationalism of our days, which maintains that reason, unassisted by Divine grace, is a sufficient guide and monitor for man on his way through life.

This heresy was triumphantly refuted by the great St. Augustine in his treatises on grace, and was also condemned by several Councils.

About the same time, under Pope Celestine, Fastidius, Bishop of London, wrote two books on this subject—"De Vita Christiana," and "De Medico ad Conservandam Viduitatem." These treatises are elegant and polished in style, but somewhat savour of Pelagianism.[2]

Whilst the peace of the Church was being disturbed, even in the British Isles, by Pelagianism, she was at the same time receiving consolation from the thousands of converts who flocked into the fold in Scotland and Ireland.

St. Palladius. St. Prosper, speaking of Pope Celestine, says that, not satisfied with exterminating Pelagianism

---

(1) Henrion, Hist. Eccles. Tome xv., p. 267.
(2) The same, p. 1214. This work is to be found in the Patrologia of Migne.

INTRODUCTION OF CHRISTIANITY. 41

in Great Britain, he consecrated a Bishop for the Scoti, or Hibernians. This Bishop, whose name was Palladius, sailed for Ireland in 431, with special instructions from the Pope to devote himself to the faithful in that country. The Christian religion had already been preached in the southern province by St. Albius, St. Declan, St. Ibar, and St. Kiaran, who had there established Christian communities.[3]

This statement is confirmed by the following incident, mentioned in the life of St. Patrick:— The great Apostle, after evangelizing the north and centre of Ireland, visited the south; but here he found a Catholic clergy and population disposed to receive him much in the same way that, later on, the Bishops of Britain received St. Augustine.

Palladius in Scotland and Ireland. Palladius landed at Wicklow, and remained there about a year, when he was forced to abandon his intended field of labour, in consequence of the persecution of some petty prince. He sailed from thence to Scotland.

If his work in Ireland was unfruitful, it was richly rewarded by the Caledonians, whose first Bishop he became.[1]

Where the Apostle of Scotland failed, St. Patrick was ordained to succeed, reaping a most

---

(1) The Scoti of Caledonia claim, like the Britains, to have received the Gospel in Apostolic times. Be this as it may, it is, however, certain that a holy Bishop, a North Briton, educated and ordained in Rome during the reign of Pope Damasus, planted the cross in the South of Scotland. His name was Ninias, or Ninianus. This saintly Apostle fixed his See at Whitehern, in Galloway, where he built a stone Church, and dedicated it to St. Martin.

abundant harvest, and winning to the faith of Christ the whole unconverted population of Hibernia.

St. Patrick Strange to say, he also landed at Wicklow, in the very territory abandoned the previous year by his predecessor. Like him, too, he had to leave and make his way to the north of the island, where, as a slave, he had suffered much. St. Patrick was accompanied by thirty or thirty-four fellow-labourers, whom he had collected in Italy, France, and Britain, to share his toils and triumph. In considering the immense work he performed, and his continual journeys and preachings, one would be led to think that he must have commenced his apostolate in the prime of life. This, however, is not the case. He had attained the age of sixty when he entered on his missionary career, being born about the year 372, and commencing his work in 432. Yet, like a conqueror, he swept through the north, converting the Pagans by thousands, and persuading even princes and princesses not only to become Christians, but to embrace the monastic life.

When the thirty missionaries who had accompanied him to Ireland became inadequate to the spiritual wants of the converts, so rapidly did they increase, St. Patrick sailed for Britain, to enlist Priests from the ranks of the clergy of that country, either as professors for the University of Armagh, or to assist him in the work of conversion.

This Apostle, so wonderful, who is even to this

day held in such love and reverence wherever an Irish heart beats, or an Irish foot has been planted, was nearly a centenarian at the time of his death. Before leaving for heaven the land he loved so well, he could say with truth—

"When at the age of sixteen I was captured and brought to this soil as a slave, there was no Christian altar at which I could kneel, or Christian soul with whom I could commune. When I fled from hence the whole country was plunged in idolatry. At sixty I returned as Bishop, and now, after labouring for forty years in my mission, I die rejoicing, for few are now the children of this land who remain unconverted to the faith of my Master."[1]

Few amongst the Apostles succeeded during their own lifetime in changing a whole nation from idolatry to Christianity. Ireland, as a people, has lost her native Celtic tongue, but most steadfastly has she preserved the faith of the Catholic Church, taught by Saint Patrick.

Although originating with a native of Britain, Pelagianism did not gain much ground in the island until an exiled partisan of the heresy succeeded, on his return to Britain, in deceiving many by an exaggerated account of the talents and virtues of Morgan, whom he represented as a persecuted defender of the truth. Agricola—such was his name—gained over several of the

---

(1) St. Patrick was born in the year 372 at Pondaven, a town now in the Diocese of Quimper, Finisterre.

clergy and laity to his views, and thus, for the first time, the plague of religious dissension was disseminated throughout the land.

<small>St. Germanus and Lupus.</small>

Palladius, writing from Scotland, informed Pope Celestine of the disturbed state of religion in that country. At the same time the British clergy sent a deputation to the Bishops of Gaul, soliciting them, as qualified to explain the orthodox doctrine of grace, to give their aid in a holy war against heresy. In consequence of this application Germanus and Lupus were sent to Britain for the purpose of upholding the true faith.

Germanus, the head of this mission, had in his youth been a lawyer, then a soldier, and subsequently, as Bishop, was eminent for sanctity and erudition.

To give greater effect to his mission, Pope Celestine named him his Vicar Apostolic in Britain. During their voyage across the channel the two Bishops were assailed by a violent storm, as though the demons of dissension dreaded their landing on British shores.

Germanus, filled with confidence in God, invoked the adorable Trinity to come to their aid, and poured Holy Water on the sea. The storm then abated, and they were enabled to reach the English shores.

The arrival of the two Bishops soon produced good effects. They preached without intermission in the Churches, in market places, on elevated spots, in the fields, under the canopy of heaven. Thousands of the people crowded to hear them, and wherever they directed their steps they were met by multitudes.

The noble forgot for the moment the pleasures of the chase; the labourer left his plough in the furrow, rather than forfeit the chance of hearing the truth from the lips of these holy and eloquent preachers. Even mothers, with infants in their arms, made their way through the throngs in order to approach as near as possible to the two Bishops.

Pelagianism rapidly lost ground in public opinion. Germanus and Lupus soon made it clear to all that the doctrine of Christ, not that of Morgan, was the true faith; that the Church, the guardian of truth against innovators, was the appointed teacher whom all must hear; and that no credence must be attached to an individual presuming to come forward and endeavour to impose his own views on the ignorant and credulous.

The missionary Bishops, however, were not only powerful in their orthodox teaching, but also in supernatural deeds. On a certain occasion a Tribune and his wife, leading by the hand their blind daughter, ten years of age, made their way through the crowd, and presenting her to the preachers, besought them, in the name of God, to restore sight to their beloved child. Germanus referred the case to the heretical teachers, asking them to comply with the parents wishes. They, of course, were unable to do so, and declined. Germanus then, filled with the Holy Ghost, invoked the name of the Blessed Trinity, and the girl at that moment was restored to her sight. Such miracles as these were even more powerful than eloquence, and made a deep impression on the people, who ever afterwards accepted the words of the Bishops as Gospel.

Germanus twice visited Britain. First in the year 425 or 426, and again, twenty years later, in 446. On the second occasion, Bishop Severus, and not Lupus, was his companion.

Such is the substance of what may be gathered concerning the Church in this island, from its first foundation down to about the middle of the fifth century.

Compared with the immense results obtained as regards Christianity, the records we possess are indeed scanty. When the last Roman soldier left Britain for Gaul the whole nation had been converted to the religion of Christ, and possessed a regularly constituted hierarchy of Archbishops and Bishops throughout the entire island. Priests were distributed in due proportion to carry on the work of the mission. This affords ample testimony that at that time the rule of Christ was firmly established through the length and breadth of Britain.

A few observations on the fall of the Roman Empire. The departure of the pro-consuls effected a great change in the temporal administration of the country. The organization established by the Cæsars ceased then to exist. It is also worthy of remark that, about the same time, the Vicar of Christ in Rome was already beginning to acquire that moral influence which, in the end, was to raise him to the temporal supremacy of the City of the Cæsars.

The colossal empire, crimsoned with the blood of Christian martyrs, was crumbling to ruin, a prey to two powerful enemies—its own corruption and the invasion of barbarians. The hand of Divine justice was armed against it, and its day of retribution had come. Christ had already punished the Jews, the first enemies of his Church. They, as a nation, had ceased to exist.

Now, in her turn, Pagan Rome was to disappear as an empire. Heaven, for three hundred years, had patiently beheld the tortures inflicted on the Christians in the Forum and Amphitheatre by these proud idolaters. The time of hard trial for the Church had passed away, and she was now triumphant. The heathen temples were deserted, or changed into Catholic Churches.

Now was heard chanted at Matins by the clergy round the altars these words of David— "Why have the Gentiles raged, and the people devised vain things? The kings of the earth stood up, and the princes met together against the Lord and against His Christ, saying: Let us break their bonds asunder, and let us cast away their yoke from us. He that dwelleth in heaven shall laugh at them, and the Lord shall deride them."[1] These words were most applicable to the doomed empire. At the fall of the Cæsars and the extinction of their rule, the fathers of the Church were forced to exclaim—"Justus es Domine et rectum Judicium tuum."

<small>What now is visible of the ruins of the past</small> The inhabitants of the earth in this, the nineteenth century, if educated, have had the growth, increase, final grandeur, and fall of that mighty empire placed before them in the school-room, but the mass of mankind knows but little if anything of its existence and doings. Now and then the scholar's attention is drawn to some ruined temple, "broken arch," rusty old coin which has been disentombed, or tesselated pavement, all of which proclaim to the gazer, "Vanity of vanities." And of the mighty "mistress of the world" nothing more now remains!

Truly dost the Psalmist exclaim, Everything under the sun is doomed to destruction, but *Veritas Domini manet in æternam.*

The Cæsars, with their legions, have passed away, but Christ and his religion remains. The Church to-day sings His glory and triumph throughout the universe. "*Te per orbem terrarum sancta Confitetur Ecclesia.*" His name is hallowed, not only in the school-room, but in the humble homes of every nation under the sun.

Once every road to Gaul was covered by the armies of Pagan Rome, on their way to Germany

(1) Psalm 2.

or Britain. Her officers crowded the galleys sailing eastward to execute the orders of the Senate of the Roman people.

Long ages have elapsed since these were things of the past. New kingdoms have arisen on the tottering ruins of the once mighty empire. But the oldest and strongest amongst them is the Kingdom of Christ.

Rome is the seat of his Vicar, and from that city he sends his officers to the four corners of the globe; for he has brethren in the faith in Japan and Norway, on the banks of the Euphrates, as well as in the mountains of Scotland.

Modern kingdoms will disappear and be replaced by others, but against the Kingdom of Christ no power can prevail. The Church is to last as long as the sun and the stars are to shine in the firmament.

CHAPTER II.

THE CAMBRO BRITONS AND THE PAPACY.

"Thou art Peter, and upon this rock I will build My Church."—
Matthew xvi.

WHATEVER information we can glean referring to the British Church, from the visit of St. Germanus down to the arrival of St. Augustine, is to be found in the western part of the island, and chiefly in Wales.

The history of the Church in Britain confined to the western part of the island, from the visit of Germanus to the arrival of St. Augustine.
The Saxons, invited over by Vortigern in 449 to fight his battles, finding the country to their liking, came in crowds. Chieftain after chieftain brought his followers across the ocean, not at the request of a native chieftain, but following the strong instinct of barbarians for conquest and plunder. The Britons, as in the time of the Roman invasion, under Julius Cæsar, were disunited, and hence no match for these numerous and bold adventurers incessantly landing on the eastern and southern coasts, and were by degrees driven from county to county, and obliged to take refuge in the mountains of Wales and Cornwall, or to cross the sea over to the western coast of Gaul, to which they have left their name—Brittany.

The conquest of Britain by these foreign races was not, however, the work of a few years, for nearly a century after the landing of Hengist (the first Saxon leader), we find the celebrated Arthur master of the western part of England—from Land's End, in Cornwall, to York. At his death in 544 the Saxons had not pushed their conquest beyond the Thames in the south of the island, or the Humber in a northerly direction.

As they advanced the scourge of war raged in its worst form in that part of the country trodden under their heels. They burnt, or levelled to the ground, Churches and Monasteries, and put to the sword their peaceful inmates. Their motto seems to have been—"Worship our gods, or perish by our swords." Those of the wretched Britons who escaped the general massacre were forced to become their slaves. The Bishops of London and York, with such of their flock as they could hastily gather together, took refuge in Cambria; and, for years to come, the Christian Church was confined to the western part of the island, and especially to Wales.

This period in the history of the British Church —fugitive, covered with blood, and clad in poverty—was a glorious one, and prolific in Saints who edified their countrymen by their holy lives, and kept the light of faith burning in the hearts of the Britons.

Three eminent saints stand on the threshold of this period; and, as we advance, we shall see their disciples nobly following in their footsteps. They are Dubricius, first Bishop of Llandaff;

Dubricius, Cadoc, and Illtyd at the head of this period

Cadoc, Abbot of Llancarvan; and Illtyd, of Lantwit Major. These are the first three bright lights of this period. Scholars, practical men, and, above all, true servants of Jesus Christ, they brought to the service of their Master in Cambria learning, piety, and zeal. Education received from them a wonderful impulse, and Glamorganshire, where they chiefly resided, became the abode of sanctity and learning.

Dubricius, consecrated Bishop by Germanus, ranked first in dignity amongst the Bishops as the Metropolitan of all Wales. Cadoc, surnamed the wise, figured as the founder of several monasteries in his own country, in Scotland, and in Brittany; and Illtyd deserved to be surnamed the "*Great Master*" in Cambria, for his university of Llantwit Major was resorted to by scholars from all parts of Europe.

By birth they belonged to the highest families. Dubricius was the grandson of Pebian, a king in Herefordshire; Cadoc's father was Gwynliew, a warrior chieftain in Monmouthshire; the parents of Illtyd reigned in Armorica. They all followed the monastic rule peculiar to the time. Dubricius and Cadoc entered the cloister very young, whilst Illtyd first took to the army, fought under the British standard, and then enlisted in the Militia of Christ.

These three eminent personages, at the end of a long and well spent career, left to their country a legion of saints, whom they had carefully trained to the service of God. David, Bishop of Menevia; Teilo, second Bishop of Llandaff; Daniel, the first Bishop of Bangor; and Padarn, of Llanbadarn, Cardiganshire, were either disciples of the school we have just mentioned, or connected with it, and continued to carry on the work of the Church in Cambria, when Dubritius, Cadoc, and Illtyd had departed from this world. About the same time Kentigern, Bishop of Glasgow, settled in the beautiful valley of St. Asaph, at the head of a large community of monks.

A great number of their disciples crossed over to Brittany, and there implanted the Catholic faith and the traditions of their country, and left their names to cities and villages, to mountains and valleys. Amongst many we may mention Samson, of Dol; Paulus Aurelianus, Maglorius, the two brothers, Tugdual and Eleanor; Gildas, the historian; St. Malo, &c., &c. The saintly lives of these eminent servants of God, and zealous propagators of the Gospel, are hardly known in Britain in our days. *The lives of these eminent men hardly known in their native country.*

Gildas, a contemporary, who, like St. Jerome, inveighed in no measured terms against the abuses of the time, both amongst some of the princes and clergy, remains silent on the virtues of hundreds of his countrymen, who, like himself, kept the commandments of God and of the Church in the most perfect manner that can be attained by human weakness. *Gildas the most ancient chronicler in Britain.*

Venerable Bede, who died in 737, is also silent on the subject. An Anglo-Saxon by birth, he devoted his talents to record the doings of the servants of God belonging to his race, and did not heed the *British* Church. Butler, in his "Lives of the Saints," merely mentions their existence. Protestant writers, in their zeal against Popery, as a rule aim at one object—to make the world believe that the British Church before St. Augustine was Protestant, entirely disconnected with the Papacy, and that it never acknowledged the Pope as the head of the Church.

The Rev. Ria Reece, an Oxonian and professor of Welsh at Lampeter College, in his *Essay on the Welsh Saints*, constantly reminds his readers that such was the case. How, having under his eyes undeniable documents to the contrary, he should have repeated such historical errors, is not within my province to explain.

The verger of Llandaff Cathedral. From time to time I like to visit the old Cathedral of Llandaff, now at the door of Cardiff; and I can the more easily indulge in this pleasure, as the village lies within the district entrusted to my spiritual care. In one of these visits I happened to go round the building in the company of the verger, the very type of a cicerone, knowing by heart the information he is expected to impart to strangers, and delivering his lesson in the best style of his profession.

As, during five previous months, I had been studying hard the history of the Church, of Dubricius, Teilo, and Oudoceus, I was seized by that impression which rushes upon the souls of most visitors when they enter under the roof of an ancient Church. The ghosts of those who prayed and taught in the place seemed to come from their graves.

Distracted by my thoughts, I happened to exclaim—"Dear me! what an ancient Catholic Church this is. The Roman legions were as yet quartered at Caerau,[1] when the Holy Sacrifice of the Mass was offered up for the sins of mankind on this spot." This ejaculation seemed rather strange to my learned friend, the verger, for he started and soon called me to order in a somewhat abrupt manner. "You are totally wrong, sir; this place has never been in the hands of Catholics, nor has this Church ever been connected with the Pope of Rome."

This historical barbarism I thought it my duty to correct, and asked my conductor whether, in the course of his life, he had ever heard or read anything about St. Fagan. "St. Fagan," he said; "yes, sure; St. Fagan's is the next parish to us." "But do you know anything about him?—who he was, where he came from, and what he did?" "You see, sir, I am not much of a scholar." "Well, I will tell you. St. Fagan was a priest in Rome. King Lucius, a real

---

(1) Caerau, a Roman camp about two or three miles from Cardiff.

Briton, thought it was better for himself and his countrymen to profess the religion of Christ rather than that of the Druids, and so despatched ambassadors to Rome to Pope Eleutherius, who was then the reigning Pontiff of the Christians, begging him to send over some priests to instruct and baptize himself and his people. St. Fagan, one of these priests, came to Llandaff, baptized many of your forefathers, and then built the first Church in this place."

Whilst this exchange of ideas was carried on, we came to the tombstone of Dubricius. I let the verger recite his ordinary lesson, and when he had done put in a rejoinder.

"Yes," I replied, "Dubricius was the first Bishop of this Cathedral, and a great man he was, highly esteemed by his countrymen from generation to generation. The old Welsh kings and princes, whenever they made a grant of land to any Church in this diocese, invariably began their act of donation by saying:—

"I grant to Almighty God, to St. Peter, to holy Dubricius [so many] acres of land, that the Holy Sacrifice of the Mass may be offered up for my soul, and the souls of my wife, children, and forefathers."

In the days of Howell Dda this Cathedral had for its Archdeacon a celebrated Welsh scholar, who put into shape the laws decided upon at Ty gwyn on Taf, near Carmarthen. This same accompanied to Rome Howell Dda and the Welsh

Bishops, who thought it their duty to pay a visit to the Pope, and have his opinion on the code they had framed for their country. No mistake about it, every Welshman in those days was a Catholic.

St. Dubricius was consecrated by Catholic Bishops from France, invited over by the British clergy to help them to convince the people that they were going astray from the Catholic Church, a task in which they succeeded.

In the year 1107 A.D., Urban was consecrated Bishop of Llandaff, and built the Cathedral on the present plan. He was an energetic and clever prelate, and by the help of two Popes—Calixtus II. and Honorius II.—to whom he applied for redress, placed the diocese on a good footing.

The Liber Landavensis[1] contains some twenty Bulls, or letters from these two Popes, addressed to the Bishop and people of Llandaff, to the people of Gower, to the Archbishop of Canterbury, to the King of England, &c., &c.

In his letters Urban says that "the Church of Llandaff, ever since the days of Eleutherius, Pope of the See of Rome, and since the coming of St. Augustine, has always been truly Catholic." It was the same Urban who brought the relics of St. Dubricius from Bardsey Island and buried them here.

At the close of this conversation, I gently hinted to the verger not to be so positive in his

---

(1) There are six Bulls of Calixtus II. and fourteen of Honorius II. concerning the ecclesiastical affairs of Llandaff Diocese.

assertions to visitors, for many of them were sure that, at one time, Wales was Catholic to the backbone. As for myself, a Breton by birth, I have to thank Welsh Bishops and Monks and others for converting my countrymen to that Catholic faith, which they practise to this very day. Yes, it was from Llantwit Major and Llancarvan, in Glamorgan, that most of those saintly missionaries who founded the Catholic Church in Brittany started on their holy mission.

One cannot expect the verger of a Cathedral to be well up in history, nor does one rely over much on what he recites. His duty is to be the custodian of the Church, and to shew kindness to the visitors, a qualification which the verger of Llandaff most certainly possesses.

However, the false statements of this guardian of a Cathedral, built by Catholics, and once Catholic, reflect to a great extent the opinions of many of his countrymen in our days. Some reason or other must be brought forth to cover with the veil of antiquity a religion of yesterday. The religion of Jesus Christ is 1900 years old, whilst that of Henry VIII. has not existed more than 300 years.

Llandaff Cathedral contains a diocesan library accessible to all the clergy of the diocese. I expected to find on its shelves the Liber Landavensis (or the Register of Llandaff), the most interesting record of the Catholic Church in Cambria, containing memoirs of the lives of most of its prelates, the acts of endowment to Churches, from the time of St. Dubricius to that of Urban in the twelfth century. However, this precious book was not to be found. In fact, on the whole, the library is a poor one. The Latin and Greek fathers now found in the private library of many a Catholic priest, thanks to the exertions of the Abbé Migne of Paris, are also conspicuous by their absence. The clergy of the diocese, if anxious to study the traditions of the Church of God from the time of Christ down to the nineteenth century, are not, certainly, to rely on what is collected together in the Cathedral of Llandaff, for the selection made will never give them a correct idea of the religious traditions of past centuries.

Any one who will call the British Church out of her grave, kneel with her clergy and people round the altar as they did, pour forth their prayer to their Redeemer, assist at their ecclesiastical meetings in some deep valley under the shadow of the oak tree (as for instance at Brefi or within the precincts of the monasteries of Llancarvan and Llantwit Major), study the history of her Bishops, Monks, princes, or people, is obliged to exclaim, "What fine Catholics these were." The Seven Sacraments as channels of grace, prayers for the dead, prayers to the Saints, the altar containing the Sacred Body and Blood of Christ, a veneration for the Pope of Rome as the great chieftain of the Church, these formed essential parts of their religion and belief.

<small>Organization of the British Church and its connection with the Papacy.</small>

Great Britain, like most of the nations of the globe gained to Christ, owes her conversion directly to the Popes. Leaving aside the obscure tradition concerning the preaching of Ss. Peter and Paul in these islands, there is not the least historical doubt that the first missionaries who converted Britain, Ireland, and Scotland, received their mission from the Pope, acknowledged him as their highest superior on earth holding the place of Christ in the government of the Church, and taught the same to the various tribes which they gained to Christ.

Eleutherius, at the request of King Lucius, in the second century, sent over Ss. Fagan and Damian to Britain. Later on another supreme Pontiff of Rome—Celestine—sent Palladius for the conversion of Ireland, and, on his settling in Scotland, appointed St. Patrick in his place.

The idea which the old Britons entertained of the Church of God was that of an immense, supernatural society, founded by Christ to lead mankind to heaven, and intended to embrace within her bosom all the nations, tribes, and tongues of the globe.

To keep together in the unity of the faith such a variety of nationalities, Christ had placed the Bishops as the teachers and rulers of that Church; and amongst these Bishops, one had power and jurisdiction over the rest; for it was then understood, as it is now, that, as no army can be kept together without a general, so the various

Churches stand in need of a chief, otherwise unity of faith and discipline is a mere dream.

Such was the plan of the Church taught to the Britons by their first missionaries, and admitted by all as true, because established by Christ Himself.

When Ss. Fagan and Damian had established Christianity in their new mission, they went to the Pope to give an account of their stewardship, and then a hierarchy, similar to that of other Catholic countries, was established in Britain, as already stated in the preceding chapter.

St. Patrick in Ireland and Palladius in Scotland, acting on the same principle, deemed it their duty to keep Rome informed as to their doings, and to consult the Pope in matters of faith, morals, and discipline, following in this the practice of the Catholic Church throughout the world.

In A.D. 314, on the first of August, was opened the first Council of Arles in the South of France. The British Church was represented by three of the leading Bishops, and they subscribed to the decrees which were sent to Rome for approbation, with a synodical letter from the Fathers of the Council to Pope Sylvester. Amongst other things, we find the following passage:— *[British Bishops at the Council of Arles.]*

"We have thought it advisable not to confine our labour to the programme set before us. We have also thought of providing for the wants of our dioceses; and so we have framed for our dioceses, in the presence of the Holy Ghost and His angels, certain regulations. But *it is our opinion that, as you have a wider jurisdiction*, it is your duty to promulgate them to all the faithful."[1]

From this it is evident that all the Bishops present, and with them *those of Britain*, recognised the supremacy of Rome. The legates of Pope Sylvester—namely, Claudius and Vita, priests, and Eugenius and Cyriacus, deacons—were present, and all, as a matter of course, thought it their duty, before separating, to give an account of their transactions to the great chief of Christianity.

<small>The first Bishops of Llandaff gave an account of their doings to the See of Rome.</small> When, therefore, we open the Liber Landavensis, and, a century or a century and a half later on, we see the Bishops of Llandaff giving an account of the state of the Diocese to the Pope of Rome, we find such a step natural enough. They acknowledged Rome, like their predecessors at the Council of Arles, as the mistress of all the Churches; and, like good Catholic Bishops, thought it their duty to keep that See acquainted with their doings and teaching.

Hence, in the lives of Ss. Dubricius and Teilo, the first two Bishops of Llandaff, we read without wonder the following phrase:—

"And *sanctioned* by Apostolic authority,"[2] in reference to privileges granted to them and

---

(1) Henrion, Histoire de L'Eglise. Tome 13, p. 584.
(2) Liber Landavensis.

accepted by them. The Pope of Rome was evidently consulted on these transactions.

The third Bishop of Llandaff, not satisfied with sending a written account, went in person to Rome to confer with the head of Christianity.

St. David is the great legislator of the Catholic Church in Wales. The laws and usages which ruled the Church in Cambria were agreed upon at the celebrated Council of Brefi, in Cardiganshire, A.D. 519. St. David was commissioned to write them down in a canonical form. This he did at Caerleon, and, when the work was complete, he called together another Council in this ancient city of South Wales, and laid before it what he had written. *(Councils of Brefi and Caerleon approved by Rome.)*

The work was unanimously approved by the Council, sent to Rome for approval, and remained for centuries the ecclesiastical code of Wales; for we read the following words in the Cambro-British Saints, p. 442:—

"Therefore, from these two synods all the Churches in the country received their method and rule, approved of by Roman authority, the decrees of which confirmed by his mouth . . .

Let us for the present leap over two or three centuries, forget chronological order, and assist at a national meeting of the Cambrians convened at Ty-gwyn, near Carmarthen, by Howell Dda (or the good). This prince may be called the Justinian of Wales; for in his life he gave his country a written civil code, which deals minutely with the respective rights and duties of every Welshman, from the prince to the lowest of his subjects.

The Welsh code submitted to the approval of the Pope.

I will lay before the reader a summary of the preface to this interesting work, as we find it in the Dimetian code.

"Howell Dda, son of Cadel, by the grace of God King of all the Cymru, observed the Cymri perverting the laws and customs, and therefore he summoned to him from every cantreff of his kingdom six men practised in authority and jurisprudence, and all the clergy of his kingdom possessed of the dignity of the crosier, as the Archbishop of Menevia, and Bishops, and Abbots, and Priors, to the place called White House on the Taf, in Dyved. That house he ordered to be constructed for him of white rods, as a lodge in hunting, when he came to Dyved; therefore it was called the White House.

"And the king, with that assembly, remained there during the whole of Lent to pray to God through perfect abstinence, and to implore grace and discernment for the king to amend the laws and customs of the Cymru.

"At the termination of Lent, the king selected, out of that assembly, twelve of the wisest laics and the most learned scholar called the Master Blegwirid...... And by the advice of these wise men, the king retained some of the old laws, others he amended, others he abolished entirely ..... sanctioned them with his authority; and the malediction of God, as well as theirs and that of the Cymru, was pronounced upon such as should not observe them, unless changed by the concurrence of the country and the Lord."

"Howell the Good, after the Law had been made, accompanied by the princes of Cymru, Lambert, Bishop of Menevia, Mordav, Bishop of Bangor, Cebur, Bishop of St. Asaph, and Blegwirid, Archdeacon of Llandaff, went to Rome to Pope Anastasius to read the Law, and see if there was anything contrary to the Law of God; and as there was nothing militating against it, it was confirmed and called 'The Law of Howell the Good,' the year of the Lord at that time, 914."[1]

That St. Dubricius, Bishop of Llandaff in the fifth century, and St. David with the Welsh clergy in the sixth, after meeting in Councils on ecclesiastical business, should communicate with the Pope, is easily understood. They were Bishops of the Catholic Church, and their flock practised the Catholic religion; communication with Rome was, with them, a matter of course. But when Howell Dda, a Prince and a layman, after framing a civil code, deemed it his duty to refer it to the Pope, lest it should contain any regulations against the Gospel, whose chief interpreter is the Bishop of Rome, one must admit that the Cambrians were thoroughly Catholic.

Howell Dda's line of conduct, far from being laughed at, should, on the contrary, command

(1) Welsh Laws. Dimetian Code. p. 341.

the respect, and draw the attention of legislators; be they kings or deputies of their fellow citizens: it contains a deep sense of justice and much practical wisdom. It stands to reason that any one legislating for a Christian community should acknowledge the fact and work upon it. The following axiom should guide him: "The first Law of all is that of God; the Laws of man are minor rules which should respect the legislation of Christ, and never enact any regulation militating against it."

The Britons thought that the best interpreter of the Law of God was the Pope of Rome, and hence they submitted their Code to his consideration.

St. Kentigern, Bishop of Glasgow, consults Rome on the validity of his consecration.

But now let us go back to earlier ages and lay before the reader the Legend of St. Kentigern, Bishop of Glasgow, and the bosom friend of St. David.

Kentigern was somewhat younger than the patron of Wales, but contracted with him one of those friendships which no events can break. It began when the Bishop of Glasgow was forced, by political events, to leave the banks of the Clyde, and take refuge in the beautiful valley of St. Asaph, in North Wales. Heaven itself smiled on that friendship; for, when St. David was called to the Lord, Kentigern, although distant, was informed of the fact by a heavenly vision, in which he saw his dear friend's soul carried to heaven by angels.

He lived several years later, and his old age, as we are told by several ecclesiastical writers, was disturbed by tormenting scruples bearing on the validity of his ordination. The circumstances were as follows:

When young Kentigern had reached the age of manhood and finished his studies, feeling in his breast an inclination for an ascetical life, he determined upon becoming a hermit. He built his cell near, or on, the spot where now stands the most populous town in Scotland, Glasgow, with its hundreds of thousands of human beings.

His solitude was soon discovered, and he was burdened with admiring and curious visitors. In the course of time, his reputation became so great, that the King and clergy of the country resolved to have him for their Bishop. When the wishes of the people were communicated, Kentigern offered the utmost resistance. It was of no use.

As there were no Bishops near, the King and clergy sent to Ireland for *one* Prelate, who consecrated Kentigern.

The Law of the Church on this matter required the presence of two or three Bishops. "Episcopum prœcipimus ordinari a tribus Episcopis, vel ad minimum a duobus. Non liceri autem ab uno constitui," says the Apostolic constitution; a rule approved by several subsequent Councils.[1]

Though the Church has for ages required the presence of three Bishops, or of *at least* two, in

(1) Henrion. Histoire de L'Eglise.

the consecration of another, she had not, however, declared *invalid*, ordination conferred only by one consecrating Prelate.

However, Kentigern, in his old age, was tormented by scruples. The idea that perhaps he was never validly consecrated, consequently that those Priests whom he had ordained were not Priests at all, any more than he was Bishop, that no real sacrifice of the Mass was offered up by them, no valid absolution given in the Sacrament of Penance to those who came to confession, disturbed the peace of his mind.

Although an old man, he did not hesitate to go to Rome, and lay open his whole life, his elevation, consecration, and all the circumstances connected with it, to St. Gregory, the Apostle of the English. The Pope confirmed his consecration, as nothing that was of necessity had been omitted; and to please the venerable old Bishop, and at his earnest request, St. Gregory, *unwillingly indeed*, supplied those small defects which were wanting in his consecration.

Professor Rees, from whose "Life of the Welsh Saints" I borrow the narrative, laughs at the following remarks made by ancient writers on the conduct of the Bishop of Glasgow.

"A more authentic proof of the respect and dependence which the British Churches had for the Roman Bishop cannot be imagined than the behaviour of Kentigern himself. For, being afflicted in his mind by the aforesaid defects in his ordination, he did not seek for counsel or remedy from any Metropolitan in Brittany, Ireland, or France, but only from Rome and the supreme Bishop thereof, to whom the custody of ecclesiastical canons was by the Church committed, and who had authority to enjoin their observation, to punish their transgression, and to supply or dispense with the defects, either by negligence or necessity, occurring in their execution."

In the mind of Professor Rees, who had a theory of his own, (that the British Church was never Catholic) such conclusions, drawn by our forefathers, are not pleasant, and the facts on which they are grounded must, as a matter of course, be looked upon as spurious. However, the theories or prejudices of an individual cannot destroy historical truths.

The Welsh were very partial to pilgrimages abroad. Jerusalem, the Holy Land, the tomb of St. Martin of Tours, and of St. Peter and Paul in Rome, were visited by thousands of pilgrims even from Wales. Devotion was the primary motive of these religious excursions; at times, the journey was imposed as a penance. A Welshman, Bishop, Prince, or Abbot, was often seen crossing Gaul and the Alps on a pious journey to Rome. Thus we read of St. Cadoc of Llancarvan that seven times in his life, the pilgrim's staff in hand, he had gone to Rome, and thrice to Jerusalem, to obtain pardon for

Pilgrimages to Rome.

the souls of his parents and companions; an evident sign, as we shall see later on, that the Welsh thought it their duty to undergo hardships for the souls of their departed relations and friends.

<small>Gildas' present of a Bell to the Pope.</small>   On a certain evening, a pilgrim named Gildas, knocked at the door of Llancarvan, asking, in the name of God, shelter for the night. He informed St. Cadoc, the Abbot, that he was on his way to Rome, and that he expected to find at the Severn Sea (as the Bristol Channel was then called) a ship to take him across to Brittany, from which place he would, with the help of God, make his way to Rome. His luggage was not very heavy; but it contained a handbell, which the pilgrim stated it was his intention to present as a gift to the Holy Father. It was of his own manufacture, and so sweet in tone, that he thought no one should have it except his Holiness.

The Abbot took the bell, admired the workmanship, rang it, and declared that never before had he heard such a sweet sound. At once he expressed a desire to possess the bell and to purchase it at a handsome price. Gildas replied that it would always be a pleasure and honour for him to oblige Cadoc the Wise, Abbot of Llancarvan, but he was sorry to say that in this case he could not comply with the inclination of his heart, for he was determined to offer it on the altar of St. Peter in Rome. St. Cadoc insisted.

"I will fill it up with as many pence as it can contain." Gildas declined the offer. "Well," added the Abbot, "I will give thee as much pure gold as it can hold." "On no account," said Gildas; "I have made a vow to God and St. Peter, and, with the grace of God, I hope to be able to give what I have vowed; for a foolish and unfaithful promise is displeasing to the Almighty." So Gildas, the legend says, started for Rome and arrived safely with his bell.

On presenting his gift to the Pope, he acquainted his Holiness with all the temptations he had been subject to on the road; how St. Cadoc, an Abbot of a monastery in his country, wanted to bribe him by offering as much gold for the bell as it would contain; but he was proof against corruption, and had brought it to his Holiness.

The Pope greatly admired both the devotion and determination of the Celtic Monk, thanked him most sincerely, and said to him—"Well, Gildas, I will bless this bell; and then you will take it back to the Abbot of Llancarvan as a present from me. I know Cadoc well; he has been here several times. Your countrymen, in course of time, will take their oaths on it; because it has been blessed by me, and has been the property of Blessed Cadoc of Llancarvan."

The Code of Howell Dda brings forward the same reverence, in the most explicit terms, in several passages. The 25th Article of the

Dimetian Code may seem very extraordinary to a modern Welshman, brought up to look upon the Pope as the harlot of the Apocalypse. It runs as follows:—

Privileges granted by law to the Pope.
"Whosoever shall commit treason against his lord, or waylay, is to forfeit his patrimony; and, if caught, is liable to be hanged...... If he repair to the Court of the Pope, and return with a letter in his possession shewing that he is absolved by the Pope, he is to have his patrimony."[1]

According to the notion of the Welsh legislators and people, the position of the Pope as the ruler of the Church, and the high estimate in which he was held by the people, entitled him to this privilege; and no Welsh prince or official was to lay his hand on any felon, whatever his guilt might have been, if the same man had been fortunate enough to obtain his pardon from Rome.

It was, again, a custom in a Welsh Court of Justice, when there was some difficulty on the part of the Judge in finding the truth between the conflicting depositions of the litigants, to take the relics in his hands, and thus address them:—

"The protection of God prevent thee; and the protection of the Pope of Rome; and the protection of thy Lord; do not take a false oath."[1]

St. Augustine and the British Bishops.
Shortly after the arrival in England of St. Augustine, the Apostle of the Anglo-Saxons, an

(1) Dimetian Code, p. 551.
(1) Venedotian Code, p. 117.

event took place which has been so far misinterpreted by Protestant writers as to induce many to believe that the Welsh people separated altogether from the Catholic Faith. I will place before the reader the substance of the facts, as related by the Venerable Bede.[1]

St. Augustine, with the help of King Ethelbert, called together the Bishops and Doctors of the Britons, and begged of them, in a brotherly manner, that, for the sake of Catholic peace, they should preach, in common, the faith to the nations, and keep the celebration of Easter on the same day. The meeting took place in Worcestershire, under an oak tree. A long debate ensued, in which the Britons pertinaciously maintained their determination to keep to their customs. St. Augustine then said:—

"Let us beseech Almighty God, who creates union in the Church, to inspire us with His heavenly gifts, that we may know what traditions are to be followed. Let some infirm person be brought forth, and let the traditions of those who shall cure him be received."

This was agreed to. A blind man taken from the ranks of the English was brought in. The prayers of the British produced no effect. St. Augustine, kneeling down, besought the Almighty to give sight to the blind man, that thereby spiritual light might be imparted to the faithful. His prayer was heard, and the blind

---

[1] Ven. Bede. Historia Eccl. Part iv. Art. iii. Cap. ii.

man restored to sight. This miracle produced a deep impression upon all; and the Britons confessed that the way of justice preached by Augustine was the right one. However, they could not lay aside their customs without consulting their brethren, and requested that a more numerous council might be convened.

At the appointed time, seven British Bishops and several Doctors and Abbots (amongst them Dinoth, Abbot of Bangor Iscoed, near Chester) came to meet St. Augustine.[1]

Previous to going to the assembly, some of them called upon a hermit, renowned in the country for wisdom, sanctity, and learning, to have his opinion as to whether they should give up their traditions to follow those of St. Augustine;—

"If he be a man of God, follow him," said the hermit, and such he is, if he be humble; for the Lord says—'Take upon you My yoke and learn of Me to be meek and humble of heart.' If Augustine be meek and humble, he carries the yoke of the Lord; but if you find him proud, do not take much heed of his advice. When you go to the meeting contrive to arrive last, and if he rises from his seat to salute you, listen to him."

It happened, that when the British Bishops came in a body, St. Augustine did not rise. This want of etiquette produced at once a painful impression on the minds of the British Bishops, and spoiled the work of conciliation, the object

(1) Sammes Britan. ant. p. 510.

of the convocation. They accused him of pride and haughtiness, and contradicted him in most of his views. In the course of the conference St. Augustine gave them to understand that he would give way in many points out of respect for their customs; but requested that they should agree with him in three things: (1) To celebrate Easter at its proper time; (2) To administer Baptism in the same way as the Roman Apostolic Church; (3) To preach with him the Gospel to the English nation.

These points were not agreed to by the British Bishops, nor would they acknowledge him for their Metropolitan; for amongst themselves they made the following remarks:—

"If he does not even condescend to rise when we come into his presence, how much more will he make little of us when we are subject to his jurisdiction."

Such is the substance of what the Venerable Bede tells us of this celebrated Council that estranged for years the British and English Churches, although both of them were Catholic.

Dr. Lingard properly observes that, "it is surprising that so many modern writers should have represented the Britons as holding different *doctrines* from those professed by the Roman missionaries, though these writers have never produced a single instance of such difference. Would Augustine have required the British clergy to join in the conversion of the Saxons if

they had taught doctrine which *he* condemned?
Bede has minutely related all the controversies
between the two parties; they all regard points
of discipline." These observations of Dr. Lingard are perfectly correct.[1]

Ireland and Scotland, as well as Britain, with
that pertinacity of temper in the blood of
all Celtic races, kept to their computation as to
the celebration of Easter, without thinking themselves out of the pale of the Catholic Church.

However, such a diversity of opinion, on a
practical question, created no small amount of
ill-feeling; and even, at times, interfered with
the peace and union in families; nor was it easy
to come to an understanding, owing to the strong
national feeling of each party. Thus Oswy,
King of Northumberland, saw with regret his
own household divided into two factions; and at
the end of each Lent, it was a hard task to keep
peace; for when one half of the Court sang the
Easter Alleluias and sat down to an Easter
dinner, the other half fasted and did penance:
for *them* it was Palm Sunday, the first day of
Holy Week.

To settle this difference, it was thought expedient to call together a synod. It was held at
Whitby in 664. King Oswy opened the proceedings by briefly stating to the assembly that, " as

[1] Some writers have handed down to us a fabricated speech, placed on the lips of Dinoth, the spokesman of the British Clergy. The document is evidently spurious, as, in the beginning it asserts that the British Bishops acknowledged the Pope, and at the end, only the Archbishop of Caerleon, they could not thus contradict themselves.

they served one God, they should observe one way of living, neither should they differ in the administration of the Sacraments; for they expected only one kingdom in heaven. Let them, then, discuss the matter and follow the truth."

Coleman represented the Scots, and Wilfred the other side. Both defended their respective opinions with warmth and eloquence, and, when they had spoken, the king closed the conference by the following conclusive and practical remarks:—Wilfred had concluded his speech by appealing to the authority of the Holy See and the practice of the universal church, as the ultimate judge in religious matters.

"Whatever your Columban, whom we admit to have been an holy man, may have thought," said Wilfred, "is, after all, his authority above that of the Prince of the Apostles, to whom Christ said 'Thou art Peter; and upon this rock I will build My church, and the gates of hell shall not prevail against it; and I will give unto thee the keys of the kingdom of heaven'?"

"Is it true," said Oswy to Coleman, "that Christ addressed these words to Peter?"

"King, it is true."

"Did He tell the same to your Columban, thereby conferring on him the same authority?"

"No," answered the Scotch Bishop.

"Then," replied the King, "both you and Wilfred agree that the keys of the kingdom were given chiefly to Peter?"

"We both agree."

"Then," concluded the King, "as the Pope is the porter of heaven, I am unwilling to disobey him. As far as I know, and to the best of my power, I shall abide by his statutes; lest perhaps that after my death, when I come to knock at the door of heaven, the porter who holds the keys should lock me out."

The British Bishops were in exactly the same state of mind, and knew full well that the Pope of Rome was the Head of the Church; yet they were, for a time, unwilling to give up some of their customs, and to recognise St. Augustine as their Metropolitan.

No doubt, they thought that St. Gregory was hard on the British race, by imposing on them as Archbishop a foreigner, ignorant of their customs and language, with another doubtful qualification in their eyes, that of being the favourite of their bitterest enemies. Pope Eleutherius, in the second century, had established a hierarchy for the Britons; and they, their descendants, expected that the same should be respected, by his successor in the sixth.

However, when the British Bishops were invited to meet St. Augustine, they obeyed; and had the zealous apostle of the Anglo-Saxons risen to greet them, the celebrated oak tree in Worcestershire might have witnessed an act of reconciliation and recognition. St. Augustine conceded as much as his conscience would allow;

but unfortunately he had wounded the susceptibility of the British Bishops, who exchanged amongst themselves the remark: "If, when we are not his subjects, he proves so haughty, what will he not do when he is our master?"

Something similar had occurred in Ireland about a century before. When the great apostle of Erin had established missions in the North and centre of Ireland, and converted the population, he directed his steps southward; but there he found the Church already established, with an organized clergy. St. Patrick had received from Rome jurisdiction over the whole island; on the other side the people of Munster were satisfied with things as they were, and said that, as they were already Christians, St. Patrick might confine his labours to the rest of the country. However, this difference on a question of jurisdiction was amicably settled. The reader would have wished a similar result from the celebrated meeting in Worcestershire.

In the case of the British and Anglo-Saxon question, a strong national antipathy between the two races, the invaded and the invaders, stood in the way of reconciliation.

Nationality is often a great obstacle in the propagation of the Gospel. The Church of Christ is intended by her Divine Founder to embrace within her fold all the nations of the globe. The commandment of the Great Master is: "Make no distinction between the Jew and the Gentile. All are brethren, or children, of Adam and Eve. Christ died for them all, and wishes all to reign with Him in heaven."

The selfish spirit of the world does not consider this, but confines rights, privileges, brotherhood, to certain narrow boundaries of territories; as much as to imply, "We are brethren, provided we belong to the same race, and live under the protection of the same flag."

After making due allowance for national feeling and human frailty, one cannot exonerate from blame a Catholic clergy, such as the British Bishops; *first*, from disobedience to ecclesiastical orders from Rome; and *secondly*, for refusing to help in the conversion of the Anglo-Saxons.

The Britons, as a nation, were perfectly justified in resisting the invasion of their island; but Catholic Bishops and Priests, the ministers of a God who wishes the Gospel to be preached to all, seem for the moment to have lost sight of the spirit of their Divine Master. Peter and Paul were by race Jews; the Romans were the deadly enemies and the conquerors of their country; yet these Apostles rejoiced to shed their blood for the spiritual good of their prosecutors.

Protestant writers have greatly exaggerated the consequences of the step taken by the British Bishops under the oak tree in Worcestershire. According to them, the Welsh Church, if ever Catholic before, became altogether disconnected with the Church of Rome. I think I cannot better answer such an historical barbarism, than by calling a Welsh Bishop from his grave and begging of him to correct the erroneous ideas of his countrymen in the Nineteenth Century.

This Prelate is Urban, Bishop of Llandaff, a man of energy, talent, and zeal. He lived in the twelfth century, and kept up a long correspondence with Rome. His first letter to Pope Calixtus II. solves the question. In the Liber Landavensis it is entitled:—*Requisition of Bishop Urban to Pope Calixtus II.* It runs as follows:—[1]

"To the Venerable Apostolical Calixtus, *chief Patron* of Christianity, Urban, Bishop of the Church of Llandaff, sends faithful service and due reverence. The Church of God, and ours under God and *you*, addresses this letter to your mercy and piety; and suppliantly requests that, for the sake of Christ the Chief King, you will order that it may be carefully read, and kindly heard by you.

"From the time of the ancient Fathers, dearly beloved Father and Lord, as the Chirograph of our patron St. Teilo does testify, the aforesaid church, originally founded in honour of the Apostle St. Peter, was always the mistress of all other churches in Wales in dignity and privilege, until at length through means of seditions and many injuries from wars . . . it began to decline,

---

(1) Liber Landavensis. p. 555.

and to be nearly deprived of its pastors, and annihilated by the cruelty of the natives and the invasion of the Normans.

"Yet religious persons always remained in it to perform Divine Service; as well on account of its being in the neighbourhood of the English from whom they differed nothing in Church service (having been brought up and educated amongst them), as because from ancient times, that is from the time of Eleutherius, Pope of the see of Rome, and after the coming of St. Augustine, (Metropolitan of the Church of Canterbury) to the island of Britain, the *Bishop of this place was always* subject and obedient, in all things, to the same Archbishop."

There is no doubt whatever that the Supremacy of the Papacy in the Church was an undisputed dogma in the old religion of Wales, as it is now in the Catholic Church. When a Bishop of Llandaff in the twelfth century sent his *faithful service*, and *due reverence*, to the *venerable Apostolical Calixtus, chief patron of Christianity*, he did nothing more than what his countrymen before had done. The civil code of his country had been sent to Rome to be approved by Pope Anastasius, 200 years after the arrival of St. Augustine. In case the Cambrians had not been Catholics, such an event would have been noticed as extraordinary. There is nothing of the kind; not a word is uttered implying that, after having seceded from Rome, they had returned to it in the days of Howell Dda. The Welshmen in the days of Dubricius, in the fifth and sixth centuries, were as Catholic as when they received the Gospel from the missionaries sent by Pope Eleutherius at the request of Lucius, and remained such for nearly 200 years after the faith had left England, in the days of the so-called Reformation.

A Breton tolerably well up in the knowledge of the early religious history of Armorica, who should come over to Cambria and read in some of the modern historians of Wales sentences such as the following—"The early Britons were never Catholic in faith or worship," would greatly wonder at such barefaced inaccuracies, for he would know well that Brittany received the Catholic faith from the early British Church, and that her first Catholic Bishops, with few exceptions, were all from Britain. *Cambro-British Missionaries establish the Catholic religion in Brittany.*

As the Anglo-Saxon invasion drove away the Britons from their country, and even long before, in the days of Conan Meriadec, legions of emigrants made their way to that Celtic country. Thousands upon thousands of exiles continued for years to choose the Armorican shores as a refuge from the sword of the Saxons. In a few years the new settlers completely outnumbered the natives, and changed the name of Armorica for that of Brittany, or Little Britain, no doubt as a compliment to, or in remembrance of, their old home.

The first Bishops mentioned in the archives of the ancient dioceses of Armorica, such as Dôl, Quimper, St. Brieuc, St. Malo, are all of British origin.[1]

The graphic pen of Montalembert describes the exodus and the influence it exercised. "A swarm of monastic missionaries descended on the cliffs, at the head of a population already Christian. They came to ask shelter from their brethren, issued from the same race, and speaking the same language. The leaders of the British monks, who disembarked with their army of disciples, undertook to pay for the hospitality they received, by the gift of the true faith; and they succeeded. They gave their name and their worship to their new country. They preached Christianity in the language common to all Celtic races, and resembling that which is *still* spoken by the peasants of Lower Brittany. They implanted in the Armorican Britain, in this Brittany of ours, that faith which remains so firmly rooted there. 'The sun,' says a Breton monk of the seventeenth century, apostrophising one of these prophets from beyond the sea, ' has never lighted a country where, since you banished idolatry, the true faith has been held with more constant and unchanging faithfulness. For thirteen centuries, no kind of infidelity has stained the language by which you preached Jesus Christ; and the man has yet to be born, who has

---

(1) Montalembert. Monks of the West. Vol. II., p. 264.

heard a Breton preach in the Breton tongue, any other than the Catholic Faith.'"

In the diocese of Quimper, there is an island called Sein, that bears not a single venomous beast; no serpent can live on its soil. It is a faithful image of the Brittany you (British Saints) have evangelized; it is a land which, since her conversion, has bred no venom against the sentiments of our Holy Mother the Church.[1]

There is not a shadow of doubt that Brittany has always been a Catholic country, and that it received the faith, in a great measure, from British priests and monks. The Celtic songs of Brittany invariably convey two ideas; that its inhabitants are proud of two qualifications—to be Bretons and Catholics.

If Montalembert had lived in Glamorganshire he would not have failed to remark that many of these holy missionaries, who preached the Catholic religion in Armorica, were sons of South Wales, or educated at Llantwit Major, Llancarvan, or other seminaries of Cambria. Glamorganshire, however, has the lion's share in the honour of having trained them for their Apostolic labours.

In our days Wales has reached a material prosperity not to be met with in her past annals. If the surface of her soil, except at the sea coast, is poor, not to say barren, the bowels of her valleys and her mountains conceal diamonds in *[Without the Pope of Rome the unity of Christendom is impossible.]*

---

(1) Albert le Grand, Vies des Saints de Bretagne.

the shape of coal and minerals. Her seaports are filled with the fleets of the world, and innumerable railways convey her minerals to crowded docks. Her miners earn wages envied by clerks in banks or in Government offices; and wherever the curse of intemperance does not extend its baneful influence, comfort is the general rule in a Welsh home.

Such is not the pleasing aspect when we come to examine the religious condition of the country. A variety of religions and creeds, almost as numerous as the coal-pits, divide the country. There is only one Christ and Redeemer, one Faith, one Baptism. Our Lord came into the world to band mankind together in one form of religion, and Britain has torn that unity into shreds, and cast it to the winds.

Amongst the most intelligent and better educated portion of the Britons there is a feeling gaining ground every day that there ought to be only one religion, as there is only one Christ, and not many; that class of men would hail the dawn of better days, when the Britons could again kneel round one altar and sing together, "Credo in unam Catholicam Ecclesiam." A large and influential party in England is striving to forward this principle. The only possible way of bringing about this result is the Papacy. To think of the unity of Christians in one religion without the Pope is an idle dream; it is to build a house on the sand, to be washed away by the first boisterous tide. "Thou art Peter, and upon this rock I will build My Church; and the gates of hell shall not prevail against it," is written. Civil governments or individuals cannot bestow on the world unity of religion. Christ did not choose them as the foundation-stone of His Church. Wherever and whenever they meddled with religion, their hand undid the unity established by Christ. The history of the east and west unfortunately proves this.

Henry VIII. took it into his head to become the supreme ruler of religion in England. What has been the consequence? In 1877 not half of the English population will hold communion with his Church, or acknowledge in him or his successors on the throne any Divine mission or spiritual jurisdiction.

Any, therefore, be it a kingdom, a society, or an individual, anxious to promote unity of religion, let him take the only road leading to it—the road to Rome. Every plan devised by the greatest genius, or the most powerful conqueror, will be an utter failure without the Pope.

The motto of Protestantism—"Let every one judge for himself"—is the most destructive engine of war ever brought against the Church of Christ. The Bible is made a laughing-stock throughout the world by this erroneous principle. Even Pagans keenly remark that "the Christian religion is the greatest absurdity ever offered to mankind, if everybody is allowed to interpret it according to his interested views, his national or individual prejudices."

Very few nations under the sun exhibit a greater love and respect for human authority than Great Britain. She venerates civil authority in all its gradations; and this fundamental principle of society has contributed in no small degree in extending and consolidating her immense power, and in keeping away from her shores continental revolutions.

<small>As a citizen the modern Briton respects authority; as a Christian he acknowledges none.</small>
An Englishman respects the Sovereign and anyone lawfully invested with authority. Take the Navy, the Army, the Civil Service, subordination to superiors is instinctively understood by all to be a duty, and orders are cheerfully obeyed.

Outside the Government influence, in a sphere in which the people feels its liberty to greater advantage, the same spirit rules its mind. A mayor during his term of office is an important personage, for he represents the community. A magistrate on the bench is respected, and even in passionate meetings the most rabid speaker bows to the chair.

In *religious questions* there is not a more insubordinate being than the modern Briton. He will acknowledge no authority, and proclaims himself as good a theologian as any one living, and thinks he must be the final judge in the interpretation of the Word of God, free to take as much as he likes, and to reject as much as he thinks proper.

With such principles unity of faith becomes an impossibility. Hence, as a Christian community, there is not a country more divided than Great Britain.

Religious dissension exists in the Established Church as well as amongst Dissenters, and makes itself felt in political and social life, and often interferes with the peace of families. Want of unity in religion is witnessed in Parliament, in elections, in town halls, at the school board, on the platform, and in the pulpit.

The sentiment that creates unity is uprooted from the mind of the nation—namely, submission to ecclesiastical authority, to the local clergy, the Bishops, and the Pope of Rome.

This is the secret of Catholic unity, which binds together in one faith the millions of the east and the west.

An influential party in the Church of England is accused of Romanising the mind of the people. The charge is somewhat correct, and the Catholics rejoice in this movement towards our faith, and hope that time will bring home the Prodigal Son, after an absence of centuries.

These gentlemen are busily occupied in the erection of a fine Catholic bridge, but the building will not hold together without the keystone—the *supremacy* of the Pope of Rome.

Before the country returns to the old faith this principle must sink deep in its mind, form a part of the thoughts and phraseology of the nation, manifest itself as of old in the writings of the historian, philosopher, and poet. This last remark brings to mind the romance of Gwen, a fair young Cambrian *belle*, whom the bard of old sends to Rome to receive penance for causing the death of her lover.

In the Iolo MSS. it runs as follows:—"Take thou thy neat ashen staff, and proceed to Rome. The Pope will demand of thee, What wickedness has brought thee here? What hast thou done? If thou wilt enjoy heaven thou must confess. Then will the disheartened *fair one* acknowledge herself guilty of the death of one who loved her; that she broke the heart of a youth of her country, who died for her love. Then will the *fair one* be clothed in horse hair, thus to perform penance for the rest of her life, for wilfully slaying the youth who loved her. And may St. Mary forgive her as I do! My beauteous maid, may heaven be to thy soul!"

CHAPTER III.

The Cambrians' Belief in the Holy Eucharist, Mass, and Communion.—Practice of Confession.

We have seen the Cambrians, in their relation to the Papacy, faithful in their allegiance to the Pope of Rome, on whom they looked as the great Captain of Christianity and centre of Christian unity. Now, let us ask the reader to accompany us into the Church, where the Priest celebrates Mass. Let us lead him to the altar, with its relics and candles; show him the tabernacle which contains the Body and Blood of our Lord Jesus Christ, carefully preserved there for the adoration of the faithful, and to be carried to the sick and dying, whether rich or poor; to the prince in his castle, to the labourer in his hut.

Within the Sacred Temple let us point out the confessional, around which, in Holy Week, or on the eve of Pentecost, the faithful are kneeling, awaiting their turn to unburden their consciences and to receive the Absolution of the Priest.

Leaving the Church, let us stroll with that reverence for the house of the dead which is so marked in the Celtic race through the cemetery, and gaze on the Cambrians of past ages, kneeling as they come from Mass at the graves of their forefathers, sprinkling them with Holy Water, and saying a "De Profundis" for the souls of the faithful departed.

I like to summon the dead from their tombs, to sit with them under the shade of the yew trees, and silently listen to the narrative of bygone generations, for the tales of the dead are impressive beyond expression.

The ancient Cambrians believed in the real presence. The Cambrians were taught by their spiritual preceptors to believe that Jesus Christ, on the eve of His death, instituted the Holy Eucharist containing really and truly His Body and His Blood for the spiritual nourishment of our souls, and that the Holy Eucharist was both a sacrament and a sacrifice.

The first Priest who ever celebrated Mass was Jesus Christ Himself, and He commanded His disciples to do the same till the end of time. It was also on the eve of His death that the Redeemer of the world gave communion to His disciples, who were the first on earth to partake of the Body and Blood of their dear Master; but one of them—Judas—made a sacrilegious communion.

The Welshmen of early days did not, like the Jews, call in question the power of Jesus Christ by saying, "How can this man give us His Flesh to eat and His blood to drink?" and when our

Lord persisted in declaring to them, "Unless you eat the Flesh of the Son of Man and drink His Blood, you shall not have life in you,"[1] went away and left Him. The Welshmen of old said with St. Peter, when he was asked by his Master whether he also would not go away like the rest, unwilling to believe in His power, "To whom shall we go? Thou hast the words of eternal life." The Welshmen of old, without exception, believed in the sacrifice of the Mass, and that when the faithful came to the altar rails to receive communion, they did really and truly partake of the Body and Blood of our Lord.

In their eyes the most exalted dignity on earth was that of the Priesthood, because the Priest had power to call Jesus Christ from heaven whenever he went to the altar, and distributed to the people the real bread from heaven whenever he gave Communion.

With St. Paul they knew that "every high Priest taken from among men is ordained for men in the things that appertain to God, that *he may offer up gifts and sacrifices* for sins."[2]

The laws of Howell Dda give the priest the title of "offerenner," or the celebrator of Mass. In the Breton language the Mass bears the same name as in the Welsh. "Offeren" is the Breton name for Mass. "Offeren" conveys the same significance in the ancient Cambrian.[3]

---

(1) Gospel of St. John, chap. vi., v. 54.
(2) Epistle to Hebrews, v. 1.
(3) In the English and Welsh Dictionary (Thomas Edwards) the Priest is called "Offireiadd."

The Welsh laws are clear and precise in their definition of the duties of a Priest. The three things named as indispensable to a king are *his Priest* to say grace and to *sing Mass*.

The judge of the court to elucidate everything doubtful, and the chief of his household for his command. (Venedotian Code, p. 177. Dimetian Code, p. 436.)

These laws, although compiled in the tenth century, are nothing else than the reflection of the faith of the Britons from the time they received the grace of conversion from heathendom.

<small>Gildas rebukes some of the clergy for not celebrating Mass often enough.</small>

The celebrated Gildas, a British monk belonging to the fifth and sixth centuries, leaves no doubt on the subject.

In his work *Increpatio ad Clerum* he inveighs with all the energy of his soul, and in that strong style peculiar to him, against certain abuses that had crept into the midst of a portion of the British clergy of his days.

"Sacerdotes habet Britannia sed insipientes quam plurimos, Ministros sed imprudentes . . . raro *sacrificantes* et nunquam puro corde inter altaria stantes."

The earnest Monk, from his monastery on the Armorican shores, denounces two abuses. He finds fault with some of the clergy for rarely celebrating the Holy Sacrifice of the Mass, and when they went up to the altar for not being endowed with that purity of heart required in those who do service in the sanctuary of God.

According to the Catholic spirit he expected his brethren in the Priesthood to celebrate daily the Holy Sacrifice. Then, the sacredness of their functions imperiously demanded that they should enter the temple of the Lord clad in the robes of an unblemished life. They were the ministers of the Church, sprinkling mankind with the blood of the Lamb of God. Their hands were to be pure.

The altar of sacrifice and the British saints cannot be disconnected. On the shores of Armorica we find these servants of God from Britain celebrating Mass in the presence of an alarmed crowd which has called on them to rid their neighbourhood from a huge dragon or a poisonous serpent. They opened the battle at the altar, offered up first the sacrifice of the Body and the Blood of Jesus Christ, who formed their sole strength; and clad in these very vestments in which they had celebrated Mass, they boldly started to meet the dangerous reptile, and gained an easy victory. Thus acted Paulus, Aurelianus, St. Meen, and many others. From the holy Eucharist they derived that personal courage the boldest of warriors lacked on the occasion, as well as supernatural power over dreaded animals.

The Britons and the altar of sacrifice cannot be disconnected.

Indeed, one cannot read the history of these islands without being constantly brought before the holy of holies.

In all the large monasteries the perpetual adoration was strictly carried out. Jesus Christ is really present in the sanctuary. He is not to be left alone like an indifferent and neglected guest. Day and night a sentinel of honour is appointed to do duty in His temple, and sing Divine praises. Such was the spirit of the ancient Britons, and that of the founders of religious houses throughout the country.

The men of the fifth and sixth centuries possessed a limited knowledge of sacred architecture. This was a science the Monks of the Middle Ages were destined to develop to a degree of perfection not even surpassed in our days. However, the Britons paid a particular attention to the decoration of the altar. The stone was often brought from Jerusalem, and the tabernacle studded with diamonds and gems of the greatest value.

St. Cadoc massacred at the altar.

Many of the saints of Britain died martyrs before the altar, and as it were mingled their blood with that of Jesus Christ. Such was the case of St. Cadoc, of Llancarvan, Glamorganshire.

Let Albert le Grand, a Breton Monk, describe the circumstances:—" The old Prelate—for he was no longer Abbot, but Bishop—was residing at Weedon, in Northamptonshire, when one night, whilst in prayer, an angel appeared to him and gave him his choice as to the kind of death he would prefer. The old man said, " As my Lord died on the cross for my sake, I should wish, if such be His holy will, to shed my blood for His sake."

THE HOLY EUCHARIST AND CONFESSION. 97

The angel replied, "Servant of God, rejoice; this desire shall be accomplished. To-morrow thou shalt pass from this miserable life to everlasting glory, and receive the crown of martyrdom." This said, the angel disappeared.

In the morning St. Cadoc communicated the revelation to some of his intimate friends, and prepared himself to celebrate the Holy Sacrifice as usual. At the appointed hour he vested and began Mass. At the same time an army of barbarians rushed on the town unexpectedly, and made their way to the Church. There they found St. Cadoc at the altar, and after swearing at and cursing the Christian worship and its ministers, they seized upon Cadoc, and slew him at the altar.[1]

When the Saxons, laden with plunder, had retired, the people came to the Church, washed away the blood, and buried him in his own sanctuary.

St. Winefrid, in the Ecclesiastical Annals of Cambria, and also in the opinion of her countrymen, ranks first amongst the maidens of Wales. What St. Agnes is in Rome, St. Genevieve in Paris, Winefrid is in her native land. From the time of her martyrdom to the present day a continuous stream of pilgrims has annually resorted to her well, in the hope of finding, on the spot where she died for her virginity, a cure for their infirmities, for at all times and every-

Legend of St. Winefrid.

(1) Albert le Grand. Vies des Saints de Bretagne.

where a virgin martyr is looked upon by the people as a soul dear to God—a spouse of Jesus Christ, able to help the afflicted who seek her intercession.

On a certain day St. Beino visited Tewyth, the father of Winefrid, with the intention of obtaining from him the cession of some land on which he might build a Church, wherein to celebrate Mass. Tewyth agreed to give the land on condition that the Priest should instruct his only child, Winefrid, in sacred and human learning. The land was situated in a valley called in Welsh "Sychnant," or the dry valley. There Beino built a Church in which he daily officiated, and he fulfilled his agreement of instructing the young Winefrid. Under the training of such a holy man the youthful virgin closed her heart and her mind against the world. She was beautiful in person, and possessed of great intelligence and a pure heart.

Her pleasure was to keep in order the Church of her pious master, and to attend to everything required about the altar. She prepared the thurible with its lighted charcoal for High Mass, and when the Holy Water stoup was drained of its contents she replenished it, placing salt and the Ritual in order that the fresh supply of water might be blessed by the Priest.

On a certain Sunday, whilst Beino was at the altar and Winefrid alone in the house, the lawless Caradoc made his appearance. The young girl contrived to escape, but was overtaken on the threshold of the Church, and barbarously slain by the wicked prince. This murder at the door of the sanctuary, and during the celebration of Mass, was not to be soon forgotten in Cambria. The Christian bards commemorated it in their verses, and the maidens of Wales, in the long winter nights, sang by their firesides, with throbbing hearts and eyes bedewed with tears, the death of the Virgin Martyr.

We may picture to ourselves the sacred bard drawing a touching antithesis between Jesus Christ shedding His blood for the sins of mankind, and Winefrid, expiring in the protection of her virginity.

"One Sunday morning," said the bard, "a father, a mother, and a people weep, in the Sychnant Valley, at the altar of St. Beino. Two victims are immolated—the bridegroom and the bride—one on the altar, the other at the door of the Church. The one is Jesus Christ, the only Son of the living God; the other St. Winefrid, the only daughter of Tewyth. St. Beino mystically immolates the Lamb of God, a victim willing to die for the sins of the world. The wicked Caradoc strikes off the head of the virgin Winefrid, unwilling to yield to his passions."

This episode in the life of St. Winefrid carries us back to another celebrated daughter of Wales —St. Ninnoc, of the royal house of Brychan, in Brecknockshire. She lived in the days of Germanus, about the middle of the fifth century, and was induced, by the example of this venerable prelate of Gaul, to embrace a religious life. She went to Brittany, and there founded a monastery for women.

Guereck, Duke of Brittany, a man who could appreciate worth and sanctity of intention, behaved generously and nobly to the young virgin, and granted her a large tract of land.

The charter conveying the deed of donation was solemnly placed upon the altar, together with a chalice containing wine, and a paten of gold. This charter expressly stipulates that "the banquet of the Body and Blood of our Lord should be offered up *in perpetuum* for the benefit of the donor's soul, and for his family, both living and dead." This deed of gift, which bears the date 458, will, later on, be placed before the reader. In form and substance it is similar to those in the Liber Landavensis.

Oaths before the Altar. The register of Llandaff abounds in instances where we see Welsh princes on their knees in the sanctuary, and there, in the presence of bishops, clergy, and nobles, taking the most solemn oaths. Such instances repeatedly occurred in the days of Oudoceus, Bishop of Llandaff.

When a feudal war was about to break out it was customary with the clergy and laity to endeavour to effect a reconciliation between the disputants, and thereby prevent the shedding of blood. On these occasions the contending parties came to the Church, and there, before the altar, in the presence of God, His ministers, and the laity, they solemnly promised to lay aside hatred and the spirit of revenge, and to live together like brothers, in peace and concord.

When such an oath, taken in such a sacred place, was violated, and murder committed, the Churches in the neighbourhood were deprived of Mass, the altar was stripped, the relics, candles, and bells were laid upon the pavement of the Churches, and thorns heaped up before the closed doors, for those who violated their promise to Jesus Christ were deemed unworthy to partake of the benefit of the Holy Sacrifice of His Body and Blood, or to receive Holy Communion.

Upon an act of such severity being exercised by a resolute Bishop, such as Oudoceus, the gloom of death seemed to overshadow the district under punishment of interdict. Sunday, instead of cheering the heart with gladness, cast a cloud over every home, and forced the people to reflect deeply on the enormity of the crime of the prince who had brought such desolation on the country. Sooner or later he was compelled to yield to the pressure of public opinion, and seek pardon from the Bishop, because his people would not remain long without the Holy Sacrifice of the Mass. The reader will find fuller details on this subject in the life of the third Bishop of Llandaff.

According to the laws of Howell Dda, when a judge was appointed, the taking of the oath administered to him was attended with greater solemnity than in our days. The life and the property, as well as the liberty of subjects, are in the hands of the judge. He decrees the ruin or justification of many. This was well understood by the legislators of Wales, and therefore, before entrusting any person with an office of such importance, they ordained that he must appear at the foot of the altar at the moment when the Redeemer was present thereon, and in that Divine presence, and before the angels of God, he was obliged to take a solemn oath to render justice to all, to the rich and to the poor alike, without distinction of rank or position. The law runs as follows:—

<small>The Magistrate to take the Oath before the Altar.</small>
"When the judge is appointed, let the Priest, the King's Chaplain, with twelve principal officers of the court, take him to the Church to assist at Mass, and after Mass and offerting by everyone, let the chaplain require him to swear by the relics, and by the altar, and by the consecrated elements placed upon the altar, that he will never deliver a wrong judgment, knowing it to be wrong, either through the entreaty of any person, or for worth, or for love, or for hatred of anyone. Then let the chaplain declare what has been done."[1]

The people of Wales believed, with the rest of Christendom, in the real presence of our Lord in the Holy Eucharist as an article of faith, and

---

(1) Dimetian Code, chap. xiv., art. 20.

therefore considered that if the word of a man could ever be relied on, it would be when in the presence of Jesus on the altar, he affirmed or denied an assertion. The law being aware of this sentiment, often cited the litigant to the sanctuary, confident that if the truth was to be told, and falsehood confuted, it was most to be at the foot of the altar.

If a woman appealed to law concerning the birth of a child, she was required to swear as to its paternity before the consecrated altar, and her deposition was then taken; for no Welshwoman, unless she had reached the lowest degree of perversity, would dare to take a false oath at the feet of the Lord.

The law again, to prevent the lodging of rash and untrue informations, which were often the result of ambition, jealousy, or revenge, imposed a caution on the informer as to the gravity of the charges he was about to make. Before the deposition was taken the Priest was enjoined to bring him to the Church, and there remind him of the duties imposed by justice and charity, and of the awful sin of perjury. *The informer cautioned before the Altar.*

The formalities to be observed on such occasions are defined as follows:—

"Whoever wills to make an information, let him go to the lord (prince) and say that a person, whose name he does not mention, has committed a theft. The lord should then summon the Priest, who is to take the informer before the Church door, admonishing him to understand and beware of the guilt of perjury. If he swear, let him first take an oath before the door of the Church, secondly in the chancel, and thirdly at the altar. This being done, let the priest go and inform the lord of it."[1]

The writer of these lines, during a sojourn of ten years in the East, in the island of Mauritius, has witnessed hundreds of times even Pagans make their way to a Catholic Church to settle their differences at the foot of the altar. They had learned from the Catholics that the *Bon Dieu* dwelt in the tabernacle, and into His presence they therefore came. As a rule they lighted two or three candles before the altar. Then the man who was accused of robbery solemnly declared to all the bystanders, generally six or seven in number, that he was aware he knelt in the house of God (la grande case du Bon Dieu), and he invoked Him as witness that his hands were free of theft.

His assertion, made in so sacred a place, was generally received as truth, and thus all further litigation was prevented. More than once the writer has heard these Indians remark, when they left the Church, "Well, now, we leave him to Almighty God. If he has told an untruth in His presence, he will have to pay dear for it."

A Church, in the eyes of a Catholic population, is more sacred than the holy of holies in the

[1] Venedotian Code, p. 247, art. 28

tabernacle of Solomon's temple was in the eyes of the Jews. A Church is in reality the house of Jesus Christ, in which He dwells—not in figure, but really and truly. Hence when a Catholic enters and beholds the lamp of the sanctuary burning before the tabernacle, he falls on his knees in adoration. " Terribilis est locus iste, hic domus Dei est et porta cæli."

In the old Celtic phraseology the Church in Wales and Brittany is called " Ty Doue, Ty Duw" —that is to say, the house of God. What a difference exists between that ancient name and the modern Welsh term " Meeting-house," which conveys the idea of a covered space suitable for any purpose, whether tea parties, fierce political discussions, or prayer. Since Jesus Christ was expelled from the temple it has lost its sacred character in the minds of the people.

The Welsh law punished, with particular severity, any misdemeanour committed in or about a Church. The sacredness of the place was considered to aggravate the transgression. Whoever shall do wrong in a Mother Church, let him pay to it fourteen pounds. If in the Churchyard, seven pounds. Whoever shall do wrong in another Church, let him pay seven pounds.[1]

Punishment of Sacrilege.

A Catholic of the nineteenth century, reading this penal code written for a Catholic population of past ages, draws this natural inference. The

(1) Welsh Codes.

severity, increasing by gradation, implies the following facts. The *Mother Church* enshrined habitually the Blessed Sacrament; hence the heavy penalty of fourteen pounds for any serious wrong committed under its roof. The Churchyard connected with the Church, and the burial places of her Christian children, was also sacred, but not in the same degree; hence the fine was only half. The other Churches wherein cases of crime occurred, which were subjected to a fine of seven pounds, no doubt were Chapels, used occasionally, but which were not privileged to reserve the Blessed Sacrament, and consequently an offence perpetrated in them was a lesser profanation.

The Church of England is spending millions of pounds sterling in the restoration of the old Cathedrals built by generations of Catholics, and wrenched from them at the time of the Reformation. No expense is spared, the highest architectural talent is employed in effecting the work of restoration, and to all outward appearance one would take them to be again Catholic Churches. That which is essential is, however, as yet absent —the Holy Sacrifice of the Mass. These Churches were built to enshrine the sacred humanity of our Lord Jesus Christ in the sacrament of the Holy Eucharist. As long as He is kept away, they do not answer the purpose for which they were erected.

THE HOLY EUCHARIST AND CONFESSION. 107

There was nothing in the world the Catholic Welshman dreaded more than dying without the Sacraments of the Church; and the Priest who had care of souls considered it a most sacred duty to attend the last hours of a dying Christian. If ever remorse gnawed his conscience it was when any of his parishioners had died without the Sacraments through his fault. This was also the opinion expressed by the legislation on the subject, for the laws of Howell Dda specify that a Priest, on his way to attend a sick call, shall be free to pass over any person's land. He may ride through gardens and cultivated fields if he thinks it necessary, for he is called to the death-bed of a Christian, who, before leaving this world, stands in need of absolution and of the Body and Blood of our Lord Jesus Christ. When upon such a holy mission no one in Wales has a right to call him to account for trespassing.

The Cambrians at Holy Communion.

When Gwynlew, the warrior, was dying in his hermitage on Stowe Hill, Newport, Monmouthshire, he called his companions around him and said—"I feel my days are coming to an end. Send to Llancarvan, and request my son Cadoc to come in haste to receive the confession of his dying father, and to give him Holy Communion before he leaves this world."

St. Cadoc at once came from Llancarvan, and when he reached the cell of his dying parent, on the hill of Newport, he found that St. Dubricius was already at his bedside. After he had received the Body and Blood of our Lord, the old chieftain thanked God and his son for his conversion, and stretched forth his hand to bless Cadoc in this world and in the next.

St. Teilo, the second Bishop of Llandaff, was on his way to Brittany at the head of a colony from Glamorganshire, when coming to Cornwall, the place from which they were to embark, he was hospitably entertained by the prince of that country. Geraint, for such was his name, took compassion on these poor exiles, forced to fly from yellow fever. The account of the awful havoc caused by this pestilence in Wales (where the houses were empty, and the Churchyards full —where kings, as well as their subjects, had fallen victims), as related by the fugitives, together with their emaciated and yellow appearance, struck terror into the heart of Geraint, for he felt that this dreadful plague might seize upon him as it had on thousands of others. He thought it advisable, therefore, to take advantage of the arrival of the Bishop of Llandaff, and settle the affairs of his conscience before he should again embark. St. Teilo assured the alarmed prince that he was not as yet to die. The Holy Prelate had received a revelation that Geraint was destined to live for seven years longer, and that he should not pass away without receiving the Body and Blood of our Lord from His own hands.

The prophecy was verified by subsequent events. At the end of seven years Geraint fell ill, and St.

Teilo, whilst returning to Wales from Brittany, met the messengers of the dying prince, who requested him to hasten his journey that he might keep his word to their master. Teilo hurried on, and arrived in time to administer Holy Communion to the sick man, who shortly afterwards expired.[1]

We might multiply, almost *ad infinitum*, the instances in which we see the dying Welshman consoled during his last moments by the presence of the Redeemer of the world, and the Judge before whom he will have to give an account of all his actions and omissions, of his words and of his thoughts, when the soul shall have parted from the body; but as these will be placed before the reader as they occur in the life of each saint, we shall not tax his patience now by useless repetition.

To be deprived of Communion, the greatest punishment in Wales.

The greatest punishment which could be inflicted on the Welsh was to forbid them to approach the sanctuary to receive the Body and Blood of our Lord.

When King Meuric had given to Almighty God, to the Church of Llandaff, and to St. Dubricius, the Bishop thereof, the tract of land situated between the rivers Taff and Ely, the grant was understood to be *ad perpetuum*, for when a Welshman gave land to religion it was for perpetuity. However, the charter clearly specified that "if ever any man, prompted by

(1) Liber Landavensis

avarice and the evil spirit, seized on such lands in any way whatever, he was to be admonished twice or thrice; and if he did not amend, was to be excommunicated and *deprived of the Body and Blood of our Lord.*" And the people who heard the proclamation of this threat cried "Amen!" for it was the opinion of all that this punishment, severe as it was, should be inflicted on persons who were guilty of sacrilege.

The ecclesiastical authorities dealt with other crimes and misdemeanors in like manner, by forbidding the offender to approach the sacred banquet until such time as he had performed penance. In the register of Llandaff we find several examples of Welsh princes who, having committed murder, were excommunicated, sent on pilgrimages, and not allowed to receive the Holy Eucharist until they had gone through their penance, as will be seen in the life of St. Oudoceus.

The history of the early Christians, both in the east and west, are full of instances showing forth the wonderful effects of the Holy Eucharist. The Fathers of the Church call our attention to the fact that the martyrs, drawn in crowds by iniquitous tyrants to torments and death, derived their superhuman endurance from Jesus in the sacrament of His love. One day their members were dislocated, the next day they were slowly burnt, then thrown to wild beasts, or tried by other tortures. But nothing could induce these

THE HOLY EUCHARIST AND CONFESSION. 111

noble heroes to renounce their religion, for they were fortified by the Flesh and Blood of their Divine Master. Hence the greatest care was taken to bring them Holy Communion before they left the prison for the amphitheatre. Nay, in time of persecutions the early Christians were allowed to keep the Holy Eucharist in their private houses, for at any moment they might be called upon to seal their faith with their blood.

St. Ignatius, Bishop and martyr in the second century, was so enamoured of his Divine Master in the tabernacle, that on his road from the East to Rome, *there* to die for his religion, he writes to his brethren in Rome—" The pleasures of this world have no longer any attraction for me. I long after the celestial bread—the bread of life—which is the Flesh of Jesus Christ, Son of the living God, the incorruptible love and life everlasting."

Later on St. Cyprian gives us several examples in which Christians receiving unworthily the Body and Blood of Jesus Christ were severely punished by heaven.

These remarks of St. Cyprian brings to mind the monstrous conduct of a British chieftain towards the two sons of Modred.

Constantine, son of Cador, kinsman of King Arthur, and his successor, said on his lips—" Forgive us our trespasses, as we forgive them that trespass against us," but in practice followed to the letter the law of retaliation, in exacting blood for blood, eye for eye, tooth for tooth. He thought himself bound to revenge the death of Arthur, who fell in a battle against Modred, on the two sons of this rebel prince.

The clergy, in the name of religion, demanded of Constantine to spare the two youths, and not call them to account for the sins of their father.

The Duke of Cornwall promised, before the altar, in the most solemn manner, to do nothing against their existence.

Yet, not long after, maddened by the spirit of revenge, he broke the gates of the monasteries the two brothers had entered. They ran into the Church, entered the sanctuary as places guarded by the Angels of God, and respected by every Christian. But Constantine had regard neither for the laws of God or man. He entered the sanctuary, in which he found his victims clinging to the altar, and begging to be spared in the name of Jesus Christ, who was there present. But Constantine listened to no entreaties, and slaughtered them in the Church.

Three years afterwards he was miserably slain, and people remarked that it was high time he should be chastised for his *sacrilegious* murders. Well might the earnest Gildas use strong language in denouncing the crime of this prince, his readiness to swear anything at the altar, and his promptitude to become sacrilegious and perjurer.

It is reported of St. Samson, that in Lent, at least during some portion of his life, he abstained

THE HOLY EUCHARIST AND CONFESSION.

altogether from any kind of food excepting the Holy Eucharist of the Body and Blood of our Lord, which he carried with him.[1] In fact, what we are told of the extraordinary mortifications of this Saint seems almost incredible and beyond the power of human endurance, if we did not keep in view the various effects of Holy Communion, which not only nourishes the soul, but at times has been the sole nourishment of certain Saints for a certain period.[2]

The Welsh code of Howell Dda says—"A child is to be placed under a confessor's care at the age of seven years," and describes the privileges of all persons who from seven years upwards are under direction of a confessor.[3]

Confession

A Catholic of the nineteenth century, who remembers the Catechism of his young days,

---

(1) Britannia Sancta.

Gorres, as quoted by Migne, says that in the case of certain Saints Communion replaced the ordinary corporal food. According to the general law of nature, we assimilate into our organisation the aliments we eat, but in the partaking of the Holy Eucharist, the reverse is the case; our nature is, as it were, assimilated to that of our Lord; supernatural life absorbs the natural life.

Certain Saints had no relish for any other food but the Holy Eucharist, and for a time have subsisted solely on this Heavenly Bread.

In 1225, Hugues, Bishop of Lincoln, on learning that there was, in the town of Leicester, a nun who for *seven* years had partaken of no other food but the Body and Blood of our Lord which she received every Sunday, refused to believe what he was told. He sent over fifteen Clerks with instructions to watch her carefully, and never to lose sight of her for the space of fifteen days. As during that time she preserved her health and strength, the Bishop became convinced of the fact.

In Norfolk there lived a holy young girl named Johanna Matles, who for *fifteen* years partook of no other nourishment but the Holy Eucharist. A Spanish nun—Louisa of the Resurrection—lived in the same miraculous manner. Many holy hermits in the deserts, such as John the Abbot, St. Mary of Egypt, and others, were favoured by heaven in like manner. St. Catherine of Sienna, St. Rose of Lima, relished no other food but the Body and Blood of our Lord.

(2) Migne, Mystique Chrétienne.

(3) Welsh laws, p. 207.

cannot help remarking the antiquity of the practice of confession at an early age. Catholic mothers are now as of old exhorted to bring their children, both boys and girls, to the confessional when about seven, for it is believed that a child who has reached this period of life is a moral agent capable of distinguishing between good and evil. The old Cambrian Catholics thought the same, and even went so far as to prescribe, in their civil legislation, the necessity of taking a child to confession at the early age of seven.

The same code, alluding to the confession of a king, says "that a Bishop is the confessor of a king by privilege."

The practice of going to confession is often mentioned in the lives of the early Welsh Saints. Thus when Maelgon, King of North Wales, sent an expedition to plunder the South, under his son Rhun, amongst other strict recommendations given to both commander and army are the following : — " When you reach the Bristol Channel you may come upon Llancarvan Abbey. Mind you respect the said territory. Touch no man or animal belonging to its community, for the Abbot is my *confessor*, and expects protection and exemption from the horrors of war from his spiritual son."[1]

It is related of Amon, father of St. Samson, that being dangerously ill he dispatched messengers to Barry Island, where his son was a

(1) Cambro-British Saints.

Monk, requesting his attendance at home, giving as reason that his coming would have the result of curing him both in body and in soul.

Indeed, it is asserted that this nobleman felt very uneasy in his conscience. In the habit of going to confession like every Christian in Britain, he had not been sincere in the accusation of his sins, and thus had made sacrilegious confessions. At some period of his life he had committed some great fault which he could not find courage to confess. He knew full well that religion required a disclosure of all mortal sins, under the pain of rendering the Sacrament of Penance inefficacious, and the absolution of the Priest void. This fact had disturbed the peace of his conscience on many occasions, but never so much as in this illness, when death stared him in the face. However, the arrival of Samson infused energy into his soul. He made a general confession of his entire life, and, accompanied by his brother, followed his son to Barry Island, to live and die religious.

Anyone who will read the lives of such men as Gwynlew, the warrior, a prince of Monmouthshire, and of Geraint, King of Cornwall, or assist at the death-bed of any Welshman from the earliest dawn of Christianity down to the Reformation, and even long after, will always find the practice of confession in force. At the hour of death a Priest will always be discovered attending the last moments of the dying man, receiving his confession, absolving him from his sins, "in the name of the Father, and of the Son, and of the Holy Ghost." The family and friends of the dead were doubly afflicted at a funeral if, when lowering the body into the grave, they were conscious that he had gone into eternity without confession and communion.

Modern Welshmen entertain very extraordinary views on this subject, and have presumed to limit the power and control the will of the Son of God, for in their opinion He cannot empower a man to forgive sins. If amongst us anyone can delegate his authority to another, and constitute him his *alter ego* as far as he judges proper, is it reasonable to deny the same power to the Redeemer of the world?

The Cambrians of old thought differently, and believed, with the Catholic Church, that when Christ told His disciples, " Whose sins you shall forgive on earth they are forgiven in heaven," instituted the Sacrament of Penance by which the sins committed by adults after baptism are really forgiven.

Penance, as a sacrament, implies the concurrence of two persons, a sinner and a Priest, with power from God to absolve. The sinner must be sorry for his transgressions, determine to do his best not to fall again, confess, and make satisfaction. Then an approved Priest absolves him, as the agent of God empowered by Him to forgive.

The Cambrian of old was also reminded by his spiritual teacher of the provident kindness of our Redeemer in securing for us a life-boat in case of shipwreck, for how few there are who preserve baptismal innocence through life.

Let us go to the graves of past generations and ask the dead whether or not they have been benefited by this noble institution of our common Master and Redeemer. Thousands upon thousands will tell us—"On earth we lived reckless and cared little for any law, human or Divine. However, in the course of time we repented, did penance, and received absolution. When called upon to give an account at the bar of Divine justice we pleaded guilty, but said on earth there is a tribunal established by heaven with power to forgive, and that tribunal has forgiven us, and thus we have escaped the eternal punishment of hell; and now we are members of the elect of heaven, and thank the Lamb of God for the wise institution of the Sacrament of Penance.

Dissenting and Ritualistic opinion on the question of confession engrosses a great deal of public attention at the present time, both in Great Britain and throughout her immense empire. A large, influential, and determined party in the Church of England are inviting their people to frequent the confessional, and that with a success which cannot be under-rated. It is true this party meets with a great deal of opposition in high quarters, and draws ridicule upon it from a certain number of Protestants, and is even annoyed by the wavering hand of the law. Dissenters, as a matter of course, side with the opponents of confession, while Catholics watch with deep interest the great change which is taking place in the public mind in favour of the Divine institution they cherish.

The Ritualists and public opinion. The Ritualist is in the right, and can say to his opponents, with us Catholics, *read the Scriptures.* What do they say in Matt. xvi. 19, xviii. 18, St. John xx., 22-23? Christ gave power to His Apostles to forgive or retain sins, to loose or bind, and whatever course they take is ratified in heaven. The words are clear and obvious, and cannot be distorted to suit our purposes.

Yes, whatever sins are forgiven in a confessional, in a sick room, on land or on sea, by those who have received power, are forgiven in heaven. Our ancestors, for 1,800 years, believed in the institution of the Sacrament of Penance. Ask the fathers of the Greek and the Latin Churches. They all speak of the power of forgiving sins—of the tribunal of penance.

In the course of the present year (1877) public opinion was somewhat occupied by this controversy in the neighbourhood of Cardiff. A celebrated Canon of Llandaff considered it his duty to come before the public and expose his views on the subject. The elegant Churchman denounced, as strongly as he could, the practice of confession as unscriptural, and unsupported by the traditions of early ages.

THE HOLY EUCHARIST AND CONFESSION. 119

This step did not meet with the approval of a large portion of the Church-people attending Llandaff Cathedral. One of them told the writer of these pages that they were sorry the Canon had committed two egregious blunders: first, in having misunderstood altogether both Scripture and history; and secondly, in having wounded the susceptibilities of many in the Church who entertained on confession exactly the same ideas as the Catholics.

I replied that I felt certain the Canon had distorted the Holy Word and the traditions of past ages, but was not aware that such a large portion of the people round Llandaff shared our Catholic views on the Sacrament of Penance. I was happy to learn that we were drawing closer and closer.

"Fifteen or sixteen years ago," I added, "I happened to be sent for to a certain institution for females, connected with Llandaff. The practice of confession seemed to be a law of the institution, as the following reason for my visiting the place will show :—

"A young inmate, Irish and Catholic, was invited like the rest to present herself for confession. This she declined, stating that it was very useful to go to confession to a Catholic Priest, who had power to forgive sins, but a loss of time to confess to anyone else. Let them send for one of her own clergymen, and she would be happy to unburden her conscience, for unfortunately, she had neglected her soul since she had left school.

"The institution, with a consideration not always met with in such establishments, wrote to the Priests of Cardiff, and one of us called in consequence.

"A well-known Catholic book treating on confession—" Gaume, Manuel des Confesseurs"— occupied a conspicuous place in the parlour, and evidenced to every visitor that confession was favourably looked upon in the house."

My impression in those days was that this Catholic custom was confined to Protestant convents; by what this informant said, I found it was extending to the Church of England at large.

I hope a day will come when England will again kneel round one altar in the unity of faith and practice.

It is out of place for any Protestant Clergyman of Llandaff to run down confession as an introduction of modern times. The Saints of that Church, one of the most ancient in Britain, might come forth from their graves and protest against such historical blunders.

St. Dubricius, first Bishop of Llandaff, in the fifth century, and St. Teilo, his successor, heard confessions.

In the days of Howell Dda an Archdeacon of Llandaff was commissioned to write down the Welsh code at Ty-gwyn as Daf, near Carmarthen,

One of the articles of the said code declares that a child is to go to confession at seven years of age.

Well might the educated portion of the Church-people of Llandaff feel uncomfortable on the benches of the Cathedral when they heard the Canon tell them that the practice of confession did not exist before the twelfth century. The very stones of Llandaff Cathedral deny the correctness of such assertions, and the traditions of past ages protest against the historical barbarism.

CHAPTER IV.

PIETY TO THE DEAD A SACRED AND GENERAL CUSTOM IN THE ANCIENT BRITISH CHURCH.

> KINDEST Jesus, Lord blest,
> Grant them everlasting rest.
> THE DIES IRÆ.

IN Llandaff Cathedral, on the monument erected over the Matthew family, lords of the Rhadyr, we read the following inscription:—

"Orate pro animabus Gulielmi Matthew, qui obiit decima die Martii . . . quorum animabus Deus Propitietur. Amen. (Pray for the soul of William Matthew . . . who departed from this world on the tenth of March . . . on whose soul may God have mercy. Amen.)

This epitaph reminds us of a devotion deeply impressed on the hearts of our ancestors, which made it a crime for the living to forget the departed when the grave had closed over them.

Piety to the departed a general custom in Wales. To offer prayer for the dead has ever been looked upon in the Catholic Church as a most sacred duty. Whatever may have been the faults or vices of our forefathers, there was one virtue they never failed to practice—piety towards the departed; and the Welsh in particular were most religious in the fulfilment of this spiritual work of mercy. They deemed it obligatory in a Christian to feed the hungry, to clothe the naked, and to offer hospitality to the traveller; but they believed that to relieve the suffering souls in Purgatory by prayer, alms, and the sacrifice of the Mass, was the greatest act of mercy that could be exercised, and one impossible to be neglected, except by the most ungrateful, who were pointed out to public execration as the scum of Christians.

In Cambria there is invariably a cemetery round a Church, or a monastery, for kings and subjects, clergy and laity, did not relish the idea of being buried in any other place. They felt convinced that if their bones were laid whilst awaiting the resurrection of the body beside the walls of the Church, the people who came to Mass on Sundays would not fail to breathe a prayer to our Lord on the altar for the repose of their souls.

The Church-yard of a monastery was also, in the public mind, a favourite spot for interment, because it was frequented both day and night by the Monks on their way to the Church to chant the Divine Office. The sacred harmony died away into the silence of nature in the following strain—Et Fidelium animæ per misericordiam Dei requiescant in pace. Amen. (May the souls of the faithful departed, through the mercy of God, rest in peace. Amen.)

To lay the body, when abandoned by the soul, within the boundaries of a Church, or in the case of the rich under the very roof of the sacred building, was deemed most important by the faithful of old, for they seemed to feel, through a religious instinct, that they could be happy near the altar on which Jesus Christ sheds His blood, both for the living and the dead.

"There are three places," says the Welsh code, "where a person is not to give the oath of an absolver. . . . The second is at the porch of a Church-yard, for the Pater (the 'Our Father') is there said for the souls of the Christians of the world; and at the Church door, for the Pater is chanted there before the road."[1]

Devotion to the dead in Armorica. To realise the extent of the devotion to the departed which prevailed in Wales in by-gone ages, one should visit the country parishes of Brittany, for there the old religious customs of Britain have been preserved in all their purity.

Every Sunday, either before or after Mass, there is not a grave but is visited and sprinkled with Holy Water. Children, whatever be their age or sex, are seen kneeling at the tomb of a father or a mother. A wife bends over the stone beneath which her husband rests; a husband over that of his wife. A mother leads her children by the hand, and they, like her, kneel

(1) Welsh Laws.

and pray, for she deems it her duty to teach them a devotion which she has herself learnt from the departed; and no doubt the thought suggests itself to her that one day, when she has taken her place in this same Church-yard, those now innocent children, grown up to manhood, will in like manner come and weep and pray for her soul.

In a Celtic country the old beggar is a type of the living faith of former days. He enjoys acknowledged privileges, and follows customs handed down to him by generations of his class. No police, no pauper guardians, can meddle with him. He is old, poor, known in the parish, born in it, and has never left it except when conscription called him to serve in the army. So he is free to go about unmolested, and to knock at every door. The farm dog will not even bark at him; they are too old acquaintances. If the dog could speak he would call the beggar by his name, and the latter politely salutes the canine guardian by the title familiar to him.

Bent on his staff, the old man can undisturbed make his way to the door. On the threshold he takes off his hat, and commences to recite aloud the Pater, the Ave, and the De Profundis, ending with the following ejaculation—"May all the souls of the faithful departed, the souls of those who lived in this village, and in this house, through the mercy of God rest in peace."

Whatever humour the landlady may be in, or however busily engaged, she will find time to go to the flour-bin, and pour from thence a measure into the wallet of the mendicant.

When a marriage is about to take place, and the time fixed for its celebration is at hand, the departed are not forgotten, nor can the festivities attendant on a wedding be opened without giving a thought to those who once also married and gave in marriage, but now lie buried in the cemetery. Two or three days before that appointed for the wedding a Requiem Mass is sung in the Church at which the bridegroom and the bride, with their respective relatives, attend, according to an immemorial custom.

Funerals. No interment takes place without the Holy Sacrifice of the Mass being celebrated in presence of the corpse; and when the body of the deceased has been laid in the grave, his family will cause Masses to be offered for the repose of his soul on every day for a week, and once a week for a year after his death. Then when the anniversary comes round, Mass is again celebrated for seven days.

Who can reasonably find fault with a practice which is so natural to the human heart, and which testifies gratitude, and keeps alive the memory of those who formerly tenanted the land in which we live—perhaps built the very houses in which we dwell—and helped, in a great measure, to bestow on us the comforts we now enjoy. Away with any teaching which condemns the dead to oblivion, and stifles thankfulness for past services in the breast of man. Let the Cambrians of old leap forth from their graves and denounce such revolting impiety and black ingratitude.

The venerable founder of Llancarvan Monastery is particularly noticed in the Welsh manuscripts for his piety towards the dead. No doubt in the history of his ancestors he met with sullied pages which made him think that many of them were detained in purgatory for a time. His prayers in their behalf were incessant, and his penances offered up to heaven for the same intention. St. Cadoc's devotion to the dead.

He must be acknowledged as the great traveller amongst the Welsh Saints. Several times he went to Rome and to Jerusalem. In undertaking such dangerous, long, and fatiguing journeys, he was actuated by no natural desire for moving from place to place, or love of learning, as is often the case. His sole motive was piety to the dead. The Pope, speaking of him to Gildas, said—"Cadoc has been in Rome seven times, and thrice to Jerusalem, to obtain forgiveness for the souls of his parents and friends."

The Liber Landavensis is full of wills and bequests to religion. These public deeds, carefully written and signed on all occasions by witnesses taken from the ranks of the clergy and Prayers for the dead constantly mentioned in the charters.

laity, illustrate in bold relief how strong was their piety towards their departed brethren.

In the fifth century Meurig, King of Glamorgan, ceded to Almighty God, to St. Peter, and to Dubricius, Bishop of Llandaff, all that tract of land lying between the rivers Taff and Ely, over which the rising town of Cardiff is now continually extending itself. The condition of tenure required by the charter is—" That daily prayer should be said, and ecclesiastical service performed, for his soul and for the souls of his parents, kings and princes of Britain, and of all faithful deceased."[1]

Under St. Teilo, successor of St. Dubricius, of Llandaff, we find Iddon, a prince living in Monmouthshire, granting land in a place near Abergavenny, at Llantellio, or Llandeilo Pertholey, stating that "his intention in making the donation is to benefit his own soul and those of his ancestors."

The charter commences thus—" King Iddon granted an alms for his soul and the souls of his *ancestors*, kings and princes, to God, and to St. Peter, and to Archbishop Teilo, and all his successors in the Church of Llandaff, Llanmawr —that is, Llan Teilo."[2]

To spare the reader too many quotations, let me introduce him into the home of the kings of Glamorganshire, and *there*, in the intimacy of

(1) Liber Landavensis, p. 311.
(2) Liber Landavensis, p. 385.

family life, he will be able to judge for himself as to the religious duties dictated to their faith with regard to deceased relatives. Their religion and customs were, without exception, exactly the same as those of their countrymen.

In that family a sacred tradition exists that is handed down from father to son, and never departed from, which embodies the beautiful saying of St. Ambrose, Bishop of Milan, who thus addresses the dead:—"We will never forget thee till such time as by our prayers and good works we have delivered thee from Purgatory." Thus Meurig, King of Glamorgan, prays for his father Tewdrig after the grave has closed over him; and when in his turn this dutiful son has passed to eternity, we find his children and grand-children calling on the Redeemer to overlook his frailties, granting land to religion and building Churches for the repose of his soul.[1]

Connected with the name of Meurig, the Liber Landavensis mentions a charter, thus worded—"Be it known to all that Meurig, son of Tewdrig, and his wife Ambrawst, daughter of Gwirgant, gave to God and Oudoceus, and to his holy predecessors, Teilo and Dubricius, and to all his successors in the See of Llandaff, for their souls and *the souls of their parents*, three modii, nearly twenty-seven acres of land."[2]

When the grave had closed over him and he had gone to eternity, the same attention was paid

(1) Liber Landavensis, pp. 384, 385.
(2) Liber Landavensis, p. 382.

to his memory by his surviving relations, for we read—" King Morgan, son of Athruys, granted the village of Guilbin for his soul and the soul of his grandfather, Meurig, to Oudoceus, the Bishop, and to the Church of Llandaff."[1]

The murderer at the graves of his victims

These two chieftains were, however, far from being blameless. They had shed innocent blood, and that too of near relations. Their Bishop, in solemn assembly of the clergy and laity, had even deemed it his duty to excommunicate them as guilty of perjury and murder. Undoubtedly at times they had no control over their wild nature, but no sooner had their passions cooled down than the action of faith told powerfully on their souls, and caused them to repent and do penance. They soon felt an intensity of remorse, and the ghosts of their victims haunted their imaginations night and day. Faith doubled the stings of conscience, for it reproached them for having sent into eternity a soul unprepared for the journey. Was it not just, therefore, that they should have prayers offered and alms given to benefit these near relatives, the victims of their swords?

Hence we find the following words in the Liber Landavensis[2]:—" King Morgan, son of Athruys, *for the soul of Ifrioc, son of Meurig, whom he killed*, and for the redemption of his own soul, having taken on him the yoke of penance in fasting, prayer, and alms-giving,

(1) Liber Landavensis, p. 391.
(2) Liber Landavensis, p. 399.

bestowed on the chief Bishop Oudoceus, and on St. Dubricius, and on St. Teilo, Lan Cyncyrill and the land of Cynfall, situated on the banks of the river Ely, in Glamorganshire."[1]

In these days of materialism the law considers the crime of murder only from a temporal point of view, and pronounces the perpetrator of it guilty, because he deprived a man of the right to live an additional twenty or forty years of life, and took, perhaps, a husband from a wife, or a father from his children. The man of faith sees it in another aspect, and says—"Here you have launched an unprepared soul into eternity. By far the most serious part of the offence is your having deprived him of the chance of putting his conscience in order by repentance, and prevented him from receiving the Sacrament of Penance and the Holy Eucharist. Temporal existence is nothing compared to eternal life. The least you can do is to pray to Almighty God for the soul of the victim of your unbridled wrath."

As I have before said, the Bretons of Armorica had Welshmen for their first Bishops and Pastors, and monastic institutions were introduced into that country, or at least owed their development to natives of Britain.

Donation of Guereck Duke of Brittany, to the Welsh nun St. Ninnoc

It is said that the first convent for women erected in Brittany was founded by a daughter of Cambria, Ninnoc, the virgin and servant of

---

(1) Liber Landavensis.

God. On this occasion kings and princes came nobly forward to help the cause of religion. There is a charter of Count Guereck to blessed Ninnoc, which we will place before the reader, as it evidences the same respect and devotion to the departed. It bears the date 458, and thus belongs to the fifth century.

"In the name of the Holy and Undivided Trinity, and of the Most Blessed Virgin Mary, and by the virtue of the Holy Cross, I, Guereck, by the grace of God, Duke of Brittany, out of my own heritage, for the *continual commemoration of the souls of my parents, either alive or dead*, for the salvation of my soul and the souls of those of my blood who are to succeed me, and for the welfare of my kingdom, in the presence of the Bishops, counts, and lords of Brittany here present, give and concede to the virgin and servant of God, Ninnoc, and her successors for ever who are to serve God in this locality, called by her name Lan Ninnoc, the whole Parish of Pluemer, with all the territories cultivated and uncultivated contained within its boundaries. Moreover, I add another gift—namely, the whole territory on which stands the Church of St. Julitta, with the Church of the same name situated in Rengruis. Towards the support of the said donation I also grant annually three hundred measures of wine, salt, and wheat, out of the estate called Dalkhgerran, to be delivered on the spot by vessels, and at my own expense.

I increase my donation by the gift of three hundred horses, or mares, and as many bullocks and cows, and other smaller cattle. To confirm, therefore, this privilege of my donation, I offer this gold chalice full of pure wine, and a patina, as a testimony and to be used in the heavenly banquet. Therefore, whoever shall violate or diminish the quantity of this donation, let him be pierced by the dart of present and eternal anathama, and let his lot be with those who burn in the unextinguished fire for their sins.

"All present answered Amen; and this was done in the place called Lan Ninnoc, in the Parish of Pluemur, and presence of the above named princes of Letavia, in the year of the Incarnation of our Lord CCCCLVIII. (458), the same Lord Jesus Christ reigning throughout the infinity of ages."[1]

(1) Albert le Grand. Vies des Saints de Bretagne, p. 361.

"In nomine Sanctæ et Individuæ Trinitatis et beatissimæ Virginis Mariæ, ac per virtutem sanctæ Crucis, Ego Guerech, Dei gratiâ, Brittaniæ Minoris Dux, ex meâ propriâ hæreditate, pro commemoratione assiduâ animarum parentum meorum, tam vivorum quam defunctorum, et pro salute animæ meæ, nec non eorum qui ex stirpe meâ successuri sunt, et pro statu Regni mei, in conspectu Episcoporum, comitum et optimatum regionis Brittanicæ hic astantium, Do et concedo sanctæ Dei famulæ et Virgini Nennocæ, ejusque successoribus, in perpetuum ibi in loco qui ex ejus nomine dicitur Lan-Ninnoc, Deo servituris, totam plebem quæ dicitur Pluemur, cum omnibus terris cultis et incultas, itâ ut penitùs continetur intrà fines suos. Adjicio insuper aliud donum, terram totam videlicet, in quâ est ecclesia sanctæ Julitæ, cum eâdem ecclesiâ quæ est in Renguis, ad sustentandam quoqve loci hujus procurationem, quolibet anno, trecentos modios tam vini quam salis, atque frumenti, de terrâ quæ dicitur Dalkh-Gerran (vel Rathguerran), similiter concedo, eosque deferri hùc usquè navigio faciam. Augeo etiam huic meo dono trecentos tam equorum quam equaram et totidem boum et vaccarum, necnon minutorum animalium. Ad corroborandum verò hujus meæ dationis priviligium, calicem hunc aureum, cum patenâ, vino mero plenum in testimonum offero et in discumbitione æternâ. Quicumque ergò hujus doni quantitatem violaverit, aut minuerit, præsentis et æterni anathematis jacula transfigatur, sitque pars ejus cum illis qui in igne inextinguili in cumulum perditionis pro suâ nequitiâ involvuntur. Respondentes autem omnes qui ibi aderant

A careful reader meditating on this will of a king in the fifth century may, perhaps, share our own feelings as regards the donor and recipient. It is beneficial to the heart of a Christian man living in the nineteenth century, an age of materialism, to see his fellow-men long since departed so supernatural in their deeds, and so Christian in the wording of their transactions.

Ninnoc, the Welsh nun, had no doubt gained the esteem of the Britons, both clergy and laity. Had she gone to Armorica, as a young and beautiful daughter of Cambria, she would have been admired, and at once have become a welcome guest amongst the nobles of that country. Young princes would have sought her hand, and bards have sung the praises of her beauty in the banquet halls; but when she lands on the western coast of Gaul, her form is shrouded in the coarse habit of the convent, her face hidden under the veil of a nun, and she is venerated. Her aim is not to please the world, but to serve God, and those amongst whom she came thought that too much could not be done for her and her companions.

The Armoricans regard her as an angel on earth, and her prayers ascend straight to heaven; and the spirits who minister around the throne of God are prompt in assisting her. Hence the Duke, in return for his donation, demands her

dixerunt. Amen. . . . Faactum est hoc in loco, qui dicitur Lan-Ninnoc, in plebe Pluemur, coram prædictis Letaviæ nobilibus, anno ab incarnatione Domini Jesu Christo CCCCLVIII regnante eodem Domino Jesu Christo per infinita sæcula sæculorum. Amen."

intercession for himself and for all he holds dear.

On the day of the official promulgation of the charter, the solemn ceremony commenced, as was usual on such occasions, with the Holy Sacrifice of the Mass. A chalice of gold, with the paten, reminded the community of what was required in perpetuity—namely, the celebration of the Holy Sacrifice for the donor and for the souls of his relations, living and dead. The *Discumbitio æterna* meant that the Body and Blood of our Lord was to be offered up for ever, according to the intentions specified by the charter.

When the Anglo-Saxons were converted to Christianity they also inherited the piety and the usages of the Britons towards the departed.

An Anglo-Saxon chieftain, although a Christian, shows at times no more control over his passions than his British *confrère*. Unfortunately in those primitive days murders occurred but too frequently amongst both races. However, as they professed the same religion and the same faith, they atoned as far as they could in the same religious manner for the crimes they committed.

<small>The same piety is manifested in Anglo-Saxon converts.</small>

Oswy, King of Northumberland, was a strange mixture of virtues and vices. Zealous for the propagation of Catholic truth, we have already beheld him presiding at the conference between Coleman and Wilfrid on the question of Easter. Yet the same prince unmercifully slew his opponent, Oswin, who had been treacherously delivered into his hands. Public indignation and bitter remorse soon brought him to the altar to ask pardon for himself and for his victim.

He erected a monastery on the very spot where the murder had been committed, and stipulated that daily prayer should be offered for both kings—the slayer and the slain. It is related that his conscience not being yet satisfied, he thought, when fifty-eight years of age, of going as a poor pilgrim to Rome, still further to atone for having slain Oswin.[1]

Reader, deride not the piety of our forefathers towards the deceased, nor the religion which implanted it and fostered its growth in the breast. Call not by the name of superstition a devotion that brings a child to kneel at a father's or a mother's grave, *there*, according to the Welsh phraseology, to say the Pater for their souls. Laugh not at a beloved and bereaved fellow-being who seeks the Church in order to plead before Jesus Christ the cause of his departed relatives or friends. It is impiety and folly, and any enlightened man who may witness the act feels indignant. May you, on your death-bed, be consoled by the idea that when you shall have exchanged a short existence for an everlasting one the living will still remember you, for in the family there is a sacred tradition which pronounces it a sin not to give a thought

Piety towards the departed an act of gratitude and justice

---

(1) Sammes, Brittania Antiqua.

to the dead or to pray for them. Happy are the father and the mother who have taught their children to kneel each night by the fireside, and who have enforced, as a religious duty, that every one should join, before retiring to rest, in prayers for the faithful departed. Such a custom may be beneficial beyond the grave to the pious soul who practices it.

We are deeply indebted to those who have gone before us. The house, the village, the town in which we were born was built by them. The general comfort we enjoy is in a great measure the result of their work. They opened our roads, and brought the country into a high state of cultivation. From them we inherit our laws and customs, and our present safety as regards life and property. Is it not, therefore, just that we should gratefully appreciate what they have done, call down a blessing on their graves, and invoke peace to their souls?

Were the dead allowed to appear again and speak, they might with truth reproach the living with being in a great degree the cause of their sufferings in Purgatory, and say—"We now undergo a term of punishment before being admitted into heaven, and this we attribute to the scandals you placed before us, and to your advice which we followed; and further, in order to benefit you in temporal concerns, we, for love of you, infringed on the rights of God and man." In such a case not only gratitude but justice bids us remember, in our prayers and good works, those souls suffering in another world because of our sins in this.

When Judas Maccabœus had put the army of Georgias to flight, he traversed the battle-field to ascertain the number of his own soldiers who had fallen, in order that they might receive honourable burial. To his own great sorrow, and also that of his companions in arms, donaries to idols were found underneath their coats. The fact that such brave men should have died guilty of such a heinous transgression grieved all the survivors.

A collection amounting to twelve thousand drachmas was made amongst the soldiers and sent to Jerusalem, in order that sacrifices might be there offered up for the sins of the dead, because Judas and his warriors knew to a man, as the Sacred Biography remarks, "*that it is a holy and wholesome thought to pray for the dead, that they may be loosed from sin.*"[1]

A day will again dawn over Cambria when the sons of Britain, re-converted to the faith of their forefathers, will restore to their country that piety towards the departed so sadly lost at the present time.

Welshmen who have recently returned to the Catholic faith, and were possessed of wealth, have already bestowed land and endowments upon Catholic missions; and, following the custom

(1) Maccabees, xii. 46.

of the children of the Church in the fifth and sixth centuries, have stipulated that in return for their donations prayers should be said, and the Holy Sacrifice of the Mass offered up for their souls and for the souls of their departed relatives.

When the tide of public opinion, directed by the spirit of God, shall have brought men to look upon Catholicity in a more favourable light, and shall have drawn more souls within the threshold of the Church, such donations will increase in number. *Amen.* We want land whereon to build Churches—schools wherein to pray and educate our rising generation. Like Beino, the master of St. Winefrid, we are under the necessity of appealing to landowners, being unable to refrain from using our utmost exertions to supply urgent needs. We ask them in the name of God to grant us at least a few *square yards* of ground on which we may erect a modest Chapel, wherein to worship according to the dictates of our conscience and the religion of our forefathers.

I will close this chapter with a Breton tale, which is often narrated in the peasant's homes by the fire-sides on the long winter nights. A tale, although but a tale, is still a medium for conveying the thoughts and religious convictions of a nation as to what a Christian should do for the faithful departed. This story is borrowed from Emile Souvestre, who has naively reproduced the customs and mode of thinking, not only of his own country, but of Celtic races in general, who have not lost the faith.

"The Bretons," he observes, "like all the rest of the world, are children of sin. However, they love their dead, take compassion on those in Purgatory, and endeavour to release them from the purifying fire."

It is in the *black month*[1] they more especially demonstrate their Christian piety. *On All Saints evening* every one gives a thought to those who have stood at the bar of Divine justice. Masses are said for them, blessed tapers are lighted, and their sad condition recommended to the intercession of the Saints. Their graves are visited by the people of the district in the company of little children, and after Vespers the Parish Priest proceeds from the Church to bless their tombs.

It is on that night Jesus Christ bestows many favours upon departed souls, and allows them to re-visit the homes they inhabited whilst on earth. During those hours the dead are as numerous in the houses as the leaves are on the deep roads, and each dwelling is set in order to receive them with hospitality.

But if we count those devoted to the Blessed Virgin and her Divine Son by thousands, children of the Black Angel (the Devil) also abound, who forget those who have been dear to them, and are no longer of this world.

(1) November.

William Postic was one of these. His father had died without the benefit of Absolution, and he was going in the right way to depart in the same unblessed manner. He led a dissolute life, and danced during Mass on Sundays, whenever he could, in company with horse dealers and the like. In the same year he lost his mother, sisters, and wife, and to console himself, like every wicked widower, he used to say, "I lost my wife, but I can find plenty more."

His Parish Priest had warned him privately, and had even denounced him from the pulpit as a scandal to every Christian; but all to no purpose; for, as the saying is, "The cracking whip drives away the loose horse."

When the feast of *All Souls* came round, every baptized Christian put on mourning and went to Church to pray for the dead. As for William, he proceeded to the neighbouring village to meet sailors without religion, and shameless women.

All the time passed by the others in pious exercise for the relief of the suffering souls was spent by him in drinking *fire water*, gambling with the sailors, and singing songs to the girls. Thus he caroused until midnight, and was the last to leave the public-house.

On his way home he chanted aloud such songs as even the boldest only whisper, and passed before the highway crosses without lowering his voice or taking off his hat. He whirled his stick, heedless whether he might strike the souls with which on that night the roads were crowded.

On arriving at a place where four roads met, he paused to deliberate, for two of them led to his village. The longer one was under the protection of God, whilst the shorter was haunted by the dead, for many in passing along it at night had seen and heard things they dared not speak of except near the Holy Water stoup. But William was no coward, and so in the end he dashed down this road.

The night was pitch dark; no stars glistened in the firmament; no moon was to be seen; the silence of death reigned around, interrupted only by the murmuring of streams, and the clattering of his clogs on the rocky path.

Whilst he was passing under the walls of an old ruined manor house the weather-cock from the tottering belfry crowed and said, "Go back! Go back! Go back!" But William went on, and when he came to the cascade the waters spoke thus:—

"Do not cross! Do not cross! Do not cross!"

Leaning on his stick, he leaped from rock to rock, until he reached the opposite side.

As he passed an old hollow oak tree the wind whistling through its branches said:—

"Stop here! Stop here! Stop here!"

William struck the old tree with his stick, and walked on till he came to the entrance of the haunted valley. At this moment the hour of midnight was tolled from the towers of the three Churches.

To cheer himself up the young man began to whistle, but at the fourth attempt he heard the noise of wheels coming in his direction; and as soon as he caught sight of the mysterious cart he perceived that it was covered with a winding sheet. Postic soon discovered that it was the *Chariot of Death*, drawn by six horses as black as ebony. The coachman, who was death himself, shouted—

"Get out of the way, or I will overrun thee."

William moved aside, but, far from losing courage, audaciously said—

"Well, Master Death, what art thou doing here?"

"I take—I waylay!" was the solemn answer.

"Then thou art a robber and a traitor," said William.

"I strike blindly and regardless of persons."

"Then thou meanest to say that thou art a fool and a brute," exclaimed the young man; "but never mind all that, only let me know whither thou art going."

"I am going," Death replied, "in search of William Postic."

The youth burst into a fit of laughter, not altogether natural, and continued his journey.

He was not long in reaching the spot haunted by the night laundresses from the other world, and he was soon convinced that what people said on this subject was correct, for he perceived young women as white as snow stretching linen to dry on the hedge.

"Hail! fair damsels," shouted William. "I see you are not shy; but pray what are you doing in these meadows at this hour of the night?"

"We wash, we dry, we sew," smartly replied the two women.

"But what?" enquired the young man.

"The winding sheet of a dead man, who as yet speaks and walks."

"A dead man! But pray do let me know who he can be?"

"William Postic."

The youth laughed as before, and continued his descent along the narrow, rocky path. As he proceeded he heard the voices of several women, mingled with that particular noise occasioned by several persons scouring on the stones of streams.

As he drew nearer he beheld them with his own eyes washing out *winding sheets*, and heard them singing the following mournful verses as they worked:—

> "If Christians to our aid come not
> Till doomsday, washing is our lot
> By moonlight, in the howling sleet,
> In fresh snow still—the winding sheet."

On seeing the stranger the fairies at once ran to him, requesting his help in wringing out their wet shrouds.

"I am always glad to oblige," answered William. "But, fair laundresses, let each of you take her turn, for a man has but two hands."

He laid down his stick, and took the end of a sheet presented to him by one of the dead, being particularly careful to wring in the same direction as the laundress, for old people say that is the only way of keeping one's arms to one's shoulders.

Whilst thus occupied William witnessed the arrival of other women, amongst whom were his own mother, his aunt, his sisters, and his wife, who screamed—

"A thousand woes to him who lets those belonging to him burn in the flames of Purgatory! A thousand woes!" And all the surrounding echoes repeated, "A thousand woes!"

This scene was too much for William; his hair stood on end; a cold perspiration broke out over his body; he lost his presence of mind, and wrung the linen in the wrong direction, when his arms became dislocated under the iron strength of the ghost.

Partly through fear, and partly through the deadly touch of the spectre, the unhappy young man fell down dead.

At his funeral the blessed candles would not light, and all who were present left his grave with the sad conviction that there was one more bad Christian in hell.

Whilst revising this chapter I happened to fall on Jones' History of Brecknockshire, and therein met with the following epitaph written on the monument of the Aubrey family:—

"*Water le Fitz Water git ici, Jesus de sa alme cit mercy. Amen. Pater Noster. Christina sa femme gist ici, de sa alme en merci. Ave Maria. Pater Noster.*"

Our ancestors took the greatest care to remind the living to pray for the departed. Speechless under the granite or marble monument they lent their voices to an inanimate stone, and ordered it to remind the visitors of their mortal remains, not to forget to recommend their souls to the mercy of God. They are to kneel on the pavement, and say—" Eternal rest give unto them, O Lord, and may everlasting light shine upon them."

St. Augustine, the African Bishop, in his *Confessions*, requests the reader to pray for the repose of his mother, Monica, and his father, Patricius. "My God and my Lord," says the great doctor, "inspire such of my brethren who may read this book to pray at the altar for the souls of thy servant Monica, and her husband, Patricius, whose blood flows in my veins."

In keeping with these pious and useful customs, the *writer* calls upon such persons who may read these lines recording the piety of the ancient Britons for the faithful departed to recommend to the mercy of God the humble Priest who spent many a night in the sweet company of the ancient inhabitants of this island. May they say a Pater and Ave for the repose of his soul when the grave has closed on him.

CHAPTER V.

Saints Honoured and Invoked in the Cambrian Church.

The Church of God, taken in the widest meaning of the word, encloses within her fold the living and the dead. *We* tenants of the earth form the *militant* Church, for on our road to eternity we have to fight the Devil, the world, and the flesh. Amongst the departed the souls in Purgatory constitute the *suffering* Church; whilst the happy souls round the Throne of God form that glorious society called the triumphant Church.

We can tell the number of our brethren on earth, but are unable to realise an approximate idea of the legions of souls either in Purgatory or in heaven. We pray for those who suffer beyond the grave, and earnestly request our brethren enjoying the vision of God to help us with their powerful influence in heaven.

The Council of Trent, in its twenty-fifth session, directs that all over the world it shall be taught "That the Saints who reign with Christ in heaven offer up their prayers on behalf of *(Doctrine of the Council of Trent on this subject.)*

men; that it is a good and useful thing to invoke them and seek for their intercession and help, in order to obtain graces from God through our Lord Jesus Christ, who alone is our Redeemer and Saviour."

This doctrine is certainly in keeping with the traditions of the Catholic Church. From the time of Christ down to our own, religion, although teaching that it is not absolutely necessary in order to be saved to pray to the Saints, still strongly recommends her children to avail themselves of the powerful influence which their departed brethren exercise in heaven. The Saints, no longer within the prison of a corrupt body, enjoy the vision of God. They are beatified spirits, empowered to behold what passes on earth, and from the heights of heaven look down with compassion on their brethren who are still navigating the stormy ocean of life. The blessed in the other world return thanks to the Lamb of God, in whose blood they have washed their garments, but do not forget those whom they left behind; and coming to the presence of Christ they bear with them the phials containing the prayers of their brethren. (Apoc. v. 8.)

Veneration for the Saints and confidence in their intercession with God is everywhere to be met with in ancient Welsh history. In Churches and monasteries their lives were read and set up as examples to be followed, and their intercession invoked in Litanies and in prayers at Mass.

Sailors during a storm called on them for assistance in the hour of danger, and their countrymen, when visited by epidemics, unfavourable seasons, or the scourge of war, implored of these Saints now before the throne of God to plead for them in the time of tribulation.

The Rev. W. Y. Rees, M.A., in his introduction to the lives of the Cambro-British Saints, very properly observes that "these and similar lives were compiled to give information how the holy persons commemorated lived, and to set their modes of living as an example for others to follow; and accordingly they were appointed to be read in the time of and as a part of Divine service, whereby the hearers would receive a knowledge of the various particulars of their conduct, and be excited to imitate them. Being thus read for the purpose of conveying religious instruction and inciting to piety, they were called legends, in contradistinction to homilies and discourses. The days of the year on which these lives of the Saints were publicly read were those of their festivals, which took place on the anniversary of their deaths, and were considered as their birth days, because they then entered into a state of happiness."[1]

Their lives written and read for public edification.

In many a Breton family of Lower Armorica this ancient custom is not yet extinct, and the lives of the Saints are invariably read before kneeling down to evening prayer every day

(1) Cambro-British Saints.

throughout the year. Several religious communities also follow this practice, and a short life of the deceased members of their order is read on their anniversary days.

Such a custom in any nation or family denotes a supernatural people who place a due value on the real end of man, and are anxious to copy the example given them by the servants of God. A soldier studies the life of an Alexander, a Cæsar, or a Napoleon, in order to learn from them how to vanquish nations and obtain perishable glory. The soul illuminated by Divine grace, scorning all such transitory considerations, takes the Saint who conquered heaven for the model of his life, and his written history for his book of study.

Beautiful sentiments expressed by the biographer of St. David at the end of his life.

Supernatural life as a rule pervades such writings intended for edification, and at times the cast of thoughts is somewhat original. Let us take as an instance the sentiment which emanates from the pen of a biographer of St. David, after the said pen had narrated his departure from this world.

"And on that Tuesday, the first day of March, Jesus Christ took the soul of St. David with great victory, joy, and honour, after hunger, thirst, cold, labour, fasts, and acts of charity; afflictions, troubles, and temptations, and anxiety for the world. The angels bore his soul to the place of light without end, and rest without labour, and joy without sorrow, and abundance of all good things—of victory, brightness, and beauty. The place where the champion of Christ is praised, and where the wicked who on earth abounded in riches are cast aside; the place where health is without pain, peace without disappointment, music without discord; the place where Abel rejoices with the martyrs, Enock with the living, Noah with the sailors; where Abraham dwells with the Patriarchs, Melchisedech with the Priests, Moses with the princes; where Aaron is with the Bishops, David with the kings, Isaias with the Prophets, Mary with the virgins, Peter with the Apostles; where Paul is with the Greeks, John with the Asiatics, Thomas with the Indians, Matthew with the men of Judea, Luke with those of Archaia, Mark with those of Alexandria, Andrew with the Scythians, in that eternal home where dwell the angels and archangels, Cherubim and Seraphim, and the King of Kings, for ever. Amen."

And as we have commemorated David in his life and works on earth, *so may he now be our assistant, and effectually give us strength before our true Creator, that we may obtain mercy hereafter.* Amen.

Nothing, perhaps, brings home to us more powerfully the veneration of our forefathers for the servants of God than the early common practice of giving their names to towns, villages, valleys, or mountains.

Anyone who will take the trouble to study a good map of Wales will continually meet such names as the following—Llan Illtyd, Llangadog, Cadoxton, Llandeilo Vawr, Llandewi Brefi, St. Asaph, etc. Now, these appellations were given to the said localities as tokens of respect and veneration for the memory of St. Illtyd, Cadoc, Teilo, St. David, and St. Asaph.

The names of Saints given to localities. The names of parishes in the neighbourhood of Cardiff point out that this part of Britain received the Gospel from the early missionaries sent over by Pope Eleutherius to King Lucius. St. Fagan and Merthyr Dovan, villages not far distant, tell us in plain terms that our forefathers never forgot the services rendered to their race by these two Priests belonging to the second century.

In Brittany the names of the following towns or villages tell the same tale—Quimper, Corentin, St. Brieuc, St. Malo, Landeilo, Lan-Iltut, and hundreds of others indicate the same custom and religious practice, for Ss. Brieuc, Malo, Corentin, and the rest had won, by their virtuous lives, the admiration of the Armoricans. They were not born on their shores, but in the island of Britain. This, however, mattered little. They were Saints, and as such gained the esteem of the people, who believed that their names being bestowed on a district would ensure for it the benefit of their protection. We find the same practice carried out at the baptismal font, for every one knows that David and Patrick are the names most frequently given in baptism to the children of Wales and Ireland.

The well, in the vicinity of which a Saint had spent a great part of his existence in prayer and contemplation, was considered a sacred spot, and resorted to by numerous pilgrims, especially when it became known that it did not arise from a natural spring, but, at the command of God, gushed forth from the mountain side at the humble petition of one of His dear servants, or, as in the case of St. Winefrid, indicated the spot where the virgin had nobly shed her blood for the sake of her Master. This well is religiously visited by hundreds every year. In times past St. David's, in Pembrokeshire, although situated on a far away, treeless promontory, was resorted to by pilgrims not only from Cambria, but even from England. The journey was long and fatiguing, but nothing deterred the "man of faith" who had some heavenly favour to obtain or sins to atone for. William the Conqueror, Henry II., Edward I., and his consort, Eleanor, accomplished the journey. In the minds of the people two pilgrimages to St. David's were esteemed equal to one to Rome. *[Pilgrimages to wells or Churches.]*

Roma semel quantum, Dat bis Menevia tantum, *and*, Meneviam si bis et Roman si semel ibis
   Merces æqua tibi redditur hic et ibi.[1]

These were couplets used to convey the general impression.

The grave of a Saint or the Church erected to his memory was also chosen as a suitable spot *[Differences settled by the grave of a Saint.]*

---

(1) The Welsh Saints. Reece, p. 202.

wherein to settle differences, lay down the sword of murder, and form a resolution to lead a religious life. I will illustrate this by the legend of St. Clydog. In the days of Bethguuin, fourth Bishop of Llandaff, there lived in Herefordshire a young prince, who kept to perfection the laws of God and of the Church. In his private and in his official life he was a model to his countrymen. He governed his subjects with justice, and watched over his officers, a duty which many of the British chieftains failed in. His private life was austere, chaste, and kindly towards the poor. A fair damsel of the district used to say openly how much she desired a union with such a prince. Amongst those devoted to him was a maiden of great wealth, who invariably put off her numerous suitors by saying that if ever she was to marry she would take no other husband but Clydog.

One of the companions of the young prince fell in love with this lady, notwithstanding her expressed resolution, but was dismissed like so many others.

He who of old tempted Adam and Eve in the terrestial Paradise suggested to the discarded lover the thought of ridding himself of the obstacle to his wishes by murdering Clydog. The demon whispered that though the lady would weep at first, yet after a month or two she would forget the prince and ultimately marry his false friend. The deluded youth listened to this evil suggestion, and determined to assassinate his master. This he accomplished at a hunting party. Clydog was alone in a solitary part of the forest, when the murderer rushed suddenly upon his unsuspecting victim and slew him. This fiendish and treacherous deed caused a general sensation of horror throughout Wales; and Clydog, although not a martyr in the strictest sense of the word, was looked upon as such by his countrymen. The people, as a rule admirers of virtue, had remarked that his life was pure and austere as that of a hermit by the side of his well, and regular as that of a monk in the cloister. A Church was soon erected over his grave, and solemnly blessed with Holy Water, and from that time the place began to be held in great veneration, as the following events will show.

About this time two persons had a quarrel, which was to be decided by an appeal to arms. The day was fixed, and the spot for the meeting chosen, when friends interfered and suggested that the affair should be quietly arranged before the altar in the Church of St. Dubricius, at Madley. The proposal was neither adopted nor rejected, but modified in this way: They would go to the Church and kneel before the altar, not at Madley, but at the Church of St. Clydog. So they proceeded thither, and before the tomb of the martyred prince laid down their swords, and swore a solemn oath hereafter to live in peace together.[1]

(1) Liber Landavensis, p. 445.

Two brothers and a sister of good birth, who resided near the present town of Cowbridge, in Glamorganshire, resolved to abandon the world and lead a religious life. When their place of retirement came to be considered, the brothers and sister were unanimous in their choice of the spot on the banks of the river Mynndy, where the body of blessed Clydog had been deposited. No doubt they looked upon the place as holy, and believed that the demons would be driven from it by the blessed spirit of the murdered prince.

Ithael, son of Morgan, owner of the territory, was so pleased that the recluses should have chosen this spot out of respect for the memory of Clydog, that with the approbation of his sons and heirs he granted the land to them by a clear and formal charter.

The description given by Geoffrey of Monmouth of the battle of Badon pourtrays, as accurately as possible, the confidence of the Britons in the intercession of Saints. When Dubricius had given his blessing to the army after exhorting them to do their duty, the men prepared for battle.

Arthur at the battle of Badon (Bath) invokes the Blessed Virgin. Arthur having arrayed himself in a coat of mail suitable to the grandeur of so powerful a king, placed a golden helmet on his head, on which was engraven the figure of a dragon, and upon his shoulders his shield called Priwen, on which *was painted* the *picture* of the *Blessed Virgin, Mother of God, in order to put him frequently in mind of her;* then, girding on his sword Caliburn, which was of wondrous power, made in the Isle of Avallon, he took in his right hand his lance named Ron, which was hard, broad, and fitted for slaughter. Then, having placed his men in order, he attacked the Saxon army, which was drawn up in the form of a wedge, as was its custom. They made a noble defence during the whole day against the onslaught of the Britons, but towards sunset retreated to the nearest mountain, which served them as a camp. . . . On the following morning Arthur, with his soldiers, rushed up the mountain, but lost many of them, on account of the advantageous position held by the Saxons, which enabled them to shower down stones upon his men with greater rapidity than they could advance against them. The Britons, notwithstanding, after a very hard struggle, gained the summit of the hill, and came to a close engagement with the enemy, who again gave them a warm reception.

In this way a great part of the day was spent. At last Arthur, provoked at seeing how little he had achieved, and that victory was still in suspense, drew his Caliburn, and, *calling upon the name of the Blessed Virgin*, rushed furiously forward into the thickest ranks of the enemy, of whom (such was the success of his prayer) very few escaped.[1]

Emile Souvestre, in his Foyer Breton, elucidates this truth in the tale of the *Old Witch* and

(1) Goffrey of Monmouth.

the *Two Orphans*. It commences thus:—" In the olden times there lived in Lan-illis a young man called Houarn Pogam, and a fair young girl whose name was Bella Postick. They were cousins, and their mothers brought them up as though destined to marry by the permission of God, when of age. They lost their parents early, and were then obliged to earn their bread as farm servants.[1]

They might have been very happy in that position of life, but lovers, like the sea, are ever murmuring.

"Had we but the means to buy a cow and a lean hog," Houarn sadly remarked, "I could rent a plot of ground, and the Priest would marry us."

"Yes," replied Bella, sighing; "but times are hard, and the cattle market rose at the last fair. *For once* God seems no longer to mind the world."

"I am afraid," rejoined the young man, " that we must wait for a long time, for when I share a bottle of wine in the public-house with my friends the last drop never falls to my share."

"Very long indeed," said Bella, "for I never hear the cuckoo."

These complaints were repeated day after day, until at last Houarn lost patience. One morning as Bella was winnowing in the barn he came to communicate to her that he was going to travel in search of fortune.

[1] The most sceptical reader may convince himself of the faith of Celtic races in the intercession of Saints by studying their traditions, as reflected in old stories told by the winter firesides at night. These tales, although abounding in fictions, still indicate the nature of the religious tendency of the mind in those early periods.

The young girl grew pale at this intelligence, and used every persuasion to induce him to change his purpose. But Houarn was obstinate, and would not listen to reason.

"The birds," he said, "fly onward until they find a corn-field, and the bees never rest unless they discover flowers filled with honey. Should man be less enterprising than these tiny-winged creatures? I also will fly till I make out the price of what I want. If you love me, Bella, oppose not my plans."

The young girl, seeing it was useless to offer further opposition, said with a failing heart— "Under the protection of God go, since it must be so; but before we separate I must divide between us the best part of the inheritance left me by my parents." Then she led the young man to her drawer, and took from it a little bell, a knife, and a walking stick.

"These three relics," she said, "have never left my family. Here is the bell of St. Koledok. Its sound is heard even at the further end of the world, and tells us the danger we may be in."

"*The knife* once belonged to St. Corentinus, and whatever it touches becomes free from charms and the Devil. The staff is the very same on which St. Vouga leaned, and possesses the virtue of transporting its owner whithersoever he may wish to go.

"The *knife* I give you as a protection against evil charms, the bell to warn me of the dangers which may beset you, and the staff I keep to carry me to your assistance if needful."

The Liber Landavensis contains hundreds of charters from the fifth century down to the twelfth. The first of these bears the date of the time of St. Dubricius, and the last is connected either with Urban or his predecessors.

The charters of Llandaff full of donations to the Saints.
Their phraseology runs as follows—"I grant to Almighty God, to St. Peter, and to the Holy Dubricius, Teilo, and Oudoceus, for the benefit of my soul, the redemption of my sins, and for the souls of the faithful departed [so many] acres of land." Such is invariably the form in which the ancient Cambrians worded their deeds of donation; and we children of the nineteenth century, living in an age of materialism, are agreeably affected in reading such phrases in the full freshness of religion and faith. Generation after generation pass before our eyes; changes, social and political, take place throughout the island; the Anglo-Saxons, the Danes, the Normans, invade the country, and introduce their customs and language. Yet each Briton who makes a will, either whilst in health or on his death-bed, keeps faithfully to the old form, so religious and edifying.

Thus in the twelfth century Urban, Bishop of Llandaff, in his long correspondence with two Popes, adheres to the sacred phraseology of his predecessors, and we find it reproduced in the Rescripts from Rome, for in the Bulls of Pope

Honorius we read such passages as the following:—

"Therefore, dearly beloved in the Lord, Bishop Urban, complying with thy rational request, we receive the Church of St. Peter, and of the holy confessors, Dubricius, Teilo, and Oudoceus, at Llandaff, over which through God you preside, into the protection of the Holy See."

An antique French sonnet on St. Gunstan, a Briton by birth, and a disciple in Brittany, of Paulus Aurelianus, runs thus:— *Sailors invoked St. Gunstan.*

> St. Gunstan (Goustan)
> Notre ami
> Ramenez nos maris.
> St. Gunstan
> Notre amant
> Ramenez nos parens.[1]

This used to be sung by the wives and daughters of sailors on the western coast of France. His memory was endeared to a seafaring population by two qualifications. In the first place he was a Saint; in the second he had been long connected with the ocean; so they considered that, having been acquainted with the hardships and dangers of a sailor's life, he would naturally when in heaven specially interest himself for hard-working mariners.

When a mere boy he had been kidnapped by pirates, and being of a strong constitution was retained by the captain as a sailor. The hard and menial work fell to his share as a matter of course, because he was a slave. He became

(1) Albert le Grand, page 783.

incapacitated for service at sea through a tumour in his foot. Being no longer of any use, he was landed by the captain on the coast of Brittany, between Morlaix and Brest, Finistèrre. When cured of his ailment he became a disciple of Paulus Aurelianus, and later on retired to lead the life of a hermit in a small island called Houadic, in which place he frequently found abundant opportunities of exercising charity.

When shipwrecked sailors were driven by a storm on the coast of this little island, Gunstan hastened to the sea shore along with his companion, and they spared no exertion in rendering assistance to the mariners, who, when safely landed, found a good fire lighted to warm and dry them, and the best provisions to be procured at their disposal. The reputation of the Holy Hermit soon spread from country to country, his charitable deeds being related by the crews whom he had not only rescued from danger, but cheered in body and edified in spirit.

The confidence of our forefathers in the intercession of Saints a natural deduction from the miracles they had seen them perform in their life. The confidence which Celtic races placed in the servants of God whom He has called from this land of exile to His heavenly kingdom may be thus accounted for. It was often a simply rational deduction from the miracles which they had seen them perform under their own eyes whilst they were yet in the flesh. Such, for instance, as Germanus commanding the winds and the waves to subside when he was crossing from France to England during a storm, and shortly afterwards restoring sight to a blind girl; or from the belief that St. David, whilst on his way to the Council of Brevi, restored a boy to life. Far from thinking that the power of their prayers was decreased by death, they, on the contrary, came to the natural conclusion that if whilst on earth they could obtain favours for their fellow-men, this privilege must be immeasurably increased when freed from the faults and defects inseparable to human nature and displeasing to God. They now, clothed in the beauty of glorified spirits, rejoiced in heaven as brothers of the Lord Jesus Christ. And hence those who suffered in mind or body sought their protection.

Such were the reflections of our forefathers, as frequently evidenced by their writings or practice. The Liber Landavensis closes the life of the first Bishop of that See with the following words:—
" As the survivors of Dubricius had venerated and looked upon him as a father when with them corporeally, so they now often applied to him as an intercessor with God, and as the defender of all the Saints in the island and throughout the entire country."

On the death of his successor in the same See, such was the eagerness amongst Welshmen to possess his body that a dispute arose between three parishes. After much altercation, Llandaff prevailed, and from the time of his burial in that Cathedral his grave was for centuries visited by crowds of pilgrims, and there frequently the sick were healed of their diseases, sight restored to the blind, and hearing to the deaf.

In this nineteenth century of ours, which boasts of having discarded all belief in the supernatural, there are still thousands and millions who venerate the grave of a servant of God, and resort thither confident that their time and trouble will not be without avail. North Wales possesses the spot more favoured and frequented by pilgrims than any other sanctuary in the British Isles. Holywell is known to everyone. Unbelievers may scoff and rail; newspapers write rabid leaders on superstition; nevertheless, in our own enlightened ages crowds will persist in visiting, or having themselves carried, to the well of St. Winefrid, the Cambrian virgin. Neither can it be denied that many are benefited in soul or body, or that miraculous cures were effected in past ages, and still take place at the present time.

Is the hand of God to be shortened because there are infidels? or is the simple confidence of the believer in His protection and in the power of His Saints to be disappointed to please blasphemers or sceptics? Of Holy Winefrid and her well the reader will hear again later on in these pages.

The Welsh Archæological Society has given us some prayers and hymns used in the Welsh Church, no doubt at a very early period, probably the fifth or sixth century. They are addressed to Curyg and Julitta, both of whom died in the East under Diocletian. The fact that Julitta was a young mother, and that her boy, but three years of age, cried out along with her "I am a Christian," and that both were victims for their faith, endeared their memory to our forefathers, who never failed to appreciate noble sacrifices for Jesus Christ. I will place a few of those hymns before the reader.

HYMN I.

In the name and in honour of our Lord Jesus Christ, and the Blessed Virgin, and the holy Curyg and Julitta, his mother, and all the male and female Saints in heaven, deliver us, Lord Jesus Christ. To-day and this night, and at all times, protect and defend us from all oppression, robbery, damage, and sudden misfortune—namely, from fire and water—and provide us with all things needful for our soul and body. Amen.

HYMN II.

Christ our Lord who reigns, Christ who vanquishes, Christ, through the merits of holy Curyg and Julitta, his mother, and all the male and female Saints in heaven, deliver us and preserve us from all evils to our souls and bodies. Amen.

HYMN V.

Lord Jesus Christ increase what is beneficial for us, and keep us from all evil, as Thou didst increase it for Thy servants Abraham, Isaac, and Jacob, in the name of Curyg, the holy martyr, and Julitta, his mother, and the male and female Saints in heaven. Amen.

HYMN VI.

Lord Jesus Christ blot out all our iniquity and all our mortal sins which we have committed in times past, and which we commit at present; destroy the incitement of the devil from us and from our household and property, in the name of Curyg, the holy martyr, and Julitta, his mother, and all the male and female Saints in heaven. Amen.

In the Celtic races devotion to Curyg and Julitta was general, for in Brittany we find Churches dedicated to them as early as the fifth century, as mentioned in the charter of Guereck, Duke of Brittany, to St. Ninnoc. It seems probable that the above-mentioned prayer belongs to that period.

This short summary of a national devotion will no doubt convince even a prejudiced reader that Saints were honoured by the ancient Cambrians, and that they availed themselves of their influence quite as much as any Catholic nation under the sun, either in primitive or modern times. The Cambrians of old knew that Saints are the work of God. The heroism through which we find them reproducing in themselves the life of their Master was also God's work. To praise their actions was to give glory to the Lord. Even an earthly architect feels nothing but pleasure in the admiration bestowed on a building of which he was the designer.

The Catholic Church is slowly but surely working her way throughout Wales; and a traveller, as he journeys along, is sometimes struck by the remark, emanating from far-seeing Protestants, that the country will again return to the Catholic faith, for it is becoming weary of a Babel of creeds.

Already that religion is represented in Cambria by two Catholic dioceses, and parishes duly constituted exist in its crowded cities and towns of importance. From these the Church of God will, according to her custom, extend her influence into the villages. Then the feasts of ancient Welsh Saints will be restored, and in their own country they will again find a place in the Missal and the Breviary.

New Catholic Churches, dedicated to St. Dubricius, St. Illyd, St. David, St. Winefrid, arise from the ground already.

When the time—not, it is to be hoped, far distant—arrives that the commemoration of these Saints shall be introduced into the Missal, or their lessons read in the Breviary at Matins, the Bishop to whom God shall have entrusted this restoration will only have to borrow in most cases a Breviary or Missal from the dioceses of Brittany, for in that Celtic land most of the Welsh Saints are to this day held in remembrance.

Many Cambrian families of wealth and position

have of late returned to the faith of their fathers, and been most generous and liberal to the Church, and by grants of land and money have forwarded the work of God. Many more no doubt will in course of time follow in their steps, and exhibit the same earnestness and spirit of sacrifice. Then again we may see revived in deeds of donation to religious institutions the ancient form of words, so pious and so Catholic—" I grant for the erection of a Church, Monastery, College, or Hospital, to Almighty God, to St. Dubricius, St. Teilo, St. David, St. Winefrid [so many] acres of land, for the redemption of my soul and the souls of my ancestors and deceased countrymen."

As Catholic doctrines gain ascendance amongst the people, the preachers of Protestantism will no longer venture to denounce the consoling belief which assures us that our fathers who surround the throne of God, far from being indifferent to our trials, temptations, and needs, spiritual and temporal, are, on the contrary, our best friends and protecting angels. He will also fail to convince his hearers that honour paid to the servant of God in any way detracts from the homage due to his Creator. The Saint is the work of God, and He is glorified through him.

Moses, in narrating the gradual formation of the world, from the creation of light to the moulding of the frame of Adam from the dust of the earth, into which the Almighty breathed a soul, repeats at the close of each day that God was pleased with his work. " Et vidit deus quod esset bonum."[1] Thus when the souls of His servants, on being liberated from their bodies, are presented to Jesus Christ, the Redeemer complacently smiles on that which is in truth His own work. Can He be displeased if we rejoice in what He has made perfect?

May the day soon dawn upon Wales when the feasts and devotion to the Saints of Cambria will resume their place in a country now oppressed with the curse of religious dissension. May the prayers of Dubricius, Teilo, Winefrid, and their companions bring back the faith to the country of their love. A Welsh lady—a convert to the old religion—beautifully illustrates this feeling in the following verses, which, with her kind permission, we place before the reader.

BRING BACK THE FAITH TO WALES.

In those old days so blessed
When Cambria's Faith was one,
They knelt around one altar—
The father and the son,
The mother and the daughter,
And all the hamlet too,
For One, the God, they worshipped,
And one, the Faith, they knew.

From all our ancient valleys,
Borne on our mountain gales,
Our cry goes up to Heaven—
Bring back the Faith to Wales!

That faith for which our martyrs
Poured forth their blood of yore,
Ten thousand of them at Caerleon,
And many, many more.

(1) Genesis.

For though not ours the glory
  Of martyrdom to be,
Yet still we hope in heaven
  Their faces bright to see.
      CHORUS.

Our saints to many a hamlet
  Have left their names so sweet ;
On mountain and in valley
  We trace their holy feet.
Who has not heard of Iltyd,
  Of Tydfil, Cadoc, Nun—
The mother of Saint David,
  Our Patron, her great son?
      CHORUS.

And those three holy Bishops,
  The first of Llandaff's See,
Long ere on Wales had fallen
  The blight of heresy ;
We'll ask them to remember
  The land their feet once trod,
For saints are they in Heaven,
  Before the throne of God.
      CHORUS.

And you to whom is given,
  For food, the Living Bread,
Pray for them, for whom Jesus
  His precious Blood has shed.
They're groping in the darkness,
  Whilst you walk in the light,
God waits but for your Prayers
  To turn to day their night.
      CHORUS.

Then let us cry to Heaven
  That Cambria's sons once more
May all be one in Jesus,
  As their fathers were of yore.
That our most sweet Redeemer
  Once more within the Fold
May drive these sheep, now straying
  Out in the dark and cold.
      CHORUS.

CHAPTER VI.

ON THE MONASTIC LIFE.

"Jesus said to him, 'If thou wilt be perfect, go sell what thou hast and give it to the poor, and thou shalt have treasure in Heaven, and come follow me.'—And when the young man had heard this word he went away sad, for he had great possessions.—Then Jesus said to His disciples, 'Amen; I say to you that a rich man shall hardly enter into the kingdom of Heaven."—St. Matt. xix., 21, 22, 23.

THUS far we have seen ancient Cambria in her relation with the Papacy; we have assisted with her at the Holy Sacrifice of the Mass; in her company we have knelt at the graves of the dead, and said the Pater for the souls of the faithful departed; in the Church our ears have heard the sweet harmony of the prayers and litanies addressed to our brethren in Heaven. Now, let us pay a visit to the Monastery and converse with such monks as St. Cadoc at Llancarvan, Illtyd at Llantwit-major, and others; and in a straightforward manner ask them why, and for what purpose, they have left the world; and learn from their own mouths their way of living, their occupation, and sundry other things.

In our days people entertain a very poor idea of a monk. What the present generation knows about him comes from enemies, or has been gathered from romances, the stage, or occasional leaders in the newspapers.

Principle of the religious state: its difference from the ordinary life of Christians.

Our Lord and Redeemer, Jesus Christ, summed up the substance of the Gospel in two words— "*Thou shalt love the Lord thy God with thy whole heart, with thy whole soul, with all thy strength, and with all thy mind; and thy neighbour as thyself.*"[1] This is the great law that is to guide the children of Adam through this valley of tears on their journey to eternity.

The Pope in the Vatican, the king on his throne, the magistrate on the bench, the soldier on the field of battle, the merchant or the humble peasant, all were created for no other purpose but to fulfil this great commandment. The same law guides the religious man in the cloister as well as the ordinary Christian in the world. The degree of glory we are to enjoy in Heaven is to be measured, not according to the position we occupy, or the kind of life we lead, but by the greater or lesser progress we make in the love of God and of our neighbour.

What, then, is the line of demarcation between the religious life in the cloister and the ordinary one in the world? It is this—Religious life implies the profession of the evangelical counsels —namely, poverty, chastity, and obedience—in order that we may attain the end of our creation, which is to love God above all things, and our neighbour as ourselves.

If one wishes to convince himself of the great advantage of travelling on the road to eternity

---

(1) Matt. xxii., 37, 39. Mark xii., 30, 31.

in the company of these three virtues, which in a vision appeared to St. Augustine after his conversion as three beautiful maidens, let him in imagination stand at the Bar of Divine justice for one day and see judgment passed on some 80,000 souls, which daily have to give an account of their stewardship.

In that crowd of souls some are condemned to hell, others to Purgatory, for a longer or shorter period, to be purified according to the state of their souls; a third part goes to heaven. He will invariably remark that those who are condemned to hell or Purgatory have been deluded into sin either by riches, pleasures, or an uncontrollable self-will. These are the three rocks on which we are generally wrecked on our weary voyage in this world. An inordinate love of riches, the source of numerous acts of injustice, proves fatal to many at the day of reckoning. Carnal pleasures not checked in their wild course, and a self-will not kept within the bounds of the commandments of God and of those of the Church, draw down thousands of punishments on the other side of the grave.

"*Love not the world,*" says St. John, "*nor the things which are in the world. If anyone love the world, the charity of the Father is not in him; for all that is in the world is concupiscence of the flesh and of the eyes, and the pride of life, which is not of the Father but of the world.*"[1]

(1) St. John, 1st Epistle, ii., 15, 16.

On the other hand, to those souls which, practising poverty, chastity, and obedience, have passed through the world free from injustice, impurity, and disobedience to the laws of God, the gates of heaven are at once thrown open; or, if they are condemned to Purgatory, the sentence as a rule is a very short one.

Serious reflection upon these facts has induced thousands, since the introduction of Christianity, to enter the cloister and form religious communities. The primary object of an Antony, Benedict, Francis, or Bernard was not to create a society of agriculturists, architects, theologians, or learned men, but to save their souls by the practice of the three evangelical counsels—viz., poverty, chastity, and obedience.[1]

If in the course of time the orders founded by them acquired a reputation in agriculture or science, Divine and human, this was only a secondary object, and the result of the love of God and their neighbour burning in their hearts, for these men looked from their cells on the wants of society, and devoted their existence to such particular works as they deemed most beneficial to the interests of the Church of God.

People form associations for worldly purposes, for the construction of railways, to build fleets of steamships, to lay telegraphs on land and across the ocean; in fact for any undertaking that will bring them money. Religious men will also

---

(1) Montalembert, Monks of the West.

associate, but for the attainment of a spiritual end—to save their souls and those of their neighbours.

As soon as Constantine had put an end to the 300 years of persecution under the Roman Emperors, or even before that, immense Monasteries arose all over the world. The deserts of Egypt became peopled by legions of monks. *Religious communities in the Church from the earliest ages of Christianity.*

When St. Antony died on the Nile, 4,000 or 5,000 of his sons wept and prayed round his grave; and we are told by Rufinus, a traveller in the East in 373—namely, seventeen years after the death of this celebrated chief of Monastic life—that there were as many monks in the desert as inhabitants in towns; that at every hour of the day and night the praises of the Lord rent the skies. About the middle of the fourth century it was calculated that some 70,000 men and 20,000 virgins followed the Monastic rule in Egypt.[1]

About the same time there was a rush from the world into the cloister, in Gaul and in Britain. St. Martin is believed to have established the first Monastery in France, and with such success that his funeral resembled that of St. Anthony, for thousands of the religious brethren of St. Martin covered the roads from Poitiers to Tours, accompanying the body of their founder to its last resting place.

In the same period St. Patrick brought the

---

[1] Migne Dict desordres religieux.—Introduction.

Monastic plant from Gaul to Ireland, in which country it soon prospered to a wonderful extent. St. Patrick had spent one year in the Monastery of St. Martin at Marmoutiers, and seven at Lerins, always dreaming of the conversion of that land in which he had been a slave. Montalembert properly observes that the Apostle of Ireland was astonished that in his own lifetime the number of the sons and daughters of chieftains who had embraced the life of the cloister at his bidding could not be counted. The celebrated Irish round towers, whose origin and use for so many years exercised the ingenuity of archæologists, modern science has proved beyond dispute to have been only the belfries of Cathedrals, Abbeys, and Priories.

Britain did not remain behind other nations in the practice of religious life. It is difficult to tell who was the first to introduce Monasticism into this land. Glastonbury, as we have already seen, was the first *ground* of Almighty God in Britain. There St. Joseph, of Arimathea, and his companions are believed to have lived in community, as far as their missionary duties allowed; and probably their successors lived much in the same manner.

Be this as it may, it is an undeniable fact that in the fifth and sixth centuries Wales teemed with religious life, and immense Monasteries rose throughout the length and breadth of Cambria.

(1) Montalambert. Monks of the West.

Llancarvan, Lantwit-Major, in the south; Bangor and St. Asaph in the north, were the centres of intellectual and manual labour, as well as the abodes of sanctity.

In those days a traveller on his way through Wales, starting from Chepstow in the south, following the Bristol Channel as far as St. David's, in Pembrokeshire, then the sea coast along the Irish Channel, and continuing his journey as far as Chester, would meet on his road almost as many religious houses as there are now important railway stations.

Shortly after leaving Chepstow, he would come to Caergwent, an ancient Roman fortress. The Roman legions are gone, and a small religious community, governed by an Irish monk, have taken their place. Coming to the present town of Newport, Monmouthshire, he will find on Stowe Hill, which commands the town, a Welsh chieftain, Gwynliw the warrior, and a few companions leading an ascetic life. At the foot of the same mountain, in the valley of Risca, at Bassaleg, Gwladys, his wife, is at the head of a community of nuns. The Flat Holmes and Barry Island, at the entrance to the present town of Cardiff, are occupied by the men of Christ, as the monks are called. The said traveller, as he proceeds westward, at about eight or ten miles from Cardiff, will come to the valley of Llancarvan. Here there is a busy monastic colony, founded by St. Cadoc, the son of those two

Numerous cloisters in Cambria.

hermits he met with a few days before at Newport, Monmouthshire. Here the axe clears the forest, and the spade drains swamps, to make room for wheat, barley, or oats. A few miles farther on the sea coast is Lantwit-Major, which was also a Roman camp, but is now the residence of Illtyd and his brethren. The spot is a scene of activity, mental and physical—labourers, builders, and students are occupied by their respective work. The valley of Neath and the neighbourhood of Swansea have their religious communities; Ty-gwen-ar-taf, where the South Wales Railway now branches off for Tenby, is occupied by Paulinus, the master of St. David, Teilo, and others. Later on Howell Dda will render the place sacred for Wales, as in its valley the Welsh laws will be compiled. Still more to the west there is a celebrated monastery—St. David, on the very limits of Wales.

On his journey northward, monastic institutions will offer him hospitality. In Cardiganshire, a mile or two from the present Aberystwith, is Lan Badarn Fawr, whose bishop and abbot is Padarn, a Breton monk. Not far off, in the bay of Cardigan, lies the celebrated Bardsey island, called the Necropolis of Welsh Saints. Anglesey, the residence of the chief druids in times gone by, is occupied by the monks. And so on till he comes to Bangor Iscoed, in the county of Chester. Should he return from north to south through the midland counties, he would still hear the praises of Almighty God in monastic churches scattered here and there throughout the country, and erected by St. David or his disciples.

No period of Welsh history has witnessed a greater percentage of the population rushing to the cloister than the fifth and sixth centuries. The monastery finds willing recruits in every class of society, amongst the princes and their tenants, and to such an extent as to be hardly believed in our days of materialism and religious indifference. A careful perusal of the "Liber Landavensis" and "The Lives of the Cambro-British Saints" will, however, convince the most incredulous reader that the enthusiasm for religious life was then at its greatest height. *The cloister finds recruits in every class of society.*

Let us take as instances two or three great families in South Cambria—that of Meurig, king of Glamorgan; then of his next neighbour, Gwynlew, the warrior chieftain, in the present county of Monmouth; and after him of the family of Brychan, of Brecknockshire.

Meurig, king of Glamorgan, exhibits in his life a mixture of virtues and vices. We see him, in the "Liber Landavensis," coming forth most nobly to the help of the bishops of Llandaff; and yet one of them, Oudoceus, is forced to excommunicate him as guilty of the blackest perjury and the most atrocious murder. He submitted to penance, not only under the pressure of faith, but also through the powerful influence brought to bear on his guilty conscience by the many monks belonging to his family.

His father, Tewdrig, who had resigned the sovereignty of Glamorgan in his favour, and thus made him king when he was yet a mere youth, was leading the life of a hermit on the river Wye. His nephew, Sampson, embraced religious life at Lantwit-Major; then, forced by circumstances to put himself under the abbot Peyro, at Barry Island, induced his father and uncle, his mother and aunt, and then his cousin Maglorius, to leave the world and follow him to the cloister. His father and uncle he brought with him to Barry Island, whilst their respective wives, namely, his mother and aunt, retired into convents.

So Meurig could say that, whatever he might be personally, his blood had given noble servants to the Church. His father, two of his daughters, two sons-in-law, two nephews, were fighting for God and the Church in the ranks of the monastic army.

To the east, the next chieftain to Meurig was Gwynlew the Warrior. The family consisted of nine brothers, who amicably, and according to custom, divided amongst themselves the landed property of their father. However, in the partition eight portions only were made, as Pedrog, one of them, surrendered a transitory inheritance for an eternal one, and, embracing religious life, would not accept of any territory.[1]

Later on the son of Gwynlew, the celebrated

[1] Cambro-British Saints.

Cadoc, left his parents' house, and, directing his steps to the west, stopped in the valley of Lancarvan, on which spot he erected a monastery. In the course of time he also induced his father and mother to quit the world.

To the north of Glamorganshire is the county of Brecknock, whose prince, Brychan, was father of a very numerous family, although it may be perhaps difficult to state their exact number.

In the "Life of St. Ninnoc,"[1] as related in Albert le Grand, fourteen of these children are said to have entered the Church, and preached the Gospel in several localities, not only in their own country but beyond the sea, and edified many nations by their saintly lives. Then the youngest daughter followed their footsteps, as we shall relate a page or two later on.

The percentage of religious vocation in these three princely families enables the reader to judge how high enthusiasm for the monastery ran in the minds of the Cambrians. It also accounts for the numerical strength of some religious communities in the country.

Thus, at Bangor Iscoed, near Chester, in the time of the Saxon king Ethelfrith, 1,200 monks were unmercifully slain for the sin of praying for the success of their countrymen in battle. Venerable Bede, speaking of this monastery, tells us that the community was divided into seven sections, each under a direct superior or prior,

Numerical strength of some monasteries.

---

(1) Albert le Grand. Les Saints de Bretagne (p. 36).

and that each of these priors had three hundred monks under him, all earning their bread by the sweat of their brow. According to this calculation, the brotherhood of Bangor, in Cheshire, amounted to more than 2,000 members.

Not far off, still in North Wales, in the beautiful valley of St. Asaph, St. Kentigern had gathered round him a numerous colony of monks, who night and day sang the praises of the Lord. They were divided into three sections—the labourers, the artisans, and the students, and mustered 965 strong.

In the south, in the county of Glamorgan, Lancarvan counted its inmates by hundreds; and at Lantwit-Major, not far off, the number was still greater.[1]

There is no doubt that the Cambrians of those days were a supernatural people, and earnest in their endeavours to secure heaven. These words of our Lord, "*What doth it profit a man to gain the whole world and lose his soul*," vibrated along

(1) In the Iolo MSS. (page 556) we find the following interesting details in reference to religious institutions in Wales :—" Here are the names of the cells of the college of Illtyd, the College of Matthew, of Mark, of Luke, of John, Arthur, St. David, Morgan, Eurgain, and Amwn. Of these eight colleges Illtyd was principal; and the place was named Bangor Illtyd, and there were *three thousand saints*. In the colleges of Dubricius there were the following choirs : that of Dubricius, of Arthur, of Julius, of Aron ; all these were in Caerleon-upon-Usk. The College of Dubricius and the College of Meugant on the banks of the Wye, and the College of Llandaff; Dubricius was principal over all, and had two thousand scholars. . . . . The College of Cattwg, in Llancarvan, with three cells and a *thousand saints*, and two cells in the Vale of Neath. . . . . The College of Dochwy, in Morganwg, with a *thousand* saints. . . . . The College of St. David, in Menevia, for *five hundred* saints. . . . . The College of Tathan, in Caerwent, with *five hundred* saints. The College of Sarlloc, in Llandaff, for *thirty* saints, and Sarlloc was the principal. The College of Elvan, in Glastonbury, for a thousand saints. The College of Teilo, in Llandaff, for a thousand saints."

every fibre of their souls, and hence they rushed to the practice of religious life, certain that it was the safest way to save their souls. Some entered religion when young, others in their old age. Thus, some were first married and then sought refuge in religion, whilst others, perhaps, had ignored altogether the allurements of the world when they put on the monastic habit. Monasteries saw several of their students enter the cloistral precincts with only the desire of acquiring human knowledge, who never after returned home, but joined the brotherhood. Others, at the end of their scholastic career, left the monastery, but soon after returned, finding in the world nothing but vanity and hollowness.

Some of these young people had the full consent of their parents, who were persuaded that it was better for their children to be in the service of God, than in that of men, and encouraged them on. Others, however, had to contend with the opposition of their relatives.

We even read of young men who, unfortunately, had conquered the hearts of princesses, and, on obeying the call of God, were importuned in their cells by disappointed damsels who made use of every art to induce them to leave.

The reader may naturally desire to have a few details of these noble souls so anxious to reach evangelical perfection.

Let us begin by Ninnoc, the beautiful and saintly daughter of Brychan of Brecknockshire; the substance is taken from Albert le grand.

St. Ninnoc.

Ninnoc was the last child of a numerous offspring, born when her parents were advanced in years. She was the gift of a supernatural grace bestowed to console, in their old age, a family that had given 14 children to religion as we have already seen.[1] When 15 years of age, a certain Irish prince came on a visit to her father and, smitten with her beauty, applied for her hand. The matter was discussed in a family council, and the offer accepted.

Brychan called Ninnoc aside and, opening his mind, informed her that such a union would be advantageous to her, as well as to both families. The prince was young, handsome, and one of the leading princes in Ireland, and a powerful ally would be gained by the family which would prove useful in time of need, for in those days, as in ours, politics and family interests played a conspicuous part in marriages.

In her reply, Ninnoc stated that the intended husband possessed every quality which could render any maiden happy; that the marriage would no doubt prove beneficial to both provinces; but she was already bethrothed, and had given her word to a divine spouse. He was aware that a promise made to Jesus Christ could not be broken, and for this reason she expected him not to be dissatisfied with her refusal. It was the

---

(1) On a Good Friday, the legend says, the chieftain knelt before the cross, and in the name of the bleeding wounds of our Lord, entreated heaven to grant him a child. . . . . In the same night an angel appeared and informed him that his request had been granted.

first time of her life she had disobeyed her father, and now he must forgive her.

The disappointed parent communicated the answer to his wife, requesting her to bring all her maternal influence to bear in altering her daughter's resolution. But entreaties, tears, and threats, proved useless, and failed entirely to shake her mind.

The young Irish prince was admitted into the secret in all its details, and then took leave and returned to Ireland, and Ninnoc was left free to follow her vocation; the parents still hoping that their dear daughter, although resolved to remain a virgin, would however live under their roof and console them in their old age. For a few years such was to be the case.

However St. Germans came to visit the court of her father, and stayed for a length of time under his hospitable roof. A spiritual friendship soon grew between the venerable old Patriarch of Gaul and the young virgin. Hearing from the bishop the edifying life led by nuns in Gaul, and their earnestness in the service of God, she determined to cross the sea and lead a religious life among them. The difficulty was to obtain the consent of her father and mother, for she was fully aware that it was the only request they would never grant. However the determined lover of the convent removed all difficulties by the following stratagem—

The first day of a new year, being also her

birthday, there was a sumptuous banquet in her honour. A number of bishops, princes, and lords were invited, and amongst them Germanus. In the presence of all the guests the young lady entered the hall dressed in her richest garments, and ravished all present by her beauty. Amidst a dead silence she went up to her father and, falling on her knees, stated that as it was her birthday she had a favour to ask, and she hoped that for the sake of all the illustrious guests present it would not be refused.

Her father raised her up and said, that for nothing in the world would he refuse whatever she might ask.

Then in a clear and beautiful voice, betraying, however, suppressed emotion, the young lady addressed her father—" Long ago I informed you how strong was my wish to consecrate myself to the service of God; now I ask your consent to cross the sea for the shores of Amorica (Britanny) and there to end my days in the service of my Jesus. I shall not cease to pray for the welfare of your souls, and those of your subjects."

This scene produced a deep impression on all present. There was a struggle between nature and grace in the breasts of father and mother, uncles and aunts, and other relations. Men were silent and women wept. Every possible argument was brought forth to force Ninnoc to withdraw her request, but they all proved fruitless assaults against an impregnable will. At last St. Germanus, seeing that this was not the over-excited imagination of a young virgin, but a purpose of long years' standing, and evidently the work of God, took her part and represented to the bereaved family, that they should yield to the call of God, Master of our existence, and make the sacrifice like Abraham, who parted with the most precious treasure he had on earth. They yielded and, tears in their eyes, gave their blessing to their parting daughter.

Whilst the vessel destined to carry her to the country she was to edify by her saintly life was being fitted out, she made such a good use of her time as to induce her god-father and god-mother, several priests, and many laity of both sexes to follow her. The little expedition safely landed in Brittany, at a place later on called Poul-ilfin, after the name of her god-father, and the chief of the colony, whose name was Ilfin. Ninnoc's success in Armorica has been referred to in preceding pages.[1]

Let us now carry the reader to the grave of old Tewdrig at Mathern near Chepstow, Monmouthshire. *Tendrig, the hermit.*

The contrast in some sense is great, although the supernatural end the same. Indeed, Ninnoc was a pure soul never defiled by the world, a virgin in all the fervour of youth; Tewdrig, on

---

[1] St. Keyna, virgin, sister of Guladys, mother of St. Cadoc of Llancarvan, belongs to the same family. It is strange that Welsh genealogists omit the name of St. Ninnoc. This may be attributed to the fact of her passing the greatest part of her existence on the Continent.

the contrary, was an old warrior whose powerful hand had slain many on the battle field, and whos' rough voice had given the word of command for slaughter.

Tewdrig was the father of King Meurig, and governed in Glamorganshire with justice. However, as he valued eternal power more than temporal, he gave up his kingdom to his son Meurig, determined to live in solitude.[1] He chose for his retreat a dense forest on the river Wye, on, or near, the spot where later on rose the magnificent monastery of Tintern Abbey, visited and admired in our days as one of the best specimens of monastic buildings.

There he built a hut beside a clear stream, and provided for his bodily wants by cultivating a few plots of ground round his hermitage, and spent his life in Divine contemplation.

In his day he had fought many a battle, and never met with any reverse, and in the opinion of his countrymen he was a bold and skilful general. In this respect his children were inferior and less successful. The southern Cambrians having sustained severe losses in some encounters against the Saxons, who were pushing their incursions as far as the Severn, and even the Wye, remarked that under Tewdrig they were never defeated, and resolved to go to his cell and there represent the danger of the country, and entreat him once more to put himself at their head.

(1) Liber Landavensis, p. 383.

Meanwhile, a heavenly messenger appeared to him at night, and said, "Go and assist the people of God against the enemies of the Church of Christ, and the foes will turn their faces in flight as far as Powll Brochwael. And thou, in full armour, stand in the battle, and when they shall see thy face and recognise it, they will, as usual, betake themselves to flight; and afterwards, for the space of thirty years, they will not dare, in the time of thy son, to invade the country, and thy people will be in peace; but thou wilt be wounded by a single stroke in the district of Rhyd Tintern, and three days after die in peace."

In the morning he rose and put himself at the head of the army of his son, encamped in the neighbourhood. Mounted on his charger, he cheerfully moved onwards with his Britons to the banks of the river Wye, at the ford of Tintern.

Both sides were soon engaged, and after a protracted battle, in which the venerable old soldier and hermit was conspicuous everywhere encouraging his men, the enemy was put to flight. In the pursuit, a Saxon, turning his face to his pursuers, threw a lance at the general, and wounded him.

The old captain requested his son to take him, if possible, to the Flat Holmes, a small island at the entrance of the present Cardiff, wishing to be buried on that rock. No doubt he felt that the monks, who came there annually to spend a few weeks in Lent, would kneel round his grave and recommend his soul to the mercy of God. However, he died on the road, and was buried at Mathern. His son Meurig built a church over his grave, and for the repose of his soul granted the land to the church of Llandaff, as stated previously.

St. Suliau. St. Suliau (Issylio in Welsh) is an instance of a religious vocation being granted at an early period of life. According to Albert le Grand, he was born in Wales, in the year of our Lord 530, under the pontificate of Boniface II. and during the reign of the Emperor Justinian I.

Brocmail[1]—his father—a chieftain in Powis, Western Wales, had many children, on whose education he bestowed the greatest care. He particularly desired that Suliau, his first-born, who was to be his successor, should be carefully trained in divine and human learning. This task was entrusted to Gwymark, Abbot of Meibot, in Montgomery, a monastery which owed its origin to the generosity of Welsh princes.

The young Suliau, whilst yet at school, had felt a strong desire to embrace the religious life, and being aware that the designs of his father ran in a different direction, considered what would be the best plan to follow in order to win him over to his views. After several attempts to gain his consent, which always met with a stern refusal, he resolved to break through all obstacles by secretly leaving home as soon as a favourable chance presented itself.

(1) Albert le Grand. Lobineau.

One day, as he was hunting with his brothers, some monks chanced to pass by, singing religious hymns as they journeyed along. This sacred music, which had so often kindled his imagination whilst in the monastic school, now, as it resounded through the silence of the woods, made such a deep impression on his mind that he resolved to carry out at once his long thought of intention. He therefore said to his companions, "I will follow these monks, and in their company spend my days in singing the praises of the Lord." His brothers, after remaining for some time rivetted to the spot in a state of stupefaction, hurried after him determined to force him back. Their efforts were, however, useless, and they were obliged to return home without Suliau. On learning the sad news, the mother wept and the father became furious, inveighed in bitter terms against monks and monasteries, and swore to be revenged.

Whilst this scene was taking place in the prince's palace, the young deserter had arrived at the monastery and informed the abbot of the bold step he had taken. Falling on his knees he begged to be at once clothed in the monastic habit, for of a *certainty* his father would soon come and reclaim him.

Gwymark—the abbot—assembled the community in order to ascertain the opinion of the brethren, and it was agreed that young Suliau should be admitted as a novice, the Chapter deciding that although such a step might draw down upon them the ire of Brocmail, they would trust in the protection of God, whose servant they were sheltering.

Shortly after they had resolved upon this step, thirty horsemen arrived at the gate of the monastery and demanded to speak to the abbot, in the name of Brocmail, Prince of Powis.

On being admitted, they reproached Gwymark and his brethren with having kidnapped a young boy, the son of their master, taking advantage of his youth to work on his imagination and decoy him into adopting a kind of life to which he was not called. They announced that they had explicit orders to bring home, alive or dead, a child unjustly taken away from his father and mother, adding that if this lawful request were refused, they would teach monks not to interfere with the family of Brocmail.

The abbot modestly, but with the firmness peculiar to his order, replied that neither he or his brethren had directly or indirectly seduced Suliau. He had come amongst them of his own free will. They should be allowed to see the son of their master, and thus have an opportunity of judging for themselves. If when in their presence Suliau consented to return home, he and his brethren would not offer the least objection to his doing so. But if, on the other hand, the youth persisted in his resolution to remain in the monastery, they could not and would not, turn him out, even though they shed their blood in his cause.

The anger of the prince's messengers was somewhat appeased by this fair but resolute reply. The young man already clad in the monastic habit was summoned before them. The soldiers testified astonishment, and said that it was not the custom for any monastery to clothe a novice before he had gone through one year's probation. Suliau, however, put a stop to all comments by the following speech :—

"Gentlemen, say to my father that I humbly confess having committed a fault against him although with no intention of giving offence; that fault consists in having left him without his consent and without his blessing. I felt myself drawn by an irresistible grace to serve God in this saintly community. I knew that my father would never give his consent, but would throw every obstacle in my way, and therefore I departed abruptly and without giving notice of my intention, having from my infancy been taught that when one is called by the Almighty to His Divine service, he must leave father and mother brothers and sisters unmindful of their tears and affliction. If, however, my dear father is so incensed against this monastery for having afforded me a shelter, and will be appeased by nothing but blood, cut off my head and carry it to him, because if any one is guilty in connection with this matter, it is myself and no person else."

This noble and touching reply of the saintly youth drew tears from every eye, and put a stop to all violence. The messengers returned to the prince and related what they had seen and heard, how they had been fascinated and disarmed by the presence and speech of the young monk, who was to have been their future king. Brocmail and his wife wept and said, " Let the will of God be done."

<small>Trials of St. Suliau.</small> Suliau's vocation proved to be a true one, and not the result of a strong imagination—not unusual with young men of twenty—which often fades away with time. He brought into the cloister a truly religious spirit. His abbot out of precaution sent him to a priory dependent on the monastery—which was situated on an island called Aber Menew, and later on Enes-Suliau (Island of Suliau) where he spent an angelic life for the space of seven years.

Guymarch on his deathbed called together his brethren and addressed to them the following words—

" My brethren and children, I loved you in life, and I could not die like a good father unless consoled by the idea that after my death you shall be ruled by a man of God. As you are aware, you will be free in the election of your new abbot, but I cannot help recommending Suliau for that office, knowing him to be a man well fitted for it."

When the last of the sacred hymn over the

grave of Guymarch had died away, the chapter proceeded to elect a new superior, and the votes were one, and all, in favour of Suliau.

He had governed Meibot Monastery for six years, when in 564, his father died, and was succeeded by his brother Jacob.

After a reign of but two years, this prince died in 566, leaving a widow but no children. This lady was destined to put Suliau's love of celibacy to the test, and to be his persecutor during the remainder of her life. The young widow, whose name was Hayarmé, was a woman of great intellectual powers, ambitious and energetic. In order to secure possession of the kingdom of her deceased husband, she informed her vassals that it was her intention to marry the Abbot of Meibot, he being the only survivor of their Royal Family.

She visited the monastery and opened her mind on the subject to Suliau, stating that the resolution she had arrived at was dictated by her desire to promote public interest and peace, and to prevent the extinction of the Royal Family of which he was the last representative. As regarded the necessary dispensation, she said she would secure that through an application to the Pope at Rome.

Suliau, as might be expected, was at first perfectly amazed at having such a proposal from the widow of his brother, but recovering from his surprise he intimated firmly that he could never accede to such a request. Was he not a monk, a priest and her brother-in-law. A young widow was free to marry again. If she decided on doing so, let it be in accordance with the laws of God and the Church. But *he* was not at liberty to break through his vows. Why should she come to seek a husband within the walls of a monastery? Were there not plenty of Princes and noblemen in Britain, not bound by religious vows, who would willingly marry one so young, handsome, and rich? By making a judicious choice from amongst the number, she could give her subjects a wise and judicious ruler. For himself, he had declined the marriage state when in his father's house, and saw no reason to change his resolution. On no account would he apply to the Court of Rome for a dispensation from his vows; he was not going to scandalise the Church and the Britons.

Whether this lady had conceived an affection for young Suliau before he embraced the religious state, and had keenly regretted his entrance into the cloister, and that her present feelings towards him were a revival of an old love, we are not told.

However, after this absolute refusal of her advances, she became possessed by the passion of hatred, swore revenge, and persecuted Suliau and his brethren; the property of the monasteries, such as cattle, was seized, and their crops destroyed.

To save his brethren from these injuries, the abbot retired to Enes Suliau; but the persecution in no degree abating, he determined to leave the country altogether, and accordingly sailed for Brittany, at that time the refuge of all who were thus troubled.

There he remained, preaching the Gospel along the shores of Armorica from St. Malo to the present town of Brest, and converting numbers of sinners. On the death of his sister-in-law, his monastic brethren in Cambria invited him to return and once more become their spiritual guide; but he declined, having been warned by an angel of his approaching death, which took place on the 1st of October, 606, at the age of 76. He was buried in his Armorican monastery, since called St. Sulian-sur-Rance, a place about six miles distant from St. Malo.[1]

The legend of Efflam and Honora reminds us of the history of Alexius, or Cecilia, in Rome, who, when forced into the marriage state, nevertheless succeeded in preserving their virginity intact, the latter through an angelic apparation, and the former through an energetic step.

Efflam was born in Ireland, about the year 448, and Honora was a daughter of Cambria. Both belonged to families of high distinction.

St. Efflam and Honora.

For two or three generations their families had only known each other sword in hand, either as pirates on the ocean, or deadly foes on the battle-field.

---

(1) The Welsh legend tells us that St. Suliau returned to Wales and was chosen to represent the British bishops in their controversy with St. Augustine. This is improbable.

The forefathers of Efflam had passed their lives in threatening the coasts of Wales with invasion, making annual descents upon her shores, during which many Christians were put to the sword, and women and children carried off to Ireland to be sold in her market-places as slaves. The Welsh chieftain retaliated, and by organised expeditions made sudden attacks on the territory of his enemy across the channel, and bore away whatever he could lay hold of. This continued plundering soon wearied the people on both sides, and discontent became so strong that the two chieftains were forced to come to terms. Peace was concluded by the betrothal of Efflam, son of the Irish king, and Honora, daughter of the Cambrian Prince. As they were both children it was arranged that the marriage should take place as soon as they were of age.

Efflam was sent to the monastic school to be educated, and whilst there felt a strong attraction towards religion, which became even more intense as he increased in years. Several of his fellow-students shared the same desire, and they encouraged each other to devote themselves to the service of Christ in the monastic life, then held in so much favour throughout the world, but more especially in Ireland.

Efflam returned home on the completion of his education, with the determined resolution that —cost what it might—he would consecrate himself to God.

Under the paternal roof, however, he was reminded of the contract signed in his name when he was an infant, by the terms of which he was engaged to marry Honora, the Cambrian princess. The contracting parties, both in Ireland and in Wales, were pledged by the most solemn oaths, and the marriage must take place. It was the condition on which peace had been concluded between the two houses so long at war. Honora was beautiful and accomplished, and would secure him many years of happiness, and the union would cement peace and friendship between those who had been bitter enemies.

This intelligence was far from pleasing to a young man whose thoughts ran in so different a direction. He communicated it to the friends who like himself had resolved on entering the cloister. They assembled in his father's house, and consulted together as to the best mode of proceeding under the circumstances. It was a juvenile meeting, and yet what serious and important matters were discussed, and what courageous resolutions adopted! The speakers demonstrated to the satisfaction of all present that full consideration should be shown to paternal authority, which could not be called in question; but that the same authority had its determined limits, and could in no way trample on the sacred rights of God in regard of children. . . . Marriage was a free contract, and those who entered on it had a right to be consulted. A match arranged by relatives between two children might be a judicious speculation according to their views, but the persons concerned should be free, when of age, either to sanction or reject such alliances.

Efflam, in his speech, informed his companions that, feeling himself called to religion, he was resolved to enter the cloister. . . . He knew his father's temper, and was fully aware that a chieftain whose will had been law to mariners on sea and to soldiers on land, would expect obedience from his children at home. Still, though most reluctant to seem disobedient, he, Efflam, was determined to follow his vocation.

It was unanimously resolved to secure a vessel and sail quietly away, trusting to God to direct them to some hospitable shore where they could land, seek out some lonely valley, and erect a church and some hermits' huts.

Whether it was found impossible to fit out a vessel before the time fixed upon for the marriage, or that Efflam thought it better, in order to avoid complications between the two families on account of the non-fulfilment of the contract, to lead his bride to the altar, is not stated.

He, however, was married, and after the ceremony had been celebrated in the church, a splendid banquet was given in the palace. Cups of the most generous wine were handed round, bards sang the beauty of the British bride, and bade her welcome to the land of Erin, and lauded the valour of Efflam and his ancestors. Later on in the evening, the numerous guests invoked the blessing of God on the newly-married pair, wished them a long succession of happy years, and retired.

When he found himself alone with his bride, Efflam commenced a conversation on the excellence of *virginity*, reminding Honora that the Redeemer of the world was a virgin, and elected to be born of a virgin. John the Evangelist, the disciple whom Jesus loved beyond the others, and permitted to repose upon His Sacred Heart, was indebted for this privilege to his state of virginity. The most glorious group around the Throne of God in Heaven consists of the guard which followeth the Lamb wheresoever He goeth, and is called in the Apocalypse the 144,000 *spotless virgins*. Thousands, in their time, cultivated this charming flower of the Church of God.

<small>Efflam quits his bride on the first night of their marriage.</small>

In Ireland, his own country, as well as in her native Wales, the monasteries were filled with lovers of chastity. "Let us," he said, "*walk in the same path*. Alexius, son of the Roman senator, left his wife the very night of their marriage; Cecilia told Valerian, her husband, shortly after their union, that an angel of God stood by her side to protect her in the fulfilment of the vow she had made to her Spouse in heaven." Honora listened to her bridegroom's words, and expressed her desire to follow these examples.

Being thus far successful, Efflam became bolder, and intimated to his wife that he, too, had taken a vow of virginity. Before the world she would appear to be his spouse, but in reality they would dwell together like brother and sister. Afterwards he told her of his intention to retire into some solitude, the better to give himself to the service of his Master. Perceiving, however, that his last announcement had brought a cloud over his young bride's countenance, he regretted having committed himself so far, and endeavoured to console her in the best manner he could. When, wearied by the fatigues of the day and her varied emotions, Honora closed her eyes in sleep, the young man made his preparations for departure. Casting one last glance on his bride, he exclaimed, "Farewell, Honora, and may God protect thee! ! ! Virgin I brought thee hither, virgin I leave thee. May thy guardian angel guard and console thee. Farewell."

Then, drying his tears, he passed through the silent halls and directed his steps to the sea-shore, where his companions awaited him in a vessel equipped for the voyage. They at once set sail, without having any definite destination, leaving themselves to the guidance of Providence. The young pilgrims landed safely in the present department Des Côtes du Nord, at the parish of Pleslen. This spot was for generations called by the Bretons Toul Efflam and Lock Mikel, in remembrance of the event; Mikel, or Michael, must have been one of his companions.

Not far from where they landed, they discovered an abandoned and dilapidated chapel. This they repaired, and around it built as many huts as answered to their number.

On the morning following the marriage, Honora found herself alone, her bridegroom had departed. As during the day he was nowhere to be seen, the whole household, the numerous guests, and, above all, Honora herself, became seriously alarmed. Messengers were despatched through the country, but no trace of Efflam could be discovered; the only intelligence they could glean was a vague report that a vessel had left the shore with several young men on board, but no one could give any information as to the direction it had taken. Meanwhile, a favourable wind was filling their sails and increasing the distance between the emigrants and their country, as, quietly seated in the barque, they chanted the Psalms of David.

Honora then remembering the conversation of the preceding night, came to the sad conclusion that he had acted up to it.

She wept and lamented, but time, which sooner or later heals the deepest wounds, failed to lessen her affliction. She could have wished that with her flowing tears the remembrance of Efflam would have also passed away. But his image remained continually before her eyes. "He asked me," the widowed bride said sorrowfully to herself, "to be a dear sister to him instead of a wife, and I promised to agree to his wishes. Why, then, did he leave me, and so suddenly?"

"I will find him; I must find him, even if it is necessary to search the whole world through."

Honora leaves her home in search of Efflam.
Like her beloved Efflam, she also secretly planned her escape, and contrived to fit out a small boat, covered with skin, and when it was ready she left home in disguise. Trusting, as *he* had done, to Divine Providence, she directed the sailors to steer for Armorica.

After being three days at sea, the little vessel drew near the coast of Brittany, and as the tide ebbed, grounded on a beautiful strand in the midst of the nets of fishermen. The manager of the fishery hastened to visit the strangers, and Honora informed him of the motive of her journey, that she was seeking for her husband, whose name was Efflam; that he was the son of an Hibernian prince, whilst she herself was the daughter of a British chieftain. He told her that at the distance of nine miles from that place dwelt a hermit, who had lately arrived from beyond the sea with a few young men like himself, that they were as busy as bees repairing a ruined church and erecting hermits' huts around it.

Having escaped pursuit, Honora reached this place, was allowed to live in a house separate from the monastery, and obtained permission to attend the services in that part of the church which was reserved for the laity. Later on she retired to the Convent of St. Ninnoc, a British nun like herself, and there ended her days. The ancient Britons used to invoke her intercession in time of epidemics.

Efflam edified Brittany by a saintly life, and died on the 6th of November, 512. His tomb became a place of pilgrimage to thousands, both from Gaul and the British isles, and God glorified his servant by granting to his prayers the requests of those who were afflicted.[1]

Most of these vocations to the cloister which we have placed before the reader were strongly opposed by parents and relatives. Others, on the contrary, were encouraged by them, fathers and mothers feeling a certain pride in the fact of their children swelling the ranks of the servants of God. Let us take two or three of these instances, and amongst them that of St. Patern, or Padarn, according to the Welsh tongue.

From his very infancy this child of predilection felt an instinct calling him to religion. It might be that love of the contemplative life was hereditary in his family, for soon after his birth his father, Petran, a prince of Brittany, with the consent of his wife, Julitta, left the world and consecrated himself to God in a monastery in Ireland; Julitta remained in the world to bring up her infant child.

Young Padorn.

(1) The Bretons have popularised this romantic legend by Celtic verse, which may be found in Albert le Grand.

When the boy came to the use of reason, hearing the name of his father mentioned, he, with that inquisitiveness which belongs to children, would ask his mother thousands of questions about him—where he was, what he was doing, why he would not come home, and say how happy he would be to see him. And *a thousand times* over his mother was obliged to answer these queries, often with suppressed sobs. She told the boy that his father had crossed the sea and dwelt in a large island called Hibernia, where he lived in a monastery. Then the child would inquire what a monastery was, and what people did there. This his mother would explain in a style adapted to his age, telling him that in a monastery lived the soldiers of Christ, waging a constant war against the devil. There every one laboured to secure a crown in heaven when he should have departed from this world, and disdained the service of kings and princes on earth, deeming it more glorious to enrol themselves amongst the servants of the King of kings.

When his mother's narrative was concluded, the boy invariably said, " When I grow up to be a man, I will follow my father, and, like him, become a soldier of Christ."

He kept his word, for in his youth we find him kneeling to receive the blessing of his mother previous to taking the habit in the Monastery of St. Gildas of Rhuys.[1]

(1) Cambro-British Saints—Lobineau—Vies des Saints de Bretagne.—Albert le Grand.

In course of time Padarn was chosen to be one of a monastic colony which was sent from Brittany to Western Wales. We find him erecting a monastery and church in Cardiganshire, about a mile from the present town of Aberystwith. In consequence of his zeal in the propagation of the Gospel, he was consecrated bishop of that district.

The numerous visitors who frequent Aberystwith in the bathing season, and may sometimes take half-an-hour's walk to Lanbadarn Fawr, which to this day retains the name of its founder, Padarn, will be struck by the size of an enormous yew tree in the cemetery, near the old church. Perhaps it was planted there of old by the Breton Bishop. From the bold mountains surrounding the valley and the high cliffs on the sea-shore, Padarn many a time gazed on the setting sun whose golden gleams rested on the green isle beyond the waves, and thought of his father, longing to see him if but once in his life. After God, it was his example that had decided his own religious vocation. At last he crossed over to Ireland and received the embrace of that venerated parent whose hair had turned to silver under the monastic habit. During his stay in Ireland he succeeded in reconciling two chieftains of the country, who had elected him as their umpire, after which he returned to Wales.

Hoel *the First*, King of the Armoricans, having been overpowered by the soldiers of Clovis, who *The family of Hoel the great.*

put his father to the sword, set sail for Cambria, and with 15,000 followers settled in South Wales, either at Caer-gwent, in Monmouthshire, or in Glamorganshire. He was accompanied by his wife, Pompeia, and a numerous family. In 513 Hoel recrossed the sea, and, landing on his native shores at the head of a large army, composed of his own subjects and volunteers from Britain, recovered his provinces and drove off the lieutenants of Childebert. Later on he returned to Britain to assist his cousin Arthur in his wars against the Saxons, and died in England in 545.

During all these events his family remained in Cambria under the care of their mother. Three of his sons—Eleonor, Twgdual, and Hoel, surnamed Jonas, were sent to Lantwit-Major, the celebrated college of Illtyd, which was held in high esteem by all classes, to be educated.

At Lantwit-Major two of these boys—Eleonor and Twgdual—hearkened to the sweet voice of Christ calling them to enlist under His standard. The world became distasteful to them, and the love of religion reigned sole sovereign of their hearts.

Their mother approved of, and even encouraged this feeling, saying she would be proud to behold her children enlisted in the service of Christ, and die rejoicing in the thought that they were safe from the seductions of a vain world within the shelter of the cloister.

They assumed the religious habit in Wales, and

during the time they remained there endeared themselves to all by the practice of every virtue that could adorn the soul.

On the death of Howel the Great, his wife, Pompeia, entered a convent, and, together with her daughter, St. Seve, consecrated herself to God. One of her sons, Hoel II., remained in the world and succeeded to his father's territory in Brittany.

Meanwhile the third brother, Twgdual, was elected Superior of his monastery in Britain, as soon as his abbot died, but was not long destined to guide his community. One night after he had retired to his cell an angel appeared to him whilst in prayer and said, " Twgdual, it is the command of God that thou leave Britain and cross the sea to Armorica, the land of thy ancestors, there to labour for the Church."

Pompeia, his mother, and Seve, his sister, being apprised of his intention, besought as a favour to be allowed to follow him, neither would his old nurse remain behind.

The light vessel which bore them across the channel touched land at the present Department of Finistère, between St. Pol de Leon and Brest. The Bretons welcomed their former queen, the wife of that Hoel whom they had called Great, and her children. 'They had seen Pompeia in her younger days, in all the splendour of royalty, and had been proud of her. But now when she landed amongst them in the coarse dress of the convent, they pronounced her to be a saint. One of her sons was now their king, but his two brothers, Eleonor and Twgdual, with their sister, Seve, by the advice of their mother had chosen what all fully appreciated to be the better part.

Hoel could not induce either his mother, brothers, or sister to accept from him any other gift than some lonely valley or sandy beach, where they might serve Almighty God according to the custom of the monastic life they had embraced.

These few examples, selected at hazard from amongst thousands of others, give us a fair idea of the spirit of the Celtic races in the fifth and sixth centuries. When converted to Christ they threw all the energy of their souls into the fulfilment of His law.

Supernatural life was strong amongst them, like vegetation in spring. Purely worldly pursuits they viewed in their true light, and pronounced to be folly and vanity. They thirsted after heavenly things; they searched for the precious pearl, and having found the bed wherein it lay, sold all things else to purchase it. The Evangelical counsels indicated to them a safe harbour against pride, licentiousness, and injustice, and they hastened to anchor within such sheltered waters.

Is it not wiser for a man who, after a few years must pass away to another world, where he must render a strict account for all his actions in this, to live in justice, purity, and humanity, rather than appear before the Judge with a heavy load of ambition and injustice and an existence sullied by impure passions, seldom or ever restrained?

The monastery offered an asylum against the corruption of the world; to it, then, they fled, as to the camp of Almighty God. They chose for their companions on their journey to eternity, not men who delight in the slaughter of the battle-field, but those who cherish meekness and innocence; not the worldly and polished lady who finds a fitting sphere amid earthly vanities, but the virgin favoured by Heaven because her only aim is to practise the beatitude; "Blessed are the clean of heart, for they shall see God."

The followers of the Evangelical counsels were divided into two classes—anchorites, or hermits, and cenobites. The first dwelt alone, in some solitary island, forest, or desert; the second formed themselves into communities. Hermits are everywhere recorded in the history of Wales. To this day the wells near which these holy men built their lonely huts and cultivated their plots of ground are clearly pointed out to travellers by local traditions.

The Hermit and the Cenobite.

The practice of a religious life was the main object of this absolute seclusion. Some old warrior whose conscience, racked by remorse, made the thought of eternity terrible, was inspired to cleanse his soul, too frequently sullied by murder and violence of every kind.

He felt that as long as he mixed with dissolute companions he could not resist their baneful influence; but in a solitary valley, shut in by mountains, there would be nothing to prevent him from keeping the commandments of God. Another time it was an innocent soul who, disgusted by what he saw around him, determined on abandoning a society ruled by the maxims of the world, and refused to share an existence spent in plunder, or in the gratification of sensual pleasures.

Very frequently we find religious men quitting the large monasteries of Lantwit or Lancarvan and retiring into solitude, as more conducive to a life of contemplation. Thus St. Illtyd, when persecuted by Merchion, withdrew to a cave in the valley of Neath, where he lived as a hermit until, being discovered by his brethren, he was forced again to assume the direction of his monastery. And so on of many others.

The aim of the religious life being the service of God and the good of mankind, the greatest attention was paid in every community to the cultivation of these two virtues. When a postulant applied for admission into a monastery, nothing was more strongly impressed on his mind than the necessity of *attaining love of God and of his neighbour.* For ten days—as we learn from the rule of St. David—he was *obliged to live in a building separated from the monastery,* and subjected to *frequent trials* in order to test his sincerity.

"For what purpose hast thou come hither?" was the invariable question put to the aspirant, and he was given distinctly to understand that if he was influenced by any idea of acquiring wealth, or reputation for learning, or science, or by the hope of finding a comfortable and easy life, he was under a delusion, and had better seek elsewhere for worldly advantages, for such were not to be found within monastic walls. *Diary of the various religious exercises in a Cloister.*

Indeed, there were two things the postulant soon learned by personal experience, if he remained, and those were, that monks prayed fervently and worked hard.

In the diurnal of the cloister a great part of the four-and-twenty hours of the day was consecrated either to public or private devotion. The Church, besides inculcating the necessity of private prayer, to every individual monk, also instituted offices to be carried out in public by her clergy, either in congregations or in monasteries. These offices consisted of prayers, which were recited or chanted by special command, and those entrusted with the execution of this were reminded that they did not act in their private capacity, but as officers of the great Christian community, doing service before the altar of God in the name of the whole Church. These prayers were distinguished by different names—Divine Office, Breviary, and Canonical Hours. They were divided into seven parts: Matins with Lauds, Prime, Tierce, Sext, None,

Vespers, and Compline. Matins and Lauds, which were said at night, were called nocturns; the other portions, being recited during the day, bore the name of diurnals.[1]

"Seven times a day," said David, "I have given Thee praise." The Church, from Apostolic times, can with truth repeat these words of the Royal Psalmist, before the face of God and man; for during the twenty-four hours of the day, seven times the choir met before the altar to sing the praises of the Lord, in accordance with the primitive institution of the Canonical Hours. At midnight they assembled for matins, at daybreak for Lauds; Prime was sung at sunrise, Tierce between sunrise and noon, Sext at twelve, None between mid-day and sunset, Vespers at sunset, and Compline at twilight.

Several of the Popes, such as Damasus, Gelasius, and Gregory the Great, employed much of their time in giving a regular form and unity to these Divine Offices. In Celtic monasteries the greatest attention was paid to ensure their being sung with devotion, reverence, and punctuality.

One of the first lessons given to a postulant was to learn the Psalms and the Lessons, as well as the sacred chant. The shores and many of the valleys of Wales resounded day and night with the praises of the Lord, and the voices of hundreds of her children ascended to heaven in

(1) Tronson. Forma Cleri.

supplication for pardon of the sins of their country and of mankind.

In several Cambrian cloisters Divine Offices were carried on not only seven times a day, but continually. Thus, in the life of St. Asaph we read,[1] "There were assembled in this monastery (founded by St. Kentigern) no fewer than nine hundred and ninety-five brethren, all living under monastic rule, serving God in great continence. . . . of which number three hundred, who were illiterate, were appointed to till the ground, take care of the cattle, and do other works outside the monastery. He assigned to another three hundred the preparation of the food and the performance of other necessary works within the walls. To the three hundred and sixty-five, who were learned, he deputed the daily celebration of the Divine Offices. He would not suffer any of these to go out without necessity, but appointed them to attend continually, as in God's sanctuary. Now, this part of the community was divided by him in such a manner, into companies, that when one division had finished another presently entered and began (it) anew; these having ended, a third troop succeeded them, so that by this means prayers were offered up in this church without any intermission, and the praises of God were always in their mouths.

In the Iolo MS,[2] we read, in like manner, that

(1) Britannia Sancta, 1st vol., p. 273.
(2) Iolo MS., p. 559.

at Lantwit-Major "praise and prayers to God were kept up by twelve saints of each college day and night without ceasing." Considering the great number of colleges and of companies, a great many Religious must have constantly stood before the altar in adoration, like the angels round the throne of God; and impressive beyond conception must have been that sacred testimony rendered by so many hundreds of voices.

Private devotion was not forgotten; for, whether in the study-room, the workshop, or the field, the monk was enjoined to keep silence as much as possible, and continually to direct his mind to contemplation. Heaven and earth were to speak to him of the greatness and beauty of God. He was to draw lessons from the sea as it dashed its mighty waves in thunder against the shore, and from the mountains which on all sides surrounded him. Even the humble flower should preach to him, for he had chanted on coming from the choir, "Oh, Lord, our God, how admirable is Thy name in the whole earth, for Thy magnificence is elevated above the heavens."

Extraordinary devotions in Lent. At certain seasons of the year, such as Lent, particular devotions were added to those already prescribed by the monastic rule. Thus, we read that several of the Cambrian monks used to spend the four weeks of Lent on some of the islands at the entrance to Cardiff, such as the Flat Holmes and others.

In closing this chapter, the writer, though his

mind is filled with the memory of the monks of the fifth and sixth centuries, cannot resist casting a glance at Monasticism in this present nineteenth age of ours.

There is no denying the fact that the followers of the Evangelical Counsels are again pitching their tents throughout Britain. Monasteries of men and women are again rising up on all sides, and Monasticism, driven away from the country, proscribed by law, reviled by the press and by the preacher, revives in the land and begins to find favour in the minds of many. The aristocratic, professional, commercial, and labouring classes are represented in our cloisters. Converts, as well as those born in the faith, swell the list of our clergy, regular and secular, and their names are inscribed in the registers of our numerous convents. Religious, both men and women, kneel in prayer before the monastic altar for the conversion of their relatives still alien to the true faith. *Revival of Monasticism in England.*

Many of the primitive founders of religious institutions in modern Britain came from France or Italy, but at their death they left behind a community exclusively native.

The large proportion of its members who, in certain families, devote themselves to the cloister recalls to mind the devotion of the fifth and sixth centuries. Without trespassing on home privacy, we will state a few instances:—

Converts are by no means backward in

estimating the advantages of religious life; they embrace it with eager enthusiasm.

A privileged family was received into the Church, thirty or thirty-five years ago. It consisted of four members, two daughters and one son, who had graduated with distinction at Oxford. The young ladies both entered convents, and the son became a priest and a religious. Their mother spent the remainder of her life near the church where her son officiated. . . . A clergyman who left the Church of England many years ago, and is still alive, pays yearly visits to a convent of which his daughter is Superioress. He is at times accompanied by his other children, nearly all of whom are priests and religious.

Another well-known and most venerable gentleman, in the county ———, is father of a large family, all of whom, with the exception of one or two, like that of the old chieftain of Brecknockshire, in the fifth century, have embraced the monastic life.

In one of the midland counties both the sons of a respectable family have become priests and religious.

One of my confrères in the priesthood informs me that seven or eight of his near relatives have entered religion. Another of my clerical brethren has had the happiness of seeing both his sisters and his brother consecrate themselves to God.

The writer himself, who is a Celt by birth,

returns thanks to Heaven for having called several of his relatives to the priesthood and to the religious life.

Monasticism cannot be uprooted. Man cannot stop the growth of vegetation in Spring. Whether he likes it or not, in due season the humble flower will bud forth in the fields, and the trees in the forests and parks will be covered with fresh leaves; for such is the law of God.

It cannot be uprooted.

In like manner, the monastic tree will and must flourish in the Church of Christ as a part of her system, and any attempt to destroy that spiritual plant must, in the end, prove a failure.

We have witnessed a regular war being waged against religious orders in our own days, and yet they are as strong and as numerous as ever. In France, during the last century, every religious house was emptied, and its inmates dispersed or guillotined. Their number is now as great, or even greater, than before.

In England, after three hundred years of proscription, monks and nuns are again seen carrying on their works all over the country.

Yearly, it is true, one or two zealous members of Parliament bring in a Bill for the suppression of monasteries, but they fail to obtain even a hearing. British statesmen are too far-sighted to countenance measures in direct opposition to liberty of conscience and public opinion at large.

Meanwhile, throughout the country religious houses daily increase in numerical strength, for

God speaks to many a heart, inviting it within the sacred shelter of His tabernacle.

When *the Spouse has whispered* to a soul these words of David, "*Hearken daughter, and see and incline thy ear; forget thy people and thy father's house, and the King shall greatly desire thy beauty,*"[1] that soul is conquered. Who, indeed, can see Jesus and listen to His sweet voice and not be enthralled by His love? He is all beauty, power, and love. A soul who has once caught a glimpse of this Spouse cannot bestow any lasting affection on anything else.

Powerful is the celestial influence exercised by grace over certain hearts, throughout the entire world, and at all times. No sooner do our Catholic missionaries form a congregation amongst the pagans, either in India or Africa, than a supernatural attraction is certain to draw some of them to the religious life. The writer has seen, with his own eyes, the bronzed maidens of India and ebony-hued daughters of Africa eagerly embrace the monastic life, happy, and giving edification in the habit of the cloister.

(1) Psalm 44—11, 12.

CHAPTER VII.

THE SAINTS AND SUPERNATURAL EVENTS.

IN the preceding chapter the Annals of Britain have agreeably surprised us, by bringing before our eyes a long procession winding its way to the doors of the monastery. We have seen the road to the cloister thronged with her children, and in the crowd have noticed the young and the old, the nobleman and the peasant, the maiden, the widow and the mother of a family. Our ears have heard the sweet harmony of Divine praise, as day and night it ascended round the altar of sacrifice. Spiritual life then was strong in the hearts of our ancestors, and they looked upon serving God in religion as a glorious undertaking, most profitable for obtaining the treasures of eternal life. Those noble souls hearkened to the voice of the Divine Spouse, and, enthralled by His heavenly beauty, forsook father and mother, brother and sister, wife and husband.

In this chapter we will call the attention of the reader to the miracles connected with the lives of the British saints.

The saints endowed with supernatural power.

Theologians divide grace into *gratum faciens* and *gratis data*. The first sanctifies the particular soul to whom it is granted; the second is chiefly imparted for the sanctification of others. The *one* cleanses us from all weeds of sins, beautifully decorates our hearts with every Christian virtue, and enkindles in them the fire of Divine love; the *other* becomes the companion of those men who are chosen by God for special missions in His Church, such as the conversion of a heathen nation, or the reformation of manners in a corrupt Christian community, or any other work which may be pointed out by Almighty God.

The Apostle St. Paul, in his first Epistle to the Corinthians, thus speaks of the latter grace:—

"*To one, indeed, by the Spirit is given the word of wisdom; and to another the word of knowledge, according to the same Spirit; to another faith in the same Spirit, to another the grace of healing in one Spirit, to another the workiug of miracles, to another prophecy, to another the discerning of spirit, to another diverse kinds of tongues, to another interpretation of speeches.*" (1 Cor. xii.)

Whether one opens the Old or New Testament he will invariably find that the men chosen by God to do His work were armed with Divine power, which manifested its presence in a variety of ways, according to circumstances of times, localities and persons.

Thus, Moses, the liberator of his brethren from the bondage of Egypt, begins his arduous task by showing to the Egyptians and their rulers that God stood by his side. He strikes the land with the ten plagues, opens the waves of the Red Sea, and performs sundry other miracles recorded in Holy Writ.

The action of fire was stopped by heavenly intervention in the case of the three Hebrew youths in the furnace of Babylon, and famished lions refused to tear to pieces Daniel, because sheltered by the protection of God.

Joseph, sold by his brethren, was favoured with supernatural light in explaining the visions of his master.

The prophets of old were shown future events, and foretold the rise and fall of mighty empires; they pointed out to coming generations, the Incarnation of the Son of God, the place of His birth, His cruel death.

In the New Testament, the four Gospels and the Acts of the Apostles are full of miracles.

Our Lord cast away devils, cured every kind of infirmity, called the dead from their graves, and when he sent his Apostles to preach the Gospel he graciously gave them the same power.

The history of the early martyrs teems with miraculous events which often converted their very persecutors. They were visited in their dungeons by angels. Their wounds were miraculously cured. Wild beasts crouched at their feet, at their deaths the earth shook, and as a rule the emperors or magistrates who so cruelly tortured them, died a miserable death struck by Divine justice.

In fact, from the first century of the Christian era, down to the nineteenth, Christ has never ceased to be *wonderful in his saints*.

St. Peter wrought miracles, and so did, later on, St. Benedict, St. Francis, St. Ignatius of Loyola, and in our days Maria Taigi and the Curè D'Ars.

Unless a biographer understands the methods which God adopts towards his chosen servants, he will be utterly unable to read, write, or comprehend their lives. He who derides supernatural action on the soul, has never studied holy men, or the history of sanctity.

Let such a man pray, and live like a saint, and in like manner heaven will visit his mind and his soul with the same favors.

In the lives of the Cambro British saints we continually read of a variety of supernatural events connected with their names. Angels alight in their cells on some particular mission from heaven. They see extraordinary visions. Power over devils—over the elements—and over beasts—is given them by their Divine Master. They command the storm at sea and a calm ensues. At their bidding miraculous fountains gush forth from the bowels of the earth; they subjugate dragons, and cure all sorts of infirmities. The afflicted gather round them whilst they remain in this world, and for centuries after they have departed from it, pilgrims are attracted to their graves.

Some modern historians question—nay even ridicule—all these *miracles*, and speak of the writers who have handed them down to us, as superstitious. The same term is freely applied to our forefathers who believed in them—and we men of faith belonging to the nineteenth century who endorse their belief, are stigmatised as simple-minded and ignorant. These critics—of course advertise themselves to the world as clear-sighted and well informed. Such men are to be pitied, in the first place for their own blindness, and in the second for their unfairness and injustice to past generations.

We fail to see why Almighty God who condescended to send an angel to an Israelite exiled by the rivers of Babylon—*or* to a virgin at Nazareth in Galilee, could not also dispatch heavenly messengers to the shores of Britain, Gaul, or Ireland. If Gabriel was the envoy of God to Daniel and to the Blessed Virgin—Jews by birth —can we deny the possibility of an angel—in the same way—holding communication with a Briton, an Irishman, or a saint of Brittany, if in time of drought Moses and Eliseus in the desert, by the power of God, obtained water to relieve the thirst of thousands; why could not the Sovereign Master of the universe impart the same power to St. David, St. Teilo, and others?

All writers who have transmitted to us the acts of

the saints, either in the East or West, bear unanimous testimony to the occurrence of miracles, which they narrate with all the circumstances that evidence their truth, no doubt of which existed in the minds of their contemporaries.

Some few hagiographers may differ in opinion as to the authenticity of *this*, or *that particular miracle* attributed to such or such a saint, but on the main point they all agree. Thus Montalembert—a layman—whose eloquent pen has so beautifully depicted the monks of the West, terms the learned Bollandists *cautious* and *reserved*, intimating that in some instances they call in question certain miracles concerning which he had no doubt.

Albert le Grand—a Dominican and a Breton—has handed down to us interesting particulars in reference to the British saints who settled in Armorica during the fifth and sixth centuries.

Difference of opinion as to the authenticity of this or that particular miracle.

The miracles attributed by him to these servants of God are, no doubt, numerous, and perhaps somewhat exaggerated. Lobineau, a Benedictine monk, writing on the same subject with greater method, finds fault with the former writer for not exercising more discretion in the reproduction of these wonders.

In a late edition of Albert le Grand, with corrections and notes by M. de Kerdanet, a Breton layman and a lawyer, he justifies the Dominican writer against the severe reproaches of Lobineau. The substance of his remarks is as follows :—

"If modern critics find fault with Albert le Grand for crowding a number of *miracles* and marvellous events into his Lives of the British Saints, it must be borne in mind that the good Religious has narrated what was piously and universally believed in his days—a time in which faith and religion flourished more than at our epoch. Then public opinion was not startled at miraculous events which illustrated the sanctity of these men and their power with God, and justified the confidence and veneration with which they were regarded in past ages. . . . Then, the authorities on which he grounded his narratives were the offices of the Church, the lessons read in the Breviary, the hymns chanted in cathedrals or parish churches. . . Miracles are found in connection with the servants of God in the Eastern and Western Churches at every period of Christianity. Why should our country be excluded? They were necessary in Britain and in Armorica, as in every part of the world. First, in the conversion of pagan nations to the faith; secondly, to confirm them in the practice of their new religion. Reason, by itself, lacks the power to convert; the senses often require to be called into action. This explains the numerous miracles mentioned in this work in connection with our saints, and handed down to us by tradition, which even in our days is vivid in these localities once trodden by our holy apostles, evidencing how deeply-rooted they are throughout the land."

These observations will be endorsed by every Christian, for it would be difficult to imagine that a servant and friend of God could be unvisited by Divine grace, or unassisted in a particular manner whilst fulfilling the mission entrusted to him.

Thus prefaced, let us place before the reader a few instances of supernatural gifts, such as we find in connection with the British saints.

<small>St. Dubricius is favored in vision with designs of Almighty God on St. Samson</small>
These holy men were at times favoured with a pre-knowledge of the designs of Almighty God, either on themselves or on some of their brethren, and this recalls the legend of Saint Samson, as related in the "Liber Landavensis." When Samson had come to attend the annual meeting of the clergy, on a certain night he fell into an *ecstacy*, during which he saw a number of persons, clothed in white, surrounding him. *Pre-eminent* amongst them were *three bishops*, who stood before him adorned with golden crowns. With great humility he inquired their names and the cause of their visit. He who was most prince-like in the assembly replied—

"I am Peter, the apostle of Christ. The Lord Jesus has pre-elected thee to be a bishop, and has commissioned us to consecrate thee."

About the same time Dubricius had also a vision. An angel of the Lord stood before him in the night and commanded him to consecrate Samson as bishop.

It is related in the life of the great apostle of Ireland that whilst in the monasteries of Gaul, Noirmoutier, and Lerins, his mind was constantly occupied with thoughts of the conversion of that land whose mariners had kidnapped him in his youth—that land which, naturally, he would not be inclined to love, as his knowledge of it was connected with the period when he worked there as a slave, with all the accompanying humiliations. Whether in the field, spade in hand, or in the choir singing the Divine praises, the remembrance of Ireland was supernaturally recalled to his mind. Sometimes a group of charming children would appear stretching forth their little hands to him, and he heard their voices crying out appealingly— *Visions of St. Patrick in relation to Ireland*

"Come to us, Patrick; we are little children from Ireland, and are not yet baptised."

The heart of the saint was touched, and he promised to comply with their request; but many obstacles occurred to detain him, and it was a long time before he was able to carry into effect his earnest aspirations to work for Ireland.

Again, it is related in the life of St. David, that St. Patrick was favoured with another vision whilst in Wales. He beheld the panorama of Ireland—with her numerous lakes, mountains, and valleys—unroll before his eyes, whilst the voice of an angel thus addressed him :—

"Patrick, the country thou beholdest is that which is given to thee to gain over to Christ, thy Master. Leave Wales to another apostle, who is yet unborn.

Most of the saintly missionaries who left Britain for Armorica in order to win that land to the religion of Jesus Christ did so in obedience to the commands of an angel. Amongst others, let us take Tugdual and Samson.

Tugdual commanded by an angel to cross over to Brittany

Tugdual, a Breton by birth, who had devoted himself to God in a British monastery, had thrown himself on his pallet after matins, when the heavenly messenger stood by his side, and, in the name of Jesus Christ, commanded him to return to the land of his ancestors and preach the gospel to his countrymen in Armorica. Next morning, when kneeling with his brethren before the altar, his mind was much occupied with what he had seen and heard during the preceding night. He poured forth his soul to his Lord on the altar, exclaiming—

"Here I am, oh, my Jesus, ready to obey; but how can I be certain that the vision of last night was a messenger of God? It may be that I am deceived."

In order to remove all doubt, he begged his Divine Master again to commission the angel to be the bearer of his commands, and that he would then at once prepare for the voyage. His prayer was granted, and the angel twice reappeared and communicated his message anew.

Tugdual summoned the community over which he was abbot, and informed them of the order he had received, and must obey. His monastic brethren did not question the reality of the vision, nor assert that their abbot was under a delusion. After hearing all the circumstances, they naturally concluded that he must fulfil the command he had received, and seventy-two of the monks at once volunteered to follow him.[1]

St. Samson, in like manner, was commanded by an angel to leave his own country and go to Armorica. As he watched and prayed in the church, on the eve of the Feast of the Resurrection, a bright light shone round him, and an angel of the Lord appeared, and thus addressed him:—

An angel commands St. Samson to go to Brittany.

"Samson, dearly beloved of the Lord, act manfully; depart from thy country and thy kindred, for thou art predestined to be a founder of many monasteries beyond the sea, and gloriously to govern the people."

Samson sought counsel of St. Dubricius, by whom he had been consecrated, and also of his old master at Lantwit-Major, St. Illtyd. Both bishop and abbot blessed him, and directed him to comply with the commands he had received.[2]

We frequently find information being sent to bishops and others, of God having great designs upon some young man whom they had trained to virtue.

(1) Albert le Grand, p. 787.

(2) Liber Landavensis, p. 299.

Apparition of the Holy Ghost under the form of a dove, foretelling the future greatness of a saint.

The bishop and all the bystanders saw a stream of fire alight on the head of St. Brienc, a young Cambrian priest, whilst being ordained, and thence concluded that he would one day shine in the Church.[1]

Such supernatural signs were seen at the ordination of St. Samson, and also at his consecration as bishop. The dove, the emblem of innocence, descended on his shoulders, and after his celebration of Mass streams of fire proceeded from his mouth. The bishop, St. Illtyd, and some others were witnesses of these extraordinary manifestations.

The Angel at the hour of death.

These contemplative souls, whom we see so highly favoured during their career on earth, who converse with God, and with whom God converses, were in a particular manner illuminated when the time for their departure from this miserable world was at hand. A worn-out frame, organs which no longer perform their usual functions without difficulty, a body failing in all its parts, warns the soul that separation is nigh. The spirit and the flesh can no longer abide together. The saints understood this law as we do, but frequently a messenger from their Master was sent to cheer them, and indicate the very day of their departure.

Vision of St. Keyna.

St. Keyna, virgin, sister of Gwladys and aunt to St. Cadoc, of Llancarvan, had spent her life in the service of her Divine Master, at Keynsham,

(1) Albert le Grand.

in Somersetshire, and later on in South Wales, edifying the Britons by her virtues. At the close of her existence a heavenly message warned her of her departure from this world.

The Cambrian virgin was asleep in her cell, on a hillock not far from Abergavenny, when a pillar of fire, whose base rested on her bed, suddenly illuminated her cottage. Then two bright angels alighted in the room, gently removed the hair cloths that covered her worn-out frame, and then clothed it with rich garments, surpassing in elegance whatever she had seen in her life. This done, the heavenly messengers pointed up to heaven and bade her follow them to the kingdom of her Spouse. Keyna wept with joy, and when the angels were departing she rose to accompany them, as she had been commanded. In the efforts she made she awoke, and felt a fire burning all over her frame. It was the fever that was to carry her away. The virgin recognised in the event her loving Jesus, whose kindness had warned her of her death. Not long after she died, and rejoined in heaven *Him* whom her heart had loved during her earthly career.[1]

St. Paul of Leon (Paulus Aurelianus), a Briton, and the disciple of Illtyd at Lantwit-Major, had run a glorious course as an apostle and bishop in Brittany. His end was not far off. He had attained the age of a hundred-and-two, and his

(1) Britannia Sancta.

body was a mere skeleton, covered with skin. The very day of his death was revealed to him.

After matins, on a certain night, as he laid himself down upon his hard mattress, an angel appeared in the room, which at once became brilliantly illuminated. He thus addressed the venerable bishop:—

<small>Death of Paulus Aurelianus</small> "Paul, thou hast fought valiantly, and blamelessly run the career. Now the time of reward is at hand, and thou shalt be paid for all by thy heavenly Master, whom thou hast faithfully served. Prepare thyself, therefore, to depart from this world on Sunday next, for on that day thy soul shall receive its crown in heaven."

Having thus spoken, the angel disappeared. Paul communicated the vision to his brethren, and encouraged them to persevere in the service of God. Having received the last Sacraments, and blessed his community in the name of the Father, Son, and Holy Ghost, he departed from this world on Sunday, the 12th of March, in the pontificate of Gregory the Great, and the tenth year of the reign of the Emperor Mauritius.

St. Meen, when in his agony, said to one of his brethren, to whom he was particularly attached, and who was extremely grieved at his death—

"Cheer up, we shall not be separated for long. Eight days hence thou shalt follow me to heaven; prepare thyself for the journey."

According to the prediction, after eight days the brother died.[1]

<small>(1) Albert le Grand.</small>

A similar fact is related of St. David. Far advanced in years, and worn out with toil and austerity, he felt his end draw near, and prayed to be delivered from the burden of his body, that he might find rest with his Lord in heaven. Like Paul, of whom we have spoken, he persevered to the last in following the religious exercises of the community.

Towards the end of February David and his brethren were singing the morning office in choir, when the venerable archbishop fell into an ecstacy; his face, pale and emaciated, glowed with saintly beauty. Then a heavenly voice was heard by the monks speaking to the saint— *St. David warned of the exact day of his death.*

"David, often hast thou prayed to be released from a miserable body and received into glory. Thy crown awaits thee whenever thou wilt have it."

David rejoiced greatly, and said, "Oh, Lord, take Thy servant in peace."

The brethren heard what was said, and fell on their knees, awe-struck by the presence of the celestial messenger. David prayed aloud a second time, saying, "Lord Jesus Christ, take my soul, for I am weary of this wretched existence.",

Then the angel spoke again: "David, prepare thyself for the first day of March, for on that day the Lord Jesus Christ will come down with nine choirs of angels to meet thee." . . . . David did really die on the first of *May*.[1]

(1) Cambro-British Saints.

St. Kentigern sees the soul of St. David taken up to heaven.

Whilst the brethren of David were witnessing the departure of his soul in Pembrokeshire, St. Kentigern, at St. Asaph, was informed of the event—not by telegraph, such did not exist—but by a heavenly vision.[1] David and Kentigern had been very dear to each other. The Scotch bishop, an exile from his country, had met in the archbishop of Wales a true friend and protector. We often find him in Caerleon during the residence there of David. On the day of his death Kentigern had a vision, and in a kind of diorama beheld the soul of his saintly friend taken up to heaven, surrounded by innumerable angels, and crowned by our Lord Jesus Christ. This he

(1) These pages, briefly recording certain visions connected with the Welsh saints, bring back to our mind what, over and over, we have read in Holy Scripture. For instance, the visions of the prophets, the apparitions of our Lord after His resurrection ; the angel bearing the message to Zachary concerning the birth of St. John the Baptist ; the angel Gabriel visiting the Blessed Virgin in her humble home, at Nazareth, on a similar errand. Schram, Gorres, and others have scientifically classified these extraordinary events in their mystical works, and laid down clear rules to discern true visions from illusions, often the effect of strong imagination, fever, weakness of mind, etc., etc. To their writings we beg to refer the reader. Our Lord, whilst yet on earth, appeared to some of His disciples in a glorified state, attended by Moses and Elias. After His resurrection, to Mary Magdalene, who took Him, at first, to be a gardener. On the evening of Easter Sunday He stood before His disciples, showing them His sacred wounds. Our Saviour suddenly appeared to Saul, on his way to Damascus, and spoke thus to him :—" Saul, Saul, why persecutest thou me ?" Saul said, " Who art thou, Lord ?" " I am Jesus, whom thou persecutest. It is hard for thee to kick against the pricks." (Acts chap. ix.) An angel also visited the prison of St. Peter, loosed his chains, bade him walk, threw open the doors of the prison, and led him away. (Acts chap. x.) An angel also assumed the form of a tutor, and became the guide of the young Tobias on his journey.

I. There are various kinds of supernatural visions—some merely *intellectual*—the senses having nothing to do in their representation. Thus, a supernatural object is seen, the eyes being closed ; a Divine voice is heard without any action of the ears. *Others* are communicated through the ordinary channel of the senses. They are called *symbolical*, where Almighty God wishes to convey to us information through the medium of objects offering a certain similitude to what is meant to be conveyed. Thus, a white dove is the emblem of the Holy Ghost and of purity. Thus, again, when St. Peter fell into an ecstacy of mind at Cæsarea, and saw the heavens opened and a vessel full of fourfooted beasts creeping things, and

communicated to his disciples long before the announcement of the saint's death was conveyed by the ordinary channel.

Many future events concerning the Anglo-Saxons were shown to this same Kentigern during his residence in Wales. Already they had established a sure footing in several parts of Britain. The holy, persecuted bishop predicted in detail a full account of the scourges they were to inflict on the Britons because of their sins. He also said that the invaders would be converted to the faith *en masse*; that the time when this change was to take place was not far distant, and

Prophecy of the same Kentigern concerning the Anglo-Saxon race

fowls of the air, coming down, and heard a voice bidding him to eat. This was a symbolical vision, which instructed him that as an apostle he was to receive into the Church all manner of nations, the uncircumcised as well as the circumcised. (Acts chap. x.)

II. Our Lord, in His state of glory, on the cross, in the sacred Host, may appear. The blessed Virgin, the angels, the saints, the devil, the souls in purgatory, etc., etc., are all objects of vision.

III. Certain rules are laid down to discern Divine and real supernatural manifestations from those which are diabolical and fictitious. Should any vision, apparition, voice, etc., intimate to us anything against faith or morals, command us to renounce the one true religion, or appeal to carnal passions, Almighty God has nothing to do with them; they come from the spirit of darkness. Neither can we rely much on visions in those living in heresy, in rebellion against God, in the proud, or in persons who lead a bad life. . . . Women, novices in the road to perfection, weak-minded people, and those with strong imaginations are often deceived in this respect; not much importance must be attached to their statements on events of this kind. When Almighty God condescends to enlighten by a supernatural favour the mind of an individual, and reveals past events or circumstances taking place at a great distance, this is called in theology revelation. Prophecy, on the contrary, refers to occurrences which have not yet taken place. It is related in the Lives of the Saints that many of them received the most extraordinary graces. To some, for instance, when in a state of ecstacy, were shown the different scenes connected with the passion of our Lord—such as the streets of Jerusalem, the crowds, their behaviour, Mount Calvary, etc. . . . Others were allowed to behold what was occurring at a distance. Almighty God has admitted some souls, whilst yet in the flesh, into heaven, hell, and purgatory, and allowed them to see by whom they were inhabited and what was there being done. A saint, for instance, was visited often at night whilst in prayer by the suffering souls in purgatory. Others were endowed with power to read the most secret thoughts of the heart. Certain laws of nature have even been revealed.

that the Saxons, when once gained to Christ, would prove themselves to be fervent Christians.[1]

This threatened scourge to Britain recalls to memory the words of the celebrated Gildas, who has so strongly inveighed against the vices of his countrymen, and threatened them with the vengeance of God. The bards of Britain claim him as a member of their brotherhood, and according to them he was highly favoured with the gift of prophecy.

The Iolo M.SS. contain the advice of Gildas the prophet, uttered before the bards of the island of Britain, when they assembled at the Gorsedd to prophecy what would befall King Arthur and the race of Cymry. As it reflects the faith of past ages, we will place it before the reader, referring him to the M.SS. for the original.[2]

Advice of St. Gildas for the obtaining of the gift of prophecy, given to the Bards of Britain. The instruction given by Gildas to the Christian bard to enable him to acquire the gift of prophecy is as follows:—"To love God with all his heart, with all his mind, and with all the faculties of his soul. . . . Let him also love his neighbour with all his energies, so far as it may not interfere with his love of God. . . . Let him be a moral and religious man in principle and disposition, cultivate a clean conscience, and strive with energy to advance in piety. . . Let his heart and mind be free from worldly principles."

(1) Britannia Sancta. Vol. I. p. 37.
(2) *Vide* Mystical writers—Gorres, Schram, Theologie Mystique.

THE SAINTS AND SUPERNATURAL EVENTS. 239

It was by following these instructions that the prophet bards of Wales acquired knowledge of future events relating to the destiny of their race.

There is much truth in this advice to the bards of Britain attributed to St. Gildas.

The first condition for obtaining access to the mysteries of heaven is to secure the friendship of God and possess a heart purified from all attachment to sin. The brighter the mirror, the greater and more powerful the light it reflects.

It would be impossible to convey to the reader a more comprehensive idea of the variety of miracles performed by Celtic saints than by quoting a hymn to St. Armel. This holy man was born in South Wales, probably near Cowbridge, in Glamorganshire, under the pontificate of Pope Simplicius, about the year 482. The hymn runs thus:— *(St. Armel Hymn)*

> Omnes ægros, bruta sanat,
> Fœminas a sanguine,
> Dæmon fugat, fons emanat,
> Monstrum mergit flumine
> Omne morbum hic explanat,
> Jesu Christi nomine

In these lines we have a *résumé* of most of the miracles connected with our saints. We can gather from them that they cured every kind of *infirmity*, exercised power over the animal creation, cast out devils, delivered the land from huge monsters which existed throughout Europe in those days. At their word miraculous springs gushed forth from the bowels of the earth; and all this was done in the name of our Lord Jesus Christ.

The Christians who lived in the time of these saints fully believed that they had received from God the power of miracles; for we find the afflicted from every class of society, both the rich and the poor, crowding around their cells. . . . Thus, when Germanus arrived in Britain, an officer in the army brought his little blind girl to him, confident that the servant of God who, by the invocation of the Holy Trinity had calmed a storm in the channel between France and Britain, could also restore sight to his young daughter, and his faith was rewarded.

How often do we see Welsh chieftains come to saints such as Dubricius, Teilo, David, and others, one entreating the cure of a child, another deliverance from the possession of the devil.

<small>Privatus' wife and daughter cured by St. Samson</small>

Nothing, perhaps, can more beautifully illustrate the general opinion of those days than the legend of a certain Privatus, a person of high position in Brittany. When St. Samson landed on her shores the life of Privatus was embittered by great family afflictions, his wife being slowly eaten up by leprosy, and his daughter possessed by the devil. Thousands of times prayers had been offered up in their behalf, but as yet to no purpose. At last he was given to understand that at no distant period a holy man would arrive from Britain, who would heal both wife and daughter. One day, as he was walking on the sea-shore, with sadness and affliction stamped upon his countenance, a boat drew near, and a party of monks landed on the beach, amongst whom was St. Samson. The saint entered into conversation with Privatus, and, remarking his sorrow, inquired kindly into its cause.

Privatus told his tale, adding that he was looking forward to the arrival of a man who was to come from beyond the sea, and as had been revealed to him in prayer, put an end to his grief.

He did not know who this servant of God who was to cross the waters and work this great miracle in his behalf could be, but as Samson had just landed from Britain, and they had met by chance, Privatus requested the bishop to follow him in case he might be the man whom God had appointed to cure his wife and daughter. The British saint followed the afflicted Armorican to his house, and by prayer and the sign of the Cross restored the two patients to health. Then Privatus knew that Samson was the stranger so powerful with God who had been indicated to him. In gratitude for this great favour, he granted to the British colonists any land they might choose for the building of a monastery. Such was the origin of Dôl, of which Samson became the first bishop.

Legends attribute a similar miracle to Maglorius, a cousin of St. Samson. Both were natives of South Wales, and grandchildren of Meurig, King of Glamorgan.

Maglorius had abdicated his bishopric and retired to Jersey. A nobleman, rich in a hundred ploughs and innumerable fishing boats, whose only daughter, though beautiful and rich, could find no husband because she was dumb, came to the holy bishop and entreated him to restore her speech.

St. Maglorius' reply to a Breton Prince.

Maglorius answered—"My son, torment me not. I am an old man, afflicted with bodily infirmities of every kind, nearly always ailing. When I lie on my bed oppressed with sickness, I know not whether I am to live or to die. How, then, having no power over my own life, can I heal the diseases of others.?"

The father of the girl, however, persisting in his petition, Maglorius followed him to his house and obtained from God the cure of his daughter.

The cases of thousands of sick persons healed by the British saints which are minutely described in their biographies are too numerous to be related here. They will be brought before the reader in the detail of each respective life.

The Hagiography of Scotland is in this particular similar to those of England, Ireland, and Brittany, as the life of Ninianus, one of her early missionaries, testifies.

The miracles of Ninianus in Scotland

Ninianus was a Christian, born in North Britain. On attaining the age of manhood he undertook a journey to Rome, probably about the time of Pope Damasus. In that city he completed his education, received holy orders, and was consecrated bishop by the Sovereign Pontiff himself, who sent him back to Britain, there in his own country to labour in the vineyard of the Lord. He fixed his see at Witehern, Galloway, and built a stone church, which was considered a marvel in that part of the country, and which he dedicated to St. Martin of Tours. His labours in the South of Scotland were blessed by numerous conversions, and his biographers tell us that he wrought wonderful miracles, for through his prayers the blind recovered their sight, the lame walked, the lepers were cleansed, the deaf heard, the dead were raised to life, and devils cast out from those oppressed by them.

Even when the grave had closed over this holy man his tomb was visited by the afflicted, and God glorified him after death by numerous miracles. It is related that a pious priest, who had a great devotion to Ninianus and often celebrated Mass at his altar, was favoured there with a vision of our Lord in the sacred mysteries, in the form of a little child.[1]

Montalembert observes that during the fifth and sixth centuries Europe was as yet an immense forest, covered with oak, elm, and pine trees. Wild beasts of great size, such as the elan, buffalo, bear, and wolf, roamed through these vast solitudes. The rivers, impeded in certain places on their course to the ocean, formed here and there extensive marshes, the resort of reptiles of every description—crocodiles and immense serpents, fifty or sixty feet in length.

The Saints in connection with wild beasts and the Dragon

(1) Britannia Sancta.

These reptiles were the terror of mankind; their aspect was hideous, nature had provided them with powerful means of defence, and their bite was often venomous. The kings and nobles of those days who, when not engaged in warfare amongst themselves, spent all their time in hunting, willingly attacked wild buffaloes, elans, bears, or wolves. This was exciting sport, which they considered worthy of warriors; but they were not so inclined to wade through marshes, amongst grass and weeds, in search of venomous reptiles. This they regarded as work for a saint, because spiritual, and not material weapons were best suited for attacking animals of this sort. The sign of the cross, the stole of the priest, the name of Christ invoked by His servants, were—in the opinion of the people—far more efficacious than sword or lance in this kind of warfare.

Montalembert, in his second volume of the Monks of the West, has dwelt at length on the power exercised by the British saints over these wild creatures.

Anyone who has visited Irish homes, whether in the courts of populous towns or amidst the solitary wilds of Connemara, is certain to have seen, a thousand times over, their walls adorned with the picture of a bishop represented driving serpents before him along a high cliff over which he forces them into the ocean. This is St. Patrick freeing Ireland from snakes, on whose soil, since that time, they can never exist.

A similar story is related of St. Tugdual. He celebrated the holy Sacrifice, and strengthened himself with the Bread of Life; then, clothed in his sacerdotal vestments, with cross in hand, went forth to conquer the dragon which filled the land with terror and devastation. The stole—the emblem of priestly power—was the only weapon he made use of.

St. Samson, at Lantwit Major, cured one of the brothers who had received a mortal bite from a snake in the harvest field, by the sign of the cross.

In the diocese of Quimper, Finistère, there is a spot which for ages has borne the name *L'abime du Serpent*,[1] because a British saint, St. Paulus, drowned a huge reptile there. This was a dragon which was the terror of the country. Issuing from its caverns, it descended upon the villages and devoured both men and beasts. The lord of the district came with the affrighted inhabitants to entreat the assistance of Paulus Aurelianus. The saint prepared himself by prayer to meet the monster, and, having celebrated Mass, set out for the cavern which was its resort, accompanied by the Count and his people. On coming near the spot none dared approach but St. Paulus and a young gentleman whose sword the saint had blessed. The dragon being commanded by the servant of God to come forth from his lair, obeyed, rolling his fiery eyes, his scales rattling on the ground as he went along, and his hisses

---

(1) Montalembert. Albert le Grand.

resounding to a great distance. Paulus walked straight up to the monster, and, tying his stole around his neck, gave him in charge to his companion. They directed their steps towards the sea-shore, and the dragon, by the command of Paulus, threw himself into the ocean and was there drowned.

Miracles of the same kind are related of St. Armel and St. Cadoc, all British saints.

The traditions of conflicts such as these between saints and dragons, or serpents, are often coloured with all the poetry of the Christian bards and of the ages of faith.

Dragons are depicted as carrying off bellowing, powerful bulls, which plough the ground and even uproot trees as they are forced along towards the den of the monster. They are also represented bearing away shrieking maidens and children through desolate marshes.

The Saints and the Devil. There is another serpent, spoken of in the first book of Genesis, and called the acutest amongst animals, who wages war against monks. This is the devil, the same devil who successfully tempted our first parents in the garden of Eden, and even dared to assail our Lord in the desert with his evil suggestions. Between him and the monks there is eternal warfare. They are sworn enemies.

This fiend of mankind adopts a variety of plans in his attacks on the soldiers of Jesus Christ, as we learn from their history. At times he takes the form of a hideous serpent, or an infuriated lion, who roars beside the cell of the hermit. Then, jealous of the angelic life led in the solitude, he disguises himself into beautiful but licentious females, to excite the carnal passions of the lovers of chastity.

We read in holy writ that he was allowed to afflict Job in property, in domestic happiness, and in health; in like manner, by the permission of God, he afflicted our forefathers, and, no doubt, in our own days he stretches his hands on many of our fellow-men. Being a spirit, he occupies even the soul, but conquers it not.

How frequently do we read of cases of this kind in the lives of the servants of God; that they cast out devils, and that it was customary for the relatives and friends of persons who were possessed to apply to them for this purpose.

Tugdual, in the beginning of his monastic life, in Britain was tormented by the devil of impurity, who, day and night continued to assault him. "Thou art but a youth," said the enemy of mankind, "thou mayest live for fifty or sixty years to come; how canst thou deprive thyself of the pleasures of the world for so long a period; thou whose passions are so strong. Go back to the world and marry." The saint prayed, fasted, and humbled himself, and vanquished the fiend.

When St. Gunstan, a Briton by birth, had retired with one companion to a desert island called Houadic, the devil followed him there.

St. Gunstan and the Devil.

In this little barren island Gunstan and his companion, like Anthony or Paul in Egypt, were visited by monsters and phantoms, whose aim was to tempt and terrify them, and thereby drive them from their holy purpose. But the young hermit was not to be daunted. He made the sign of the cross, and repeated the following verse of David:—"*Super aspidem et basiliscum ambulabis et conculcabis leonem et draconem,*" which he had so often chanted in the monastic choir.[1] Then the phantoms in all their various forms at once vanished. On a certain day, as he was journeying through his little island, Satan appeared to him in the shape of a man. Introducing himself to the hermit, he seemed at once to take the deepest interest in him, and spoke of the desolate and dreary aspect of the place, remarking that it was not a fit habitation either for man or beast. The disguised demon expressed his surprise how a young man like him, who should take care of himself and indulge in some comfort, could dwell amongst these rocks, where none was to be had. The hermit, making little of his observations, and not in the least giving in to the opinions of the fiend who seemed so kindly disposed, the latter became furious, threw off his mask, and showed himself in his true colours.

"You men of Christ," howled the demon,

---

[1]. Psalm 90—"Thou shalt walk upon the asp and the basilisk, and trample underfoot the lion and the dragon."

"stand in our way all over the world. You have driven us from Britain, from Rome, and from Gaul, and you now come to persecute us even on a desolate island."[1]

St. Gunstan at once interrupted him, and, in the name of his Master, Jesus Christ, commanded him to leave the island. This stern decree was at once obeyed, and the devil vanished.

Whoever is descended from Celtic blood, has lived among the Christian Celts, studied their history, or travelled in their country, must have heard or read something about "*holy wells.*"

The holy well is constantly mentioned in the records of past ages, and in our time is pointed out to the traveller in Britain, Ireland, and France. Our forefathers went in crowds to these sacred spots; and the present generation may be seen in our railway trains on a pilgrimage to the miraculous fountains of Lourdes, in France, or that of St. Winefrid, in North Wales. These facts cannot be denied.

Sacred Wells.

I cannot close this chapter on miraculous events without calling the attention of the reader to the subject, and inquiring into the origin of the holy well.

Rain water, after moistening the surface of the earth, and supplying the wants of men, beasts, and plants, either makes its way to the next river, which carries it to the ocean from which it was taken, or enters the earth, sinking through

(1) Montalembert.

various beds, till it comes to impermeable strata; then, stopped in its downward course, it forces its way onwards, forming subterranean rivers or even lakes, and at length finds its way to the surface in greater or less quantity, according to the size of the chink that allowed it a passage.

These waters, passing through beds of sulphur, iron, copper, or other minerals, absorb a certain amount of their chemical properties, and thus form our various mineral springs, so much appreciated by medical science. Such are the natural springs, the result of a providential law of God, whose kindness has taken the greatest care to supply us with an element so necessary to vegetable and animal life.

Hydrology was not an unknown science to our forefathers, who were great observers of nature. Springs vomited forth their incessant streams in their time as well as in the present day; nay, as Europe was not yet shorn of its immense forests, which attract the clouds, they were more numerous than they now are, and their laws were as well understood in those days as in ours.

A "sacred well" is so called either because a saint, in the name of God, ordered it to come forth from the bowels of the earth, or owing to the fact that a holy hermit served his Divine Master by its side, and when he died God was pleased to show forth the sanctity of His servant by endowing the waters of the fountain with miraculous power.

In the mind of the people something supernatural is connected with the holy well, either in its origin or in the miraculous power of healing it possesses. An ordinary mineral spring may be recommended by doctors for this or that complaint, according to the nature of the disease and the properties of the waters; but the man of faith makes his way to the sacred well, not on account of its chemical attributes, but trusting in the power of God and in the prayers of the saints.

The mind of the past generations of faith is clear and explicit on the subject. They tell us that in such a spot there was no water, to the great injury of animals and plants, when suddenly it oozed out by the power of God. No subterranean river or lake had ever made its way to the surface in that place, till ordered to do so by supernatural power. They could not tell, any more than we, where lay the river or lake out of which the water was taken; whether it was distant or close to the surface, or miles deep in the bowels of the earth. They simply tell us that it was a miraculous well, and not found by the digging of persevering miners, as in the case of our modern Artesian wells.

In most cases the generations in whose lifetime the event took place flocked to the spot; and so did those that succeeded them for centuries. The crowds of pilgrims to the holy wells went there, as a rule, with interested motives—viz., the lame, the blind, the leper, the paralysed, the consumptive, in the hope of finding a cure; and it cannot be denied that many returned restored to health, leaving behind as tokens or *ex-votos* the stretcher on which they were carried, or crutches without which they were previously unable to walk.

The Church, as a rule, does not interfere with the faith of the public in these matters. If ever she steps in, it is to prevent abuses, which in the course of time arise everywhere.

In our days, at Lourdes, in the French Pyrenees, public opinion forced the local bishop to inquire into the apparition of the blessed Virgin in that locality, and the springing up of a miraculous fountain in connection with the said apparition. A commission was named to inquire into the facts—viz., first, whether there was a fountain before in the grotto of Massabielle; secondly, what was the supposed cause of the existing one; and thirdly, whether its waters had really cured the infirm. The commission drew up its report, and sent it to the bishop, who published it; thus, the facts being laid before the public, everyone is left to form his own judgment.

Thousands upon thousands all over the globe entertain no doubt whatever on the subject. Our modern infidels may scoff, and the press may cry down the revival of superstition, but the people will persist in going to Lourdes in spite of the comments passed upon them.

THE SAINTS AND SUPERNATURAL EVENTS. 253

The strong faith of past ages may, in many instances, have carried their credulity too far, even to such an extent as to have entailed on them the censures of the Church. Thus we see ecclesiastical authority obliged to interfere with practices carried on in Ireland, in the cavern connected with the life of St. Patrick.

Miraculous fountains, or waters endowed by heaven with curing properties, are often mentioned in Holy Scripture, and recorded in the history of the Church from the first century down to the ninth. When the people of God murmured bitterly against Moses in the desert for want of water, God commanded their leader to strike the rock of Horeb, when a plentiful stream gushed forth from the mountain and supplied the wants of the twelve tribes of Israel, amounting to more than a million of human beings, together with their cattle.[1] Sacred Springs spoken of in Holy Scripture and in early traditions.

In the fourth book of Kings, chapter iii., we are told that the prophet Eliseus procured water without any rain for the whole army.

The Probatica pond at Jerusalem, as we read in the gospel of St. John, possessed supernatural and miraculous powers of healing every sort of infirmity,[2]

St. Peter, a prisoner in the Mamertime dungeon, converted to the faith of his Master his gaoler, who requested to be baptised. As there

---

(1) Exodus, chap. xvii.
(2) St. John, chap. v.

was no water in the deep dungeon, through the prayer of the apostle a stream rushed forth from the rock, and flows to these days.

St. Clement, his disciple, drew upon himself the anger of Trazan owing to the numerous conversions he made. Relegated to the marble quarries of Chersonesus, he met there 2,000 Christians condemned like himself to extract and cut blocks of marble for the Roman Government. As the place lacked water, St. Clement ascended a neighbouring hill, and by his prayers obtained a fountain from the Lamb of God. Many of the pagans were so struck that they believed in Christ.

In our incredulous age, and in the lifetime of most of us, the blessed Virgin has caused two miraculous fountains to gush forth in France— one in the Alps, at La Salette, the other at Lourdes, at the foot of the Pyrenees.

Wherever the old British saint set foot, it is not uncommon to find the sacred fountain, connected with his name in lifetime and visited by pilgrims for ages after.

St. Meen. St. Meen was a native of South Wales, and a contemporary and near relation to Samson, Archbishop of Dôl. He emigrated to Brittany, and resided for a time at Lan-Meur, a few miles from Morlaix. Later on he built a monastery, dedicated to St. John the Baptist. Whilst the building was being raised, the workmen complained that they were greatly delayed by the want of water, which they had to bring from a great distance. The mortar was never ready in time. When St. Meen heard of this, full of confidence in the kindness of God, he knelt down and addressed his prayer to heaven; then, driving his staff into the ground, a plentiful fountain oozed forth from the spot.[1]

Pilgrims afterwards came to this fountain, which for centuries was admitted by all to cure a kind of cancer called prosa by medical men, and by the common people the evil, or fire of St. Meen.

St. Teilo, second Bishop of Llandaff, is reported to have obtained by his prayer two miraculous springs; one near his cathedral at Llandaff, and another near Dôl, in Brittany, during his seven years' residence in that country. The "Liber Landavensis," speaking of the residence of Teilo with St. Samson at Dôl, says: "He left there some beneficent proof of his sanctity, that is, the salutiferous fountain called Caï, which he obtained from the Lord to flow; at which the sick recovered in the name of God and St. Teilo."[2]

St. Teilo's Wells.

As St. Teilo had in his lifetime undertaken long voyages, been to Jerusalem, crossed several times from Wales to Brittany, the sailors for

---

(1) Le Père Candide has thus versified the legend in French :—

"Les ouvriers étant en peine / Et d'une vertu merveilleuse
D'aller chercher de l'eau fort loin / Pour le mal qu'on nomme St. Meen.
St Meen fit sourdre une fontaine / Une dame étant affligée
Tout proche d'eux pour leur besoin. / De ce mal infect et hideux
Cette source miraculeuse / Buvant de cette eau fut purgée
Est un remède souverain / De sa lèpre selon ses vœux."

(2) Lib. Landavensis, p. 346.

centuries had a great devotion to him, and asked heaven to grant them prosperous winds and a safe passage, through St. Teilo. In return, the mariner whom business brought to the Bay of St. Malo, and so to the neighbourhood of Dôl, deemed it his duty to keep his fountain in good repair. I have been told by ancient inhabitants of Llandaff that not many years ago a brewer wanted to take water from Teilo's well to mix with his barley in malting. The inhabitants of Llandaff have no particular repugnance to beer; however, as the well of Teilo has, even to this day, retained some of its sacred character, people thought it was not proper that its waters should be used in a brewery.

Moses sweetened the waters of Mara in the desert; so St. David, by blessing the waters of Bath, which heretofore had proved most deleterious to health, rendered them most salubrious to persons washed by them.

Traditions still alive on the subject. After noting in various works, such as the "Liber Landavensis," the "Cambro-British Saints," and others, the various sacred wells connected with the British saints, and which are too numerous to be brought before the reader, I thought of inquiring whether any traces of the old Welsh traditions still remained amongst the people. I consulted old, illiterate Welshmen about Cardiff, and from them learned that there are more sacred wells than I had heard of. If I wanted to see a holy well, I had not far to go. I would find that of St. Teilo at Llandaff, that of St. Cadoc at the foot of the Garth mountain, at Pentyrch. There is one at Pen-y-lan, on the north-east of Cardiff; others at Penarth and Sully; at Llantrissant, on the top of a hill, there is a holy well which, to my knowledge, is visited by sick people from Cardiff. A traveller who should undertake a tour through Wales, and make inquiries on the subject, would be shown the well of St. David, in Pembrokeshire, and others along the coast as he goes northward, till he comes to the fountain of St. Winefrid, at Holywell, known all over Great Britain.

The writer of these lines visited it in August, 1876. One is struck by the great mass of water that oozes out gently from the rock, and one must travel a great distance before meeting another fountain so abundant as this. I have seen only one spring that nearly equals Holywell in this respect, and that is in the island of Mauritius (Indian Ocean), at Shoenfeld, a sugar estate in the district of Rivière du Rempart.

Holywell yields one hundred tons of water a minute, and turns a powerful mill a few yards from its source.

On the road from the railway station to the well, I met an Irishman, lately returned from America. To ascertain his views as to the supernatural character of the spring, I stated that several people did not believe there was anything connected with the fountain, beyond the purity and freshness of its waters. "Well," he smartly replied, "people may say what they like; but the world will never be able to stop the infirm from coming over to this place, in the hope of being cured by the power of God and the prayer of St. Winefrid. The well has been visited for centuries by the blind and the cripple; and as long as England, Ireland, and Scotland continue to be inhabited by man, pilgrims will make their way to Holywell."

On coming to the spot, I minutely examined the place. In a covered gallery, above the spring, I found crutches and stretchers, left there by invalids who previously could not walk without them, but, being cured on the spot, had left them behind as an encouragement to others.

Some people, free from all human vanity, had deemed it their duty to publish to all comers the favours received at the well, and had written the cure obtained on the very arches that covered the fountains. Thus, the visitor may read the following inscription:—" T. M. Carew, Esquire, cured here October, 1831."

I inquired of the guardian whether any book was kept on the premises recording the cures obtained, and was shown a register of recent date, out of which I copied the following extracts:—

"May 30th. Mary Conway, of Monkside, cured of paralysis."

"I, William Ward, hereby certify that my wife, Honora Ward, was cured of fits through coming to Holywell and bathing in St. Winefrid's. Dated this 22nd day of June, 1876."

"Lewis Colquhan, Edinburgh, visited St. Winefrid, July 14, 1876."

In the same book I met with the following Latin words, so expressive of faith :—

> "Christus vincit, Christus regnat.
> Sancta Maria, Mater Dei, Ora pro nobis.
> Sancta Winefrida, Ora pro nobis."

Others, in going away, wrote, "Thy will be done." Perhaps these words, conveying full resignation to the will of God, imply that the visitors had not obtained the grace which they had come to seek.

One person writes that "he visited the place, and begged both spiritual and temporal favours.' A convert certified that he "had received much benefit." Two nuns of the Holy Family, from Bolton, inserted their names. On the day of my visit several visitors must have been at the well, for the guardian's room was full of wet towels. There are two ponds by the well; one connected with it, another lower down, and covered over by a glass roof. The pilgrim whom faith has brought to Holywell will not bathe except in the first; ordinary bathers and excursionists are not so particular, as I was informed by the guardian.

As I had come from Cardiff, I was recognised by two Cardiff women and a young boy; they informed me that they had come from South to North Wales to obtain some favours from St. Winefrid.

The Catholic Church does not present to the faithful as articles of faith the miracles connected with her saints. Everyone who reads the various circumstances of such facts, and witnesses the belief of all ages, is able to form his judgment on the subject. It is not the power of working miracles that makes a man a saint, but keeping the commandments of God and the Church. In the process of the canonisation of saints, so ably treated by Benedict XIV., the first point examined is, not whether such a person worked miracles, but whether in his life he practised, to an heroic degree, the three theological virtues— Faith, Hope, and Charity; and then the cardinal virtues—Prudence, Justice, Fortitude, and Temperance. When the commission sitting on the life of a man reputed to be a saint arrives at the conclusion that he was to an heroic degree a man of Faith Hope, and Charity, and to an eminent degree gifted with Prudence, Justice, Fortitude, and Temperance, then they examine into the various miracles connected with his life.

Hence, St. Paul says: "*If I speak with the tongue of angels, and have not charity, I am become as a sounding brass or a tinkling cymbal; and if I should have prophecy, and should know all mysteries and all knowledge, and if I should have faith so as to remove mountains, and have not charity, I am nothing.*"

The power of miracles, by itself, does not render a man holy. Judas performed miracles, and was a reprobate.

However, as a rule, this power is granted by

God to such persons as observe His laws to perfection, and are generally connected with the lives of those who served their Master in an eminent degree, either in past ages or even in our own days.

CHAPTER VIII.

A FEW REMARKS ON THE SERVICES RENDERED TO SOCIETY BY THE EARLY BRITISH MONKS.

"*Principes persecuti sunt me gratis.*—Ps. XVIII."

IN the preceding chapter we have glanced at the saints as spiritual men; in the present we will study them as men of business—active, intelligent, zealous, and persevering in the various works undertaken by them.

Nothing can be more unfair and unjust than the ideas of modern society in reference to religious orders. On their side we see heroism, self-sacrifice, prolonged labour, and talents of all kinds consecrated to the welfare of mankind. On the other, ingratitude, calumny, and contempt.

The unfairness of modern times in regard to Religious Orders. Those monks, who have not been surpassed as scholars, architects, agriculturists, artists, or missionaries by any class of society, either past or *present*, are stigmatised as ignorant, slothful ambitious, or dissolute. In speaking of them, we may truly say with David, "*Principes persecuti sunt me gratis*"—(princes without cause have persecuted mc.)

The monks were not oppressors, shed no blood, seized not the property of their fellow-men, lived chaste and pure, like the angels in heaven, and yet the world has branded them as tyrannical, luxurious, and enemies of God and man; it has even carried injustice so far as to deprive them of the fruit of their labours, and cast them into dungeons, which they often never quitted until led to the scaffold.

In the fifth and sixth centuries Wales abounded in religious men, who have never since been surpassed. Whether taken as bishops, scholars, missionaries, fearless defenders of the rights of God, or protectors of the people against the tyranny of chieftains, none since in their country have ever equalled them.

It is only at this period that a Dubricius, a Samson, or an Illtyd can be met with in the history of Wales. In the present time of great material prosperity, Cambria cannot show to the world universities like those of Dubricius at Mochross, in Herefordshire, or Lantwit-Major, in Glamorganshire. Where are now the thousand scholars, not only from *Britain, but from Gaul and Armorica?* Who in our days flock to such seats of learning? With the monks they disappeared, and cannot now be recalled.

Nor do we find at the present time such vast schools of farming as those of Bangor, St. Asaph, and Lancarvan, in which thousands of God's servants not only sang His praises, but laboured with spade and axe, reclaimed large tracts of land from pathless forests or unhealthy swamps and transformed them into delicious gardens and productive fields.

In the minds of these holy men *spiritual* works of mercy took precedence of *corporal*. The soul before the body is the motto of well-regulated charity. To feed the hungry, cover the naked, and visit the sick, are praiseworthy works; but to instruct the soul, point out to it the way to heaven, and clothe it with sanctifying grace, is far more important.

A traveller, writing from a pagan country, gives a painful account of what he saw there. "The people are badly clothed, badly fed, and badly governed; they can neither read nor write, and all arts tending to increase the comforts of life are utterly unknown amongst them. They are wretched socially and politically." The visitor is rightly grieved at witnessing this miserable state of things, but his is merely a human compassion, or what is known in our days as philanthrophy.

A Catholic missionary who, speaking on the same subject and about the same people, grieves also, and is deeply moved; but his sympathies take a wider scope. His first care is for the immortal soul, unregenerated by baptism, and plunged as yet in the darkness of paganism.

He, also, would wish to introduce into that benighted land the more advanced civilisation of

Europe; but his first and chief aim is to establish the Christian faith and win those infidel races for his heavenly Master, because he does not forget the precept, "Seek first the kingdom of God and His justice, and all else will be added unto you."

The traveller possesses the virtue of humanity; the missionary is endowed with that of charity, whose basis is supernatural benevolence, from which springs natural kindness, both being included in Christian love.

We have already related the vision of little children through which St. Patrick was invited to Ireland. St. Brieuc, a contemporary of his, a native of Western Wales, is another instance of the spiritual zeal so manifest under the monastic roof. Brieuc had in his youth followed St. Germanus to Gaul, and been ordained priest in Paris. On the day when he celebrated his first Mass, filled with the impressions which rush on the mind of the young priest when for the first time he holds in his hands his Creator and Redeemer, he thought of Cambria, the country so dear to him, of his father and mother, his relatives and countrymen, and prayed most fervently for them all.

Zeal of St. Brieuc

It is asserted by some writers that the parents of St. Brieuc were still pagans. It is more probable that, although Christians, they persisted in adhering to some national customs which were heathenish, and condemned by the Church in Gaul and Britain. This grieved the heart of the zealous young priest. He was a minister in the Church of God, whilst the laws of his Master were being disobeyed by his father and mother. If ever he poured forth an earnest prayer, it was on this day.

He felt within him an ever-increasing desire to revisit his native land, in the hope that he might win his parents to Christ. Heaven smiled on this aspiration, for an angel appeared to him, and in the name of God bade him set forth. Brieuc consulted his superiors, and they advised him to fulfil the mandate.

"Go, my son," said the Abbot, "whither God calls you; and may you, by your zeal and fidelity to His grace, succeed in the mission entrusted to you."

On arriving at his father's house, he found the family celebrating a pagan feast in honour of Janus, which lasted three days. It was numerously attended, and the time was spent in various sports. Some of the men wore masks to represent gods; others, habited as wild beasts, ran through the country affecting madness, terrifying some and amusing others. These games terminated with a rich banquet in the evening, and the greatest part of the night was spent in drinking and carousing.

St. Brieuc refused to take any part in the entertainments, on the plea that his conscience, as a Christian and a priest, would on no account allow him to engage in a pagan festivity.

His father and mother, and the friends of his youth, were glad to see again, after so many years, a beloved son and former companion. But they remarked how his thoughts and manners were changed, and considered it rather sad that his foreign education should not only have extinguished in his heart the love of national customs, but created within it a distaste, even amounting to hatred, for practices which they considered an honour to their country. In consequence of this, his eloquent appeals against paganism were without effect.

Almighty God, however, supplemented all drawbacks by endowing him with the gift of miracles. A young man, of noble birth, being thrown from his horse, was greatly injured. St. Brieuc healed him by the sign of the Cross. Later on, a boy who had been bitten by a mad dog was seized with hydrophobia. On being taken by his parents to the young priest, he was cured by him in the same way; for Brieuc, trusting in the power of God, sucked the bitten finger, and every symptom of the disease at once disappeared.

These miracles produced effect throughout the country. The people began to look upon him with veneration, his own father and mother not excepted. From that time his preaching produced fruits, and hundreds of conversions were the result. During the fifteen years Brieuc spent in Wales he built several churches and monasteries, which followed the same rules as those of Gaul.

On the night of Whit-Sunday, St. Brieuc, overcome by fatigue, dozed in the choir after matins, when an angel appeared to him in his sleep and commanded the zealous priest to cross the sea to Brittany, there to work in the vineyard of the Lord.

With his usual simplicity, he at once communicated this vision to his brethren, and one hundred and sixty of them immediately volunteered to accompany him. He carried on his mission in Brittany as he had previously done in Wales until his death.[1]

The present town and diocese of St. Brieuc, so called out of respect to the memory of this zealous monk and bishop, is under his especial patronage.

We are here reminded of the legend of St. Malo, as related by Albert le Grand.

Malo was born in the present county of Monmouthshire, near Chepstow, and seems to have been a relative of St. Samson.

Being educated at Llancarvan, he, at the conclusion of his studies, embraced the religious life in that monastery. Some disagreement appears to have arisen in the community, and he with the abbot and about seventy of the brethren, left Llancarvan and dedicated themselves to the conversion of the heathen.

(1) Lobineau. Albert le Grand.

SERVICES RENDERED BY THE MONKS.

According to the geographical knowledge of those days, it was supposed that somewhere in the far ocean, westward, were to be found large islands, whose inhabitants were still unconverted. It is difficult, in our time, to indicate the supposed position of these unknown territories. According to some, it was the Canary Islands, and others imagine it to have been the Orkneys. At that period, however, the undiscovered tracts were known by the name of the Fortunate Isles.[1]

St. Malo fits out ships for the discovery of the Fortunate Islands.

St. Malo and his companions determined to set out on a voyage of discovery in search of these regions, with the view of converting the natives to the Catholic faith. They, accordingly, fitted out a small fleet and started on their expedition, which, though it proved unsuccessful, shows how strongly at that time the missionary spirit existed within the cloister. Whenever one or two recluses felt inspired to visit foreign countries in search, not of gold or silver, but of souls to win to the Almighty, numerous volunteers were sure to offer their services.

The Cambrian monks were great travellers and men of enterprise. We read of St. Pedrog journeying not only to Jerusalem, which was visited by many of his countrymen, but pushing on even to India. Having lived there for seven years, he returned to his native country, and died at Bodmin, in Cornwall.[2]

(2) Perhaps our ancestors felt, by a kind of instinct, that large continents lay to the west, and, like Columbus later on, fitted out expeditions for discovery.

St. Maglorius perplexed in his old age.

St. Maglorius, a relative of St. Samson, and a student of Lantwit-Major, had grown old in Brittany in the service of God. For fifty-two years he had been abbot, and for three archbishop, when he determined to retire into solitude, there to prepare for eternity. He, accordingly, resigned his dignities, and in order the better to secure himself from intruders, selected for his retreat a spot surrounded by marshes and difficult of access. The people, however, found him out, and by their constant coming and going soon opened a road to his cell.

The venerable archbishop was perplexed as to what course he should pursue. In his heart he longed for solitude, but love for his neighbour pleaded that it might be uncharitable to refuse him any service he could render. Being unable to arrive at a decision on the point, he determined in this difficulty to consult the bishop who had succeeded him in Dôl, and abide by his judgment.

He accordingly visited this prelate, and complained to him of the importunities by which he was beset. "I have left the world," he said, "to give myself entirely to God, but the world follows me. I am no longer bishop, but my privacy is intruded upon now much more than when I was a pastor. Would I not be justified in secreting myself in some distant spot, or on an island inaccessible to visitors?"

Budoc, the bishop, being anxious that

Maglorius should remain in his diocese, reminded him of his former missionary zeal, and thus delayed his departure.

"Contemplation," the Bishop said, "is undoubtedly sweet, and it is good to sit, like Magdalene, at the feet of our Lord. Visitors incessantly breaking in upon you from morning to night do certainly interfere with your peace and privacy; but remember that our Master left the bliss of heaven to work and suffer for mankind.

"After spending the day in preaching and healing the infirm, the only way in which our Lord could obtain rest was to cross the lake and retire into the mountains. Even there the people followed him, and, far from being turned away, miracles were even performed to feed them in those deserts. Our Saviour carried the stray and weary sheep upon His shoulders. If uneasy consciences and wounded hearts come to you for advice or encouragement; if the sick and the afflicted, trusting in your power of prayer, flock to you to be cured, are you justified in shutting the door of your cell against them? To serve our neighbour is to serve God. Our Saviour sacrificed Himself for us; let us do the same for our fellow-men."

Budoc, in appealing to the zeal of Maglorius, had struck the right chord, and thus persuaded him not to abandon the mission.

Nothing more strikingly evidences the ardent desire of monks for the salvation of souls and

Bishops generally chosen from the cloister.

their aptitude for missionary work than the fact that the early Celtic Church chose their chief pastors from the Monastery, for all the early bishops were religious. Dubricius, Teilo, David, Paternus, and Daniel were members of religious communities, as were also the first bishops of Armorica, most of whom came from Britain.

<small>Particular care taken of the spiritual wants of the people in the neighbourhood of a monastery.</small> In Cambria the monks watched with paternal care over the spiritual needs of the people in their vicinity. At Llancarvan, Lantwit-Major, and St. Asaph, provision was made for the spiritual instruction of the inhabitants of those districts.

St. Cadoc, Abbot of Llancarvan, divided the country round his monastery into parishes, over each of which he appointed a priest, with a necessary revenue, in order that he might attend to their souls.

St. Kentigern, in like manner, whilst residing at St. Asaph chose some of his brethren who were in holy orders, and possessed talents for preaching, to devote themselves to missionary works, in order to enable them to carry on which they were exempted from the severities of monastic rule.

In the fifth and sixth centuries the crowds who gathered round David in Llandevvi, or St. Brevi, or who followed Samson, Gildas, Maglorius, or Tugdual to the shores of Armorica, were for the most part in a very primitive state of civilisation. As a general rule, they could neither read nor write, nor did they feel any need of it. They were quite content with supporting their families by their manual labour. But they were aware that learning was necessary for a priest or monk, whose office it was to instruct and preach, and also to chieftains, magistrates, etc. Printing had not been invented in those days. Books were scarce and costly, and the teaching of the people devolved upon the missionary, who had no means of imparting instruction or the knowledge of Christian doctrine but those of oral preaching and teaching, in which they followed the example of the apostles of our Lord, who were the first missionaries.

In order to impress their lessons more forcibly they availed themselves of the aid, so powerful more especially in Celtic races, of poetry and numbers.

Whilst Britain was yet pagan she glorified her bards; when converted to the Christian faith she still honoured them, and they continued to occupy in Christian society the same position they had possessed in that of the pagans. *The Christian Bard.*

In Celtic nations poetry has always exercised a most powerful influence, and bards, in consequence, were held in the highest esteem. Privileges of byegone days are accorded to them even now, in Cambria, Brittany, Ireland, and wherever the Celtic element prevails.

When danger threatened the State, it was the bards who roused the patriotic spirit into ardent zeal to fight in defence of fatherland. It was they who sang the praises of the victorious warriors in the banquet-hall, or poured forth lamentations over the tombs of the slain. They also acted as censors of morals or customs, choosing as themes, if occasion required it, the murderer who had shed innocent blood, denouncing his crime, and exemplifying the justice of God and man by pointing to his shameful end. When a Briton forsook the customs of his ancestors, the bard reviled and ridiculed him through the medium of sarcastic verses.

On the conversion of the Celtic races to Christianity, the clergy largely availed themselves of the aid of poetry in imbuing the minds of the people with the precepts and practices of the faith of Christ. Thus, the commandments of God and of the Church, the Seven Sacraments, and other points of doctrine, were clothed in verse. The lives of the saints and the wonders wrought by them, the histories attached to miraculous fountains, and the cures obtained at sacred wells, were favourite themes with the Christian bard whereon to exercise his talent; and his verses, inspired by such subjects, were committed to memory by the people and sung at the doors of the churches, at fairs, or other social gatherings, and by the fireside during the long evenings of winter. Christianity thus became identified with even the every-day life and occupations of the people.

In Lower Brittany, where the native language is still spoken, great use is made of poetry in the rural districts even at the present day. The professional singer, with his hundreds of hymns and songs, travels from village to village and from fair to fair. He has a diary of his own, and knows the feasts of every saint in all the parishes of Brittany, and also the month and the day of every fair throughout the province. He has no fixed abode, but rambles about the country, deriving his living from his songs, which he teaches and chants according to occasion. At the doors of the churches, on Sundays, he sings religious hymns after Mass and after Vespers, and if he can supply a canticle on a saint, or sacred well in the neighbourhood, it will take the place of all else.

At a fair the local bard mingles the profane with the religious and semi-religious; but, as a rule, his songs are always serious, the music inclining to melancholy. Before offering a hymn or a song for sale, he sings it himself, in order to instruct his customers in its melody, after which he invariably succeeds in disposing of his collection.

In that part of Armorica where the Breton tongue is still the language of the pulpit and of the people, sacred hymns are even now sung in the original Celtic version, supposed to have been the composition of the British missionaries of the fifth and sixth centuries. Such, for

Hymns composed by British saints of the fifth century still sung in the churches of Brittany.

instance, are the "Cantic ar Barados," "Cantic un Ifern" (hymns on heaven and on hell), which are of monastic origin, and describe so beautifully the longing of the soul for Paradise, and its passage through the moon and the stars as it wings its flight to heaven, there to be united to the saints of Britain, or terrifies the sinner by revealing hell opening beneath his feet.

The Welsh bards claim to include such saints as Cadoc, Gildas, Suliau *(alias* Issillio), and others within their order; for, like their cousins of Brittany, poetry was amongst them the natural handmaid of religion. They, too, had their sacred hymns, and their bards consecrated their gift of song to chanting the praises of their Redeemer and of His servants.

A few specimens of these poems have been handed down in the Iolo Manuscript. Amongst them is one in which the life of St. Illtyd is condensed. Mention is also made of similar compositions having reference to St. Teilo, St. Cadoc, and St. David. In Albert le Grand's "Lives of the British Saints of Armorica" the reader can find many which are written in Latin, Breton, or French verse. However, these compositions are in several instances modern.

Our forefathers transacted business in the open air. King Gwynliw dispensed justice under the oak trees on the mountains surrounding Newport. His son, the Abbot of Llancarvan, held spiritual conferences with his brethren within a hazel grove, and the missionaries also often preached and catechised their flocks beneath the canopy of heaven, in valleys or upon the slopes of hills. It was thus that the Council of Brefi was held.

Armorican writers have given us some specimens of the method adopted in teaching by numbers. The reader will see by the following extracts that the teachers were very courteous towards their pupils:— *(Religious instruction imparted through the medium of numbers.)*

Question: "Fair son of Britain, what is number one?"
Answer: "One God, creator of heaven and earth."
Question: "Fair son of Britain, what is number two?"
Answer: "Two natures in Jesus Christ, the nature of God and the nature of man. Two Testaments—the Old and the New. The old embraces four thousand years, and the New will last to the end of the world."
Question: "Fair son of Britain, what is number three?"
Answer: "Three persons in God—the Father, the Son, and the Holy Ghost. Three sons of Noe—Sem, Cham, and Japhet; we fair sons of Britain are descended from Japhet. Three theological virtues—Faith, Hope, and Charity."
Question: "Fair son of Britain, what is number four?"
Answer: "Four great Prophets—Isaias, Jeremias, Esechiel, and Daniel. Four Evangelists—Matthew, Mark, Luke, and John. Four cardinal virtues—Justice, Prudence, Fortitude, and Temperance."
Question: "Fair son of Britain, what is number five?"
Answer: "Five Books of Moses. Five populous towns destroyed on the spot which is now covered by the Dead Sea, in consequence of the crimes of their inhabitants. Five wounds of our Lord. Five virgins who were wise and five who were foolish."
Question: "Fair son of Britain, what is number six?"
Answer: "God created the world in six days."
Question: "Fair son of Britain, what is number seven?"
Answer: "On the seventh day God rested after the creation of the world. The seventh day is Sunday. Seven years of

plenty and seven years of famine were foretold to Pharaoh. The great candelabro in the Temple had seven branches. Seven Sacraments were instituted by Christ—no more, and no less."

Question: " Fair son of Britain, what is number eight ?"

Answer: " There are eight Beatitudes. Eight persons were saved at the time of the deluge, four of whom were men and four women."

Question: " Fair son of Britain, what is number nine ?"

Answer: " Nine choirs of angels surround the throne of God."

Question: " Fair son of Britain, what is number ten ?"

Answer: " There are ten commandments, which were delivered by God to Moses, on Mount Sinai."

Question: " Fair son of Britain, what is number eleven ?"

Answer: " For above eleven months the face of the earth was covered by the waters of the deluge, in the time of Noe."

Question: " Fair son of Britain, what is number twelve ?"

Answer: Twelve Apostles were chosen by our Lord, and there are twelve articles in the Apostles' Creed."

This mode of instruction, so simple and at the same time impressive, might perhaps be usefully employed even now.

In studying the lives of the British saints we find that they cultivated the law of kindness to a remarkable degree, protecting to the utmost of their power not only men but animals.

In the solitude of the forest wild beasts, such as wolves, boars, and more especially deer, became the natural friends of the monks, as in the primitive state of the world, before the fall of Adam and Eve, when animals acknowledged man as king of all creation, and man regarded them as fellow-creatures of a lower grade.

The hermit never pursued the deer, and the timid creatures looked without suspicion on the stranger who had settled in his wood, and, becoming familiar, liked to browse around his dwelling and ruminate at his door. *The monks protected the weak animals and their fellow-men*

An intimate friendship sprang up between the two, and when in the hunting season hounds and sportsmen visited the neighbourhood, the stag often took refuge in the cell, and sometimes in the church itself. When this occurred the monk deemed it a duty to protect the weak creature against his enemies, and asserted in his behalf the inviolable rights of hospitality. The hounds might howl and the hunters rage and threaten, but the recluse never yielded. We read that St. Illtyd on one occasion forgot that he was a monk and a man of peace, and this was when a stag ran panting up to his feet for safety. He seemed once more to become the heroic knight in the army of King Arthur, and sternly defended and secured the safety of the animal against all attacks, whether of man or dog.

St. Ninnoc, a Welsh nun, evinced equal courage in protecting a deer which had fled into the church for shelter whilst the sisterhood were singing the Divine Office. It can easily be imagined that those who extended protection to the beasts of the field could not look with indifference on the sufferings of their fellow-men.

Thus, from the earliest ages we find religion extending her shield to shelter the weak and persecuted, both in the east and in the west. Persons in distress, from any cause whatsoever, prisoners of war, run-away slaves, or sufferers of any kind, felt themselves in safety the moment they set foot on church or monastic territory. No military array was needed to enforce this right of sanctuary; moral and religious power alone sufficed to maintain it.

In the fifth and sixth centuries we find the law of refuge established everywhere throughout Britain; it was specified in charters, and formed part of the national code. At times we read instances of its violation by princes, such as those recorded of King Arthur, Maelgon of North Wales, and others; but such infringements were universally looked upon as scandalous transgressions of sacred rights, condemned by public opinion, and punished by excommunication. The guilty parties, as a rule, made reparation.

Privileges granted to St. David. When, on the resignation of St. Dubricius, St. David had been elected Bishop at Brefi, the grateful Cambrians conceded to him almost unlimited privileges as to the right of refuge. They decreed that it should be lawful for him to grant shelter to murderers and wicked persons of every kind who were fleeing from place to place, even before saints, kings, or men of any degree; and it was ordained that any one who violated St. David's right of sanctuary should be excommunicated and cursed.[1]

(1) Cambro-British Saints.

In all the charters granted by the kings of Glamorgan to the diocese of Llandaff the right of affording refuge is clearly laid down. The "Liber Landavensis" distinctly states, in the life of the third bishop of that See, that the privilege of sanctuary secured an asylum in which a fugitive might find safety without any other protection, not for a limited time only, but as long as he required it.

Later on, Howell Dda in his legislations retained this sacred custom which was so long maintained by his countrymen.

In an age when Britain was divided and subdivided into petty kingdoms, each governed by independent sovereigns continually at war with each other, when the sword was resorted to on the least excuse of grievance, real or imaginary, religion asserted her right to protect the children of God. Unable to prevent warfare, murder, or hasty executions, she instilled into the minds of the people that blood should not be spilt on consecrated soil; such territory must be neutral to all contending parties. The servants of God did not use the sword or sacrifice human life, therefore within their bounds all must dwell in safety. Thus, amidst social and political turmoil the weak had an assured refuge in the church or in the monastery. It cannot be denied that this privilege proved most *beneficial* to Britain and all other Christian nations, and that many owed their safety to it.

Indomitable courage displayed by the monks in the protection of life.

Some Welsh monks showed indomitable courage in the defence of those who were in danger. The life of St. Cadoc, as found in the "Cambro-British Saints," abounds in instances of his undaunted bearing on such occasions. He gave shelter at Llancarvan to a general who had slain some of the soldiers of King Arthur. His brethren warned him that this might excite the wrath of the king. "Let us do our duty as servants of God," was his reply, "and God will take care of us. Fear not him that kills the body but has no power over the soul;" and he continued to protect the fugitive.

Seven years later on, a contest arose between Cadoc and Arthur, the particulars of which will be related in his life.

St. Samson undertook a weary journey to the court of Childebert to defend the rights of the oppressed,

St. Meen and the prisoner.

The holy monk, St. Meen, was on a certain day visiting the different cells of his monastery when, as he passed along, his attention was attracted by the sound of bitter lamentation. On inquiry, he found that the cries came from the dungeons of Prince Hoel, whose castle was in the vicinity of the monastery, and that the victim was a poor man who, having in some way incurred the displeasure of his lord, was confined there.

St. Meen sent two of his monks, begging in the name of God that the captive might be liberated.

The request being sternly refused, Meen and his brethren betook themselves to prayer. Through the intervention of heaven the prisoner made his escape, and sought protection in the monastery.

The prince, on hearing what had taken place, sent some of his soldiers to demand his captive. Meen replied that he could not, before God and man, surrender a fugitive who had claimed the rights of hospitality. He was in conscience bound to protect him.

Hoel, enraged, came in person to the door of the church, which he forced open, and, rushing to the altar, followed by some of his men, dragged the object of his vengeance back to his former dungeon. It was in vain that Meen and his brethren appealed in behalf of the unfortunate man, the prince would not release his victim. Then the abbot, as if inspired from above, told Hoel to *put his conscience in order*, for in *three days* he would die and have to render account to the great Master before whom kings are but as dust.

The wild young prince mounted his horse to depart, jeering at the prediction of the old priest as dreams and nonsense.

On arriving at his castle, whilst still under the influence of his passion, he spurred his horse so violently that the animal threw him, and he was so much injured by the fall that he became for a time insensible. When he came to himself the ominous words which St. Meen had spoken at the door of the church reverted to his mind. He ordered his prisoner to be set at liberty, and begged of him to return to the abbot, relate what had taken place, and entreat him to forgive the outrage. The saint at once went to the prince, and saw at a glance how serious was his case. He, however, endeavoured to cheer him; but, though he refrained from reproaching him in words, this thought forced itself upon his mind: "Hoel, the hand of God is upon you. You profaned the altar, refused mercy to the afflicted, would not hearken to my entreaties. Moved by indignation, I cited you before the tribunal of God; you laughed my words to scorn, but I fear they will prove true."

The abbot exhorted the wounded prince to repent of all his sins, heard his confession, and administered to him the last Sacraments of the Church. He died on the third day, and the people recognised in his doom the just judgment of God.

Light-houses built and maintained by the monks.

The Celtic monks were bold navigators, and, dwelling in stormy regions and on shores exposed to the fury of the wild Atlantic, they had practical knowledge of the dangers of the deep, naturally sympathised with sailors, and provided food and shelter for the crews of vessels shipwrecked along their coasts. The erection of light-houses was one of the most important services rendered by them to mariners. They built towers on the most conspicuous points, and the bright flames which from thence cast their gleam over the troubled waters during the fogs and darkness of winter were the means of saving many a gallant ship and hardy crew in times when such modern inventions as reflectors, or electric, or lime lights were not dreamt of.

The fires in these primitive light-houses were fed with wood, cut by the monks in the forests, and piled in readiness around the base of the towers. Thus, we read that the fire on the Flat Holmes, at the entrance to Cardiff, was kept up by the monks of Glastonbury at their own expense.

Tanneguy and his brethren, who lived at Relec, near Morlaix, in the days of St. Paul of Leon, having inherited a large tract of land at the entrance to the roads at Brest (Finistère), built there a monastery. The monks of St. Matthew, as Montalembert remarks, kept up a light-house for the safety of mariners in those dangerous seas opposite to that terrible strait of the bay which no man, according to the Breton saying, has ever passed without fear or grief, and which has inspired the well-known petition, " My God, help me to cross the bay, my boat is so small and the sea so great."

Light-houses in our days are erected and kept up at the expense of Governments; they are constructed on the best principles, and carefully attended to. In an age when kings and princes gave little thought to such a subject, and probably had no means at hand to carry out the system of beacons which at present exists under all civilised governments, it is impossible not to admire the forethought and devotedness of the monks, who spared no trouble in order to secure the safety of seafaring men.

As regards labour, both mental and physical, the monasteries were the greatest institutions of those days. There every one, from the abbot to the youngest novice, worked, and that according to system.

The principle of division of labour, which is a subject so often under discussion in our days, was then well understood by the monks. Professors, artisans, and workers of every kind, had their respective avocations and responsibilities.

<small>Every article necessary for life produced within the walls of the monastery</small> Every article necessary for the community was produced within the monastery. At the forge, blacksmiths manufactured spades, axes, etc.; in the field, husbandmen sowed and reaped; carpenters, bakers—in fact, every trade had its monastic representative. A great deal of time was devoted to the copying of manuscripts, printing being then unknown. The paper and skins used for this purpose were also prepared in the cloister, together with the chalices, church bells, and all that was required for divine service.

A beautiful treatise, written by a Benedictine monk, still exists which treats on the art of working in gold and silver, and also on that of painting on glass. This work may be even usefully consulted in our day.

But in no branch of industry did the monks excel more than in that of farming. They were the best agriculturists known at that time; they cleared forests, drained swamps, and astonished their contemporaries by the gigantic extent of their works.

At a period when Europe lay uncultivated, being overrun by Franks and Anglo-Saxons, who lived as the wild huntsmen in America now do, husbandry was the great lesson needful, and the people beheld with amazement these hundreds and hundreds of monks toiling from the early dawn, in the fields and forests, and saw the most barren districts becoming transformed under their hands, as though by magic, into rich cornfields, gardens, and orchards.

Thus, the country round Llancarvan and Lantwit-Major was cultivated into fertile farms during the lifetime of St. Cadoc and St. Illtyd, and St. Asaph, in North Wales, during that of St. Asaph.

St. Illtyd was the first who introduced the plough into Wales, and when a great famine desolated Brittany he was able to provide food for the starving, and seed-corn for that country from his granaries at Lantwit-Major, and nobly to supply the necessities of others, out of his own abundance.

In speaking of the monks of the middle ages as

the best architects ever known, Montalembert observes that "they combined the greatest beauty with durability." To this fact the cathedrals which they erected bear ample testimony. No buildings of the present come up to them.

In the fifth and sixth centuries monastic edifices were simple, and often consisted of wooden buildings clustering round the church as a centre. Timber was plentiful and close at hand. Settlers in Australia and America lodge after the same fashion at present.

Stone was by degrees, however, substituted for wood in Lantwit-Major; for round the present village the traveller finds many remains of ruined walls, and, at even the distance of three miles, the plough now and then comes in contact with buried masonry which once formed halls for study or workshops for labour.

CHAPTER IX.

St. Dubricius, the First Bishop of Llandaff.

"*Omnis enim pontifex ex hominibus assumptus constituitur in his quæ sunt ad Deum, ut offerat dona et sacrificia propeccatis.*"
Heb. v. 1st verse.

"For every high priest taken from among men is ordained for men in the things that appertain to God, that he may offer up gifts and sacrifices for sins."

Dubricius—in Welsh Dyffrin, or Dyfrig—is, in order of time, one of the first among the early saints of South Wales whose biography strikes the reader of ecclesiastical history. He was contemporary with St. Patrick, though somewhat younger, for the Apostle of Ireland began his missionary career about the year 432, and Dubricius his episcopal life in 446 or 447. St. Patrick's mission was to convert to the faith of Christ a pagan nation, which Palladius, an Italian monk, had in vain laboured to instruct in the truth. The work of Dubricius, on the contrary, was to preserve from the errors of Palagianism a people already Christian, to re-establish ecclesiastical discipline amongst them, and to give a new impulse to education. His career was long, and most fruitful in good works. It opened in the beginning of the fifth century, and did not close until the early part of the sixth. Bishop of Llandaff in 447, he transferred his see to Caerleon in 490, and died a centenarian at Bardsey Island, in Cardigan Bay, probably in 522.[1]

According to the "Liber Landavensis," Dubricius was born at Madley, a parish on the south side of the river Wye, in Herefordshire, seven miles south-west of Hereford. Pebian, his grandfather, surnamed Spumosus, or the frothy (in Welsh Claforawg), is said to have attempted, in a fit of passion, first to drown and then to burn the mother and her unborn son, afterwards Dubricius. However, by the intervention of Almighty God, he did not succeed in his wicked design, for mother and child were miraculously preserved.

Birth of Dubricius.

When this same boy had attained the age of manhood, and become the most eminent personage in South Wales, his grandfather remembered with bitter regret how, prompted by passion, he had stifled the very sentiments of nature whilst making this lamentable attempt.[2]

Little is known of the early life and education of Dubricius; the same may be said of the time and place of his ordination. According to Dugdale, after completing his studies he resided and taught with distinction in the neighbourhood

(1) Professor Rees. "Liber Landavensis."

(2) According to some authors he was born at Miserbdil. Migne. "Hagiographie."

of Warwick. Be this as it may, South Wales was to be the theatre of his labours, both as a scholar and as a bishop.

Whether his own inclination or circumstances prompted him to return to his native district, or whether he did so in compliance with the wishes of his grandfather and other relations, is not mentioned; but, undoubtedly, his arrival was hailed with joy by Pebian, who felt a certain pride in the public report which declared that amongst the young British clergy none excelled Dubricius in virtue and science. His grandfather placed at his disposal as much land as he should require for the service of religion.

Dubricius selected a wooded solitude near the river Wye, Herefordshire. This place was called, in the old Celtic tongue, Mochross, or the land of the swine, probably from its being the haunt of wild boars. There the servant of God built a church, which he dedicated to the Holy Trinity, as also a monastery and colleges. Scholars from all parts of the country flocked to this new seat of learning, and in a short time Dubricius found himself at the head of a seminary numbering more than a thousand students. Here he spent his life, dividing his time between teaching, praying, and preaching to the people of the district. He instructed both clergy and laity, and was the greatest luminary of that period throughout Britain, being consulted on the most important affairs of the country. Events, however, were taking place in the island which ultimately became the occasion of his leaving both his college and students.

In those days the island of Britain happened to be visited by two scourges—namely, a great political revolution in the State, and religious dissensions in the Church.

The Roman rule had ceased in Britain, and the legions had been withdrawn from the island to defend the falling empire, attacked on all sides. Pro-consuls and other imperial officials had gone home with the army, leaving the country to its own resources.

The Britons, after so many centuries of bondage, were unprepared for self-government. In the first enthusiasm of liberty they took down the Roman eagles from the public buildings, and hailed lustily the dawn of independence.

State of Britain at the time. Unfortunately, they did not possess those social and political virtues necessary for the formation of a great country. During the Roman occupation they grumbled, but obeyed the conqueror; when he had left, they refused to be governed and ruled by their own countrymen. Each chieftain declared himself independent. It is true they formed a kind of confederation, with a king at its head; but in most cases his authority was not acknowledged. They had no standing army able to protect the country against the repeated inroads of the Irish and Caledonians.

Often they had called on the Armoricans to

come to their help, and at last had invited over the Saxons who were to conquer their island. Such was the political condition of Britain in the first part of the fifth century.

At the same time the Church was disturbed by religious dissensions. If in our days every erroneous religious theory finds ready adepts in England, and that by thousands, such was not the case up to the fifth century.

Britain could *then* boast that there was no Christian community under the sun which had kept the purity of faith with greater respect; for it may be said that Pelagianism was the first heresy to strike any root in this island.

The British clergy, naturally, opposed the errors of Pelagius; but, on the evil increasing, they looked across the channel to the French Church, and implored help. The bishops of this country were aware that the French prelates were more advanced in theological dissertation than themselves, and thus they invited some bishops from Gaul to come to their assistance, and, amongst others, Germanus.

Palladius, originally a deacon in Rome, who had great influence in that city, wrote to the Pope, urging him to exercise his authority in sending Germanus to Britain, as the man best qualified by his talents and virtue to crush the spreading evil.

Pope Celestine ruled the Church at the time, and commanded Germanus and Lupus to comply with the request of the bishops of Britain. To give greater authority to the defenders of the faith, he named the Bishop of Auxerre his Vicar-Apostolic, with unlimited powers.

Such was the complicated state of Britain, civilly and religiously, when Dubricius was selected to become the first Bishop of Llandaff and Metropolitan of Cambria.

Dubricius consecrated Bishop of Llandaff by St. Germanus.   St. Germanus justly thought that nothing was better calculated to preserve purity of faith and doctrine than a good episcopate. As the proverb says, "A good bishop and a good diocese." The Abbot of Mochross was highly recommended to him, both by clergy and laity, as a man of God, well versed in divine and human knowledge, and possessing great influence throughout the country. He, accordingly, consecrated Dubricius Archbishop of Llandaff, with jurisdiction over the entire of Wales, and strongly urged him to turn his mind to the development of sound education in his diocese. After that St. Germanus bade farewell to Britain, and died shortly after in Italy.

Antiquity of Llandaff   Llandaff, with its cathedral restored, is now a neat village, close to Cardiff, but looks humble beside one of the greatest sea-ports in England. However, if we seek for its origin, we must trace it up to the introduction of Christianity into Britain.

The first church ever built in this locality was erected in the second century, during the reign of King Lucius, by one of the missionaries sent by Pope Eleutherius to that British prince. Amongst these was St. Fagan, who is still patron saint of the village, which bears his name, and who was either the first or second priest connected with the district. However, as the bishop resided at that time at Caerleon, in Monmouthshire, Llandaff was only a dependence on that see, ministered to by some missionary under the episcopal jurisdiction of Caerleon, from which place it is about twenty miles distant.

It was reserved for St. Dubricius, in the fifth century, to raise Llandaff to the dignity of an episcopal see.

The student of history is bound to acknowledge a debt of gratitude to Llandaff and its bishops, who carefully chronicled the events of their days, and thereby enable him to glean precious information as to the religion and customs of the early Christians of Wales and Britain. The "Liber Landavensis, or Book of Teilo," is an invaluable manuscript.

At the time of the Reformation, when it was held praiseworthy to destroy everything connected with the Catholic Church, piles of documents, carefully written and preserved by the faithful clergy of that ancient see, were gathered together and burnt at the close of an evening revel, for the amusement of the ministers of the new religion, their wives, and their guests. This grievous act of Vandalism afforded pleasant recreation to the partisans of the Reformation.

The erection of an episcopal see in Llandaff was looked upon as a great event, and the nomination of Dubricius as its first bishop hailed with joy along the coasts of the Bristol Channel. Nor was public feeling manifested only by empty applause, for the people came forward most generously to provide everything necessary for divine worship.

Generosity of the Cambrians of old in religious matters. In glancing through the records of the "Liber Landavensis," one is impressed with the belief that the inhabitants of Glamorgan and other counties were a noble, generous race, devoted to their bishop, and taking the deepest interest in their religion. Throughout the whole diocese grants of land were at once made to the prelate for building churches and monasteries and for parochial purposes. We trace the Catholic spirit everywhere in these deeds of gift. The laws and customs of the Church are strictly adhered to, the Welsh charters being compared with similar documents in Gaul, Spain, and Italy; such, for instance, as that made by Clovis in favour of religion; are all alike in spirit and form. This king of the Franks, after his conversion, in 491, made a concession of land for a monastery to the uncle of Lupus, the companion of Germanus in his mission to Britain. The charter runs thus:—
"Dwell in your country, in the land I give you, in the name of the Holy, Undivided, Equal and Consubstantial Trinity. . . . We grant you

this domain that you may pray to Almighty God for our preservation and that of our dear spouse and children." The Cambrians were equally generous, and framed their deeds of gift in the same style and spirit.

During the episcopacy of Dubricius[1] King Meurig summoned an assembly of the clergy, nobles, and leading people of Glamorgan, and, with their consent, ceded large tracts of land to the new bishop for the service of religion. This included the plain between the river Taff and Ely, on which a portion of the present town of Cardiff stands. A study of such documents as these, in all their details, is very interesting, and, at the same time, most edifying, for it gives us an insight into the religion of our forefathers.

King Meurig of Glamorgan

I. They are solemn, public deeds, carefully drawn up by the best intellects of the time, with that earnest simplicity peculiar to the early Church. They were invariably signed by several witnesses on the part of the clergy as well as on that of the laity, and placed upon the altar during Mass. They were regarded as most sacred transactions; for, as a general rule, a curse is pronounced on those who shall violate them, and the blessing of Almighty God invoked on all who respect their provisions.[2] In the

A few remarks on the leading characteristics of British charters.

---

(1) The longevity of Prince Meurig has somewhat puzzled chronologists. He lived under the episcopacy of three bishops, one of whom ruled his diocese for a long period. The only explanation that can be given is, that he was very young, a mere infant, when his charter to the first Bishop of Llandaff was written, and *very old* in the days of St. Oudoceus, and that the said charter to Llandaff may not have been written immediately after the consecration of St. Dubricius.

(2) "Liber Landavensis."

intention of those concerned, the agreement is to last for ever. Property given to religion is never to be used except for the service of God, and it is consecrated to Jesus Christ without any limit of time.[1]

II. The intention of the donor, as a rule, is specified in the charter; sometimes it is recorded that he wishes to atone for his past sins—as alms cover a multitude of iniquities—or to have his name inscribed in the Book of Life; or, again, it is a thank-offering for victory obtained over the enemy of his country, or in remembrance of some favour received from heaven. In some deeds the testator makes his bequest for the benefit of the souls of his father or mother deceased, or for the soul of someone he has murdered in an inexcusable encounter, or under the influence of passion.[2]

III. It is specified that such a territory is to be a place of refuge, not only for persecuted innocence, but even for great criminals. The sword is not to be used on land consecrated to Jesus Christ, nor is it to be stained with human blood. Even the cattle of any man who has sought shelter under the protection of the sanctuary cannot be molested when within its pastures. The Church is essentially pacific, and wherever she exercises immediate authority, war and its attendant evils are not allowed; for she

(1) "Liber Landavensis."
(2) "Liber Landavensis."

is the teacher of peace to all men of good-will. The poor were never forgotten; valuable privileges were secured to them by these charters, every indigent person in the diocese being allowed to fish in the rivers, cut wood in the forests, and pasture his cattle on the commons.[1]

IV. The form of donation was as follows:—
"King —— makes an offering of such or such territory to God, to St. Peter the Apostle, and to Dubricius, Bishop of Llandaff, for ever." When a bishop died his name was still mentioned in the deed of gift. Thus, in the time of Oudoceus, third Bishop of Llandaff, we read such testaments as the following:—"King Ithael, son of Morgan, and his sons . . . give to God and to St. Dubricius, St. Teilo, and Oudoceus, and all their successors in the Church of Llandaff for ever, three uncias of land" (about 324 acres).[2]

Dubricius and Teilo were then dead, and the see was governed by another bishop. The testator, notwithstanding, does not forget his deceased prelates, but appeals to their intercession in heaven. He feels that those saintly bishops who during their lifetime took such an interest in the eternal welfare of their people, will not forget them now before the throne of God in heaven. Such, amongst the Cambrians of old, was the spirit and form of donations to the Church. The "Liber Landavensis" has handed

(1) "Liber Landavensis."
(2) "Liber Landavensis."

down hundreds of them, thus transmitting to future generations unmistakable testimony of the deep religious feeling which prevailed throughout the country in former days.

In the first charter of King Meurig, which, unfortunately, is handed down to us only in fragments, we find the limits of the diocese clearly defined, and the cession to the Church of the entire district extending between the rivers Taff and Ely distinctly stated. The grant specifies exemption from service, regular or secular, and right of weirs, fisheries, etc. One condition, is, however, attached, which is that daily prayers shall be offered and ecclesiastical service performed for the soul of King Meurig, and those of his parents, of kings and princes, and all the faithful departed.

It also decrees that all donations, whether from bishops, princes, offerings of the people, or any other just source, shall be preserved faithfully and in full for perpetuity.[1]

The charter goes on to state that it shall on no account be lawful for anyone to disturb the aforesaid church, or take away any part of its possessions, or retain such as may have been taken from it, or diminish, or harass it with vexatious proceedings, and that all things, together with the boundaries of the diocese, shall be preserved intact.

Therefore, if any ecclesiastical or secular

---

(1) "Liber Landavensis."

person shall in future rashly violate these decrees, and on being admonished twice or thrice, does not amend and give due satisfaction, he shall be deprived of all dignities, powers, and honours, and liable to the Divine judgment for the crimes he has committed, and shall not be allowed to partake of the most *holy Body and Blood of the Lord our God and Redeemer, Jesus Christ*, and be subject to severe punishment at the final judgment. With respect to those who shall preserve to the Church the property justly belonging to it, "May they be blessed in this world and in the next."[1]

Promulgation of charter. On the day appointed for the promulgation of this charter, nobles, freemen, and bondsmen deemed it their duty to assist at the ceremony, and pay their respects to their chief pastor. Early on the preceding evening the country round Llandaff was transformed as if by magic into an immense camp; the hills were covered with the tents of hundreds of Welsh chieftains. From the summit of each pavilion floated the banner which indicated the name and rank of its occupant. The horses, turned loose after their long journey, grazed quietly around, and the whole scene was not unlike a huge encampment. When night fell the country was illuminated by fires kindled wherever the tents were pitched. As the multitude had assembled for a religious festival, an unusual gravity could be discerned

(1) "Liber Landavensis."

in their demeanour, and before retiring to rest all knelt down before the expiring embers, and religious hymns, sung to the accompaniment of the harp, sounded sweetly and solemnly through the gathering darkness, after which the silence of the night remained unbroken until early dawn, when all directed their steps to the church of Llandaff.

In those days religious buildings were very limited in dimension; but even had the church of Llandaff been built upon the vast scale of our modern cathedrals, it would not have afforded accommodation to the vast crowd of worshippers.

The holy Sacrifice of the Mass, therefore, was celebrated in the open air, and during the ceremony the charter of King Meurig was proclaimed aloud. When the people heard that the extensive plain extending between the Bristol Channel and the rivers Taff and Ely was the munificent gift bestowed upon the Church by King Meurig, on the condition that the Sacrifice of the Mass should be daily offered for the living and the dead, they were greatly edified. When the deed of gift had been read, a solemn procession was formed. The clergy, robed in their clerical vestments, and preceded by the cross, led the way, carrying the relics of saints; after them walked Dubricius, the new bishop, with pastoral staff in hand. Then came King Meurig, bearing the Book of the Gospels, and surrounded by his nobles. The people brought

Procession along the banks of the rivers Taff and Ely.

up the rear of the procession, which passed around the boundaries of the land conceded to the diocese of Llandaff; and as it proceeded from point to point, the limits were sprinkled with holy water, and dust collected from the pavement of the church was scattered here and there along the banks of the rivers Taff and Ely. In those days this was the form used in taking possession of a property consecrated to the Church. Finally, when the procession returned to Llandaff, a solemn curse was pronounced on any person who should violate the covenant entered upon that day, and the blessing of heaven invoked upon all who should religiously respect it.. To this the people, in accordance with a custom mentioned in other parts of the " Liber Landavensis," loudly responded " Amen," thereby testifying the strong instincts of a religious nation.

Impressive beyond description must have been this ceremony, attended as it was by the sons and daughters of Cambria, assembled together from all parts of the nation round their spiritual father. What a deeply devotional feeling filled their hearts as they generously pressed forward to help the cause of religion, and how unreservedly they consecrated to Almighty God the gifts they bestowed on His Church for ever! In keeping with its teaching, they—like Judas Maccabæus and his brethren—did not forget the dead, but enjoined that daily prayers and the daily Sacrifice of the Mass should be offered up for the living and the deceased whether rich or poor, princes or vassals, all must be held in memory within their church, as in all other Christian sanctuaries. There, also, the weak must be secure from persecution, and even the criminal find a refuge. Neither must the sword smite any child of God on ground dedicated to Him. As the Saviour of the world pardoned His bitterest enemies, His children are not to execute vengeance in or about His temple.

The faith and customs of Cambrians in those days were entirely Catholic. They dedicated their cathedral to St. Peter, the head of the Church. The bishops of the See of Llandaff recognised his successor in Rome as inheriting his primacy. Dubricius, and those who came after him, acted in accordance with the laws and customs of the universal Church in transmitting to the Pope an account of the state of their dioceses; and when, in the twelfth century, Urban, Bishop of Llandaff, found it necessary to appeal to Rome for redress against the encroachments of the Bishops of Menevia and Hereford, he could say with truth that all the Bishops of Llandaff, from the time of Dubricius to his own, had ever been devoted to the Holy See.

Work of Dubricius in South Wales.
The new bishop, when fairly settled, set at once to work in the vineyard entrusted to his care. He erected parishes throughout the whole diocese wherever they were needed. The princes

of Herefordshire, Glamorganshire, and Carmarthenshire generously met the wishes of the bishop in his zeal for the advancement of religion. The "Liber Landavensis" mentions ten or eleven grants made to Dubricius.

Pebiau, the grandfather of the archbishop, is most conspicuous amongst the donors, and the ardour of feeling which is manifested in his deeds of concession is most touching. In conceding Llan Junabü, near Herefordshire, he commences thus:—"King Pebiau, being penitent, with a humble heart, mindful of his evil deeds, and desiring to change his life for the better, gives, in exchange for the kingdom of heaven, the mansion of Junabü to Dubricius and his successors in the See of Llandaff."[1]

And again: "King Pebiau, in conformity with the Scripture which saith 'Give and it shall be given unto you,' bestowed, for the salvation of his soul and the hope of future reward, four uncias of land at Conloc, on the banks of the river Wye."[2] The reader cannot help feeling that the remembrance of his brutality to his grandson and his mother is constantly recurring to the mind of the old chieftain, and that he feels he cannot be too generous towards his intended victim, who was saved by the intervention of God, and, by divine dispensation, called to be his spiritual father and the chief prelate of his country.

(1) "Liber Landavensis."
(2) "Liber Landavensis."

The great speciality of the first Bishop of Llandaff was education, and St. Germanus, who on his visits to Britain, had strongly recommended the necessity of instilling sound principles into the minds of the growing generation, had the good fortune of placing the right man in the right place in Wales.

<small>Education the speciality of St. Dubricius.</small> Dubricius, as a bishop, does not come before us as a great orator, fascinating the people by the power of his eloquence; he is a patient organiser of a sound system of education throughout his diocese. It would be hard to point out in the whole history of Britain a bishop who met with greater success. Indeed, in the monastic colleges of his diocese, and under his eyes, grew St. Teilo, David, Daniel, Samson, and hundreds of others, who formed that brilliant generation of British saints of St. David's time.

Providence had raised up two illustrious saints —Illtyd *the Knight* and Cadoc *the Wise*—to share with him the labours and the glory of carrying with prudence and success this work of the Church in Cambria.

In Chapter VI. we called the attention of the reader to the great percentage in the Cambrian population rushing to the cloister—chieftains leaving their estates, the student in the monastic school never returning home, or, if he did, shortly after going back to the cloister. Immense monasteries existed throughout the land, in which the praises of God were chanted day and night.

THE FIRST BISHOP OF LLANDAFF. 307

All this took place in a great measure during the episcopacy of St. Dubricius, and under his spiritual guidance.

Womanhood did not remain indifferent to the religious enthusiasm of the age. Indeed, it would be a wonder to find the daughter of Eve less devout than the son of Adam. At all times the beauty of virginity has fascinated woman as much as man; nay, as a rule, more women embrace religious life than men. In our days, throughout Europe, there are more *nuns* in the convent than *religious* in the monastery. *[A great number of women enter the convent.]*

The ancient records of Britain are sparing in their details of the life led by British nuns; but this *lacune* does not destroy the fact that the cloister of those days sheltered the virgin as well as the widow.

How many of these convents throughout Britain were burnt down by the Anglo-Saxon, yet pagan, and how many of these defenceless women fell under his sword?

Indeed, in reading the history of Britain we constantly meet women of every class of society on their way to the convent. In the lifetime of the first Bishop of Llandaff the female crowd rushing to the cloister is truly amazing; in the throng we perceive the maiden, the widow, and even the married lady. Every county is represented in the cloister, which shelters the daughter of the prince, of the nobleman, and of the commoner.

At Bassaleg, near Newport, Monmouthshire, Guladys, the mother of St. Cadoc, is at the head of a convent; her two sisters, St. Keyna and Ninnoc, are both nuns.

The mother of St. Samson and his aunt entered the cloister when their respective husbands had joined the religious community of Barry Island, near Cardiff, as we have already noticed in Chapter VI. The mother of St. David ended her days in a convent, and the wife of St. Illtyd followed the example of her husband by leaving the world; and so on of many others it would be too long to mention.

We read in the "Liber Landavensis" that St. Dubricius was called upon to give the veil to a young virgin called Dulon, living in Glamorganshire.

The parting between the parents and their daughter is termed a sacrifice in the old record. There can be no doubt that when Almighty God calls to the cloister a young and dearly-beloved child, perhaps the cream of the family, the separation is a sacrifice. No matter how strong may be the faith of the parent, or how deep his conviction that his *dear one* is safe for ever from worldly trials and temptations, nature cannot remain insensible. Like Abraham, he sacrifices a second Isaac. Humanly speaking, the cloister is a grave, for it separates in this world father and mother from a beloved son or a cherished daughter.

Such ceremonies were carried out with great solemnity. St. Dubricius on the occasion was attended by the nobility of the neighbourhood. Gwerdog, the father of the young novice, gave to the convent in perpetuity, as the dowry of his daughter, four modii, or about thirty acres of land. According to the invariable rule of the Welsh Church in such transactions, the deed of gift was carefully written and signed by the clergy and laity. Amongst the latter we find the name of King Merchion. The blessing of God was called upon those who should respect the provisions contained in the charter, and the curse of heaven upon the guilty ones who should violate them. It was admitted in those days that conventual property could not be alienated, for it was consecrated to religion.[1]

Solemnity of taking the veil.

On a certain occasion a rich nobleman, called Gwyddgenew,[2] came to St. Dubricius to lay before him a tale of sorrow. His young daughter, Arganhell, was possessed by a demon. The poor girl, under power of the evil spirit, was thrown at times into the water and into the fire. She tore everything she could lay hands on. To save her from danger she was bound by strong cords, but these she often burst asunder like so many threads. The unhappy father threw himself with great humility at the feet of the bishop, and besought him, as a servant of the Lord Jesus Christ, to deliver his child from this fearful suffering.

(1) "Liber Landavensis."
(2) "Liber Landavensis."

On coming to the house, St. Dubricius knelt down and implored the Almighty, through the intercession of St. Peter, Prince of the Apostles, to grant the cure. The evil spirit at once left the maiden, who recovered her health of mind and body. Filled with gratitude to God for this great favour, she abandoned the world and consecrated herself to the religious life, in which she persevered until death.[1]

Dubricius transfers his See to Caerleon. The saintly Bishop of Llandaff, after forty-three years' residence in that locality, transferred his See to Caerleon, in 490.[2] In taking this step he was probably influenced by the wishes of his people, who suggested that Caerleon—the capital of Cambria—should again become the residence of the Metropolitan, as it had been since the time of Lucius, in the second century.

(1) Possession by the devil, as a fact, is testified by Holy Writ and history. The Gospel narrative abounds in instances of the Saviour casting out devils and delivering persons who were possessed by evil spirits. His enemies even accused Him of doing so through the power of Belsebub. When He sent forth His disciples He transmitted to them this power, and they rejoiced especially in it; for, when returning to Him to render an account of their mission, they said, "The devils even are subject to us in Thy name." Ecclesiastical history abounds in similar statements, recorded in the lives of the fathers of the Greek and Latin Churches, as also do the books of the Old Testament. This is particularly evidenced in the history of Job, where Satan is represented as appearing before the Throne of God and seeking divine permission to try the holy patriarch—first in his goods, then by domestic afflictions, and lastly in his own person, through loathsome diseases. Diabolical possession may be the result of vile and unrestrained passions. A wicked man often opens the door of his soul to the demon, courts his friendship; and when once this false guest has effected an entrance it is hard to put him out. The great enemy of mankind may even be allowed to persecute the lover of perfection. Trials of this kind are sanctioned by God to purify His servants, and thereby enable them to merit eternal rewards. The effort to withstand these attacks arouses all their heroism and fortitude. But he cannot get beyond certain boundaries. Thus, in the case of Job, the Lord assigns a limit to the devil's power. "*Serva animam ejus*"—Spare his life. In the Apocalypse Satan is represented chained like a dog, the chain being lengthened as far as it pleases God, and no further. There is a difference between *possession* and what is

(2) "Liber Landavensis" (Notes).

In a political and ecclesiastical point of view, the history of the ancient city is most interesting. It is situated on the banks of the river Usk, four miles distant from the present town of Newport. The Romanesque appearance it presented in those days, with its high walls, amphitheatre, baths, temples, and schools, forced the Britons—who compared it to Rome itself—to acknowledge the intellectual superiority of their conquerors, of whose rule in Western Britain it was the head-quarters. The Questor resided in the city, and all questions of justice and finance were transacted within its walls.

It was also the head-quarters of the Second Legion, called Augusta. This legion had been brought from Germany by Claudius in the year 43, for the protection of the Roman rule in the western part of the island, and remained for four hundred years on the river Usk. This circumstance led to the city being called *Civitas*

termed *obsession*. The latter implies *external* annoyances from the evil spirit, the former *internal*. In it the devil enters the body and takes possession of it, either wholly or partially ; whilst in obsession he acts externally. A few examples will render this more clear to the reader. We read in the "Lives of the Fathers of the Desert," and also in those of later saints, that the devil appeared to them in various shapes—sometimes as a roaring lion, or a serpent, or a dragon, to terrify them ; whilst at others the demon transformed himself into the most beautiful and seductive forms, in order to excite their carnal passions. We are even told that some of the champions of Christ were severely beaten by His sworn enemy. This, in the language of theology, is called obsession. The Gospels speak of persons being blind, or deaf and dumb, from the fact that a devil occupied the organs of sight, hearing or speech. When the evil spirit was cast out those organs were restored to their natural powers. In other cases the demon substituted the instincts of animals for those of man, and souls thus visited became tormented by all the appetites of wild beasts. Persons possessed by the devil have also at times spoken foreign languages hitherto unknown to them ; illiterate, stupid human beings have suddenly become imbued with intelligence and scientific knowledge ; and those suffering from debility have manifested superhuman physical powers. This is called possession.—*Vide Schram, Gorres.*

Legionem, or, in the Celtic tongue, Caerleon, which name it retains to the present day. Even still, in this once celebrated spot, the plough and the spade constantly bring to light Roman coins, columns, tesselated pavements, and mutilated statues of the gods of pagan Rome.

In connection with the Christian religion, Caerleon was looked upon as sacred. From the earliest period of its introduction into Britain, in the second century, the Metropolitan of Cambria resided within its walls, and the beautiful valley surrounding it could boast, perhaps, of possessing the largest Christian population in the kingdom. When the persecution under Diocletian broke out, the Forum of Caerleon became the theatre of martyrdom, where thousands of the followers of Christ shed their blood as witnesses to His faith.

That a seminary for the education of priests existed in this city we are led to infer from the "Life of Amphibolus, Martyr, and Patron of Winchester," in which it is stated that he had been professor in the college of Caerleon.

It is not unreasonable to suppose that the inhabitants should have urged Dubricius to transfer his See to the ancient metropolitan town, and that at last, yielding to their wishes, he left Llandaff and fixed his residence in the City of the Legions.

For some time he governed both Sees, but his advanced age, and the reluctance of the people of Llandaff to be deprived of a bishop, induced him, in the year 512, to consecrate St. Teilo its second episcopal pastor.

Caerleon preserved all its splendour up to the fifth century, for King Arthur selected it for his coronation, as being the finest city in Western Britain. *Coronation of King Arthur at Caerleon.*

Geoffrey of Monmouth gives a glowing account of the crowning of King Arthur at Caerleon, by the venerable Metropolitan of Wales. The festivities took place about Pentecost, that day so dear to our forefathers. The City of the Legions, with its beautiful river—which was navigable for the largest ships built in those days—its charming position, its palaces, and its churches, was decided upon by the British Confederation as the most suitable place for the consecration of the king. The Archbishops of London and York, with many other prelates, were invited. All that concerned the religious part of the ceremony was conducted by Dubricius, the Royal court being within his diocese.

At the time appointed, the prelates proceeded to the palace of the king, and conducted him to the metropolitan church of St. Aaron. Long and imposing was the procession which wound its way through the streets of Caerleon, while the solemn strains of sacred music filled the air. Clergy and laity in due order preceded the king, who was supported by two archbishops, and by four chieftains carrying golden swords, the insignia of royalty. *Coronation of King Arthur by St. Dubricius.*

The Queen's *cortege* formed a second procession. This wended its way to the Church of St. Julius, to which was attached a choir of virgins dedicated to the service of God. It, also, was accompanied by bishops. Four queens, bearing four white doves, according to ancient custom, walked before the bride of Arthur; and a crowd of women followed with every demonstration of joy.

The holy Sacrifice of the Mass was offered up, and every ceremony prescribed by the ritual of that day minutely carried out. When divine service had concluded in both churches the king and queen, relieved of their crowns, and arrayed in lighter ornaments, prepared to participate in the amusements in honour of the festivity.

The banquet took place in two separate palaces, the king sitting down with the clergy, nobles, and men of all classes; the queen with the ladies, the Britons still observing the ancient custom of Troy which enjoined that men and women should celebrate their festivals apart.

St. Dubricius and King Arthur were known to each other, notwithstanding their disparity of age. Whether the young prince had been educated in one of the colleges of the venerable prelate is not certain, but there can be no doubt that Arthur, like the other British chieftains, rejoiced in securing the presence of the archbishop in dangerous and critical events. It was a custom of the clergy, as we may infer from the history of Bangs, St. Teilo, and others, to follow their countrymen to the battle-field when the cause of combat was a national and just one, in order to rouse the courage of the soldiers and pray for them during the struggle. It was not in keeping with their mission to use the sword, but they could intercede for the warriors, and this the Britons expected.

We are told by Geoffrey of Monmouth that the Archbishop of Caerleon followed Arthur to Bath, and was present at the battle of Badon. Before the combat the soldiers were gathered together like soldiers under review, and were thus addressed by St. Dubricius:—

"You who have the honour to profess the Christian faith, keep fixed in your minds the love which you owe to your country and fellow-subjects, whose sufferings through the treachery of the pagans will be an everlasting reproach to you, if you do not courageously defend them. It is your country you fight for, and for it you should be ready, when required, voluntarily to suffer death; for that is in itself victory and salvation to the soul, because he who dies for his brethren offers himself a sacrifice to God, and has Christ for his example, who condescended to lay down His life for His brethren. If, therefore, any of you should be killed in this war, that death itself which is suffered in so glorious a cause shall be to him penance and absolution for his sins." *[Speech of St. Dubricius before the Battle of Badon.]*

The last important act of the administration of Dubricius was the convocation of a National Council of the Cambro-British Church at Brevi, in Cardiganshire.

Convokes the Council of Brevi.

The venerable Metropolitan was induced to take this step before he died in order to frame a code of religious laws for the province, and also to crush and extinguish the embers of Pelagianism, which still smouldered in the western part of Wales.

Landewi-Brevi, nine miles from Lampeter, which forms the boundary of three or four counties, was, from its geographical position, chosen as the most advantageous place for the proposed meeting.

Dubricius opened and presided over this celebrated synod, which defined the ecclesiastical laws that were to rule the Church of Cambria for centuries, up even to the time when she lost the faith. The most active part in this meeting was taken by younger bishops and priests, such as David, Teilo, and others, most of whom Dubricius had taught as children in his schools at Mochross, Lantwit-Major, and Llancarvan.

The Council of Brevi.

David was chief exponent of Catholic teaching at this Council, and Dubricius recognised in him the man who was to be his successor as Metropolitan, and felt that the government of the diocese must be entrusted to younger and more energetic bishops.

His, indeed, had been a noble and glorious

career. He was now a centenarian, and had been bishop for seventy-one years.[1] He knew that the time was come for him to resign the care of the souls of others and prepare his own for the great day of eternity. Therefore, he did not return to Caerleon on the conclusion of the Council of Brevi, but set sail for the Island of Bardsey, in the Bay of Cardigan.

Bardsey—or Enlly, as it is named in Welsh—was in olden times called the Necropolis of Wales, and it is recorded in the "Book Landavensis" that the bodies of twenty thousand confessors and martyrs were buried on its shores. It is a small tract of land, three miles and a-half in length by one and a-half in breadth, distant about three miles from the mainland. Dubricius thought that a place so lonely and distant was admirably suited for his purpose. It was beyond reach of the troubles and cares of this world, and the soul could there aspire to the highest regions of contemplation.

His stay at Bardsey was not to be for long. His reward was at hand. Two or three years after his settlement there the holy Dubricius died in the Lord on Sunday, the 14th day of November, 522.

In the year of the Incarnation of our Lord one thousand one hundred and seven (A.D. 1107), on the 11th day of August, Urban was consecrated Bishop of Llandaff, at Canterbury.

The relics of St. Dubricius removed from Bardsey Island to Llandaff.

(1) Dubricius was consecrated bishop by St. Germanus about the year 447-448, and the Council of Brevi was held A.D. 519.

This energetic prelate, having reorganised his diocese, considered it his duty to transfer the relics of St. Dubricius from the lonely island where he had died to the cathedral of which he had been the first bishop. Encouraged by the approbation of the Metropolitan of Canterbury, he obtained permission from the Bishop of Bangor, and also secured the consent of Griffith, King of North Wales, and on the 7th of May, 1120, the grave of St. Dubricius at Bardsey Island was opened, and his relics reverently placed in the vessel appointed to bear them to Llandaff, where they arrived on the 23rd of May, in the same year.

We are already acquainted with the solemnity of the brilliant procession and of the imposing ceremonies which attended the installation of Dubricius into his cathedral church in the fifth century. In the twelfth, the translation of the mortal remains of the same holy bishop was the occasion of a solemn religious function. The people came in crowds to seek the intercession of him who had been the pastor of their forefathers.

The country at that time was suffering from a prolonged drought. Although spring was far advanced, vegetation was backward. There was danger of the cattle perishing for want of grass, and the crops presented a yellow and sickly appearance, for in the district of Glamorganshire it had not rained for more than seven weeks.

THE FIRST BISHOP OF LLANDAFF.

No sooner, however, had the relics of Dubricius arrived at Llandaff than the country was blessed with abundant rain. The rivers Taff and Ely, the channels of which had been almost dry, rapidly filled, and their waters rolled in torrents to the sea. The faded and dying vegetation soon revived, and this was regarded by all as a favour obtained through the prayers of the saintly bishop.[1]

His body was placed before the altar of St. Mary, facing the north. When Urban rebuilt Llandaff Cathedral on its present magnificent scale, the relics were removed, and now lie against the south-east pillar of the sanctuary, near the high altar, as it would be called by Catholics.

His feast was formerly celebrated by his countrymen on the 14th of November.

As the Catholic faith is again being preached in South Wales, and a deanery and parish church

(1) The power possessed over the atmosphere by some saints is thus described by the Apostle St. James:—"*Elias was a man passable like unto us, and with prayer he prayed that it might not rain upon the earth, and it rained not for three years and six months. And he prayed again, and the heavens gave rain, and the earth brought forth her fruit.*" (James, chap. 5.) It is related of St. Francis Xavier, the Apostle of India, that, visiting an Eastern prince who was besieged in a town, and in great want of water, he announced, on the part of his Master, that, if the prince had faith in the divinity of Christ, he would obtain that abundant rain should be given. The potentate and St. Francis accordingly proceeded to the most elevated part of the city, there planted a cross, and prostrated before it in presence of all the people. Clouds gathered immediately over the town, and rain in plentiful showers poured down for the refreshment of men and animals. The enemy, on this, abandoning all hope of reducing the fortress, raised the siege and retired. It is recorded that a Christian legion by prayer obtained rain for a Roman army, and thus saved it from destruction. How often we read that our forefathers, in the ages of faith, ordered public processions, carrying the relics of saints, to obtain the cessation of a long drought. Very frequently their prayers were heard, and the event recorded in their archives, or commemorated either by building churches or celebrating particular festivals.

has received the name of Dubricius, we may hope that a day will dawn upon Cambria when his memory will be once more revived in the Breviary and the Missal.

The "Liber Landavensis" remarks that the British Church looked upon St. Dubricius as their chief advocate with God and the protector of all the faithful in the island when the grave had closed on his mortal remains.

Indeed, anyone who reads the register of Llandaff, containing hundreds of charters, is struck by the deep veneration of the Cambrians for the memory of their first bishop. His name is scrupulously mentioned in every deed of gift to religion.

<small>St. Dubricius venerated after death</small>

The following formula invariably strikes the reader:—"I give to Almighty God and to St. Dubricius such a territory." The people associate their first pastor in all their good works, in order to secure his intercession before the throne of God. Centuries roll on, social and political events take place, the country has to bow to the Saxon, to the Norman; but it never loses its devotion to the first Bishop of Llandaff.

It is to be regretted that ancient records have not handed down to us fuller details concerning the doings and spiritual life of this wonderful man—the model of a bishop. Chosen by Almighty God to crush the errors of Pelagius on his native shores, he succeeded in the work entrusted to him. But it is as the spiritual father of a legion of saints that Dubricius shines in the annals of Western Britain.

Before his death he had the consolation of seeing a considerable number of the pupils educated in his diocese raised to the episcopal dignity or at the head of prosperous and holy monasteries.

Almighty God at times revealed to him, through supernatural signs, the eminent sanctity which some of his pupils would attain in after life. In ordination time, he saw more than once the Holy Ghost alight on the young deacon or priest so carefully trained for his respective dignity in the Church. Even in this world heaven was thus pleased to reward the patient and skilful master.

The venerable prelate did not neglect to attend to his own spiritual welfare. At the beginning of each Lent, according to a practice often spoken of in the "Lives of the Early British Saints," he used to retire to Barry Island or Lantwit-Major, in order to examine the state of his own soul. This was the annual retreat, so dear to the Catholic Church, and now commanded as a duty to every bishop and priest all over the world.

The compiler of this biography has the honour of representing the Catholic faith in the vicinity of Llandaff, and feels a certain pride in being the first resident Catholic priest in this district since it has lost the Catholic faith. The population of

Cardiff is daily extending on the land situated between the rivers Taff and Ely, and the boundaries of the town have nearly reached the old city of Dubricius.

<small>The writer appeals to the public for help to build a Catholic Church between the rivers Taff and Ely.</small>
This same tract of land was granted, as we have seen, to the first Bishop of Llandaff for Catholic purposes.

With the exception of Glastonbury, it would be difficult to find, in the whole island of Britain, a spot more anciently connected with the Catholic faith than this.

Llandaff recalls to mind the memory of Pope Eleutherius, of St. Fagan, and of King Lucius, who, in the second century, consecrated these shores to the faith of Christ. The generosity of that prince to religion naturally presents itself as the foremost thought in reviewing those bygone days.

May Almighty God inspire nobles, merchants, and the public at large with the zeal and munificence which then actuated Meurig and Morgan, and help us to restore the worship of our forefathers on the banks of the Taff and Ely!

Fifteen hundred Catholics, mostly of the labouring class, are scattered over Canton, Grangetown, Llandaff, and Ely, and practise throughout these districts the religion of Lucius, St. Fagan, St. Dubricius, and St. Teilo.

The holy Sacrifice of the Mass is offered up in temporary buildings, such as school-houses, both in Canton and Grangetown. Such chapels are not in accordance with Catholic customs, nor do they fully answer the end proposed.

The holy altar should be enshrined in an appropriate building, and the Sacrifice of the Mass offered up in Temples worthy of the Real Presence of our Lord.

Catholic custom, wherever it can be carried out, enjoins that churches should be erected on freehold land; because a building which has been the sanctuary of the blessed Sacrament should never be used for any other purpose. It is clearly shown in charters and other documents that such was the spirit of our forefathers.

CHAPTER X.

St. Teilo, Second Bishop of Llandaff.[1]

"The memory of the wise man shall not depart away, and his name shall be in request from generation to generation. . . Nations shall declare his wisdom, and the Church shall show forth his praise."—Eccles. xxxix. 13, 14.

The "Liber Landavensis," or, as it is often termed, "The Book of Teilo," commences the life of the second Bishop of Llandaff in the following manner:—"This holy man (Teilo), dearly beloved, was from his infancy a worshipper of God; nor is it to be wondered at, for before he was born he was predestined to be His servant. . . . Therefore, he carried on his warfare by being urgent in prayer and by giving to the poor whatever he possessed, . . . reserving nothing to himself of his own, he exchanged *perishing* for *eternal* things. What a merchant he was who gave his own to God that he might receive a hundredfold! what wisdom and knowledge he possessed who distributed to others that he might be himself enriched, who

[1] This Life is compiled from the "Liber Landavensis," Lobineau, "Britannia Sancta," Rees' "Essay on the Welsh Saints."

consented to become poor in order to make others rich! In his infancy he was good, in his youth still better, advanced in age, the best of all."

One cannot help remarking whilst reading the life of St. Teilo how strong and Catholic was his faith, and that of the nation to which he belonged. Teilo had been a great traveller. When a young priest he had journeyed over a considerable *part of Europe*, on his way to Jerusalem, in company with St. David and Bishop Padarn. Driven by pestilence, with a part of his flock, into Brittany, he was everywhere received as a priest and a bishop of the Catholic Church, and welcomed as a distinguished member of the great Catholic community.

St. Teilo, in all probability, was born in Pembrokeshire, in the neighbourhood of Tenby. Ensic, or Ecnic, his father, and his mother were descended from families of great distinction in South Wales. The utmost care was bestowed on his education, and when quite a boy he was sent to the seminary of Dubricius, at Mochros, on the river Wye, in Herefordshire.

<small>Birth and early days.</small>

There is no doubt that young Teilo possessed talents of the highest order, and soon became a student of the first class at Mochros. His biographers state that when his master, Dubricius, met with passages in the holy Scripture which he had a difficulty in solving, it was his custom to summon his youthful disciple, so much did he rely on the acuteness of his mind and the extent of his learning.[1]

Dubricius considered Teilo the person most fitted to be his successor at Mochros. In this, however, he was disappointed, for the young man felt a strong attraction to the contemplative life, and accordingly left Mochros to place himself under the direction of Paulinus, at Ty-gwyn ar Taf, now Whitland, near Tenby.

The highest branches of theology were particularly attended to in that college, and this attracted such scholars as David and Teilo. It was there they contracted a friendship which, like that of Basil and Gregory Nazianzenus, lasted as long as life. Prayer, study, and manual labour filled up their time.

At this period a certain Irish chieftain, named Boya, who was an adventurer, and not averse to plunder, like many of the princes of those days, landed on the Welsh coast. He headed a large piratical party, and devastated the country, burning churches and dwellings, and putting the defenceless inhabitants to the sword.

The Cambrians were not more particular in this respect, for during the lifetime of St. Patrick a Welsh leader suddenly landed on the Irish coast and carried away a large number of young Christians to whom the bishop had just administered the Sacrament of Confirmation.

Boya, finding the country suited him, settled

(1) To this brilliancy of intellect may be traced the surname of Ἥλιος (Helios), by which he was known amongst his fellow-students.

in it, built for himself a permanent habitation, and soon became acquainted with the Monastery of Tygwyn, where Teilo and David resided. The life followed by the religious community was, as a matter of course, ridiculed by these men, whose ideal of perfection was daring courage, skilful swordsmanship, and their accompaniements of plenty of booty and pleasures; for carnal men, as St. Paul says, cannot rise above the level of concupicense.

The angelic and pure life led by Paulinus and his companions was much commented upon by the household of Boya. It was pronounced to be highly unnatural, or, at least, extraordinary for men to allow themselves no pleasure in this world, spending the day in labour and the night in prayer. During an evening revel someone suggested the idea that they were like the rest of mankind, accessible to earthly delights. Boya considered this a happy thought, and directed his wife to send her maids to tempt the virtue of the lovers of virginity. The command was obeyed with alacrity, and for several days these women hovered about the monastery, resorting to every wicked device to attract the pious monks and lead them into sin. They, however, sought protection from these snares by beseeching heaven to deliver them from their importunities.

Virtue of the servants of God put to the test.

Feigned madness was one of the plans adopted by these women to attract the notice of the community, and for this they were severely punished by being stricken with real insanity, which so terrified the household of the chieftain that they began to reflect on the impropriety of the lives they were leading, and perceive the necessity of reforming them. Boya and his family sought instruction from the religious whose virtue they had so wickedly assailed, and were baptised.

The history of the lives of the monks of Wales, and of their brethren in other parts of the world at the same period, abound in incidents bearing upon their relations with the wild beasts of the forests. Living in solitude, apart from human companionship, a friendship was often formed between the stag and the recluse. If, on the one hand, the follower of Christ respected the right of existence of these animals, they, on their side, frequently repaid his kindness by assisting him in various ways. The following legend connected with St. Teilo gives an instance of this:—

The monks and the stags. On a certain afternoon Teilo and Madoc were reading the Lamentations of the Prophet Jeremias in the court-yard of the monastery, when the cook came to inform them that wood was wanting for the preparation of the evening meal of the community, and that they must at once proceed to the neighbouring forest and carry back a supply. The students were at first somewhat vexed, because the evening was rather advanced; but, overcoming these feelings, they departed. On the road they were met by two stags, which, instead of running off, awaited their approach, as if to say, "We are ready to help you to drag the wood from the forest." The young men sang the praises of the Lord, and, harnessing the two animals to their vehicle, hastened to the forest and soon returned with a heavy load of fuel. These stags lived ever after near the monastery, like tame oxen, and willingly performed similar service whenever it was required.

Strangers visiting Ty-gwyn ar Taf—naturally moved to wonder at so unusual a circumstance—were wont to remark, "These holy men, by the power of God, render wild animals obedient to their will; we can kill them in the hunting field, but cannot bring them under subjection. When these apostles of Christ preach to us we do not hearken to their instructions; the beasts of the field listen, and show themselves in this to be our superiors."

In the narration of this legend it is impossible not to be struck with the simplicity of these peasants, which makes them *naively* confess that they were led to God not so much by the teaching of His ministers as by the example of irrational animals. The preaching of the Gospel failed to convert them, but when they beheld wild beasts yielding obedience to the monks they became convinced of the necessity of attending to the instructions of these holy men.

In a church dedicated to St. Teilo, in the

diocese of Quimper, Brittany, the saint is represented riding upon a stag. This is, no doubt, in pious allusion to the above legend of Ty-gwen, or Taf.

The early Christians of Britain had much devotion to pilgrimages, especially to Jerusalem and Rome. They allowed nothing to deter them from following this pious practice. The disciples of Paulinus, from the very nature of their sacred studies, had mentally to travel over those regions of the East sanctified by the footsteps of the Redeemer of the world. During the hours of study, they beheld in vision Jerusalem, Nazareth, Bethlehem, and the Jordan, and the same holy places formed the theme of their conversation at the time of recreation; then the much-desired privilege and happiness of visiting them, out of love and respect for our Lord, and the length and dangers of the journey, were freely discussed. Teilo, David, and Padarn came to an agreement to overcome these difficulties and accomplish their desire. At what period of life they started is not easy to ascertain, but the fact of their going to Jerusalem seems beyond doubt.

Pilgrimage to Jerusalem. But little preparation was needed. These pilgrims were not about to travel as tourists in search of amusement or distraction, or for the purpose of killing time by visiting unknown countries. They set forth as penitents and as loving disciples of the Lord Jesus, with the sole wish of adoring Him on the spots where, for them, He had shed His blood and died. A staff in the hand, a wallet on the shoulder, in which to receive the food begged along the road as Christian alms, in the name of the Redeemer whose tomb they were about to visit, constituted their luggage. One requisite—indispensable then as now—must not, however, be forgotten. This was a certificate from their abbot, Paulinus, and also one from their bishop, Dubricius, testifying that they were priests of the Catholic Church, men of pure lives, who observed the commandments of God and of His Church. Without such a certificate they could not be allowed to celebrate the holy Sacrifice of the Mass, or even approach, like simple laymen, to the rails of the sanctuary for the purpose of receiving the Body and Blood of our Lord Jesus Christ.

The Council of Arles, convened during the reign of Constantine, in 314, and several other Councils, are particular on this subject. Thus, in the seventh Article of the Council of Arles, we read that *any one of the faithful named by the civil authority* to be governor of a province, should take with him a letter from his bishop to certify that he lived in the communion of the Catholic Church.[1] The Roman Empire, so vast, necessitated the constant transfer of officers, civil and military, from one part of the world to another, and the Church considered such a

---

(1) Migne, Dict. des Conciles, Arles.

measure necessary to protect the purity of the faith. At all times she has taken the greatest care to preserve her altars from unworthy ministers, and not to bestow the Body and Blood of our Lord on laymen of whose purity of faith or morals doubts might exist.

In our days there have been instances whereof Ritualists presented themselves in Catholic churches, both in Rome and Paris, and requested permission to celebrate the holy Sacrifice of the Mass. Some of these gentlemen are so well up in Rubrics as to render detection difficult. Let them submit to the Church of God, receive the Sacrament of Ordination, and then, when duly authorised, we shall rejoice to see them approach the altar of sacrifice.

Teilo, David, and Padarn crossed Gaul and other parts of Europe, leaving behind them wherever they passed a most edifying example of sanctity.

The pilgrims sleep for three nights on the pavement of the church.

After a long, tiresome, and dangerous journey, they at last reached Jerusalem. For the first three days the pavement of the church was their only bed. They remembered, no doubt, that our Lord had spent three long hours upon the bed of the cross, suspended by three nails, and thought it not too much that they, hardy Britons that they were, should sleep for as many days on the stones which covered the holy spot.

This act of piety, manifesting as it did, a deep religious faith, produced a great impression in the holy city. It must be admitted that there were particular reasons why a Briton should be welcome in Jerusalem. A lady of their country, St. Helen, mother of the Emperor Constantine, had built the Church of the Holy Sepulchre, over the tomb of Jesus, and erected many others in several parts of the Holy Land.

On presenting to the Patriarch their papers, giving proof that they were priests from the island of Britain, educated and *bene-nati*, and, above all, true servants of God, living in a monastery, they found themselves welcome, and soon gained public veneration, and were even invited to preach.

St. Teilo appears to have been the first of the three who edified the Eastern Church by a clear and moving exposition of Catholic truth. His two companions, in like manner, seem to have been requested by the people to preach the Gospel to them.

The "Liber Landavensis" observes that the teaching of these saintly Britons of Cambria produced a deep impression. They proved to the East that the religion of their island was that of Leo the Great, the reigning Pope; of Germanus of Gaul, of St. John Chrysostom, the Cicero of the Church, and of the great African bishop, St. Augustine.[1]

---

(1) The "Liber Landavensis" remarks that the three British pilgrims received during their stay in Jerusalem the gift of tongues. We read in the second chapter of the Acts of the Apostles that the beloved disciples of our Lord received the gift of languages on the Day of Pentecost. The thousands of strangers from all parts of the world who had come to

"These men," justly observed the Patriarch of Jerusalem, and all the men of intelligence in the city concurred in this opinion, " come as pilgrims from a distant country far away towards the North Pole. They preserve the purity of the Gospel as a sacred treasure. Pelagius, their countryman, and his erroneous doctrine on grace are rejected by them, because contrary to Scripture and condemned by the Pope and by the Church. Unity of faith amongst Christians is undoubtedly a blessed sight amongst angels and men. Nothing shows to greater advantage the influence of Divine grace in gathering all the nations of the globe into one fold.

The power of God *alone* can unite in one faith *and one baptism* the children of Adam, divided by languages, customs, interests, and prejudices.

Jerusalem were greatly surprised in hearing ignorant Galileans speak the idioms of the East, of the islands in the Mediterranean, as well as Latin and Greek. Commentators tell us that St. Peter and the other apostles may have conveyed the doctrine of their divine Master in two ways—either by speaking the respective languages of the various nationalities present, or by these various nationalities being enabled by a miracle to understand the apostles in using their own idiom. *E.g.*, let us suppose St. Peter or St. Stephen to have spoken to the people in Syro-Chaldaic, yet the Cretes, the Elamites, the Arabs, and others understood them as if they had spoken their native idioms. We read of St. Vincent Ferrier, a Spaniard by birth, who, preaching in Brittany in the beginning of the fifteenth century, made use of his maternal language, and was yet understood by Moors, Arabs, Englishmen, Germans, and others, who knew only the language of their respective countries. Teilo, David, and Padarn were scholars, and according to all probabilities knew Greek, which was taught in the colleges of those days, as it is in ours. But their proficiency in that language may not have been of such a high standard as to enable them to speak in public and *extempore*. Then, it is not unreasonable to suppose that the pronunciation of Greek in Britain was different from that in the East. In our days, the best Greek scholars in England could hardly be understood in France or in Italy. If, then, the three saintly priests acquired such popularity in the East as apostolic orators, are we to disbelieve the ancient records which assert that the Holy Ghost had bestowed on them the gift of languages? Amongst the various gifts spoken of in the New Testament, for the edification of the Church, is that of languages. Could not the Holy Ghost communicate it to Teilo and his companions for the spiritual benefit of the Christians collected round the sepulchre of our Saviour, and many of whom had not the least knowledge of Greek?

The primary object of the Incarnation was nothing else but the redemption of mankind and the creation of unity of religion."

Before leaving Jerusalem, St. Teilo and his two companions were consecrated bishops. Some historians throw doubt on the fact, as being contrary to the canon law; but we find it mentioned in the three respective lives of Teilo, David, and Padarn. *(Teilo chosen to be Bishop of Llandaff)*

Perhaps the Patriarch of Jerusalem, who occupied a See of which the Redeemer had been the first pastor, and under whose walls he had shed his blood, enjoyed particular privileges, or assumed them.

On his way home, St. Teilo, passing through Brittany, stayed a while with his brother-in-law, Budic, and strongly recommended his sister to bring up her children in the fear of God. He had no idea then that Almighty God destined one of these young children to be one day his successor in the See of Llandaff, as we shall see later on.

In the preceding chapter we related how Dubricius, yielding to circumstances, had removed his See from Llandaff to Caerleon. For some time he governed both dioceses, but being now far advanced in years, and the people in Glamorganshire being anxious to possess a bishop of their own, Teilo was elected to fill that See about the year 512.

The ceremony of installation in his case was

conducted with the same pomp as attended that of Dubricius, with processions round the boundaries of the diocese, and confirmation of privileges already bestowed, a custom strictly adhered to at the accession of every prelate.

The new bishop entered at once, heart and soul, on the administration of his diocese, and carried on with activity the work of his predecessor, until it was interrupted by one of those scourges which cause more havoc in the country afflicted by it than the most merciless war. This was the yellow plague.

The Lord is the ruler of the earth; fire, hail, snow, ice, stormy winds, pestilence, and inundations execute His vengeance on guilty nations, as the prophet says.

The Plague. This yellow plague broke out first in North Wales, sparing neither man or beast. People fled from the North to the South, thereby, no doubt, disseminating the pestilence through regions yet healthy.

King Maelgwinn-gwynedd fled to Carnarvonshire, and there died of the plague in a church. Terror filled every heart. Imagination, excited still more by the bards and poets, exaggerated even the extent of the scourge. The bards represented the plague under the shape of a woman carrying destruction through the country. Her hair, teeth, and eyes—in fact, her whole person—was yellow. Like the Angel of Death in the time of Pharaoh, she passed alike through the castle of the chieftain and the humble dwelling of the poor. Whatever she touched was doomed to instantaneous death. However terrible the Saxon might be, he could be met face to face, sword in hand; but this hideous hag hovered about unseen, and extended her poisoned hands when least expected, striking her victims in their beds and in the fields. King Maelgwinn had incautiously looked at her through his windows, and forthwith was smitten. So the bards affirmed, and they were implicitly believed.

South Wales was exempted in the beginning, only to be more severely afflicted in the end.

St. Teilo spared no exertion in visiting the sick and relieving distress. He tendered hospitality to the thousands who fled from the North to the South to escape the raging epidemic. He ordered prayers to be offered, and proclaimed a fast throughout his diocese, and cried out to the Lord, saying, "Spare, oh, Lord, spare Thy people, whom Thou hast redeemed with Thy precious blood, for Thou willest not the death of a sinner. Give not Thine inheritance to perdition."

But as the plague, however, extended to the southern district, a general emigration ensued, carrying thousands to Ireland and to the western shores of France. After battling against the disaster for a long time, St. Teilo judged it advisable to emigrate, along with his clergy and people, to Brittany, and there await with patience the return of better days.

Emigration to Brittany.

The exiles, with Teilo at their head, crossed the Bristol Channel and directed their steps to Cornwall, being certain of finding on that coast a sufficient number of vessels to carry them over to the western shores of France.

The Prince of Cornwall, Gerennius, or, in Welsh, Geraint, extended generous hospitality to the afflicted Cambrians, and supplied their wants until such time as they had completed all necessary arrangements with the owners of vessels. It is evident that he did not allow terror at the thought of communicating with a plague-stricken people to influence him or impede his generosity.

Geraint confesses his sins to St. Teilo.

Gerennius and the Bishop of Llandaff soon became intimately acquainted, and before the embarkation of the holy prelate the Cornish prince, according to Catholic custom, desired to unburden his conscience to his venerable guest, and thus addressed him:—"Before thou departest, I request and desire that thou wilt receive my confession in the Lord."[1] St. Teilo complied with the wishes of the king, who seems to have had a deep conviction that his days on earth were numbered. The confessor, however, with that profound religious prevision which is the special attribute of the servants of God, bade his royal penitent be of good heart, because he had been favoured with a vision intimating that Gerennius would not leave the world until such time as he (Teilo) should return from France.

(1) "Liber Landavensis."

"I am going to Brittany," said the bishop, "and shall return to my diocese at the time appointed by the Almighty. King, thou shalt not die before thou hast received from my own hands the body and blood of the Lord consecrated by me in the holy Sacrifice of the Mass."

These words of the prelate were verified, as we shall see later.

On landing in Brittany, St. Teilo was everywhere met by his own countrymen. The wife of Budoc, Count of Cornouailles, was his sister, Samson, Bishop of Dôl, had been his fellow-student and intimate friend. Most of the dioceses around him were, or had been, governed by bishops from his native land, and the inhabitants in general were descended from British blood.

St. Teilo first visited the husband of his sister, and secured a settlement in his territory for many of his companions. This done, he repaired to Dôl, in order to follow the monastic rule with the brethren of St. Samson. His sister could not persuade him to remain in Cornouailles. It was more congenial to the habits of his life to dwell in a monastery than to share the hospitality of earthly princes in a castle.

Prayer, manual labour, and, when necessary, the exercise of episcopal duties, filled up the period of his absence from Cambria. He was long remembered in the neighbourhood of Dôl as an indefatigable and skilful agriculturist. He himself worked with axe and spade in clearing

Occupation of St. Teilo in Armorica.

forest land and preparing the soil for the production of a rich harvest. Montalembert states that the Bishop of Llandaff, aided by Samson, planted with his own hands an immense orchard, or, as the legend terms it, "a true forest of fruit trees," three miles in extent. To him also is attributed the introduction of the apple into Armorica, where cider still continues to be the national beverage. This orchard existed in the twelfth century, under the name of *Arboretum Teliavi et Samsonis*.

Connected with the same plantation is the fountain of Cai. Popular tradition attributes this spring to the prayers of St. Teilo. Seafaring men for centuries regarded it as a duty to keep this sacred well in repair, and clear away from around it any over-growth of vegetation, and when starting for a voyage it was their custom to invoke St. Teilo for a prosperous journey and favourable winds.

From time to time the Bishop of Llandaff found it necessary to lay aside his agricultural dress and avocations, and assume the crosier and the mitre. St. Samson was often called away on important business by the Frank kings, or summoned to assist at councils of the Church. The Bishop of Llandaff fulfilled the duties of the episcopate during his absence, and this led some historians to state that he had been a bishop in Brittany.

Meanwhile, the yellow plague by degrees

disappeared from Wales, and progressive improvement was constantly reported. This cheered the exiled Cambrians with the prospect of a speedy return to their native shores. When the bishop thought this could be done with safety, he sent messengers throughout France to gather together his dispersed countrymen. This was not a very easy task, for they were scattered all over Gaul. Some of them had even crossed the Alps and settled in Italy.

At this period of his life he left Dôl, and fixed his abode on the sea-shore, at a convenient port. There he established his head-quarters, hastening the preparations for crossing the sea, and providing food and shelter for his brethren in exile as they arrived from day to day. *[Teilo returns to Britain.]*

The formation of this camp and the collecting of a fleet of vessels announced to the Armoricans that Teilo was about to depart from their shores. That exiles should return to their native land appeared to them to be natural enough, but they were unwilling to lose the holy bishop. His sanctity and gift of miracles had endeared him to them, and measures were taken to retain him in Brittany, if possible. Samson, the archbishop, and Budic, the brother-in-law of Teilo, were commissioned to endeavour to prevail on him to remain amongst them. St. Teilo, without giving any formal promise, delayed his departure, and returned for a time to Dôl. But he still continued his preparations for leading back his countrymen into Wales.

Meanwhile, when in prayer one day, an angel appeared to him and recalled to his mind the promise he had made to the Cornish prince, seven years before. "Teilo," said the Divine messenger, "seven years have elapsed since, in the name of the Redeemer, thou didst promise Geraint that he should not die until he had received from thy hands the body and blood of the Lord, consecrated by thee in the holy Sacrifice of the Mass. Geraint lies now upon his death-bed, and expects thee to fulfil thy promise. Hasten, therefore, thy return, and delay not."

The bishop, having communicated this vision to St. Samson, at once departed from Brittany. After his embarkation he met at sea a vessel which had been despatched by the Cornish prince with a message urging him, in the name of God, to come to him with the greatest speed possible. When St. Teilo landed on the coast of Cornwall he repaired at once to the dying chieftain, whom he found in the last extremity. On the following morning he celebrated the holy Sacrifice of the Mass, and administered with his own hands the body and blood of the Lord Jesus Christ to King Geraint. Thus the truth of the two visions were realised, and Teilo faithfully kept his promise to a prince who had so generously extended hospitality to a plague-stricken people whom others would have shunned from fear of the infection spreading through their own country.

St. Teilo, on arriving at his diocese, found the country in a frightful condition—in fact, it was one vast desert, through which the traveller could walk for days and scarcely meet a single human being. Castles and villages were deserted, and the silence of death reigned over the land. Many parishes were without priest or inhabitants; an undergrowth of wood had sprung up on the roads to the very doors of the churches. For seven years these sacred buildings had never sheltered a Christian worshipper, nor had the prayers of the afflicted been heard around their altars. They were in a dilapidated condition; the cemeteries around them were crowded with the remains of the thousands who had been carried away by the plague, and luxuriant plants bloomed above their graves. It was a great work of restoration which awaited the sorrowing bishop; but, like Zorobabel, he at once commenced to rebuild the ruined walls. Several priests had accompanied him from Brittany. These he dispersed throughout the country to serve in places where the population had been spared, or had returned to their homes at an earlier period.

Amongst these priests were three of his nephews—Ismail, Tify, and Oudoceus. The reappearance of the bishop restored confidence throughout the diocese, and brought back the emigrant Cambrians to their native shores, and in a few years scarcely any vestiges of the terrible plague could be traced. Tradition, however, stamped its memory on the district for ages. Bards made it the theme of verses, which were chanted by the itinerant poets who exercised their art at the doors of the churches after Mass on Sundays, at fairs, at the firesides alike of nobles in their castles and peasants in their huts during the long nights of winter. When surviving witnesses described the harrowing scenes in the fervid and poetic idiom of the Celtic tongue, their hearers trembled and almost fancied they beheld the horrid hag still stretching her poisoned hand over man and beast.

The archbishop soon reorganised Divine worship throughout the country, and the princes, with their usual generosity to religion, nobly helped him in the glorious work. The register of Llandaff has handed down to us in full detail the account of seven or eight large concessions made to churches during the life of the second bishop of that See. King Iddon is mentioned as one of the principal donors. Many a hard battle had he fought against the Saxons, who now and then showed themselves along the banks of the river Wye, ready to cross at any part left undefended.

At one time, when St. Teilo happened to be at Llanarth, near Abergavenny, this king, encamped in the neighbourhood, came to him there and requested him to pray that he and his army might be preserved in safety, because he was on the eve of an engagement with the Saxons, who mustered strong in the neighbourhood. St. Teilo accompanied the prince to the scene of action, ascended a mountain seven miles from Monmouth, and *there*, like Moses, extending his hands to heaven, he besought the Almighty to grant victory to his countrymen, who were fighting for their homes, their wives, and their children.

Iddon gained a complete victory, routed his enemies, and carried off from them a great quantity of plunder. The Welsh chieftain, as a thanksoffering to God, granted about twenty-seven acres of the land surrounding the hill where the bishop had knelt in prayer during the battle to the church of Llandaff. This prince held the dead in great consideration, for in this and other deeds we find that he bestows his gifts on religion and on St. Teilo, for his own soul and the souls of his ancestors. These grants include the spots where some of his intimate friends were buried.[1]

God is wonderful in his saints, and is pleased to reveal His power through their instrumentality. If faith is able even to remove mountains, how must the devils tremble before a true servant of God. Whatever public opinion may now-a-days put forward on the subject of

The power of miracles

---

(1) "Liber Landavensis."

miracles, an historian would fail in his duty if he withheld the statement of facts recorded and and believed by our forefathers.

The reputation of St. Teilo's gift of miracles was general throughout both Wales and Brittany. People used to take their infirm friends and relatives to the holy bishop that through the imposition of his hands they might be restored to health. When in the county of Caermarthen, he is said to have raised a person named Distinni from the dead.

On a certain Sunday, when the saint was in the church of Radh, in Pembrokeshire, a man was brought to him who had for a long period been afflicted by palsy. The bishop, in the presence of a large assemblage of people, prayed to the Lord Jesus to have mercy on the sufferer. Then, extending his hands over the head of the patient, the man was at once restored to the use of his limbs.

Nor was the Almighty slow in making severe examples of those who persecuted his servant. It is related that a woman having grievously insulted him, died suddenly in presence of the people.

A chieftain named Gowaeddan, who committed acts of violence and desecration in the church of Llandeilo Fawr, was ignominiously struck down in its very cemetery.

<small>Death and burial of St. Teilo.</small> St. Teilo, full of merit before God and man, died in Caermarthenshire, on the river Towy, at a

place which even to this day bears his name, being called Llandeilo Fawr.[1]

St. Dubricius, his predecessor, was, as we have seen, a centenarian at the time of his death. It is probable that St. Teilo attained a still more advanced age. We find him a student at Mochros, on the river Wye, when St. Dubricius was at the head of that seminary, in 447 or 448. St. Teilo was then at least ten years old. He gave up his soul to his Maker in 563 or 566, and this leads to the conclusion that he had then reached the venerable age of one hundred and twenty or one hundred and twenty-three years. It is a remarkable fact that the early monks, both of the East and of the West, were very long-lived. Those who gratify the fanciful desires of the body hurry it to the grave much more rapidly than spiritual persons, who, by mortification and regularity of life, keep its unruly appetites in subjection. Self-indulgence causes a greater number of deaths than does the sword in a field of battle.

St. Paul, the first hermit, spent ninety years in a cavern, during twenty of which he lived on dates, and forty on a loaf which was brought to him every day by a raven; his only drink was water from a neighbouring spring. Yet he lived to the age of one hundred and thirteen.

His contemporary, St. Anthony, who led a similar life of austerity in the desert, was one

(1) "Liber Landavensis."

hundred and five at the time of his death. St. Patrick was also an old man, according to our present ideas of longevity. He was more than sixty when he commenced the work of converting the Irish. His travels, labours, and long nights of prayer are well known; yet he reached the age of ninety-two. St. Remigius, Bishop of Rheims, ruled that See seventy or seventy-one years.

Immediately upon the death of St. Teilo a dispute arose as to his place of burial. The honour of possessing his remains was claimed by three churches. Such altercations were by no means rare over the coffins of the early saints. The people of Pennalan, Penaby, near Tenby, Pembrokeshire, asserted their right, on the ground that the ancestors of Teilo had for generations been interred in their church, and that it was right his bones should await the final resurrection beside those of his relatives. The parish of Llandeilo Fawr claimed his relics because this place was a favourite residence with him. In his old age he had selected it in a particular way as a retreat wherein to prepare his soul for heaven, and it was at Llandeilo he had expired.

The inhabitants of Llandaff came forward in their turn, and urged the principle that a bishop ought to be buried in his cathedral. The church of Llandaff was the first in dignity and in privilege in Wales, and therefore it was fitting that the saintly prelate should rest within its walls, before the altar whereon he had so often offered the holy Sacrifice of the Mass.

After much altercation this claim was allowed, and the mortal remains of St. Teilo were solemnly borne to Llandaff and entombed within the church. They now lie close to the second pillar, on the south-west of the sanctuary, at the Epistle side.

· The "Liber Landavensis" remarks that for centuries it was the custom of the Welsh people to flock to the tomb of their holy bishop to be cured of their infirmities. The blind and the deaf and dumb approached his grave with faith and often came away benefited both in body and soul.

To this day the visitor to Llandaff will be shown the fountain of Teilo by any person of whom he may inquire.

The feast of the second Bishop of Llandaff was celebrated on the ninth of February in Britain, and on the twenty-ninth of November at Dôl, in the diocese of Quimper, Finistere,

In years gone by, Wales bestowed the name of Teilo on several localities along the Bristol Channel. In Brittany, also, Churches and towns have been called after and dedicated to this saintly prelate.

The parish of Landelo, in the diocese of Quimper, is under his patronage.

As far as can be gleaned from history, this is

the substance of the life of the second Bishop of Llandaff, the antique Register of whose cathedral is often called the "Book of Teilo," probably because he understood the necessity of compiling a record of the events connected with his diocese, and thus originated that precious collection which was continued by his successors up to the time of Pope Urban, in the twelfth century.

His countrymen never failed to specify his name in their charters, as follows:—" I give to Almighty God, to Dubricius, and to Teilo," so many acres of land. This is an evident proof that, in their estimation, he was a saint in heaven —a powerful intercessor before the throne of God.

CHAPTER XI.

ST. OUDOCEUS, THIRD BISHOP OF LLANDAFF.

"I am the Good Shepherd; the Good Shepherd giveth his life for his sheep, but the hireling and he that is not the shepherd whose own the sheep are not, seeth the wolf coming and leaveth the sheep and flieth, and the wolf catcheth and scattereth the sheep."—JOHN, x. 11, 12.

IN the fifth century, a prince of Cornouailles (Kerne), Brittany, was driven from his country, and, with his followers, settled in the district of Dyfed, on the western coast of South Wales. During his exile he married a Welsh princess, named Ananmed (Anne). She was a sister of St. Teilo, second Bishop of Llandaff. Ismael, one of the sons of this marriage, is believed to have succeeded St. David in the See of Menevia. Another son, called Tyfy, after embracing a religious life died a martyr, and was buried at Penaby, in the county of Pembroke, not far from the present watering-place of Tenby.

After an exile of about twenty years, Budic was recalled to his native land by the unanimous voice of his countrymen. His brother having died, the people looked upon him as the rightful heir to the throne. The prince, after collecting a fleet, left Cambria about the year 490, and, having driven away a horde of barbarians from Nantes, which they had made their stronghold, ruled over the western coasts of France as its undisputed king. Ananmed accompanied her husband to Gaul, and gave birth to Oudoceus immediately after landing in Armorica.

Adversity is a good teacher, creates within the heart a deep sense of the vanity of this world, and leads men to aim at objects above the reach of human inconsistency and caprice. Oudoceus, like his brothers, had been consecrated to God before his birth by his parents, who earnestly hoped that he would, like them, devote his life to the service of religion. Of his early youth little is known beyond the fact of his receiving a classical education, and entering holy orders.

When, after a sojourn of seven years in Brittany, St. Teilo returned to Llandaff, he brought with him several priests to fill up the vacancies which the yellow pestilence had made in the ranks of the Welsh clergy. The bishop appealed to the zeal and piety of the priests of Brittany. Amongst those who generously offered their services were three sons of King Budic, the brother-in-law of Teilo, namely, Ismael, Tyfy, and Oudoceus.

Election of Oudoceus.

Oudoceus, who was the youngest of the three brothers, must have won the esteem of the Cambrians by his zeal, kindness, and talents;

for, on the death of St. Teilo, when, according to the custom of the Catholic Church in those days, the leading men of the diocese, both clergy and laity, assembled to elect a new pastor, Oudoceus was selected to fill the vacant See. The abbots of Lantwit-Major, of Docunni, and of Cadmell, King Meurig, and many other princes whose names are mentioned in the "Liber Landavensis," decided on proposing the youngest nephew of the deceased prelate as his successor, and Oudoceus was, in consequence, consecrated Bishop of Llandaff.[1]

His installation, like those of the two first bishops, Dubricius and Teilo, was the occasion of a solemn ceremony, such as has been already described. King Meurig, with his Queen, Onbrawst, their two sons, the abbots of the three large monasteries, the princes of the kingdom, and all the clergy were present. After the celebration of the holy Sacrifice of the Mass, all the privileges and donations granted to St. Dubricius and St. Teilo were again publicly confirmed and signed on both sides; the usual procession passed round the boundaries of the church property between the rivers Taff and Ely, the cross being borne in front, and after it the relics of the saints; then came the new bishop, and following him walked the king, carrying the four Gospels. As on former occasions, the dust of the church was scattered here

---

(1) "Liber Landavensis."

and there, and the boundaries sprinkled with holy water.[1]

The third Bishop of Llandaff was much advanced in life when called upon to undertake the direction of the diocese. Born in 490, he was raised to the episcopal dignity in 565 or 566, and was at that time about seventy years of age.[2] His life as a bishop, though short, was by no means untroubled, the period of his administration being marked by much greater disturbances than had beset his predecessors. Disputes, murders of the most cruel description, and violations of solemn treaties, both in civil and religious matters, seem to have been of frequent occurrence. But the venerable prelate proved equal to all emergencies. Though of a mild and kindly nature, he became like a lion when the interests of God or justice and charity to his flock demanded it. He may be called the Ambrose or Gregory of the Church of Llandaff, for, like those saints, he mounted guard as a valiant soldier on the ramparts of the sanctuary, and withstood the tyranny and misdeeds of kings and princes. Energetic and undaunted, he at the same time possessed remarkable prudence and great knowledge of human weakness, for which he made all due allowance.

During his episcopacy several councils were held in the diocese of Llandaff. The occasions of

---

(1) "Liber Landavensis."

(2) "Liber Landavensis," p. 625.

these councils, the persons by whom they were attended, and the manner of proceeding in such matters, are most interesting to the student of history, inasmuch as they afford considerable insight into the moral, intellectual, and social condition of Cambria.

After the departure of the Proconsuls and their legions the political constitution of Britain underwent a great change, and its unity of administration was lost. The country became divided and sub-divided into small, petty states, governed by chieftains independent of each other. *State of Britain after the departure of the Romans.*

It is true that a certain confederation existed, with a king at its head, but his power was more nominal than real—a fact which rendered the conquest of the island by the Anglo-Saxons a comparatively easy task.

At this period the Britons were all Christians, though many of them were very indifferent practisers of the precepts of their faith. Montalembert's description of the Merovingian princes and of the Franks of that day would admirably suit the British chieftains and their people.

The Welsh princes, like those of Gaul, interfered very little in spiritual affairs. In this they were unlike their compeers of the East, who considered themselves better theologians than their bishops and clergy. The Cambrians respected their pastors, and, as a rule, did not seek unduly to influence their election. Princes, however, who made external profession of the Catholic faith frequently, without scruple, violated all its precepts, and even the simplest laws of Christianity. After prostrating before the tomb of some martyr and giving a grant of land to religion, they are often to be found exhibiting all the instincts of a savage nature, perpetrating acts of cold-blooded cruelty and treachery of the most revolting character; then they pass with incomprehensible rapidity to passionate demonstrations of contrition. This is, unfortunately, illustrated by the sad events which took place under the episcopacy of Oudoceus. The historical facts are as follow:—

The three murderers and the bishop. King Meurig, the benefactor of two bishops, Dubricius and Teilo, in the latter part of his life allowed himself to become entangled in quarrels with Cynfeddew, which ended in the murder of the latter.

Later on his grandson, Morgan, killed his uncle Frioc.

Two brothers contended for the sovereignty, and after a long dispute one of them took away the life of the other.

The third Bishop of Llandaff met all these sad cases with firmness, but also prudence. He did not act under the spur of the moment, but with all the dignity and calmness of a bishop, following the wise regulations of the Canon Law in such circumstances. He invariably exerted himself by kindness and persuasion to prevent the evil, but when he failed to bring about any good result, he did not shrink from the painful duty of exercising a stern severity.

Excommunication is the highest ecclesiastical penalty the church can inflict. Unlike the civil power, she has no standing army, or large staff of police to enforce the execution of her decrees, or punish their violation. She is a spiritual power, and visits with spiritual punishment those *within her fold* who rebel against her laws. A public sinner who, after being duly warned, persists in an evil course, is by her cut off from the communion of the Church, and not allowed to receive her Sacraments until such time as he amends his ways and gives satisfaction.[1]

<small>Measures taken by Oudoceus before pronouncing sentence of excommunication.</small>

When it came to the knowledge of the holy Bishop Oudoceus that serious dissensions, entailing loss of life, existed within his diocese, he, like a good shepherd, at once set to work to restore peace and effect reconciliations. The Welsh Princes, although quarrelsome, and revengeful, were not destitute of religion, and the voice of a Bishop or Abbot possessed more influence over them than that of a potentate at the head of a powerful army. In fact the people look upon their bishop as the natural umpire in such cases.

<small>(1) Theology defines a censure : *Pœna spiritualis et Medicinalis quâ homo Baptibatus delinquens et contumax, quorumdam Bonorum spiritualium usu privatur* (Gury). A censure is a spiritual penalty, which deprives a guilty and contumacious christian of certain spiritual benefits, according to the kind of the censure. The adjective, *Medicinalis*, implies that the punishment is intended as a correction to bring back the prevaricator to the observance of the law. As a rule the delinquent must be guilty o contumacy, for such is the spirit of the legislator. Hence in the charters of Llandaff, when mention is made of excommunication, we often read :—
After being admonished *twice* or *thrice*.</small>

Oudoceus appealed to their Christian feeling, and in the name of religion persuaded them to present themselves in the church and approach the altar, sheltering the body and blood of our Redeemer. The invitation of their chief pastor was law to these simple but irascible chieftains, and was seldom disobeyed. A day was appointed for meeting in the church, in presence of the leading men, both clergy and laity. The relics of the saints were placed upon the altar, together with the Book of the Gospel, and after prayer to Almighty God, the giver of good counsel and the subduer of hearts, the bishop addressed to those at variance an exhortation to live hereafter in peace and brotherly love. He reminded them that the commandments of God and of the Church forbade useless strife in which the lives of thousands were often sacrificed, and spoke of the law which prohibits the shedding of blood. He said that though a Prince carried a sword he should only use it to protect the innocent and maintain justice, but should never turn it into an instrument of revenge for exaggerated wrongs or private anger. A ruler should be the first to set a good example to his subjects by abstaining from useless wars.

The adverse Princes, in presence of the clergy and principal chieftain, approached the altar, placed their hands on the Book of the Gospel, and swore in the most solemn manner that for the future they would live together in peace

and brotherly love, like childrs peacefully with
Redeemer, that they would disbandich, Meurig,
and resign all further attempts on ear and fair
lives.   urdered
   In the case of King Meurig and Cynfeu
this ceremony of reconciliation took place in the
Cathedral of Llandaff. Morgan and his uncle,
Frioc, took the same solemn oath before the altar
of Lantwit-Major,² Glamorganshire.
   Such were the measures adopted by St.
Oudoceus to bring about reconciliations between
contending chieftains by appealing to their
noblest feelings, that of religion, and it was at
the foot of the altar that he despoiled them of
their swords.
   These transactions, semi-religious and semi-
civil, were looked upon by the Welsh as most
sacred in their nature, and witnessed as they
were by the leading members of the clergy and
the laity, stood in the eyes of the nation as legal
agreements, which could not be violated without
exposing the transgressor to be dealt with as
enemies to their God and to their country, hence
a murder after such solemn promises rendered a
chieftain unworthy to rule over his countrymen.
   When Wales was still Catholic, deep was the
veneration of her people for the sacred temple
which enshrined the blessed Sacrament. The
altar was to them the Holy of Holies, never to

(1) "Liber Landavensis," p. 390.
(2) "Liber Landavensis," p. 395.

Oudoceus appeared with fear and trembling, and in the navy where justice was dispensed was present the worthy of respect, but the Church and the altar were looked upon as the places most to be venerated on earth.

Howel Dda, the Justinian of Wales, retained in his code the old Cambrian respect for the Church and Altar, as we have seen in a preceding chapter.[1]

Some of the Welsh Princes, however, were not sufficiently masters over their passions, or proof against surrounding influences. Notwithstanding their solemn vows, they at times broke their promise. King Meurig was the first to violate his word, by murdering Cynfeddew.

This aroused the indignation of St. Oudoceus, and the whole country joined with him in reprobating such terrible crimes. A council was convoked in both instances, the clergy of the diocese and the leading men of the State being summoned to attend.

The charges against the chieftain were of the gravest nature. At the foot of the altar, and in the presence of his Redeemer, with his hands upon his gospel, he had called upon Him, and upon his assembled countrymen, to witness the solemn promise to respect the life of his adversary.

The unfortunate victim, relying on the security of the most sacred oaths, had not entertained the least suspicion of danger, but had disbanded his

---

(1) *Vide* Chapter III., "The Welsh and the Holy Eucharist."

soldiers, who occupied themselves peacefully with husbandry. Notwithstanding which, Meurig, forgetful of every principle of honour and fair dealing, had suddenly rushed upon and murdered him.

Had this attack taken place in open war, the council might have found extenuating circumstances, but as the case stood nothing could be urged in mitigation of this act of treachery and cunning, the victim of which had respected his oaths, while the guilty Prince had held nothing sacred.

Meurig was, therefore, solemnly excommunicated, and the same penalty extended to all who should in any way abet him. Their churches were ordered to be closed, the bells taken down and laid upon the pavement, and the relics and crosses removed from the altars.

In cases of such grievous crimes we often find it recorded that the whole assembly hurled such curses as the following on the delinquents:—
"*May their days be few, may their children become orphans, and their wives widows.*"

For more than two years King Meurig[1] disregarded the excommunication pronounced against him at Llandaff. Princes have, at all times, been surrounded by courtiers, who seek to advance their own interests by flattering and inflaming the worst passions of their sovereigns. Persons of this class represented to Meurig that

Resistance of Meurig.

(1) "Liber Landavensis," p. 390.

he was a powerful Prince, master of his own kingdom, and had little to fear from the curses of an old bishop. In order to assuage his irritation at the public verdict, they resorted to the means ordinarily adopted under such circumstances, namely — those of amusing the King and occupying his mind by feasts and pleasure parties arranged on a large scale. These, after a time, failed in producing the desired result. Meurig became gloomy. The spectre of Cynfeddew, covered with blood, seemed to arise before him at every festive scene. Besides which, he could not help remarking that Glamorganshire was no longer the same. Now, as he passed through the country, he no longer met a cheerful population rejoicing to meet their Prince. He was everywhere received in silence, but this very silence seemed to say, "There goes King Meurig, once so good and so beloved—now a murderer, cursed by the bishop, and an enemy to God."

His home was overshadowed by the same ban. His chaplain could not celebrate the holy Sacrifice of the Mass, and the people throughout the country were becoming clamorous at the long privation of all religious ministrations they were compelled to endure on account of the sacrilegious and impenitent murderer who ruled over them.

His own family was a cause of bitter reproach to the unhappy man. Many of them, by their saintly lives, had a right to remonstrate against the course he was pursuing. As we have already seen, the house of Meurig had given several of its most illustrious members to the service of religion. His father had retired from the world to lead the life of a hermit; his grandson, Samson, was a religious at Lantwit-Major and at Barry Island. His two daughters and their husbands had parted from each other for the purpose of practising the Evangelical counsels. He could not repel the reflection which constantly arose in his mind, that it was befitting a man whose family could boast of so many saints, to cease from being a scandal to the Church and the country. After struggling against the merciful inspirations of God for two years, his soul became keenly alive to the sense of his guilt, and lifting up his voice, like David, he wept with deep contrition. He threw himself at the feet of Oudoceus, acknowledged his sins, and declared himself ready to submit to any penance which might be imposed upon him, provided he might again be restored to the communion of the Church.

The bishop decided on the reconciliation taking place in public, and summoned the abbots of the three principal monasteries, Lantwit, Lancarvan, and Docunni, together with many other persons of note, to assemble in the cathedral of Llandaff.[1] *His repentance*

Meurig, kneeling before the altar, confessed his guilt, and acknowledged the additional sin of pride which had so long prevented him from

(1) "Liber Landavensis," p. 390.

submitting to the laws of the Church, and professed himself ready to perform any satisfaction that might be required of him.

After receiving the King's promise to amend his life, the bishop imposed upon him penance in the form of prayer, fasting, and alms. As he had launched an unprepared soul into eternity, he must now offer prayers, fasts, and alms in its behalf.

Meurig complied with these injunctions, for we read in the "Liber Landavensis" that he gave four villages for religious purposes, to benefit his own soul *and the soul of Cynfeddew*, whom he had murdered.[1]

The spot on which the unfortunate victim had fallen under the sword was consecrated to God, as was also the place where the King's son had committed a sin.

When the Bishop of Llandaff had settled everything connected with the sad crime of Meurig, tranquillity reigned in Glamorganshire, until it was again disturbed by the son and grandson of the same Prince.

King Morgan. Frioc and Morgan quarrelled. The cause of dissension between uncle and nephew is not clearly indicated. Some daughter of Eve seems to have been at the bottom of it. St. Oudoceus again endeavoured to re-establish peace and avert bloodshed. The contending parties presented themselves before the altar in the Church of

---

(1) "Liber Landavensis," p. 391.

Lantwit-Major, and there in the most solemn manner in the presence of God, of the bishop, and of the nobility, promised to live for the future in peace with each other. On this occasion the council, in consequence of previous experience, warned the relatives now publicly reconciled, that in case either committed perjury and murdered the other, the guilty person should not be allowed, on any plea, to redeem himself *either with land or money*, but should resign his dominion, and pass the entire remainder of his life in pilgrimages.

Morgan, unfortunately, yielded to temptation, and killed his uncle; but he did not show the same obstinacy as his grandfather in resisting authority. He hurried at once to Oudoceus, at Llandaff, and sought pardon for his two-fold sins of perjury and murder. The council of the nation was again convened,[1] and Morgan came in person, accompanied by the nobles of Glamorgan, to await its decision in his regard. The agreement which had been decided upon at Lantwit-Major left, however, no liberty of action to the council. It was of necessity bound to condemn the guilty prince to resign his kingdom, and start as a pilgrim, staff in hand, for a foreign land, there to weep over his sins. Several members of the council, however, represented that if this sentence was carried out, Glamorganshire would be left

(1) " Liber Landavensis," p. 395·

without a ruler, and deprived of its natural protector. The Saxons were at their door, and the country would be exposed to their inroads more than ever.

This consideration had great weight with Oudoceus, and it was unanimously agreed that, under such circumstances, Morgan, although guilty, should still retain his authority and reign over the Principality, after having performed the same penance that had been imposed upon his grandfather, Meurig. This resolution having been adopted and communicated to the king, Morgan, in the presence of the nobles of Glamorganshire, approached Oudoceus. The bishop stood before the altar, holding the four Gospels; the king knelt, and, placing his guilty hand upon the sacred volume, promised, with tears in his eyes, that he would do penance for his sins, and never again commit such crimes. He also swore to rule his people with clemency and justice. As it was probable that he had many a time violated the monastic rights and the sacredness of refuge, he most solemnly pledged himself to respect for the future all the privileges of the saintly abodes of St. Cadoc, of Iltyd, and of Docunni which had been conferred upon them in the days of St. Dubricius and St. Teilo.

All these transactions were committed to writing, according to the invariable custom observed by Welsh assemblies, and the proceedings were terminated with the usual blessing and curse.

The Iolo MSS. speaks in very high terms of this Morgan. He gave his own name to the district he governed; was good, valiant, merciful, and courteous, and established wise and just laws for the welfare of his dominions. One of his enactments was that no one should kill an enemy unless he could not conquer him otherwise, and it was ordained that whoever took the life of an enemy, unless no other alternative remained, should thereby forfeit his military immunities and right of refuge. Another ordinance of this code enjoined the appointment of twelve wise men to determine the just settlement of all claims, the King being at their head as supreme counsellor.

This act was called the apostolic law, because it is thus that Christ and his twelve apostles judge the world.

When young, Morgan was of a wild and impetuous disposition, but subsequently repenting, and amending his errors, he became one of the best Kings that ever lived.

Gwaednerth, who killed his brother Merchion, was treated with greater severity than Morgan. He remained under excommunication for three years, and when he applied for absolution was sent on pilgrimage into Brittany for a year. The church of Armorica took compassion on the penitent exile, and granted him sealed letters of remission, on which he returned to Wales; but Oudoceus would not release him from the excommunication, because he had not completed the year of penance. However, on the death of Oudoceus, his successor in the see of Llandaff absolved this Prince at the request of Morgan and others.[1]

The records of those times reveal, as Montalembert observes, a strange mixture of the most abominable crime, with a great deep spirit of contrition. Those Princes were impelled by a semi-savage nature to commit sins of so heinous a character as to find no parallel, except amongst African chiefs or Indian despots. Yet they reverenced a power which invariably led them to atone for their misdeeds. A bishop, a monk, exercised greater influence over them than the warlike powers by whom they were surrounded. At times they even went so far as to plunder monasteries, and violate the most essential laws of Christianity; but in the end they were sure to publicly come and, kneeling before the altar, shed tears of repentance. In the mind of the nation the bishop and the monk were natural umpires in the quarrels of potentates, and when Kings could not settle their dissensions, they looked to the Church as the final judge in such contentions. In a word, it was the triumph of moral over brute force, for princes stood more in awe of Christ and His ministers than of Kings and their armies.

(1) "Liber Landavensis," p. 430.

THE THIRD BISHOP OF LLANDAFF.

Dubricius and Teilo, the two first Bishops of Llandaff, in accordance with the custom of the Catholic Church, were in the habit of giving an account of their dioceses to the Bishop of Rome as Head of the Church of Christ.

Oudoceus, not satisfied with sending a deputation, or corresponding by letter, went in person to the Limina Apostolorum. He was far advanced in years, but neither age or infirmities deterred him from undertaking the journey. This cannot appear extraordinary to the student of Welsh history. The nation was Catholic, and intimate relations with Rome were natural. *(St. Oudoceus journeys to Rome.)*

Like the first Bishop of Llandaff, St. Dubricius, Oudoceus feeling the infirmities of age stealing over him, resolved to resign the administration of his diocese into younger hands, in order to devote the remainder of his life to the welfare of his own soul. He accordingly retired to the banks of the River Wye, in Monmouthshire, and whilst living there in solitude a stag, closely pursued by Prince Einion, sought shelter beneath the cloak of the venerable bishop. The chieftain, meeting his ancient pastor under such interesting circumstances, not only spared the stag, but gave a grant of land to St. Oudoceus for the purpose of founding a monastery and a church. Several persons placed themselves under his direction, no longer as a bishop, but as the leader of a saintly community. *(St. Oudoceus retires into solitude in Monmouthshire in order to prepare for death.)*

His retreat was often visited by hundreds of

widows and orphans, who came to him for advice and protection, and also by crowds of persons afflicted with infirmities, either physical or spiritual.

Few details have reached us concerning his last days. It is true that his disciples collected with reverence the records of the miracles performed by him; but these writings, with many others, were subsequently burned during the Saxon invasion, or else carried away by the exiles, who fled to countries which offered them greater security than their own.

St. Oudoceus died on the second of July. It is difficult to state the exact year of his demise, but it must have been at the close of the sixth century. Lobineau is much mistaken in fixing upon the year 564. This date corresponds with the time when he was consecrated bishop on the death of St. Teilo. His feast was formerly celebrated on the second of January.

Parallel between St. Ambrose of Milan and St. Oudoceus of Llandaff The student of history is naturally led to remark a striking resemblance between the energetic Ambrose, of Milan, and the equally firm Oudoceus, of Llandaff. It is true two centuries separate them, and one had to deal with the Christian monarchs of the great Roman empire on those territories in the plains of Lombardy, at the foot of the Alps, and the other with independent Christian chieftains in Cambria, along the British Channel. However, a similarity of temper, circumstances, and actions, cannot but strike the reader who has studied the lives of both prelates.

St. Ambrose was holding a council at Milan in 390, when the news of a great disturbance at Thessalonica, in which several officers had lost their lives, reached him. The archbishop and his brethren, knowing how severely the law of retaliation was carried out by imperial officials, wrote a joint letter to Theodosius, requesting him, in the name of Christ, to forgive the unreflecting crowd through whom the disaster had occurred, or, at least, to act with leniency in a case where there was no premeditation. The emperor promised to forgive the rioters, but yielding later on to the importunities of Rufinus, his chief minister, secret orders were given to the commander of the province, directing him to take a signal revenge. The military accordingly received instructions to rush upon the circus when crowded with the citizens of Thessalonica. The command was obeyed, and the soldiers entering in the middle of the game, slew all whom they could reach with their swords, without distinction of guilt or innocence, age or sex. The massacre lasted for three long hours. Seven thousand victims were sacrificed, and the amphitheatre changed into a sea of blood.

The Emperor was then absent from Milan, but was expected to return in a few days. As he entered the city by one gate, the archbishop left it by another, being unwilling to meet a prince crimsoned with the blood of his subjects. Theodosius, however, addressed to him a most pathetic letter. Neither angel or archangel could wash away his sin; repentance was his only hope—the Monarch requested to be allowed to do penance. When the Emperor presented himself at the door of the cathedral, Ambrose confronted him on the threshold, and forbade him to advance, because he was not worthy to approach the altar or partake of the body and blood of the Lord, being guilty of the murder of seven thousand of His children. Theodosius replied that although David had committed adultery and murder, he had been forgiven. "Yes," replied the intrepid archbishop, "but he did penance. Do thou in like manner, and deserve pardon."

This happened in April, 390. Theodosius accepted the penance imposed, and for eight months mourned over his sin. As the Christmas festivities drew nigh, he became still more sad at the idea of being excluded from the communion of the faithful and shut out from the altar of sacrifice. He thought of presenting himself at church, though certain of being humbled, for he knew how inflexible Ambrose was. However, he did go, and was publicly rebuked, but in the end absolved.

Happy the Church whose walls are defended by such intrepid champions of justice and humanity. Only one who was a saint, a lover of Jesus Christ, and a true shepherd, devoted to his flock, could display such energy in time of need. St. Oudoceus evinced the same firmness when dealing with guilty potentates. Like Ambrose, when he suspected a crime was about to be committed, he exerted himself to avert it by fatherly advice; but if this had no effect, and the sin was perpetrated, he cut off the criminal from communion with Christianity. Fear of drawing revenge on himself was powerless to deter him from the execution of his episcopal duties, and, like St. Ambrose, he closed the door of the Church against guilty Welsh princes, not once, but on no less than four occasions, until such time as they had undergone the penance imposed upon them by the council. During the greater part of his administration some portions of his diocese were under interdict; one, in the neighbourhood of Gower, for three years, a part of Glamorganshire for two. No power on earth could induce him to absolve a Christian prince until he had made full satisfaction, like King David and the Emperor Theodosius, for the crime of which he had been guilty.

Notwithstanding St. Ambrose's severity, Theodosius could not withdraw his admiration from him. He alternately resided at Milan and at Constantinople, and he could not avoid seeing the difference between the Patriarch and the Archbishop. The acute monarch was accustomed to observe, "At Constantinople I am surrounded by flatterers, at Milan I am told the truth;

there is not under the sun a bishop like Ambrose."

The Cambrians also, as a rule, approved of the energy and firmness of Oudoceus. They flocked around their prelate at the altar of St. Illtyd at Lantwit-Major, or that of St. Peter at Llandaff, and supported him in the execution of his pastoral duties, and when he pronounced sentence of excommunication on the guilty, they acknowledged the justice of the decree. With the exception of those parasites and courtiers who always live on princes, the people of Glamorganshire received with veneration and awe the just severity of their bishop, aware that he was the representative of Christ, and when, on Sundays, the Gospel of St. John, describing the difference between the good shepherd and the hireling, was read to them, they were wont to remark, "Oudoceus, the Bishop of Llandaff, is the good shepherd who flieth not when the wolf approacheth the fold, but remaineth at his post and will not allow any of his sheep to be touched."

The Cambrians in their charters introduce his name along with those of St. Dubricius and St. Teilo. Ancient records speak of him as one of the three saintly bishops of Llandaff.

The early Cambrians, whatever may have been their other defects, respected the priest as a person invested with the most exalted dignity on earth, and looked upon him as the coadjutor of God,[1] *the dispenser of his mysteries.*[2]

(1) 1 Cor., iii. 9   (2) 1 Cor., iv. 1.

He was the possessor of power over the body and blood of Christ in the Sacrifice of the Mass.

He cancelled sins in the sacrament of penance, and was the ordinary minister of the seven Sacraments, and in the Church of God he was a ruler and a teacher.

In our modern times a Welshman recognises no authority in religious matters. He judges for himself, he discards the sacraments of the Church established by Christ, he has no need of any priesthood, and is impressed with the idea that no sacerdotalism should exist in his temples.

Christ and his own ancestors have taught a different lesson.

The feast of St. Oudoceus was celebrated on July the second, the day of his death.

The life of Oudoceus closes the career of the first three Bishops of Llandaff, mentioned as saints in the archives of their diocese.

Let us now leave the old Cathedral, and invite the reader to accompany us to Llancarvan and Lantwit-Major, and make the acquaintance of Cadoc, the wise, and Illtyd, the knight. A few miles to the west along the British Channel will bring us to their monasteries.

CHAPTER XII.

SAINT CADOC, FOUNDER OF LLANCARVAN
MONASTERY, GLAMORGANSHIRE.[1]

IN the earlier part of the fifth century there lived in the present county of Monmouth, South Wales,[2] a Cambrian chieftain named Gwynlyw, son of Glywys. He was the eldest of eight or ten children. When dying, their father divided his territory equally amongst them, in compliance with the custom called gavel-kind. One of the brothers, however, named Pedrog, declined his portion, having determined on embracing a religious life, in which he lived and died.

To the share of Gwynlyw fell that tract of land lying between Newport, Monmouthshire, and the present town of Cardiff; how far it extended towards the north is not stated. This estate at present is in possession of the Tredegar family.

On entering into this inheritance the young chieftain considered the time had arrived for him to marry and settle down. His choice fell

(1) This Life is compiled from the works of Lobineau, Albert le Grand, and from the "Cambro-British Saints."

(2) Monmouthshire is here placed in Wales, for in the times we allude to the river Wye formed the frontier of Llandaff diocese,

upon a young lady named Gwladys, who belonged to the family of Brychan, prince of Brecknock, a lady in every way accomplished. His proposal for her hand being declined by the family, the impetuous lover determined to carry her off by force.

Such cases of abduction were not uncommon in those days, and their repeated occurrence induced the Catholic Church to introduce into the marriage code the *impedimentum raptus*, for the purpose of protecting the free will of womanhood, necessary to the validity of marriage.

Gwynlyw having successfully accomplished his romantic feat, a deadly war was the result, as a matter of course, and many lives were sacrificed in consequence. Friends, however, interfered to restore peace, and on the lady declaring that she would never marry anyone but Gwynlyw, an agreement was arrived at, and the young couple united in lawful matrimony.

Of this marriage was born a son, Cadoc, or Cathmail, as he was named in baptism, who became the celebrated founder of Llancarvan Monastery, and to whom future generations were to apply the title of *Wise*.[1]

This child, with St. Dubricius, first Bishop of Llandaff, and Illtyd, the Knight, whom, later on, he was to induce to forsake the world and its vanities, was destined by Divine Providence to

---

(1) According to the Breviary of Vannes, Cadoc was born in the year of our Lord 421.—*Vide* Albert le Grand.

become one of the most illustrious sons of the Catholic Church of Wales in the fifth century.

Cadoc was baptised by Tathai, a monk living at Caer-went. As this priest exercised great influence over the future career of our saint, it may not be out of place to narrate the circumstances under which he became intimately acquainted with the house of Gwynlyw,

Tathai was at the head of a small religious community at Caer-went, near Chepstow, once an important Roman fortress. At this period the far-famed legions had departed, never to return, and their settlement was occupied by the men of Christ, as the monks were called. As yet the number of religious was small, and they possessed property of no consequence.

Cadoc baptised and educated by Tathai.
One night some of the followers of Gwynlyw—good soldiers, no doubt, but bad citizens—started on a plundering expedition. Directing their steps eastward, they came to Caer-went, broke into the enclosure of the monastery, and carried off the few head of cattle belonging to the monks. This event took place on the very night Cadoc was born. His father had had a dream, in which he beheld a venerable-looking priest enter the hall of his castle. As he gazed upon him, somewhat amazed, he heard a voice which said, "Be kind to this holy priest, and let him baptise the new-born child, for he will be the guide and teacher of his youth."

Tathai, on being informed on the following

morning of the outrage which had been committed during the night, and of the plunderers being in the service of Gwynlyw, at once started off to lay his complaint before their master, and claim restitution.

The arrival of the priest at the castle accorded exactly with the dream of the chieftain, who, having heard his statement about the cattle, and given him satisfaction for the theft, asked Tathai to baptise the child.

The monk seemed to have a prevision as to the future destiny of that infant, for, on restoring him to his father, he strongly recommended the chieftain not to neglect the education of his son, but have him brought up in the pursuit of literary knowledge. Gwynlyw promised not to forget this advice, and added that amongst all the seminaries of Britain to none but the monks of Caer-went would he entrust the early training of his son.

When seven or eight years of age, Cadoc was accordingly sent to Tathai's monastery, where he graduated through the various stages of education imparted in those days.

Manual labour was a custom seldom departed from in monastic schools; hence we find young Cadoc, though of noble birth, engaged in the humble occupation of lighting the fires, like a servant. The legend tells us that on a certain day the young student was sent to fetch some fire from a neighbouring cottage. He was there told that he could not have any unless he carried it away in his breast. This Cadoc did, without either his garments or his body being in the least burnt.

The noble youth remained in the school of Caer-went for twelve years, and did not leave it until he had completed his studies. He was then nineteen or twenty, a good scholar, and proficient in learning, both Divine and human. He was innocent, and beloved by all. The parting between master and pupil was affecting. Tathai had baptised Cadoc, and watched him as he grew up under his eyes. Stretching his hands over the young man, he implored Almighty God to protect him, and His holy angels to be his companions on the road of life; then, giving him his own blessing, he wished him prosperity in whatever career he might be called to pursue.

Contrast between the monastery and the home of the chieftain.

Young Cadoc, on returning home, soon began to feel the difference between the monastery and the mansion of a chieftain. In the former, every hour was usefully occupied either in manual labour, study, or prayer. At the castle, his father and friends spent their days either in hunting or warfare, and their nights in banqueting. In the monastery no plundering of any sort was allowed, for those whose lives were passed in doing good to others could not permit the least act of injustice to be perpetrated.

The chieftain, on the contrary, closed his eyes to the misdeeds of his followers. Provided they stood under his banner and fought valiantly in time of war, he was satisfied, and did not interfere with their liberty unless they committed themselves in a way to bring discredit on him before the world. In fact, whilst he looked well after his own interest, he neglected that of God. His son, with a mind enlightened by the Holy Ghost, and well grounded in the Gospel precepts, was at a loss to understand how his father and his friends could take such delight in the battlefield and set such a value on the slaughter of their foes, and in such other worldly pursuits.

Gwynlyw, by his deeds of valour, had shed a halo over his country which had been so appreciated by the people that they added to his name the title of *Warrior*. To the young man all this was *vanity of vanities*. More than once he indicated his feelings to both his parents, and urged on them the necessity and utility of serving God, but his words produced little effect; the time had not yet come.

Cadoc seems to have made up his mind to enter religion whilst at Caer-went, but how long he remained at home after the completion of his studies is not stated. Some writers incline to think that the following circumstances[1] decided the young nobleman to leave home suddenly:—

Some difference had arisen between Gwynlyw and a neighbouring chieftain, which, as usual, was to be decided by the sword. Cadoc was

Cadoc departs from home.

(1) Albert le Grand.

appointed to the command of this expedition, but he declined, on the plea that he was a soldier of Christ. His Master, he said, had shed His own blood for the redemption of mankind, but never used the sword for the destruction of the children of Adam; it was his wish to follow this Divine example. Aware that his father, a stern soldier, would never forgive this answer, he resolved to leave home, and thus at once commence the religious life. This abrupt decision reveals in the son the determination of character of the father, but turned to a better cause.

With a few friends who entertained the same idea, he set out, and, directing his steps westward, passed through the present town of Cardiff, and studied the localities of that district along the Bristol Channel. This part of Glamorganshire is undulating, and abounds in hills and valleys, which in those days were in great part covered with wood.

The swineherd and Cadoc. Cadoc made a minute inspection of the country, crossing hills and diving into valleys, but could not find a place suitable for his plans until he came to Llancarvan, three or four miles from Cowbridge. Here he discovered a swampy valley, rarely visited by anyone, and which, by the very nature of the ground, was adapted to secure the solitude so prized by monks. Staff in hand, he examined the place, wading through the swamps and forcing his way among briars and thorns. Tired out, at last he lay down to rest on a rising spot where the ground was dry and shaded by a wild apple tree, and fell asleep. A herd of swine, which was feeding not far off, came to the spot, and seeing the prostrate figure were frightened and ran away. Their guardian seeing this, suspected the presence of thieves or wolves, and began searching about the place, finding Cadoc, who by this time was on his knees in prayer. The man at once concluded it was thieves, and not wolves who had startled his flock, and that the young man on his knees was one of the gang. After showering abuse and curses on the stranger, he grasped his spear, determined, as he said, to rid the country of one of its worst robbers.

The legend adds that, whilst in the act of aiming a blow, his arm became stiffened and he also lost his sight. He at once perceived that the object of his attack was specially protected by the Lord, and soon found that he possessed the charity of a saint; for Cadoc consoled him with the assurance that the God who struck was also able to restore to him the use of his eyes and arm. When informed by the shepherd that the name of his master was Doulpenythen, Cadoc replied that he was his uncle. He then told the man to go home, and recommended him to tell his master all that had occurred.

When Doulpenythen heard the narrative, he ordered twelve horsemen to accompany him to Llancarvan, for which place he at once started.

The uncle and the nephew.

The meeting between uncle and nephew was by no means free from embarrassment. The chieftain was distressed that his swine-herd should have shown disrespect and even violence to the son of his brother; but when, instead of a gay young nobleman, surrounded by hounds and sporting friends, he saw a few youths, meanly clad and neglected-looking, he guessed the purpose for which they had come to that locality, and felt still more embarrassed.

After a few preliminary remarks on both sides, which indicated how matters stood, the chieftain thought it his duty to recommend his nephew to return home. He bade him remember that a brilliant career was open to him. He was the child of a celebrated warrior, who expected that his son should be worthy of the father, and win a reputation for bravery in the battle-field and courtesy in domestic life; that, having now reached the age of manhood, filial duty required he should comply with the reasonable wishes of his family.

Cadoc replied that his mind was irrevocably made up as regarded his future life, and that on no account would he forsake the service of religion for the allurements of a deceitful world, prefer earthly to heavenly attractions, or risk the loss of eternal bliss for the enjoyment of temporary pleasures. He had himself witnessed with sorrow the lives led by many noble youths, who were far from assimilating themselves with the Gospel of Jesus Christ. "All," he added, "that I desire is a small corner of God's earth on which I can build a hut, wherein to pray, live an innocent life, and die."

His uncle, being much edified by the young man's steadfast piety, said—

"If thou hast need of land, choose and take as much as thou requirest out of my territory."

Cadoc thanked his uncle, and replied, "My companions and myself have minutely inspected this district in search of a place suitable for the religious life we purpose to lead. This valley will answer our purpose. It is far from human habitation, and here we can devote ourselves undisturbed to the service of our Divine Master."

Having arranged this matter to their mutual satisfaction, the chieftain bade farewell to his nephew, and returned home.

Cadoc and his companions recognised in this event the finger of God, who had provided them with a home. At first sight, the place selected was not an inviting spot. The valley was a watery moor, producing nothing but reeds and bulrushes, and swarming with reptiles and snakes. Here and there a few dry and elevated mounds rose above the surface of the marsh; these served as places of resort for wild boars. It was called by the natives the Valley of the Deer, because in the hunting season, when these animals were closely tracked by the hounds, they were wont to take refuge in this almost inaccessible swamp,

Foundation of Llancarvan Monastery

which was dreaded alike by huntsmen and dogs.

The servants of God, however, were glad to have a place they could call their own, and thanked their heavenly Father for His gift. They passed the following night in prayer, imploring light to enable them to decide on the best place whereon to erect a building for His greater honour and glory.

As Montalembert observes, animals were often made the medium of indicating to religious the site of monasteries predestined to become hereafter great centres of piety and learning. Thus, the position of Fecamp, Hautvillers, and other convents in France were pointed out; one by a stag, another by an eagle, and a third by a dove.[1]

The site and position of the great monastery of Llancarvan were, in like manner, marked out by a wild animal.

The legend records that an angel appeared to Cadoc, and said, "To-morrow thou shalt be shown the spot whereon God wills thee to erect thy foundation. On coming to a piece of dry ground thou shalt find a wild boar, which will run away affrighted. There thou shalt build a church. The boar, as he retreats, will twice stop for a moment. On the first spot thus indicated erect a dormitory, and on the second a refectory."

This prediction was fulfilled, for as Cadoc journeyed along on the following day he did

(1) Montalembert's "Monks of the West."

really meet a bristly white boar. He marked the spot on which the animal stood, as also the two places where, as the angel had foretold, he halted in his flight, and thereon, in course of time, arose the various buildings connected with the monastery of Llancarvan.

The first erections were simple, being constructed of wood from the forests on the adjacent hills, the roofs being formed of reeds or bulrushes from the moor.

The fame of Cadoc's sanctity soon spread throughout South Wales, and crowds of disciples, eager to follow the evangelical counsels, flocked to Llancarvan. By degrees the appearance of the country was completely changed. A deep trench, cut in the centre of the valley, formed a channel for conveying the stagnant waters into the sea; the sloping ground was also drained, and roads or footpaths were formed which opened easy communication with the neighbouring country.

However scanty may be the records of monastic foundations, it is always to be remarked that one of the first works undertaken by the monks was the formation of an enclosed cemetery, and near, or within it, a church. No doubt, those who had renounced the world for ever remembered that it was within the cloister that they were to live and die, and, therefore, the church and the cemetery were linked together in their minds. It was fitting that the brethren who had passed away should await the resurrection in the vicinity of the altar whereon the holy Sacrifice of the Mass was offered for the repose of the souls of the faithful departed, and near the church from which their prayers had so often ascended to God.

Round the church and the cemetery, as round a centre, the other buildings which composed the monastery were erected. The plan of Llancarvan was identical with that followed by most of the religious houses in those days, and included a monastery, a college, and an hospital.

We can discover no record in the "Lives of the Cambro-British Saints" of the amount of land granted to Cadoc by his uncle Poulentus, but we have reason to believe that its dependencies became greatly enlarged through various donations, and that the boundaries extended beyond the Valley of Llancarvan. Even in the lifetime of Cadoc we find that the monks had cultivated the land in the neighbourhood of Penmark as far as the shores of the sea. On the west they carried their works through St. Athens, Lambthery, and on to Lanfythen; whilst on the east they extended as far as Molton.

It is probable that round Llancarvan, as a centre, rose various priories, each under the rule of a prior, for we read that in course of time a separate building was erected for the residence of St. Cadoc as abbot, and called Cadoc's Castle.

The buildings first constructed being merely

huts formed of green wood, were very perishable, and as the community increased a monastery formed of permanent materials was substituted.

The biographers of St. Cadoc inform us that in the Valley of the Deer great use was made of those animals; they dragged timber from the forests and stones from the quarries. No longer tracked by hounds and huntsmen, they willingly assisted the monks in their various labours. Persons who visit Llancarvan and neighbourhood at the present day must feel convinced that in former times men highly gifted with physical strength and intellectual power must have tenanted that locality. This is exhibited in the ruined churches, halls, and extent of land enclosed within walls, forming immense parks, whilst huge mounds of earth raised within the valleys retained the waters and formed lakes and reservoirs.

It must not be forgotten that, as a rule, the peasantry willingly became tenants on monastic territory, influenced by its many advantages. There they found peace, security, and exemption from military service; and also good masters in the science of farming, and safe teachers in spiritual matters. They found that Cadoc was a better ruler as a monk than he would have been as a wild chieftain like his father, Gwynlyw, and others.[1] He was, indeed, the spiritual life of the

(1) The Iolo MSS., page 557, speaks thus of the numerical strength of this monastery:—"The College of Cattwg, in Llancarvan, with three cells and a thousand saints, together with two cells in the Vale of Neath."

brethren and others of Llancarvan, as also a model to many monasteries.

Cadoc, like the rest of the religious, did not disdain manual labour. In the house of religion none were allowed to eat the bread of idleness.

Not far from Llancarvan was a field specially called the "White Field" (Erwgwen), a name which was religiously preserved for centuries. The clearing and cultivation of that field was the work of the blessed Cadoc.

<small>Travels of Cadoc.</small> The primitive monks of Britain were indefatigable travellers; we find them in Gaul, Italy, Rome, and Jerusalem; and, considering the few facilities for locomotion which existed in those days, we are bound to confess that they were men who possessed great energy and extraordinary physical powers. They crossed stormy oceans in small open boats, and traversed immense continents on foot, if no other facility was open to them. Devotion or love of learning were their chief motives for undertaking these labourious journeys; and Cadoc, the founder of Llancarvan, holds the first rank as a traveller amongst the abbots of Wales. We meet with him in Ireland, Scotland, and Brittany, seeking instruction for himself, preaching the Gospel to others, and building monasteries. He kneels at the tomb of Saints Peter and Paul in Rome, and in Jerusalem follows, in tears, his Saviour along the Via Dolorosa. Again and again

during his life does he renew these pilgrimages.

When the Monastery of Llancarvan was thoroughly established, the abbot thought of visiting Ireland because the religious houses and colleges of that country were famed for piety and learning. The founder of a monastic institution could but profit by a personal knowledge of establishments which were looked upon as models. He remembered the words of holy Scripture, "Son, acquire learning in thy youth, and thou wilt find wisdom with thy grey hairs, and it will be to thee as a father and as a mother."

Cadoc's monastery being a new foundation, he considered it expedient to examine into the spirit and administration of the most celebrated cloisters in Ireland. Taking with him some of his brethren, he visited Lismore, which then enjoyed a well-deserved reputation as the perfection of a monastic institution. Here he resided for three years, conforming in all things to the rules of the house.

On his return to Wales he brought back with him several Irish monks and British priests, who had a desire to become members of his community. Amongst them were the celebrated Professors Finian, Macmoil, and Guavan.

This practical common-sense, which we note with pleasure amongst the saints of Cambria, contributed in no small degree to their attainment of a high standard of perfection, both religious and scholastic; and, in course of time, they gained a great reputation as masters of Divine and human sciences.

Some persons are inclined to think that there is nothing to be learnt beyond the narrow limits of their own country. According to their opinion, science has fixed her abode amongst them, and, as a matter of course, there is nothing they can acquire from others.

Cadoc's feeling on the subject was very different. He knew that much was to be learnt in other lands and from their inhabitants, especially on subjects about which they possessed greater experience than his own.

On returning from Ireland, the saintly abbot passed some time in Brecknockshire, the birthplace of his mother, Gwladys. Love of learning prompted this new absence from Llancarvan. There lived in Brecknockshire a celebrated professor, who had spent several years in Rome, and Cadoc wished to acquire from him the real pronounciation of Latin, and also the Roman style of psalmody, in order that he might secure Liturgical correctness for his brethren.

We also find him making pilgrimages to Jerusalem and Rome. Devotion was his chief motive for undertaking these journeys; for at all times a natural religious instinct attracts the devout to the sacred spot trodden by the feet of our Redeemer—to Bethlehem, the place of his birth, and to Calvary, the throne of his conquest over death and hell.

Pilgrims to the East, as a rule, carried back with them relics—especially altar-stones—which had touched the holy sepulchre or been taken from the quarries on the spot. Cadoc brought *three such altar-stones* on his return to Wales, two of which he gave to his monastic brethren, Macmoil and Elly, keeping the third for his own use. The Cambro-British MSS. assert that seven times in his life did this holy man visit the Liminia Apostolorum, and Jerusalem *twice*.

His pilgrimage to Jerusalem and his visit to Rome, on his way back to Britain, took place, according to Albert le Grand, in 462, in the beginning of the pontificate of John the Third, by which Pope he was kindly received.[1]

The following remarks on the motives which incited Cadoc to undertake these long journeys show how deeply rooted in the hearts of the Britons of those days was devotion to the faithful departed. According to his biographer, the abbot performed these pilgrimages as a penance for the repose of the souls of his departed relatives.

He undertook other journeys also—one to Scotland and another to Brittany. Having knelt at the holy sepulchre in Jerusalem and at the tombs of St. Peter and St. Paul in Rome, he wished to pray at the Church of St. Andrew in

---
[1] Albert le Grand, p. 666.

Scotland, and with three of his brethren started for the North. His devotions being over, he remarked that the faith in certain portions of central Scotland was lukewarm, or, at least, was little practised. The holy abbot prayed, therefore, for light to know if he should consecrate a part of his life to missionary labour amongst these people.

He prolonged his stay, accordingly, and preached the Gospel throughout the country; and, that the work he had done might not be lost, he established a branch of his order, to insure its being carried on in the future. His stay in Scotland lasted five years.

It is also on record that the Abbot of Llancarvan built a monastery on a small island in the river Ectell, Brittany, in the diocese of Vannes. For many centuries this island bore the name of Enes Cadog, or Cadvog, in memory of the saint who is said to have connected it with the mainland by a bridge or causeway, which, for length and beauty, was looked upon in those days as a prodigy of engineering skill.[1]

(1) By the Breton firesides, during the long nights of winter, the legendists used to narrate how, in the execution of this work, Cadoc cheated the devil. The saint was spanning the distance to be bridged over, and calculating the immensity of the work he was about to undertake, when Satan appeared before him, and at once entered upon the subject. "So you are thinking of throwing a bridge across the strait! A gigantic work! It will require thousands of men to quarry the stones, all the oxen of Brittany and Wales to convey them to the spot, and a forest of wood for the lime-burning. Who will dig for the foundations through mud and water? If you agree to my terms, I will do it; and that, too, in the short space of one night. As remuneration for my labour, I require that the first that crosses the bridge shall become mine." The saint well understood that what Satan wanted was a soul to take with him to hell; but, as he did not clearly specify such a demand, Cadoc determined to outwit and give him a lesson in verbal exactitude. So he bade him

The saints, as we have seen in the preceding pages, were great lovers of souls.

St. Brieuc offered the most fervent prayers for the conversion of his father and mother, the first time he celebrated the holy Sacrifice of the Mass.

At Llancarvan, St. Cadoc often thought of his parents' home near the river Usk, in Monmouthshire. When, in choir with his brethren at night, he chanted the Psalms of David which so beautifully pourtray the miseries and vanities of this world, the mind of the holy abbot often wandered from the church to the parental dwelling.

Cadoc induces his father and mother to leave the world.

It was especially during Lent, and when at the Flat Holms, near Cardiff, that the heart of the pious priest was pierced with sorrow, because in the penitential season his mind was most occupied with and penetrated by the eternal truths; and from the island of Flat Holms he could behold the territories of his parents. They were advancing in years, but were they securing for themselves a happy eternity? He had induced hundreds to follow him in the practice of the Evangelical Counsels, and he could not but desire that his own father and mother should lead good, Christian lives, at least in their latter days.

build the bridge. Satan at once summoned a legion of demons from hell and set to work during the night. Next morning, after Lauds, Cadoc found that the bridge was completed, and perceived the devil on guard at the extremity which opened on the island. "You have kept your word," said the abbot, "and now I will fulfil my part of the compact." He went back to the monastery, and shortly after returned carrying a cat, which he threw on the bridge, and the frightened animal at once darted across it. "Take him, if you can catch him," exclaimed Cadoc. "He will rid you of all your rats." Satan vanished, discomfited; and thus it was that the abbot cheated the devil.

No man is a prophet in his own country, and but few are considered such in their own families. Acting on this maxim of our Lord, Cadoc hoped that some of his clergy might exercise greater influence over his parents than himself, and accordingly sent Finian, Guavan, and Elly to visit them. These envoys were well received by Gwynlyw and Gwladys. They were the followers of their son, and the pleadings of nature told in their behalf. They spoke of the holy life led by Cadoc, and of the number of devoted men who served God under his direction in the Valley of the Deer, and said one thought ever predominantly occupied the mind of their saintly son, and that was anxiety for the eternal welfare of his father and mother.

This revelation made a deep impression on both parents, but in a particular manner affected his mother, who impressed it upon her husband. "Let us trust to our own dear son," she said. "Let us listen to his advice, and he will be a father to us in heaven. Let us amend our lives, and enjoin that at our deaths our bodies shall repose in his cemetery, near the walls of his church. He and his brethren will remember us in their prayers when in this world we have ceased to exist, and recommend our souls before the altar to the mercy of God."

To this touching appeal of Gwladys her husband replied, "Whatever thou recommendest let us do it, and wherever thou goest I will follow."

A messenger was forthwith despatched to Llancarvan to inform Cadoc of what had taken place; he hastened to his parents with all the joy of a general who had gained a great victory; and through his exhortations they were incited and strengthened in their resolution to spend the remainder of their lives in a pious and saintly manner.

Supernatural grace told powerfully on these two souls. Of course, they had penance to perform—the guilt of past sins to wash away. As we have already seen, the very earliest days of their married life bore the stain of blood, and their after hours had been devoted to worldly pleasures and pursuits; neither had they profited by the good example set before them by so many of their relatives. One of Gwynlyw's brothers was a monk; the holy nuns Ninnoc and Keyna were sisters, or nearly akin to Gwladys, and Cadoc, Abbot of Llancarvan, their own son. The inspirations of God, no doubt, filled their minds with such serious reflections in connection with these facts that in the end they determined to abandon the world, and, by mutual consent, separated, and led a life of chastity.

As we have already mentioned, the chieftain retired to Stowe-hill, Newport, Monmouthshire, where he built a few huts and an oratory.

Gwladys, his wife, founded a church and an hospital in a valley at the foot of the same hill, and, being joined by a few other pious women, there ended her days as a nun.

Gwynlyw, once renowned as "The Warrior," could never appreciate too much the singular favour he had received, through his saintly son, of a call to religious life. On his death-bed he sent for him and for his bishop, Dubricius, and entreated them to prepare his soul for death. After making *his confession*,[1] and receiving holy Communion and Extreme Unction, the dying hermit raised himself on his pallet, and, beckoning Cadoc to come nearer to him, told the bystanders that for years he had slighted his son's advice, but that it was to his unceasing prayers and solicitations he owed his return to Almighty God. Then, addressing the holy abbot, he said, "Blessed be thou, my son, because through thee the Lord has had mercy upon me, and thou hast obtained for me the Divine favour. I grant to thee this monastery and all that belongs to it; and it is my desire that kings, princes, nobles, and warriors be buried at thy altar, at Llancarvan. Whoever shall respect this, my will, let him be blessed, and may he who violates it be cursed." All present answered, Amen.

Nothing can be more touching than the supernatural love exhibited in the lives of this father and son.

When the grave on Stowe-hill[2] had closed over

(1) "Cambro-British Saints."
(2) St. Wolloos, Newport.

the warrior-hermit his son did not cease to remember him, but devoted himself to prayer for the repose of his father's soul.

According to Celtic custom, the lives of Gwynlyw, Gwladys, and Cadoc were celebrated by the bards, who reproduced their history in verses, which, being adapted to favourite melodies, were sung at the doors of churches, at markets and fairs, and at the firesides.

There was, indeed, much to inspire a poet, and to edify a deeply religious nation, in the career of the noble warrior, the fair Gwladys, and the saintly Cadoc. Sacrifices made for the service of God were sure to meet with ready sympathy from the Cambrians, and the spectacle of a devoted and generous son leading to the cloister the proudest warrior of his time and the fairest lady in the land excited their warmest admiration.

It may not be without interest to review the relations of Cadoc with some of the leading men amongst the laity, such as the valiant knight Illtyd, Maelgon, King of North Wales, and King Arthur. He possessed great influence over them, through which he succeeded in enlisting the more worthy into the service of his Divine Master. There were others with whom he could not maintain friendship. They were men devoted to the world, and the views of such often clash with those of a staunch servant of God. *Cadoc and the Princes.*

It was the Abbot of Llancarvan who persuaded

the Breton Knight, Illtyd, a distinguished officer in the army, to give up the world and its vanities and consecrate himself to the service of a better Master, as we shall see in the following chapter.

During the life of St. Cadoc, Maelgon, King of North Wales, and probably at that time chief of the British Confederation, sent an army into South Wales, either to avenge some quarrel, or perhaps collect the tribute assigned to him as leader.

With regard to the commissariat, it was clearly laid down that the army was to be supplied with food by the districts it would pass through. One territory, however, was exempted from this imposition, for the following reason.

Before the expedition started Maelgon reviewed his troops, which were under the command of Ehun, his son, and thus addressed them:—

"An army must be supplied with food, and the country through which its course lies must provide for it the necessaries of life. It is, however, my command that you respect the territory of Cadoc. He is my *confessor*, and without his permission you must not touch a single animal belonging to him. He and his brethren expect this consideration from me. Elsewhere you will find men and cattle hidden away in the forests, terrified at the tidings of your coming; but when you arrive at the domains of the monastery no one will feel the least alarm at the appearance of Maelgon's soldiers. Labourers will continue to work in the fields, and the cattle graze undisturbed in the pastures, for all know that your sovereign is the friend of Cadoc, and that *a spiritual covenant* exists between him and me, which will preserve them from suffering in the least from the horrors of war."

Ehun and his soldiers, with the exception of a party of twelve men, respected the wishes of their king. These troopers went one day to water their horses at a brook near Llancarvan. Being themselves thirsty, they said to each other it was a pity that soldiers should have nothing but cold water to drink when there was plenty of milk at hand, and, going to the steward of the monastery, rudely demanded some. Being displeased at their impertinent language, he refused what he would no doubt have given willingly otherwise. The soldiers went away, cursing and swearing, and even carried their resentment so far as to endeavour to set fire to the barns.

Ehun and his followers were much distressed on hearing of this attempt at incendiarism, and the Prince, in atonement for the misconduct of his men, made several offerings to Cadoc.

In the "Cambro-British Saints" we find mention of a very interesting contest between King Arthur and the Abbot of Llancarvan. When divested of its romantic colouring, the narrative runs as follows :— *[margin: Cadoc and King Arthur.]*

For some unspecified cause, a brave general of the British army, named Ligessawc, the "Long

Hand," slew three soldiers of Arthur. The King tracked the murderer from place to place, and the unfortunate man, being unable to find safety elsewhere, came as a fugitive to Cadoc, to whom he confessed his sin and represented his danger. The Abbot received him into the monastery, though some of the brethren dissented, on the plea that to do so would draw down upon them the ire of the King. Cadoc replied, "Let us show hospitality, as recommended by the spirit of religion, and rely on the assistance of God for our own protection. It is written, 'Fear not those who can kill the body, but cannot touch the soul;' and let us not miss an occasion for saving the life of a fellow-creature."

The general had remained with the monks for seven years, when someone revealed his place of refuge to Arthur, who despatched messengers to Llancarvan to demand his expulsion, or, at least, obtain the tax required from every man who had committed murder.

Both these demands being refused, the King became very indignant, his anger being, very probably, fanned by the courtiers around him. But he refrained from actual violence, through a kind of religious fear, for people spoke of Cadoc as being guarded by angels from heaven, and of the woe attending those who molested him.

After much negociation between the King and the Abbot, it was agreed that the matter should be submitted to arbitration. David, Teilo, Oudoceus, and others defended Cadoc.

The judges assembled on the banks of the river Usk, and the subject was so warmly discussed, and the excitement became so intense, that it was deemed judicious that the adherents of each party should keep the river between them.

Whether the guilty general had abandoned his sanctuary, or lost his right to its privileges after seven years; or whether, influenced by fear of Arthur, one of the judges proposed that the King ought to be content to receive three very good oxen for the loss of each one of his three men. This proposition was seconded by many, whilst others asserted that human life was so precious in the eyes of Britons that a hundred cows was the least atonement which should be offered for each man, and this decision was ultimately accepted.

In course of time Arthur repented of his unfairness towards Cadoc, and made satisfaction for allowing himself to act on the unjust maxim, too often adopted by the powerful, that might presumes right.

The King, when his anger had cooled, could not fail to see that the Abbot of Llancarvan, in sheltering a man who had fled to him for protection, was but following the rule of the cloister, sanctioned by the customs of the time, which granted to monasteries the right of refuge;

also, that although the shedding of human blood, except in lawful war, was taxed according to the value of the victim, yet St. Cadoc, who had nothing to do, either directly or indirectly, with the murder of his three men, had been forced to pay for their death. Ligessawc was the guilty man, and Cadoc and his brethren had been taxed for a crime which they abhorred.

These reflections haunted the mind of Arthur, and induced him to make an ample apology for the injustice he had been the author of. He gave full recognition to the monastic claim of right of refuge, and a better understanding was come to as to the nature and length of such rights. This was committed to paper, and signed on both sides, with the usual invocation of the blessing of God on those who should observe the rules, and curses on their violators.

As we have already more than once observed, it was the custom of the British saints to recollect themselves at the beginning of Lent, and consecrate the first weeks of that penitential season to a spiritual retreat.

Cadoc retired to Flat Holms, at the entrance of Cardiff, or to Barry Island, close to the same town, during those days of entire seclusion from business and the world. The administration of Llancarvan and his other monasteries entailed many cares and troubles, and he thought it would benefit his own soul to retire completely from the world, at least for a time.

On Palm Sunday he returned to his monastery to celebrate the mysteries of Holy Week. Crowds visited Llancarvan during these sorrowful commemorations, when the Church places before us with such solemnity the Passion of our Lord. No doubt men were then instructed in their religion, made their annual confession, and received the body and blood of their Redeemer. *Life Cadoc during Lent.*

During these religious festivals the community of Llancarvan exercised the greatest hospitality towards strangers, and hundreds of pilgrims were fed daily. The labour of the monks had transformed the waste valleys of Llancarvan and neighbourhood into productive fields. They had acquired wealth by the sweat of their brow, and on all suitable occasions those riches were generously shared with their neighbours.

In the latter part of his life, the Abbot of Llancarvan retired from the first and most celebrated monastery which he had established. We have already followed him on his journeys to Jerusalem, Rome, Brittany, and Scotland. One of the brethren was selected to rule temporarily as abbot, or prior, during these absences; but now that he felt himself called to serve God in another locality, Elli was elected to succeed him as permanent head of the religious community of Llancarvan.

It was on Palm Sunday that Cadoc formally intimated his determination of leaving them. The usual procession with the relics of the saints had proceeded through the country early in the morning, before Mass, and the solemnity had drawn crowds to the monastery. Cadoc preached on that occasion with unusual earnestness; then Mass was celebrated, and Holy Communion administered.

Later on in the day he assembled his religious brethren in the abbot's house, and informed them of his resolution to depart, and appointed Elli to succeed him as abbot.

Cadoc retires from Llancarvan.

"I am now advanced in years," he said, "and though ignorant of the day on which I shall be summoned from this world, I feel convinced that a younger ruler will be better fitted to guide you in the path of perfection. Obey, in all humility, the new abbot. I recommend to you, in the name of the Lord, that no power of king, or bishop, or noble may ever be called upon to adjust any dispute arising amongst you. Let any contentions which, in consequence of human frailty must unfortunately occur occasionally, be examined into and decided upon by judges taken from amongst yourselves.

"You are all familiar with the hazel tree planted by me not far from the monastery; it is under it that we have been accustomed to assemble for the discussion of matters concerning the community, and God stood by us in these councils. Let that still continue to be the place of judgment. Let the abbot and the brethren continue to meet beneath the shade of that tree, and you will still feel under the protection of heaven."

The book containing the rules of the monastery was then brought and placed upon the altar, and Cadoc said, "May you follow what is written in that book, and may your ruler guide you according to the prescriptions therein contained."

This explicit recommendation would seem to the ordinary reader to imply that the founder of Llancarvan discarded any right of the bishop to interfere with the administration of a religious community existing within his diocese, whereas, in the Councils of that period all over Christendom, monasteries were subjected to the jurisdiction of the bishops.

Perhaps the injunction given to his brethren by the Abbot of Llancarvan may be explained by the rule which in our own days fixes the relations of a bishop with certain religious orders. A bishop is the chief spiritual officer in a diocese, and no one can exercise any spiritual jurisdiction in the said diocese without his permission. In cases of scandal, no matter from what quarter they may proceed, he possesses power to check it.

However, at the present time even the bishop does not interfere with the *internal arrangements* of religious houses if under the immediate power of the Pope. This is what St. Cadoc implied in his parting advice to his brethren.

We are told that on leaving Llancarvan he went to Beneventum, and there was again forced to place himself at the head of a monastery, and ultimately consecrated bishop.

The exact locality of Beneventum has somewhat puzzled the hagiographers of Cadoc. Some go so far as to think it was the town of that name in Italy, others incline to the belief that it was Caergwent, but Weedon (Benevenna), in Northamptonshire, seems really to have been the place.[1]

Of the episcopal career of St. Cadoc little is known, with the exception of his death taking place at the altar whilst in the act of celebrating the holy Sacrifice of the Mass. For all particulars we beg to refer the reader to Chapter III.

The founder of Llancarvan Monastery was buried at Weedon, and his tomb was visited in crowds by the sick, blind, lame, and afflicted.

His brethren at Llancarvan greatly desired to have his body interred in his principal monastery, but their pious wish was frustrated. His grave at Weedon was guarded, and it was difficult for a Cambrian to get access to it, so great was the fear entertained that they would remove his coffin.

Cadoc holds a conspicuous place in the traditions of his land. He possessed great qualities, and had he remained in the world would have long been remembered as a brave and skilful warrior and wise administrator of the

---

[1] "Cambro-British Saints."

laws. But when all these great natural gifts were directed and influenced by the grace of the religious state, they stamped him as one of the most eminent of the Cambrian saints.

He was looked upon by his own countrymen as the Solomon of his race; amongst them he bore the name of "Cadoc the Wise." Perhaps ancient biographers recorded more minute details of the actions and hidden life of this holy servant of God than are at present extant. The bards deemed it their duty to celebrate his memory.

The Iolo MSS. have handed down a few of Cadoc's parables, and twelve fables, which denote a clear and practical mind. Like Æsop, he was a great observer of Nature, and possessed the talent of imparting good moral lessons through the medium of animals and inanimate objects. He, no doubt, had studied the ancient fablists. Most of his own might take their place beside those of Æsop and Lafontaine in the instruction of British youth. *[Fables attributed to Cadoc.]*

Whilst referring the reader to the Iolo MSS. for more copious information, it may not be uninteresting to place extracts of two or three of these fables before the reader, as specimens of the holy bishop's turn of mind and style of composition. One of these is headed, "The Man who killed the Greyhound."

A Welshman—his wife having gone to church—was left in the house with only a little child in the cradle, and a greyhound. A stag, pursued by dogs, rushed past, and the man, hoping to share the venison, joined in the chase.

A wolf meanwhile entered the house, and was about to devour the child, when the greyhound attacked and killed him, thus saving the life of the infant. During the struggle between the animals the cradle was overturned. When the man returned home the dog ran to meet him, wagging his tail, but covered with blood, as was also the floor of the room. The horror-stricken father seeing this, and that the cradle was upset, came at once to the conclusion that the hound had killed the child, and, in a moment of rage, drew his sword and stabbed him to the heart; but when, on raising the cradle, he found his boy alive, and perceived the dead wolf stretched upon the ground, he at once understood that he had slain the preserver of his child, and became almost frantic with grief.

Hence arose the proverb, "Before taking revenge, first investigate the cause, and reflect *twice* before striking *once*." Another saying refers also to the same story: "As sorry as the man who killed his greyhound."

A person who suffers passion to get the better of reason is likely to commit acts which he will never be able to undo. It is necessary to bridle rage, lest the vengeance proceeding from it prove, as in this fable, unjust.

Another parable, which is called "The old Woman and the Yarn," is a striking illustration of the power which results from union in families.

An old woman had several children and grandchildren, but discord and strife prevailed amongst them. One day she summoned all to her presence, and they assembled to the number of twenty. "Bring me here," she said, "each of you a ball of yarn." They did so, and having taken one of the balls, which consisted of a single thread, she tied together with it the hands of the feeblest of her grandchildren, but the little child soon broke through this bond. Then she bound his hands with stronger thread from another ball, but this, also, he easily burst asunder. In like manner she tried threads from all the balls successively, but they were invariably broken by the child. The old woman then desired that the yarn of all the balls be twisted together, and the whole formed into a rope. When this was done, she bound with it the hands of the most powerful of her sons, but by no effort could he break it.

"Behold," she said, "how much stronger the threads are when united than when single. Even so, my children and grandchildren, as long as you remain at variance and act in opposition one to another, any person who wills can overpower you, and there is not one in a thousand but will endeavour to do so; but if you cling together, like the twisted thread, your strength will be such that no enemy will be able to conquer you."

Three proverbs are derived from this fable: "Stronger the thread of double than of single twist;" and, "There is no strength without union;" and, "It is an easy matter to cast a mountain into the ocean after separating each stone from the others."

The last fable attributed to St. Cadoc is as follows:—

There once dwelt in Cambria a maiden, fair as the loveliest of Eve's daughters. She was universally extolled, and all were anxious to see her; but before doing so they had already made up their minds as to the particular style of her beauty, and, not finding that she corresponded with their pre-conceptions, they were disappointed. Each began to paint her according to his own taste, until she became transformed into the ugliest of women, and was no longer sought for in marriage as before. The maiden perceiving this, examined her face in a mirror, and saw how much she had been disfigured, so she washed off all the paint, and refused to allow anyone to colour her for the future. She soon bloomed forth again in her former beauty, and was admired as before, except by those who had disfigured her. They would not acknowledge her charms, because it is difficult to make a fool own his folly.

So it is with respect to truth. Every man professes to love it, yet each one disfigures it according to his inclination, until it becomes transformed into a falsehood, and is hated by all. . . . Men of this character are the last in the world to confess their mistake, acknowledge their error, or admit their prejudice; because, as the proverb says, they make pretence of being in the right. He who has sworn the crow to be white, will not allow that she is black although he knows she is of that colour. He who deceives others deceives himself much more. All seek after truth, but all will not suffer truth to be truth.

These telling deductions, we regret to state, may be in our days applied to the land of the Abbot of Llancarvan.

The *modern Cambrian* is a religious man, like his ancestors; but the *modern Cambrian* paints religion according to his fancies, interests, or prejudices. Nay. he claims the right of doing so, and boasts of a liberty which allows any man to give any colour or any interpretation he likes to the Word of God.

Indeed, he has made an extensive use of the right of colouring faith, by giving the Britons hundreds of religions.

Every chapel in Wales, and one knows how numerous they are, has, or may have, a Christianity of its own. If our forefathers were to leap from their graves, they would no longer recognise the Christian teaching of our days as the doctrine of their Divine Master. Nay, if a pagan from Japan were to land amongst us, and demand the religion of Christ, Wales (without the Catholic Church) could not give him the true faith, for the country does not agree on the subject.

The doctrine of our Lord is one, and, by its very nature, unchangeable, because true; and so one regrets to see so many guilty hands occupied in colouring it to suit their ideas.

May a future day dawn which will bring back unity of faith, and lead the Cambrians to kneel at the same altar as members of one religion.

Visit to Llancarvan.
On November the fifth, 1878, whilst the Life of St. Cadoc was in the hands of the printer, the writer, in the company of a brother priest, paid a visit to Llancarvan. The valley is, indeed, picturesque, and runs northward from Penmark to the high road to Cowbridge, bending a little to the east about midway. At Llancarvan village the two hills almost close, and then immediately open, so as to form a large basin, which could easily be transformed into a deep lake by erecting a mound of earth across the village from east to west. This work would be a trifle for a railway company.

In the fifth century, when the valley was uninhabited, what a fine place for a contemplative life! How the lover of solitude and silence must have felt at home between these hills, covered with timber the hand of man had never touched! Nature seems to have purposely built huge walls to shelter a house of prayer from the intrusion of the world.

Our visit had a double object—first, to trace out, if possible, the various localities mentioned in the Life of St. Cadoc; then to ascertain how far the traditions of the past still existed in the mind of the present generation. We did not call upon any of the gentry or clergymen in the immediate neighbourhood. We wanted information from the people, and not from the scholar; for we were anxious to test the tenacity of Celtic tradition in the mind of the masses.

A Welshman, like a Breton, is civil to strangers, but reserved. One must know how to take him before getting any information, for he does not tell his mind to everybody. We soon got round this peculiarity of the Celtic character, and learnt from the villagers that *Cadoc's Castle* stood in a field quite close to the present parish church of Llancarvan. If we wanted to see the *Great College* of Cattog, we were to follow the river for a while, and turn to the left, and call on Mr. Lougher, the farmer. This we did, and found in Mr. Lougher a kind and intelligent exponent of the local traditions of the past.

His farm, he said, occupies the site of the college. He pointed out to us countless walls, scattered here and there, and mostly on a level with the ground, although some actual constructions reveal still the grandeur of the past.

In the house there is no need of a water company, for a beautiful well oozes out of the ground in the dairy, and supplies the house with the purest of water.

Higher than the farm, on the top of the hill, we were told that bones are constantly being dug up, the hair preserved. We inquired what they did with these bones—they are religiously re-interred, was the answer.

Perhaps an archæologist might come to the conclusion that the spot was the cemetery of the monastery.

Mr. Lougher pointed out the house of St. Dubricius, lower down in the valley.

We were strongly advised to visit two sacred wells in the neighbourhood. One of these wells possessed the supernatural virtue of curing erysipelas, the other the king's evil. On this matter there was no doubt in the mind of the people, for every year sick people came to the wells, and every year cures did take place. So we were told, with an expressive conviction we could not but admire.

An intelligent observer, or a keen historian who could spend a few weeks about Llancarvan, and other historical localities, might throw light on the history of Wales, by securing the confidence of the people and winning their affections; for traditions of important events are handed down from generation to generation especially by the firesides of the Celtic races.

CHAPTER XIII.

LIFE OF ST. ILLTYD THE KNIGHT, FOUNDER OF LLANTWIT-MAJOR.

"On thy walls, O, Jerusalem, I have appointed watchmen; all the day and all the night they shall never hold their peace. You that are mindful of the Lord hold not your peace."— ISAIAS, chap. lxii. verse 6.

THE name of Illtyd is still borne by several parishes in Wales, and also in Armorica, in memory of him who was first an illustrious soldier, and after his conversion became a true servant of God, practised the ascetical life, was a celebrated scholar, and the spiritual father of a legion of bishops and other eminent disciples of the Lord Jesus Christ. *(Illtyd is a name held in veneration by Welsh tradition.)*

A noble family in the neighbourhood of Llantwit preserves to this day a traditional custom—handed down from father to son—of bestowing the name of Illtyd on the first-born son of each marriage.

The birth, early life, conversion, and labours of the saint who originally bore this honoured name will form the subject of this chapter. Llantwit-Major, about eighteen miles west of

Cardiff, was the chief scene of his missionary labours.

<small>Birth and early life.</small>

The birth-place of Illtyd is veiled in obscurity. The different historians of his life do not agree on the subject, and, strange to say, British biographers indicate Brittany, whilst Lobineau assigns this honour to Britain. Having duly weighed the grounds for these different opinions, we may reasonably come to the conclusion that Armorica was his native country. His father was named Bycanus, and his mother, Rienguilida, was the daughter of Solomon, king and martyr.[1]

These virtuous parents, having remarked the natural piety with which their son's mind was imbued from his earliest years, to which was added a great love of learning, earnestly hoped that, at the termination of his scholastic course, he would devote himself to the religious life. They were, however, for many years disappointed in these expectations, for, on leaving school, Illtyd decided on entering the army.

Military life, with its changes and adventures, is at all times full of attraction to a young man of twenty, and the brilliant uniform of a soldier is not without a charm. This proved the case with Illtyd, for, on his return home, and associating with the young warriors who served under his father, he was dazzled and led to abandon any generous resolutions he might have previously entertained of serving God in

---

(1) Rees' "Essays on Welsh Saints." "Cambro-British Saints."

the Church. The helmet, sword, and charger, dangers in the battle-field, and victorious returns from it, seemed to him the *supremum bonum* on earth.

Political events and the wars they entail summoned Illtyd to the island of Britain, and Almighty God made use of the young soldier's love of adventure to endow Cambria with one of her most illustrious saints.

In the fifth century military service in Britain found favour with the Armorican sons of Mars, whose ancestors had emigrated from that island. The old people in those days were in the habit of enlivening the firesides during the long evenings of winter with narratives of their exodus from that beautiful country, surrounded by seas, the subsequent conquest of Armorica, the wreck of the immense fleet which carried Ursula and thousands of maidens and women. All the thrilling scenes attendant on the emigration were described in the poetical and forcible Celtic dialect, and were listened to with breathless attention.

The island, however, when abandoned by the Romans, was unable to protect itself against the repeated invasions of the Caledonians and Irish.

Gwethelin, Bishop of London, endeavoured in vain to infuse a spirit of union and courage into the British princes; but, failing in his patriotic endeavours to organise them into a strong and compact confederation, sufficiently powerful to drive adventurers from his native land, he passed over the sea to Brittany, in order to appeal to the Bretons.

Aldroen, the fourth King since Conan Meriadec, was offered the sovereignty of Britain, which, on his declining, was accepted by his brother, Constantine, who sailed over to that country with as large an army as his native land —at that time threatened by the Gauls—could spare. The various branches of the administration were soon re-organised, and the hardy mountaineers of Scotland and the Sea Kings of Ireland taught to respect the rights of their neighbours.

Constantine died a violent death, leaving three children—Constans, Aurelius Ambrosius, and Uther Pendragon. The eldest of these was treacherously murdered by order of Vortigern. The two others fled to Brittany, but in course of time returned with continental troops, and re-conquered the kingdom of their father.

It is probable that one of these expeditions from Brittany brought Illtyd over to England, with the sole object of acquiring military glory; but, in the designs of heaven, a far more brilliant career awaited him. He arrived as a fierce warrior, not having the least prevision that in a short time he was to be changed into a meek disciple of Him who came on earth to preach peace to men of good will. At first he drilled soldiers for battle and bloodshed, and later on trained missionaries, abbots, bishops, for the service of the Church.

Illtyd was followed to these shores by an unseen mentor, whose orders were never to lose sight of the young knight, but whenever opportunity offered to whisper into his ear that all these feats of war were but vanity. This invisible friend was his guardian angel.

Illtyd, who was ardent, brave, intelligent, and strong of constitution, soon acquired reputation in the ranks of the British army. The old romances represent him as a model of chivalry, and affix to his name the title of "Knight," as much as to imply that his valour and noble qualities gave him an exclusive right to the title.

Whilst in Britain he married a lady named Trynihid, supposed by some Welsh writers to be daughter of a Glamorganshire prince. We find a somewhat detailed account in the "Cambro-British Saints" of his life as chief of the household of Paulinus,[1] in the same county.

Paulinus and Illtyd lived on the best terms, the chieftain placing the utmost confidence—and most deservedly—in his first officer, for, in truth, a better administrator could not have been found. As his biographers remark, the heart of the soldier beat in accordance with the precepts of the Gospel. His outward garb was that of a warrior, his inward soul was effulgent with

---

(1) This Paulinus seems to be identical with Poul-peuychen, which name might in our days, perhaps, be translated into "Paul of Cowbridge," or, rather, Oxbridge, uncle of St. Cadoc, who bestowed the valley of Llancarvan upon his nephew.

intelligence and justice, which ranked him amongst the first men of Britain. He was faithful in the observance of the commands of God and of the Church, and desired that they should be followed by those under him. He did not sanction either plunder or exaction, and respected the rights of the poor as well as those of the rich.

Meeting of St. Cadoc and Illtyd at Llancarvan.

We now come to the event which was the cause of Illtyd undertaking that work in Glamorganshire which, in the order of God's providence, he was destined to fulfil.

The young knight, in company with the household of Paulinus, was hunting in the neighbourhood of Llancarvan, when, wearied of coursing through the hills and valleys, and feeling need of refreshment, the sportsmen sent messengers to the monastery requesting a supply of provisions. Illtyd was not present at the time, being engaged in flying his hawks on the seashore, which was a favourite amusement of his. The soldiers meantime assailed the doors of the monastery more like combatants in time of war than travellers in search of hospitality, and commanded that the best of everything should be brought forth, or they would themselves seize upon what they wanted. St. Cadoc, although highly displeased at their insolence, complied with their demands, and the men withdrew to their camp to feast at the expense of the community.

Illtyd, on his return, was at once informed of what had taken place, and, having severely reprimanded his soldiers, hastened to the monastery for the purpose of apologising to the abbot for the misconduct of those under him. St. Cadoc very quickly learned to appreciate the young warrior, and, according to his custom, engaged him in a long discourse on the all-important object of the life of man upon earth—the salvation of his immortal soul—endeavouring at the same time to convince him how infinitely preferable was the service of God to that of kings and princes of this world.

Illtyd, who was naturally inclined to piety, listened with the greatest attention, and, opening his heart to the holy abbot, confided to him his early desires of consecrating himself to religion; but said that his vocation had melted like snow before the brilliant dazzle of military glory. On this, Cadoc reminded him that it was never too late to correct the errors of youth.

Illtyd was deeply moved by this discourse, and on returning to the court of Paulinus, everyone remarked that he was no longer the same. He continued to discharge, with the greatest care, the duties of his station, but from that time forward refrained from taking any part in the amusements of the palace.

What he had seen at Llancarvan, and what he had heard from the lips of the leader of that saintly community, ever haunted his mind. His early impressions when, as a boy, he had dwelt in the monastery of Germanus, in Gaul, recurred to his memory like a vision of the past. During his college life his parents had been desirous that he should embrace the religious state, and often, especially before the altar, he had felt within him the workings of grace urging him to consecrate his life to the service of the Church of Jesus Christ.

Then he remembered how fleeting was the life of this world, and how false the brilliancy of military glory. To serve as a soldier in the train of kings and princes was all delusion and vanity, and he seemed to hear the voice of his guardian angel whispering reproachfully in his ear: "Illtyd, thou wast not made to do battle for earthly monarchs, but to enlist in the service of the King of kings, Christ, the Redeemer. Thy hand was not formed to wield the lance and the sword of the warrior, but the pen of the scholar. Thy voice was not bestowed on thee to urge thy fellow-men to deeds of slaughter on the battle-field, but to lead the chosen of the Lord in the sacred psalmody of the choir. Thou hast been in this world a distinguished captain; what hast thou gained but vanity and fading laurels? Cadoc of Llancarvan was, like thee, of noble birth, yet he did not allow himself to be deluded into attaching himself to the perishable attractions of this world."

Influenced by the constant pressure of these

thoughts upon his mind, Illtyd left the court, accompanied by his wife, Trynihid, and determined, if possible, to consecrate himself to the service of religion. But difficulties of an unusual nature stood in his way. Illtyd was not alone in the world; he was married, and it was no easy task to tear himself away from the ties of human affection. Still, ever in his ears there rang these words of the Redeemer: " He that loves father or mother, brother or sister, *wife* or children more than Me, is not worthy of Me." He knew that a life of continence was that held most in honour by Christ and the more favoured of His disciples; still, marriage was also instituted by God, and raised by the Redeemer to the dignity of a sacrament. Trynihid, his wife, had knelt with him before the altar, and both had there promised in the most solemn manner to share together the trials and the joys of life until death should separate them. The Catholic religion, which he professed, and which was the only religion in the country, did not sanction the separation of husband and wife, except by mutual consent; and Dubricius, then Bishop of Llandaff, under whose jurisdiction he was, would, no doubt, take this view of the case.

Trynihid seems for some time to have opposed the wish of her husband, but in the end consented to retire into solitude, and built for herself a convent and a church.

In an age so material as ours, such proceedings

may appear extraordinary, if not unnatural. This is a generation eager in temporal pursuits; the greed of money and pleasure engrosses it. Our forefathers, during the early days of Christianity, set greater value on eternal interests, more frequently condensed their views on that point where time ends and eternity begins, and, after serious reflection, adopted a line very much in opposition to the ideas of a votary of materialism. Married people, who do not experience in that state the happiness they had expected, or have been visited by unexpected trials, often separate, and the world finds no fault; but in cases where religion is in question, the same world finds nothing to justify the same step, and is unsparing in its criticisms and denunciations. The saints, however, are uninfluenced by the opinions of sensual society, but followed the spirit of Christ.

The hermit. When husband and wife had parted, never to meet again on this earth, Illtyd directed his steps towards the Bristol Channel, south-west of the present town of Cowbridge, and plunged into the forests which at that time covered the country. On coming to a spot suitable for his purpose, he built a hut on the banks of a stream, and resolved, if possible, to spend the remainder of his days in solitude. At this period of his life he was not likely to foresee the designs of Almighty God, or imagine that on these very shores, once occupied by the Roman legions, he was destined hereafter to erect another camp—not in the interests of the pagan Cæsars, but one where soldiers were to be trained to the service of God —a camp which was to become the celebrated University of Lantwit.

How long Illtyd succeeded in following that instinct which led the early monks to bury themselves in forests or amongst craggy rocks on the sea-shore, in order to remain unknown to the world, is not stated; but for some time he must have had no other companionship than the birds of the air and the wild animals of the woods, especially the deer, which are so susceptible of becoming the friend of man, and which we so often find introduced into the lives of the saints in Britain, Gaul, Spain, and Italy.

The following narrative will show how it was that a stag was the means of introducing Merchion, a Welsh chieftain, to the founder of Lantwit:—

This prince, who was one of the first benefactors, though, later on, a persecutor of Illtyd, was a man of eccentric disposition. His countrymen had named him "Mad Merchion." Like most of the chieftains of his age, he passed his time either in war or in the chase; and it was whilst indulging in the latter sport that he encountered Illtyd.

His hounds had started a fine stag, which, seeking to escape, came to the spot where Illtyd dwelt. Tracked there by the dogs, the panting creature entered the cell of the hermit and lay down at his feet, facing the hounds, who paused at the entrance, ceased their yelping, and lay down upon the ground, looking at their prey.

When Merchion and his companions arrived on the spot, they were greatly amazed at the sight of the stag quietly enjoying the hospitality of a man, and the dogs, spell-bound, gazing on the scene.

Merchion imperiously demanded his prey, and ordered the hermit forthwith to drive the stag out of the hut.

The solitary resolutely replied that this request could not be acceded to. "Here," he said, "is an animal, a creature of God, which, in great distress, has sought my protection and hospitality. Would it be noble on my part to drive forth my guest to be devoured by your dogs?"

The prince broke out into reproaches, asserting that the land belonged to him, and he could not understand how strangers and vagabonds, of whom he knew little or nothing, could venture to settle upon it without his permission.

Quite undismayed by this attack, Illtyd continued to plead the cause of his *protégé* with an earnestness and eloquence which indicated a man of rank and of cultivated mind. He attracted the attention of all present; and as soon as he perceived that their anger had cooled down, he asked, in the name of God, and as a favour to himself, that the life of the animal might be spared. Perceiving that they remained silent, he quietly begged of them to share the hospitality he had given to the stag, and partake of such humble fare as he could offer. Both of these requests were granted; the stag remained unmolested, and the invitation to dinner was accepted.

It was but an humble feast that Illtyd could place before his guests; it consisted of brown bread, vegetables, and a few fishes; whilst, instead of wine, the clear water of the spring furnished them with drink. The huntsmen, being accustomed to high living, were not sparing in their comments on this ascetic fare.

Merchion and his party, however, becoming aware that their entertainer was no other than Illtyd, "The Knight," the celebrated companion in arms of King Arthur, were somewhat ashamed of their rude behaviour to a nobleman and an illustrious soldier, who in every respect was the equal, if not the superior, of Merchion himself. Illtyd, no doubt, narrated his own story—how, in the course of a hunting expedition in the neighbourhood of Llancarvan, he had come in contact with St. Cadoc, and how the deep impression which the conversation of that renowned servant of God had made upon him had induced him to forsake for ever the world and its vanities.

The soul of Merchion was much moved by this meeting with Illtyd. Again and again would he see the stag tranquilly reposing in the cell, the hounds, spell-bound, at its entrance, the courageous resistance of the hermit, and his saintly conversation. His soul was filled with admiration for Illtyd; and, far from thinking of driving from the land, where he sought to serve God, this holy recluse, he felt it his duty to endow him with that spot on which he had settled. The Welsh chieftains were, as a rule, noble-hearted, and appreciated supernatural action.

The guardian angel of Merchion, as the hagiographer remarks, seems at this time to have whispered into his ear the necessity of reforming his life, and making satisfaction for his many transgressions of the laws of God and of the Church, and to have reminded him—the lord of the surrounding territory—that the spot upon which Illtyd had settled was of no use, being inhabited only by wild beasts, and that it was his duty to offer it for the service of God. The holy hermit, once the knight of King Arthur, would, in course of time, transform it into blooming gardens and cultivated fields.

The chieftain obeyed this inspiration, and, following the example of a neighbouring prince, uncle of St. Cadoc, who had ceded the territory of Llancarvan to his nephew, bestowed upon Illtyd the plain of Lantwit, or a portion of it.

The charter of this grant cannot now be discovered, but it must have existed, and been similar in form to hundreds of such deeds as they are to be found in the "Liber Landavensis."

The monks of old, as their lives attest, were wont to bury themselves in forests and desert islands. Their object was to fly from the world, but invariably, when their place of retreat was discovered, they were joined by pious disciples; and Illtyd the Knight was not exempted from this general rule. Numerous souls, eager to advance in the service of God, visited our saint, and by degrees he found himself at the head of a religious community.

Dubricius, first Bishop of Llandaff, faithful to the precepts of St. Germanus, who strongly urged the spread of sound religious education throughout the country, was thankful to Divine Providence for bestowing upon him such a man as Illtyd. He was quite aware of the brilliant education, the high talents, of this new votary of the religious life, and determined to turn them to the best account for the benefit of his diocese.

Dubricius and Illtyd.

He urgently pressed upon Illtyd the necessity of persons who were devoted to God and His Church consecrating themselves to the education of the rising generation, and informed him that such were the instructions he had himself received from Germanus.

Illtyd received the behest of his bishop as the command of God, and the necessary steps were soon taken for laying the foundation of the University of Lantwit-Major, which was to shine over Britain for many centuries to come as a beacon of learning and sanctity. Dubricius invested Illtyd with the monastic habit, and admitted him to the tonsure and various minor orders, crowning all by ordaining him priest.

It may not be out of place to introduce here some of the traditions which have been handed down in connection with the antiquity of Lantwit-Major. This district, in the time of the Romans, was called Caerworgorn. In the vicinity there still exists an ancient Roman fortress or camp, with triple ramparts, the position of which it would have been nearly impossible to force at a time when artillery was unknown.

Antiquity of Lantwit-Major, according to Welsh tradition.

According to the Iolo MSS.,[1] Christianity found entrance into Caerworgorn even in the times of the Apostles. Thus, we are told that a daughter of Caractacus (Caradoc), named Eurgain, followed her captive father to Rome, and there became a Christian. On her return to Britain, she built a church in this part of the country, and also a college for twelve saints.

In the second century, King Lucius enlarged the College of Eurgain, and endowed it for the maintenance of a hundred saints.

The Emperor Theodosius also favoured this foundation, which was sometimes called the College of Lucius and sometimes that of Theodosius.[2]

Welsh tradition goes so far as to assert that St.

---

(1) Iolo MSS., p. 555.   (2) Iolo MSS. p. 442.

Patrick was resident in this locality at the time he was kidnapped by the Irish pirates.

During the decline of the Roman power in Britain these coasts were exposed to the ravages of pirates, who were constantly cruising in the Bristol Channel, and on one of their marauding expeditions they set fire to the college, which was reduced to a heap of ruins. It was afterwards rebuilt, and called the College of Illtyd.

No doubt, the associations connecting this place with the early history of the Christian religion in Britain influenced Dubricius and Illtyd in selecting it as a suitable position for a college. The Bishop of Llandaff came in person to mark out the boundaries of the future university. A place was fixed upon for a cemetery, and the plot of ground on which the church was to be erected was enclosed by a quadrangular ditch. Round, the sacred edifice as a centre, the various buildings of the establishment were to be constructed. A clear stream flowing at the western side of the church afforded an ample supply of water.

Like similar institutions of the period, that of Lantwit was to comprise a monastery, a college, and an hospital—all on a huge scale. The stream separated, to a certain extent, the monastery from the colleges and the monks from the seculars. Though the professors were under the necessity of coming into frequent contact with the scholars, still they lived apart from them when not actually engaged in teaching.

Any stranger now visiting the ruins of Lantwit must be struck with the beautiful position chosen by its founders. It proves them to have been men of cultured taste and of practical good sense. It commands a splendid view of the Bristol Channel and the wooded hills of Somersetshire.

The soil is good in that part of the country, and by the constant and intelligent labour of the monks this became one of the best cultivated districts in Glamorganshire.

Rees, in his notes on the " Liber Landavensis," justly remarks that this seminary, founded by St. Illtyd in the fifth century, acquired so high a reputation that scholars flocked to it from all parts of Christendom, amongst whom were sons of British nobles and foreign princes. So numerous were the pupils that at one time their number amounted to upwards of two thousand, for whose accommodation no fewer than four hundred houses of residence were provided, together with seven large halls or colleges.

The various colleges were often designated cells: there was the cell of Eurgain, the pious daughter of Caradoc; then there were the cells of King Arthur, of Dubricius, and of Illtyd. During the lifetime of the founder this last was called Bangor Llewersant, or the Monastery of St. Lucius, whose conversion to Christianity, in the second century, we have already narrated.

Other names seem at times to have been adopted as the indication of particular cells; for instance, we have the College of Matthew, of Mark, of Luke, of John, of Arthur, of St. David, of Morgan, of Eurgain, and of Amon. Many of these had, no doubt, been benefactors to the monastery, in gratitude for which their names were attached to certain divisions of the establishment.

These various colleges, any one of which mustered as many students as the total number to be counted in a modern seat of learning, were each under the rule of its own separate prior, and all the priories worked together under the guidance of Illtyd.

As we have already seen, the early Celtic monks regulated the hours of prayer in such a manner as to ensure the praises of Almighty God being sung both by day and night in their churches without any intermission. A guard of honour was in constant attendance before the altar, because Jesus in the tabernacle must not be deserted. It was St. Illtyd's desire that a deputation from each college or priory should alternately succeed each other in thus offering homage to the Almighty.[1]

[1] The following somewhat puzzling description of Lantwit-Major is found in the Iolo MSS.:—"Illtyd founded seven churches, and appointed seven companies for each church, and seven halls or colleges in each company, and seven saints in each college.

Otherwise:—Seven Churches	...	7
Seven Companies	...	7
Seven Collegiate Halls	...	49
		343
Seven Saints	...	2401

Prayer and praise were kept up without ceasing day and night, by twelve saints, men of learning, of each company." (Iolo MSS., p. 555.)

The spiritual wants of the inhabitants of the district were not neglected, fifty-six canons being appointed for missionary work, to look after scholars, pilgrims, and settlers; to instruct the people, hear their confessions, and attend them at the hour of death.

Standard of education at Lantwit The Lantwit standard of education was much the same as that adopted in the schools of the present day. The college admitted pupils from the earliest period of life, and kept them until their education was finished. The course of study included Latin, Greek, rhetoric, philosophy, theology, and mathematics; and these were taught with so much success that Lantwit was looked upon by the most eminent persons as the first college in Britain. Most of the great saints and apostles of the country who lived in the generation succeeding that of Illtyd had been educated by him; and these included St. David, St. Samson, St. Gildas, St. Tugdual, St. Daniel of Bangor, and many others; and from Lantwit emanated, in a great measure, the bishops and abbots both of Wales and Brittany.

The scholars of Illtyd were taught to handle the spade as well as the pen. The rule of the college did not sanction exemption from manual labour, no matter what rank or position the student might occupy. Thus we see the junior pupils employed—like St. Samson—in driving sparrows from the corn-fields, and others cutting grain and binding sheaves in harvest-time. It was the importance attached to manual labour, and the vigour and constancy with which it was pursued, which gave so high a reputation to the monastery for producing architects and builders. The cloister was believed, with reason, to furnish the best mechanics in every branch of industry.

Some monks—like those of St. David—made no use of animals in the cultivation of the soil; but Illtyd employed both deer and oxen in ploughing, drawing timber, and many other forms of labour.

At the foot of Lantwit is a narrow but long valley—now forming beautiful grazing meadows—which separated as by a natural trench an ancient camp on the sea-shore from the mainland.

Illtyd, wishing to reclaim this land, built an embankment, consisting of stones, cemented with clay as mortar. A small bridge in the centre spanned the opening left to carry to the sea the waters of the stream. Three times was this embankment washed away and destroyed during storms, and Illtyd feared it was useless to wrestle against the power of the mighty ocean. However, he made a fourth effort, and, taught by experience, constructed a more solid sea-wall, of sufficient strength to resist the action of the waves. This piece of successful engineering was considered almost miraculous by his contemporaries.

We have already narrated that Illtyd and his wife separated by mutual consent, in order that

St. Illtyd visited by Trynihid.

both might embrace the religious life. The pious Trynihid, like her husband, retired to a convent, in company with some others of her sex who wished to serve God in the cloister. However, after several years, she became desirous of once more seeing the companion of her youth, in whose society she had spent so many happy days. She visited Lantwit; but her former husband would neither see her nor allow her to see him, neither speak to her nor be spoken to. He said that, as they had parted for ever in this world, they could not meet again except before the throne of God, when summoned to receive the reward of their sacrifice.

Trynihid, however, insisted on seeing him, at least at a distance. When her eyes rested on him who had been her husband they found the late gallant knight clothed in skins as a labourer, his hands and face covered with mud. His appearance indicated a severe life; he was bent and emaciated, and a snow-white beard covered his breast. The lady wept as the contrast between his present state and that of former days forced itself upon her mind. She remembered him as a noble soldier in the train of King Arthur. She had listened to the bards as they sung in the banquet-hall of his bravery in the battle-field. He had been honoured with the name of Illtyd "The Knight," because of his courage in war and his courtesy in peace, and she had gloried in being the wife of such a husband. Now his appearance was that of a hardy, but rude, peasant. Still, as she recognised in this transformation the effect of Divine grace, and the result of a fixed determination to serve God, and gain heaven by the practice of the three Evangelical Counsels, she returned to her convent in order to follow the example of her husband.

Persecution is a necessary appendix in the life of a saint. Those who wish to live piously as servants of Jesus Christ must, like their Master, take up their cross and carry it along the road to Calvary, and make up their minds to suffer persecution.

Persecution.

Strange to say, the hand which afflicted Illtyd was that of the first benefactor God had raised up to help the saint in his mission.

Merchion, as we have already seen, granted large tracts of land to Illtyd; but in course of time, when the monastery had been established on a solid foundation, this same prince turned against the saint whom he had so much admired, an instance of the mutability of human favour which recalls to mind that saying of holy Scripture, "Woe to him who trusteth in man, or in the powerful of the earth." [1]

This prince, fretful and inconstant, was entirely in the hands of his officers, in whose choice he was unfortunate. He either could not or would not open his eyes to their evil deeds, a fact which made him unpopular

(1) Jer. xvii. 5.

amongst his subjects. Two of these unworthy favourites, at different times, broke up the friendship which existed between Illtyd and Merchion. Their names were Cefygid and Cyflym. In the old Celtic vernacular the latter appellation is equivalent to an acute hound—*fin limier* in French.

The duties of these men consisted in bringing to their master the tributes to be paid by his subjects. It was an office sufficiently respectable in itself, because in every society taxes of some sort must be imposed and collected. But these officers behaved more like pashas serving a Sultan than the ministers of a Christian prince ruling over Christian subjects. Under the pretext of executing the orders of their master, they worked for their own private interests. Their journeys through the country were marked by exactions and misdeeds of every kind; neither property nor person was safe in their hands.

The aggrieved inhabitants came to the Abbot of Lantwit, as to a father and protector, and begged him to use his influence in convincing Merchion of the unworthiness of his ministers, because any complaints *they* might make would obtain no other result but an increase of vexations.

To enrich themselves, these unscrupulous men impoverished their master, whose tribute yearly decreased; and to make up for deficiencies they conceived the plan of forcing the abbot and his community to supply corn and cattle for the use of the king. The monastery was rich in both, because there hundreds of God's servants worked hard and industriously.

Illtyd could not consent to this imposition. His possessions belonged to God and to the poor; the charters, laws, and customs of the country exempted all such lands from any tribute. It was to his labours and those of his brethren the productiveness of the soil was due; and if the followers of Merchion had spent their time in a similar manner, instead of devoting it to hunting and other sports, his territory would be quite as fertile. Illtyd declared that the rights and privileges of his monastery were entrusted to his guardianship, and he could not allow them to be violated.

His opponents were not so easily to be checked. They carried on their plunder and vexations in various ways. Under the plea, for instance, that the cattle of Lantwit-Major had trespassed on the ground of Merchion, these cattle were seized and "pounded," nearly starved to death, and then returned to their owners in mockery. Things went on in this way for several years, when both agents successively died unnatural deaths, which was looked upon by the people as a punishment from heaven.

Merchion, who attributed their fate to the curse of Illtyd, resolved to be revenged. He publicly declared his regret at having permitted the monks to build on his land, saying that if Lantwit had been left to the wild beast, wolves, and deer, he would have had both sport and peace. He was prevailed upon by his courtiers to place himself at the head of his soldiers and march to the monastery to drive away Illtyd and his brethren. On several occasions he thus appeared at Lantwit with threats of war, but we do not find that he committed any actual violence.

We regret to learn that this chieftain's death is also described as a chastisement from God. His first intercourse with Illtyd denoted the possession of noble qualities, and one would wish to see him at the latter part of his life true to the sentiments of earlier days. Through the influence of unscrupulous ministers he was induced to persecute a saint, and endeavour to undo a work which he had fostered in its infancy.

Illtyd secretly departs from his brethren.
When the founder of Lantwit became aware of the machinations of Merchion, and the motives which prompted them, he came to the resolution of leaving his monastery. As these attacks were chiefly directed against his person, he hoped that his retirement might abate the anger of the prince and facilitate satisfactory arrangements between the monks and the chieftain. This circumstance offered also a favourable opportunity of following his attraction for a solitary life. Aware, however, that his religious brethren would on no account sanction his departure, he kept it as a secret, and arranged his plan in such

a manner as to preclude the possibility of anyone forming any idea of what direction he had taken on leaving.

Away from his brethren, without a home or a friend, the saint wandered about the country until he came to the banks of the Ewenny, a river which flows into the sea below Bridgend. After further roaming, under the concealment of the woods, he discovered a cave, which he looked upon as the home provided for him by Divine appointment.

He felt happy. Once more he would be enabled to lead the life of a hermit, free from all those cares which the administration of a large community necessarily entail. Now his soul, undisturbed, could penetrate into the mysteries of Divine love, and no creature in the world could intrude on his conversation with his dear Redeemer. He lived much in the same way as Paul and Anthony in the deserts of Egypt. According to the legends, every ninth hour a loaf of bread was miraculously provided for him, and after his frugal repast he visited a neighbouring spring and, with the aid of his hands, drank of its clear waters.

The secret of his retreat was revealed through the following circumstance:—Gildas, the historian, was both a master of letters and of the art of foundry; he had cast a bell, which he intended for St. David, then residing at Menevia. A brother was dispatched there with the present.

On arriving near the retreat of Illtyd, the bell rang, and its sweet tone, echoing through the silence of the forest, attracted the attention of the hermit, who came out of his cave to investigate the cause of the sound, and fell in with the brother and his present to St. David.

This was a pleasant circumstance to the monks and to the people at large, who looked upon Illtyd as the defender of their rights. They had already searched the whole country, and interrogated sailors at every seaport, but all to no purpose. As soon as his place of retreat was known, a deputation started off at once to bring him back to Lantwit, whether willing or unwilling.

No account of the last days of this celebrated servant of God, or the year and place of his death, has been handed down by the Welsh MSS. Society. Some mention is made of his having established a branch of his order at Ty-gwyn ar Taf, chiefly for the study of the higher branches of theology; also, that the Paulinus so often mentioned in the lives of St. David and St. Teilo is no other than Illtyd, and that under that name he assisted at the Council of Brefi, together with Dubricius, as one of the elders amongst the clergy.

Some maintain that Illtyd died and was buried in Brittany, others in Wales[1].

Illtyd's memory remained sacred in the minds of future generations, as preserved in the

(1) An archæologist, living in Cardiff, maintains that the tombstone of Illtyd is to this day to be seen in Brecknockshire.

traditions of Britain and Armorica. Soldiers were proud of him, because, in his early life, he had reflected lustre on their ranks, and to them he ever remained "Illtyd the Knight." The clergy reverenced him as an eminent scholar and clever administrator; monks looked upon him as their model, and the Celtic Church recognised the great services he had rendered to religion; for he had trained up, as his successors, a legion of saints, bishops, and founders of religious houses, as we have already seen.

The Archbishop of Dôl was the intimate friend of Illtyd, and, it is believed by many, that in token of gratitude to his old master, Samson erected an elaborate monument, at Lantwit, to his memory. Excavations have lately brought to light his memorial-stone, and the inscription, still extant, testifies that it was erected by a dear disciple to the master of his youth.

Lantwit, after the death of its founder, continued to flourish up to the time of the Norman invasion, then a part of its revenues were given to Tewkesbury.

To this day a little bell is exhibited at Lantwit, which is said to have been placed there in the time of Illtyd.

His feast was religiously observed both in Britain and Armorica; in the diocese of Dôl on the 16th of November, in that of Leon, on the 7th and also the 14th of the same month.

CHAPTER XIV.

St. David.

David, in Welsh Dewi, successor of St. Dubricius in the See of Caerleon, and subsequently the first archbishop of (St. David) Menevia, belongs to that generation of Welsh saints who became the leaders of the Church in Cambria, when Dubricius, Cadoc, and Illtyd, advanced in years, had either retired from public duties or gone to receive in a better world the reward of a well-spent life in this.

His contemporaries in Wales were St. Teilo, second Bishop of Llandaff; Daniel, first Bishop of Bangor; Padarn, of Llanbadarn; and Kentigern, Bishop of Glascow. In David's time the last-named prelate resided at St. Asaph, in North Wales, at the head of a large religious community.

Some of his countrymen, or, probably, fellow-students, such as Samson, Paul of Leon, Gildas, Eleonor, and Tugdual, were either bishops or at the head of prosperous monasteries in Brittany.

(1) Compiled from the "Cambro-British Saints," "Britannia Sancta," Rev. O'Hanlon's "Life of St. David."

ST. DAVID. 447

David is to this day the popular name amongst the Cambrians. We cannot convey a clearer idea of the high esteem in which he was held by his countrymen while he lived, than by quoting their own words at the Council of Brefi. When from his platform (composed, not of wood, but of the upper garments of the thousands assembled) the clear voice and eloquence of David had fascinated his audience, and uprooted for ever the Pelagian heresy from their minds, they, in their enthusiasm, pronounced him to be the greatest man their country had ever produced. "God," they said, "had given Peter to Rome, Mark to Alexandria, Martin of Tours to France, Patrick to Ireland, Samson to Brittany, and David to Wales." *[David the popular name in Cambria.]*

When in the grave veneration clung to his memory. We all know that amongst the Irish Patrick is the name most in favour at the baptismal font; so, in the Cambrian household the most used—we may say the national—name is David.

In reading the life and times of St. David, one cannot help noticing another British celebrity, who figured in the political world, and stands by the side of the patron of Wales in national popularity. It is the far-famed Arthur. This bold captain, who is made by the romancer the type of chivalry, came into the world and departed from it about the same time as David; for Arthur, born about the year 456, died in 542

—dates tallying with the birth and death of David. Both the patriot and the servant of God entered on their respective careers early in life; for Arthur at fifteen is met with in the battle-field, and David embraced monastic life whilst yet very young. The warrior fought for the independence of his native shores; the saint, fighting for truth against error, extirpated heresy and reformed his country. Both of them, out of devotion, went in pilgrimage to Jerusalem; and after their departure from this world, David and Arthur remained the two most popular names in the annals of their race.

Birth. It is rather difficult to point out with accuracy the locality and the year in which the patron of Wales came into the world. There is no doubt whatever that he was born in the south-west of Wales—Cardiganshire.

Pembrokeshire and Carmarthenshire also claim the honour of having given birth to this eminent servant of God. His father was Santus, or Sandle, a Cardigan chieftain, and his mother, who was called Nun, or Melaria, was a daughter of the Brythan princes ruling that region we now call Brecknockshire. His birth and baptism are said to have been honoured by miracles.

For example, it is related that a tyrant of Dimeta planned the destruction of David at the time of his birth. This wicked man had learned from the British magi that the whole country around must one day become subject to that infant; they even pointed out the exact place where his mother would live at the birth of this highly-favoured child. The tyrant and his associates devised means to ensnare the babe. The Almighty, however, protected the mother and child, and frustrated the designs of their enemies; for, at the very moment of St. David's birth, a fearful tempest, mingled with lightning, thunder, hail, and rain, swept over the country. This frightful storm so interfered with their wicked plans, and so terrified them, that they abandoned the whole scheme.

Furthermore, the ancient legends tell us that the birth of David was revealed to St. Patrick by an angel, after the manner in which the birth and mission of John the Baptist was revealed to Zachary.

The future apostle of Ireland was staying in the valley of Glyn-Rosin, near or in the present town of St. David. He had laid out the plan of a monastery in that place, and was beginning, with the earnestness peculiar to the monks, to carry out the buildings, when an angel appeared to him and said:—"Patrick, God has not appointed this place for thee, but has reserved it for a child, not yet born, nor to come into the world till thirty years are past."

St. Patrick felt somewhat displeased, not to say disheartened, for the angelic message produced the impression on his mind that Almighty God, whom he had served from his youth, had thrown him aside, as a useless servant, while He preferred to bestow His favours upon a child not yet born. In the eyes of St. Patrick this seemed to be very bad usage. However, the angel bade him to cheer up, and, pointing to the west, set before his eyes a beautiful panorama of Ireland, with its bays, mountains, and plains. "That island, Patrick," the heavenly messenger added, "is to be the theatre of thy future labours. It was the land of thy captivity in thy younger days; there, for six years, thou didst tend the cattle of Milcho; there, for the remainder of thy career, thou art to be the guide of kings and princes, and the instrument of God for the salvation of thousands. Begrudge not this land to the unborn child."

In the event of this vision having taken place about the time of his appointment to the Irish Missions, we find at once the exact date of St. David's birth; for St. Patrick began his mission in Ireland in 432; thirty years more, and we have 462 as the year St. David was born. But there is no conclusive evidence that St. Patrick was favoured with this vision at the time of his departure for Ireland. As we read previously, he had visited Britain several times.

St. David at Lantwit-Major and at Tygwyn ar Taf. Our saint received his education at the college of Illtyd, at Lantwit-Major, and it was in this religious house that he, very probably, embraced religious life, and took the several grades of holy orders up to the priesthood.

When the son had thus chosen a settled life, the mother emigrated to Brittany, in which country she spent the remainder of her life, weeping over the fault she had committed in her younger days. That fault was this: Melaria, or Nun, had consecrated herself to Almighty God in her youth; but, unfortunately, her beauty was so great that she fascinated Sandle, the Cardigan prince, and thus became the mother of St. David. Subsequently, when her duties as a mother no longer detained her in the world, she resolved to fulfil her promise to God and the Church, and to return to the kind of life she had chosen in her maiden days. She embarked for Brittany, and there ended her days in a convent. Her biographers have pinned to her name the epithet of "penitent." The people of Armorica for centuries pointed out to visitors the rocks on which she used to pray and weep.[1]

In the "Lives of the Cambro-British Saints" mention is often made of Ty-gwyn ar Tâf, or Whitland, in Carmarthenshire, as a seminary for higher studies. Paulinus, a disciple of St. Germanus, founded and governed this college, supposed to have been situated in a narrow but beautiful vale, formed by hills, about a mile from the present Whitland railway station.[2] St. David resided ten years in this locality as a

---

(1) Lobineau. "Vies des Saints de Bretagne."

(2) Several ancient historians have erred in making Whitland the Isle of Wight. Whitland, or White Land, is the English name for Ty-gwyn ar Tâf, or the White House on Taff.

member of the community. St. Teilo, the second Bishop of Llandaff, amongst many others, was his companion in this solitude. Several incidents connected with the life led at the *White House* have already been related in the biography of St. Teilo, to which we must refer the reader.

<small>St. David restores sight to his master.</small>

During the residence of David in this locality, an event took place which powerfully brings forth the humility of St. Paulinus. It also shows the confidence he had in the prayers of holy youths who had been brought up from their infancy in the love of God, and some of whom had, perhaps, never lost the innocence of their baptism.

The aged principal had so far lost his sight that it was difficult for him even to celebrate the holy Sacrifice of the Mass. Aware that his disciples were holy youths, and confident that, as such, their prayers were powerful in heaven, he called them all in turn to make the sign of the Cross over his eyes, that they might enable him to again put his soul in external communication with the visible works of God. They complied with the wishes of their master, but obtained no result until David came, last of all. Paulinus said to him, " Look at the state of mine eyes. I cannot see, and they pain me so much that it is with the greatest difficulty I celebrate the holy Sacrifice of the Mass." The young priest replied, " We are now ten years together, and never yet have mine eyes met thine." Paulinus, struck by the religious habit which this evinced, said to David, "Well, since it is so, as thou art a dear friend of God, make the sign of the Cross on mine eyes and I shall be cured." David obeyed, and Paulinus recovered his sight.

It is no easy matter to place in a proper chronological order the various events connected with the life of St. David. The ancient MSS. are not very particular in this respect; so it is rather difficult to state at what period of his life he visited Jerusalem. According to the "Liber Landavensis" (Life of St. Teilo), it would seem that David, Padarn, and Teilo started on this pilgrimage during their stay with Paulinus.

We have already spoken of this pilgrimage to the Holy Land, and of the reception given to the three British pilgrims, and have seen how they strengthened the wavering faith of the East by their preaching to the heretics, and even to the Jews. Among the presents given by the Patriarch to St. David was a portable altar on which he consecrated the body and blood of our Lord. David afterwards presented it to the church of Glastonbury.

David, who had been in the earlier part of his life a persevering student and an edifying religious, proved also to be a hard-working missionary, when once launched into public life. His start in this new course was thus brought about:—

After the saint had spent ten years in the forest of Whitland, an angel appeared to him and said, "Beloved of God, it is now time to turn to account, for the salvation of souls, a talent entrusted to thy care." The subsequent works of David prove how he corresponded with the call of heaven. Monastic institutions all over South Wales, from Raglan, not far from the river Wye, to St. David's, in Pembrokeshire, bear testimony to his zeal and energy of thought and act. He built twelve monasteries in his lifetime.

St. David at Glastonbury.

The first place we find him at work in, is Glastonbury, the cradle of Christianity in Britain, termed by our ancestors "the first ground of God" in England. It was there, as we have seen, that Joseph of Arimathea and his companions erected the first Christian temple to Almighty God.[1]

The building already there was small in dimensions and simple in structure. It was made of timber, roofed in with reeds or rushes. The palisades that supported this simple roof were decorated with the bark of trees, more or less artistically arranged. This modest chapel of the first apostles of the Britons seems to have been at times somewhat neglected. Although repaired at different periods, it was no more than a ruined edifice when St. David went to Glastonbury. The saint's first idea was to pull down the whole fabric and build a new church

---

(1) "Cambro-British Saints," p. 63. Sammes. Cambden.

altogether; but a religious respect for the past, and a warning from an angel, bade him leave intact as much as possible the work of the first missionaries of Britain. However, as the place was becoming every day too small for the religious requirements of Glastonbury, David added a new chancel, forty feet in length; and in order that future generations might not forget the church of St. Joseph, he placed a column in the centre, which pointed out the limits of the old church and the additions he had made. This chancel was dedicated to "Mary, Virgin, and Mother of God."

The temple thus enlarged did not reach the dimensions which Gothic cathedrals were to attain at a later time under the genius and energy of the monks of the Middle Ages.

The structure of Joseph of Arimathea was sixty feet by twenty-six or thirty feet; and the forty feet more added by St. David, with a proportionate width, covered a respectable area for those days—namely, about one hundred feet by thirty feet. Considering the little comfort people of those times required in their homes or their places of worship, the church could accommodate hundreds.

Particular mention is made of the great care David took in the decoration of the altar. In a Catholic church the altar is the chief ornament; for on it is immolated the Lamb of God for the sins of mankind. The stone of this altar was a present David had received from the Patriarch of Jerusalem. We are also told that the tabernacle was beautifully decorated, and even inlaid with sapphires of the greatest value, procured by the zeal of Glastonbury's restorers.

The connection of David with Glastonbury brought this cradle of Christianity once more prominently before the minds of the Britons. King Arthur, on his death-bed, wished to be buried in this locality; and his tomb there was brought to light by the excavations carried out by Henry II., King of England. A stone, in the shape of a rude cross, was discovered, with the following inscription :—

"Hic jacet sepultus inclytus rex.
Arthur IV. Insula avaloni."

When the Anglo-Saxon race was converted to Christ Glastonbury showed forth a brighter lustre. King Ina, in the year 698, pulled down the old church, and in its place erected a stately temple, dedicated to St. Peter and St. Paul. He also built a college for the education of English youths, and brought over from Ireland celebrated professors. To defray all these expenses he laid a tax of a penny on every household.[1]

Glastonbury was made by St. David the great depôt in which he trained his first disciples, and out of which, in the course of his wonderful career, he took the various subjects who were to aid him in establishing so many religious institutions throughout Wales.

(1) Sammes, p. 212.

The monastic establishment of Glastonbury placed on a good footing, David thought of establishing branches of his order in other localities. He went to Bath, and there placed some of his brethren. Everybody knows that Bath is a fashionable resort of the aristocracy in our modern times, and that it is much frequented by rich invalids. The ancient legends tell us that the springs of Bath, which are now so popular, were once deleterious to health, but through the prayers of St. David they became most salubrious to persons who washed in their waters.[1]

Monastic life of St. David.

From Bath our saint crossed the Severn Sea, which we now call the Bristol Channel, and took a northern direction. The regions now known as Radnorshire and Herefordshire felt the beneficial result of his zeal. Monasteries and churches rose from the ground under his energetic will. Leominster heard, at night, the sweet accents of Matins and Lauds chanted by his brethren. Then he came to Raglan, in Monmouthshire, and there established another religious community.

We find him next directing his steps towards his native shores in the west. However, on his way to the present Pembrokeshire, he stopped at Llangyvelach, in the district of Gower, not far from the present town of Swansea. There he marked out a new camp for the soldiers of

(1) "Cambro-British Saints."

Christ. Then he continued his journey to the extremity of Wales, to Glyn-Rosin, which has since lost its name and taken that of St. David.

Anyone who knows anything about religious institutions, the work they entail, the confidence they inspire, marvels how a single man could have wrought such wonders. A religious community, especially in the fifth and sixth centuries, contained a great number of men, all trained to follow a severe rule distasteful to flesh and blood, and all fully persuaded that the life they led was the best fitted for the salvation of their souls. Everyone in these institutions was there by his own free will; no compulsion was used to force him to embrace this severe mode of living. Yet hundreds upon hundreds, taken from every rank of society, noblemen and bondsmen, clergy and laity, rushed with enthusiasm after St. David, fascinated by his virtue and eloquence, and consecrated themselves to God under his direction, confident that he was a safe master of spiritual life.

Irishmen crossed the sea and came over to Wales to serve God under the guidance of St. David. Princes left the world and put on the monastic dress. Amongst others, mention is made of Constantine, the Cornish prince so severely rebuked by Gildas.

The rule of St. David. These various monasteries followed one common mode of living. The rule was much the same as that of St. Martin of Tours, and of

St. Patrick, with such alterations as were required by climate and customs.

Every monk was to earn his daily bread by the sweat of his brow. "He that does not work, let him not eat" was a favourite maxim of David. Labour screens man from many temptations, such, for example, as impure thoughts.

Everything was to be common—no mine nor thine. He required no dowry, nor would he allow any presents to be received. There was plenty of uncultivated ground about Wales that would supply their wants.

Contrary to what he had seen practised at Lantwit-Major by his master, Illtyd, who made use of oxen and horses in cultivating the country, David wished that the land of his monastery should be tilled only by the spade. During work, on the road to or from the fields, a strict silence was kept, much the same as amongst the Trappists in our days.

The time marked out for work over, the brethren returned home, and spent whatever time remained either in studying, writing, or prayer. In the evening they all went to the church. Then came the time of supper; afterwards evening prayer and rest. At cock-crowing they rose for Matins and Lauds.

Their diet was simple and wholesome, and much like that of the poorer classes. It consisted of bread and vegetables, cooked according to the custom of the time; water and milk were their only beverages. However, in case of old age and infirmity, the rule became indulgent—a better fare was allowed, and animal food could be served.

The partisans of vegetarianism find in this kind of life a strong argument in favour of their system. These ancient monks never tasted animal food, except in case of sickness, and yet sickness and infirmities were rare things amongst them, and most of them died, if not centenarians, at least nearly so.

The brethren were expected to disclose their inward thoughts and temptations to their superiors.

When a postulant knocked at the door of a monastery, instead of being cajoled into becoming a novice, he was, on the contrary, to be tried in humility and sincerity of purpose. For ten days he was kept at the door, and dealt with in such a manner as to bring down his pride. When he stood the trial, he was handed to the master of novices, to be trained to spiritual life and broken in to the customs of religion, till such time as he was qualified to be admitted as one of the brethren.

This ancient rule for the admission of new members into a religious order closely resembles that used in our own days. There is a time of probation, in which the order tries the postulant, and the postulant tries the order. This probation in our modern times lasts about two years, or even thirty months. Would it not be desirable that persons entering the marriage state should, in like manner, take time to consider?

David himself, the founder and ruler of these religious houses, was the first to show them good example. Among other evidences of the fact, we read that, not satisfied with the keeping of these rules, already severe enough, he was in the habit, like Illtyd, of plunging his body into cold water, usually about midnight, the better to subdue his passions. His days were spent in reading, teaching, and in the government of his brethren. Divine love burnt so strongly in his heart as to become reflected on his countenance, especially when, at the altar, he offered up the holy Sacrifice of the Mass. In prayer, he seemed to be speaking with the very angels, and at times tears bedewed his cheeks. The passion of our Lord, His love for mankind, and the ingratitude of the world, the sins of his own countrymen, so powerfully denounced by one of his contemporaries and fellow-Briton, called these tears from his eyes.

The Council of Brefi, in Cardiganshire, was the most celebrated ecclesiastical congress ever held in Wales, as it laid down a code of Church laws and religious customs which for ages remained deeply engrafted in the minds and customs of a people naturally conservative. When Howell Dda, about four centuries later, endowed his country with a code, he religiously respected the canons of Brefi and Caerleon.

The Council of Brefi.

The council was held in the year 519, Hormisdas, the fifty-fourth Pope, occupying the chair of St. Peter, and Justin being the Emperor of the East.[1] The errors of Pelagianism, not then uprooted in the west, were the immediate cause for the assembling of this council. We have already seen that Pelagius and his false doctrines on grace were triumphantly refuted in Wales by Germanus and his companions, and we have also seen that a sound education was imparted to the Cambrian youth at Llancarvan and Lantwit-Major. They were less fortunate in the west, where some of the old clergy and a large proportion of the laity continued for a long time to be infected with the heresy.

Before leaving the world, Dubricius, then residing in Caerleon, thought it advisable, in the interests of religion, to call together, in a national council, the clergy and people, with the double object of confirming Welshmen in the true Catholic faith, and of reforming relaxed morals, by enforcing the ecclesiastical laws already in existence, or enacting such as were demanded by the times; for continual wars and the incessant irruptions of the Saxons had partially obliterated the laws of the Church.

It was, no doubt, a noble task on the part of Dubricius and his clergy to use their utmost endeavours to bring their flock to the observance of the Gospel, and to restrain, by ecclesiastical

(1) O'Hanlon.

means, the uncontrollable passions of the people, and especially of the princes, then all-powerful. Letters of convocation were addressed by Dubricius, as archbishop, to all bishops, abbots, clergy, and laity, to assemble at Brefi at a specified time, probably about Whitsuntide.

The geographical position of Brefi, or Llandewi Brevi, as it is now called, rendered it a most suitable place for the council. Three counties border it. A traveller starting from the present town of Lampeter cannot fail to reach the spot by following a good road along the river Teify. The valley throughout is picturesque and well cultivated. After eight miles' walk he will reach the Cwm Brevi Mountains, at the foot of which runs the river Brefi, on whose banks the church of St. David, standing on a raised plateau, points out the very spot where the council was held.

Shortly after the opening of the council the solitary valley was changed into an immense encampment, and a visitor could best obtain a just idea of the scene by climbing the mountains behind the river Brefi, whence his eye could command a view of what was going on below. The valley and the slopes of the hills were covered with tents, the respective occupants of which it would take too long to enumerate. A larger tent than the rest indicated the temporary chapel, in which the holy Sacrifice of the Mass was offered up before opening the business of the day.

The council lasted several weeks, and led to the neighbourhood an immense concourse of human beings; people were coming and going in crowds. Some stayed at Brefi a few days, and then returned home, but their places were soon filled up by fresh comers. Our modern exhibitions may give us an idea of the scene. There were prayers, singing, and daily instructions to the people on the necessity and manner of serving Christ. The unity of faith was the leading theme of the discourses. The fall of man, the necessity of grace, the institution by Jesus Christ of seven Sacraments as channels of grace, occupied a great portion of the time, and were proved by Scripture and by the traditions of past ages. Particular sessions were held by the clergy and leading laity, in which measures for the reformation of morals were proposed, discussed, and finally adopted or rejected.

For some time little progress was made in communicating to the crowd that enthusiasm which softens the heart and renders it fit to take in religious truth. The clergy felt they wanted a speaker who should become the mouthpiece of the Council. There were thousands present, but not one priest endowed with a voice that could penetrate through the crowds. They wanted a human trumpet, whose stentorian tones would thrill the masses. David was not present. Old Paulinus *(alias* Illtyd) solved every difficulty by the following suggestion, which was at once adopted by the bishops:—"There is in the country," he said, "an apostle and a bishop, who is not present. It is David of Glyn Rosin (Menevia). He should have been here; but his humility and love of solitude keep him away. A disciple of mine for many years at Ty-gwyn ar Taf, I know him to be sound in the faith, well versed in Holy Scripture and in the Fathers. Nature has gifted him with eloquence and a stentorian voice. He has preached the Gospel throughout Britain, and even at Jerusalem, in which place he was consecrated bishop."

Messengers were despatched to Menevia, conveying to the abbot the general wish of the Council, and requesting his presence. David declined the first two or three invitations "Who am I," he said, "that so much should be thought about my capacity? If the leading clergy of Wales have failed, as you say, in electrifying the people, is the Monk of Menevia so proud as to think that he can succeed better than a Teilo of Llandaff, or a Daniel, or many other members amongst the clergy." However, at last, called upon by Dubricius and Daniel, he could no longer refuse, so he departed, recommending himself to the prayers of his brethren. The ancient chroniclers relate that, when not far from Brefi, and on the banks of the river Teify (perhaps in the valley between Lampeter and the spot on which the Council was held), the curiosity of David and of the deputation was excited by

<small>David forced to the Council.</small>

<small>On his way to the Council David calls the dead from the grave.</small>

cries and lamentations coming from a cottage not far distant. The saint's heart was touched; here people were in sorrow, and he must see whether any consolation could be given them. The deputation objected to any delay on the road, as the bishops and people were anxious for his arrival.

"Go," said David, "before me, and inform them of my coming; I must meanwhile relieve my suffering neighbour." On arriving at the cottage, he found a mother, surrounded by women, weeping over the corpse of her only dear son. The mother besought the bishop, in the name of God, to bring her young boy to life again. The servant of God, full of faith, knelt on the ground and humbly asked Almighty God to display His power by restoring life to the dead. His prayer was granted, for the youth was restored both to life and health. And the mother, transported with joy, exclaimed, "My son that was dead, through God's favour and yours, is now alive." David then departed for Brefi, accompanied by the same youth whom the power of God had raised from the dead.

His reception at the Council was respectful; and, as all the trouble taken to bring him to Brefi was chiefly on account of the popular eloquence he was gifted with, the bishops soon induced him to exercise his talent in preaching. The legends narrate several prodigies that took place on the occasion. As we do not see any reason why we should call in question the narrative of our ancestors, or doubt that the power of God is displayed at suitable times, we will mention some of them. On a certain occasion, when he rose to preach in the presence of the multitude, a snow-white dove seemed to come down from heaven and at length to alight on the shoulder of David.[1] Again, it is said that the mound on which the present church of St. David stands, at Llandewi Brefi, rose under his feet so as to form a miraculous platform, from which he could effectively address his audience. When a visitor to Llandewi Brefi looks at this ground he sees it to be about an acre, on the banks of the Brefi, forming a mound, at some places fifteen or twenty feet above the rest of the ground.

The eloquence, the fine countenance, and the stentorian voice of David, resounding like a trumpet through the crowds, soon captivated the audience. He quickly reduced to their proper level all the arguments of heresy, and brought forth in the brightest light the truths of the Catholic Church.

By the preacher stood a young boy, who carried the Gospel and acted as acolyte to David. His history soon spread about, and when it became known that the boy had been dead and was called to life by the man of God, the veneration of the people knew no bounds.

[1] Rev. O'Hanlon.

Previous to this communication, David stood before them as a wonderful orator, but now he was also a living saint. From that moment the words of the preacher were to all present as pure Gospel. Had an angel came from heaven, he could not have exercised a greater influence. Pelagianism, with its subtilities, appeared to all in its falsehood, and was for ever rejected by the people. As we have already mentioned, several resolutions for the reformation of morals were adopted at Brefi, and David was requested to put them in canonical form.

David elected Archbishop.

At the end of this council Dubricius, far advanced in years, abdicated, and sailed for the island of Bardsey, there to end his life in solitude and prayer. David was unanimously elected by the nation to fill up the vacancy. He tried in vain to decline the position, but, willing or unwilling, he was made Archbishop of all Cambria. Settled in Caerleon, the metropolitan See, he wrote with his own hands the ecclesiastical laws agreed on at Brefi; and when the work was completed he called a second synod, in the City of the Legions, on the river Usk, and there submitted the canons to the assembled clergy. This Council is called in history the Council of Victory, no doubt from the fact that it crowned a double work—the destruction of Pelagianism and the reformation of manners. The Council of Brefi and its consequent of Caerleon, or Victory, fixed, as we have already seen, the religious customs and discipline of the Church in Wales. That of Brefi was held in 519, Hormisdas being then Pope. It is not easy to ascertain the precise year in which that of Caerleon was held, but the time probably was not long after that historically assigned to the first.

The old manuscripts are particular about remarking that these decrees were sent to Rome, and there approved and confirmed by Papal authority.[1] We do not record this fact as indicating an extraordinary line of conduct. The Britons practised the Catholic religion, and, as a matter of course, were in communion with Rome, where the head of the Church resided. Even Howell Dda, who was not a priest, and who did not legislate in that capacity, thought it his duty to submit his code to the Pope of Rome, lest it should contain anything militating against the laws of God or the Church.

A copy of the decrees of these two Councils had been for a long time kept in the archives of St. David's Cathedral, but was at last destroyed by pirates.[2] In fact, most of the ancient records of Britain's history have been thus destroyed by the flames, which generally followed the track of war in times past. In how many articles or canons the decrees of Brefi were embodied it is now hard to tell. In spirit and form they were like other councils that had been held in Ireland, Brittany, and Gaul about the same time.

(1) "Cambro-British Saints," p. 443.
(2) Rees' "Lives of the Welsh Saints."

The spirit of these ecclesiastical laws is reflected in the "Liber Landavensis," or the Register of Llandaff, and may be thus summed up:—

I. All ecclesiastical matters, such as doctrine of faith, discipline of the clergy, had to be settled by the Church. No ecclesiastic was to appeal to the civil power; if guilty of any misdemeanour he was to be judged by the bishop and his court. The bishops were to meet once a year on business connected with the Church.

II. The right of refuge was granted to churches and monasteries—there the sword was not to strike. These territories were consecrated to the religion of Jesus Christ, and the children of Jesus Christ were safe as long as they remained within their limits. The privileges of refuge thus granted to St. David by the National Council of Brefi were almost boundless, as we have already seen.

III. The relations between the ecclesiastical and civil powers were also defined. In case of quarrels between chieftains, the bishop was to use his best endeavours to bring them before the altar, and there, in the presence of God, the clergy, and nobility, to exact a promise that they would settle their differences amicably, and live in peace like brothers. If any one of them broke his promise, he was excommunicated, and often forced to abdicate. Several such instances occurred during the life of Oudoceus, third

Bishop of Llandaff, which the reader will find in his biography. In such cases Church and people worked hand in hand—a council settled all their differences.

IV. From the Iolo MSS. we may infer that the canons of St. David strongly urged the chieftains to lessen the horrors of war, and to procure security in judicial matters; for we find that Morgan, King of Glamorgan, who reigned shortly after the Council of Brefi, issued orders that an enemy should not be killed except when it could not be helped. He also gave orders that any man accused of a crime should be judged by twelve persons. In the laws of Howell Dda we likewise find the judge surrounded by twelve officers. Wales, for generations, had reason to be grateful to her clergy, and particularly to St. David, for what was done at Brefi. To commemorate the event, the old Cambrians built a church on the spot on which St. David preached, and, later on, a monastery. By the west door of the church stands a pillar, eight feet high and twelve inches square, to commemorate the patron of Wales. The natives call it the *staff* of David. To this day the language used by Dubricius, David, and others at the Council of Brefi is the vernacular of Welshmen in the valley and neighbourhood. Unfortunately, it conveys no longer the same religion—one, holy, catholic, and apostolic. The present vicar restored the church, but a Catholic who visits this ancient and venerable spot laments the absence of the Catholic altar for the holy Sacrifice of the Mass. Formerly the Church of Llandewi Brefi had five altars.

The Archiepiscopal See removed from Caerleon to St. David's.

Caerleon, since the second century the Metropolitan of the West, witnessed the Archiepiscopal See transferred to Llandaff for a few years, and then obtained the residence of Dubricius within its walls. St. David was destined to be the last Archbishop of Caerleon. After residing some time in that city, he resolved and obtained leave from King Arthur to transfer his See to the Monastery of Menevia, in Pembrokeshire, where he was to die and be buried.

St. David, whose sphere of action became widened as archbishop, continued through life to work hard in the vineyard of the Lord. His monasteries thrived more than ever throughout the country. "Everywhere," as Ricemark, one of his biographers, remarks, "the sounds of prayer were raised to the stars; everywhere good deeds were, on unwearied shoulders, carried to the bosom of the Church, and gifts of charity were, with powerful hand, distributed to the poor. . . . To the student he was learning; to the poor, life; to the orphans, nourishment; to the widows, support; to the country, a head; to the monk, a rule.[1]

God glorified David even during his mortal career, by bestowing on him the gift of perform-

---

(1) Ricemark's "Cambro-British Saints."

ing miracles. While yet he lived he is said to have restored sight to a Welsh chieftain; and we have already seen how, on his way to Brefi, he raised the dead to life. David's name is also connected with many of the sacred wells of Britain. On a certain day the brethren came to David, complaining sadly of the want of water in the fields they were cultivating; a rivulet passed not far off, and in winter was full of water, but in summer it nearly dried up. Man, beast, and vegetation suffered greatly. David had recourse to his usual mode of proceeding whenever he wanted to obtain a favour—prayer. An angel came down and pointed out a spot in which water would be found. The saint knelt, and, with out-stretched hands, asked of Almighty God to grant him what was wanted. As he prayed, a fountain of most clear water flowed.

A farmer, finding himself in the same predicament as the monks, and having heard how St. David had given them a plentiful well, went to the saint, requesting that he would render him the same service. He was a hard-working man, and lived with his family on the produce of his land. David accompanied him to his village; there, with the point of his stick, he opened the surface of the ground, and a clear stream of water bubbled forth. These wells were visited by the sick and infirm, many of whom were cured, through the intercession of St. David.

The precise year in which David departed this *His death.*

life, and the number of years he had lived on earth, have given rise to some difference of opinion. David probably died in 544, at the age of ninety-seven. Some think he reached the extraordinary age of one hundred and forty-seven years.

His last days were visited by extraordinary graces. On the eighth of the Kalends of March, corresponding with the twenty-second of February, the old servant of God was in the choir with his brethren, at the Night Office, when he fell into an ecstasy, and his countenance beamed with a Divine light. An angel stood by him, and said: "The hour thou hast sighed after is now at hand." This was a welcome communication to the venerable bishop. In a transport of joy, he replied, like old Simeon in the Temple, "Now, O, Lord, take thy servant in peace."

The monks, hearing this Divine colloquy, stopped the singing of the Office, and fell on their knees. David spoke a second time in an audible voice, and said, "Lord take my soul, and leave me no longer in this world of misery and danger." The angel spoke a second time, and told the servant of God to be ready for the first day of March, for on that day the angels would come and take his soul to heaven. This extraordinary apparition soon got abroad, and people rushed to Menevia, anxious once more to have a glance at the holy bishop.

From the time of the angelic vision to that of

his death he continued in the church, instructing the people and praying. During this time, like St. Paul, he seems to have been lifted up in mind, and shown the state of Britain and Ireland. On the Sunday following, he celebrated the holy Sacrifice of the Mass, blessed the congregation, and exhorted them to keep the laws of God and of the Church. "On Tuesday next," he said, "I am to depart from this world. I leave you to the guardianship of the Lord Jesus, who will strengthen you in keeping what I have taught."

Tuesday had dawned, when the whole city was roused from slumber by angelic voices, which resounded through the air with heavenly harmonies, and delicious odours filled the atmosphere. David had departed from this world, and his soul was then on its way up to heaven.[1] The monks, when they assembled to sing Lauds, felt, as it were, a foretaste of heaven and gathered new strength in the service of God full of what they had heard. At the same time, the intimate friend of David, St. Kentigern, living at St. Asaph, in North Wales, was favoured with a vision, in which he saw the holy bishop's soul taken up to heaven.

(1) These wonderful phenomena which sometimes occur at the death of a saint, extraordinary as they may seem, are not to be looked upon as legendary inventions, used with the view of embellishing the narrative. They are often facts, well attested by thousands of witnesses, and are not confined to one particular saint, country, or race. We find them mentioned in the history of the Church from the earliest centuries to the present. When the soul of the great St. Martin of Tours departed from this world, many—and amongst the rest Severinus, Bishop of Cologne—heard a chorus of the most harmonious melodies: it was the solemn, angelic procession leading it to glory. An angelic choir was heard in the air, chanting over the body of St. Samson when it was committed to the grave, as we shall

St. David was buried in Menevia, and the ceremony was solemn and imposing. His body, like those of St. Anthony and Martin of Tours, was followed to the grave by thousands of his countrymen of every class of society, and by hundreds of his monastic brethren. Nor was his memory to be ever forgotten; his tomb for centuries afterwards was visited by pilgrims, the afflicted in mind or body. Indeed, this veneration so grew that in the course of time St. David's, in Menevia, became the most general pilgrimage in the West of Britain. A visit of devotion to the saint's shrine was deemed holy; a journey to the tomb of the patron of Wales came to be generally looked upon as highly meritorious; hence the saying that "Two pilgrimages to St. David's equalled one to Rome." Even the kings of England visited the tomb of St. David.

The confidence of his countrymen in his intercession in heaven was unbounded. Soldiers on the battle-field, sailors on the sea, appealed to his protection in time of danger. Thus, we read of a certain Welshman, belonging to the diocese of Menevia, who was captured by the Saracens,

see in the next chapter. The body of St. Didacus (whose feast occurs Nov. 13th) exhaled the sweetest fragrance after death, and that for months; for the crowd of pious visitors to his mortal remains was so great that the authorities were prevented from burying him for some time. It is useless to endeavour to explain such phenomena by natural causes; they are only to be understood in supernatural agency—or, in other words, they are the work of God. The sacred harmonies resounding in the air over the death-bed of a saint were chanted by angels; the sweet odours perfuming the room or the air were not the effects of aromatic drugs used by affectionate friends; no human perfumer was called upon to exercise his skill. We beg to refer the reader for more particulars to such writers as Gorres, or Migne's "Mystique Chrétienne."

and bound with iron chains.[1] In his distress, he cried day and night, "Dewi wareth" (David, help me). In a short time he obtained his liberty, and returned to his country, proclaiming that he had been delivered by the intercession of St. David. A German, his companion in captivity, had so often heard the words "Dewi wareth," that he also repeated them incessantly. Suddenly he was restored to his country, in a manner he could not explain. Later on, in Paris, he met with Welshmen, and asked them the meaning of "Dewi wareth." It was explained to him. He returned thanks to Almighty God, and resolved to set out on a pilgrimage to the shrine of his deliverer in Menevia. There he met his companion in captivity, and both acknowledged that they owed their deliverance to St. David.

When a plague broke out in the country, it was not unusual to invoke St. David, expose his relics, and appeal to his intercession. The faith of the people was often rewarded by the cessation of the scourge.

In Catholic times, St. David held, in the estimation of Welshmen, the same position as St. Patrick in that of Irishmen. In their mind the country had never produced a more eminent servant of God. His name was and is, as we have repeatedly said, the popular one in Cambria. His festival, kept on the first day of March, was

(1) O'Hanlon.

a feast of obligation all over the country; nay, the first three days of March were marked in the religious annals of Cambria as sacred. The first day of March commemorated St. David; the second, his mother; and the third, St. Lili, called in the old Celtic language "Gwas Dewi" (the man of David), he being his favourite disciple.

Ireland and Brittany erected churches to the memory of the patron of Wales, and in both these countries parishes are called after him. But the grandest church ever erected to St. David is that which rose over his grave in Menevia. It is the noblest temple built to the honour of God in the whole Principality. Kings, princes, and nobles contributed to its erection. The structures at St. David's Cathedral, College, and Bishop's Palace bear witness to the deep veneration of the Cambrians for their patron saint. The country in itself offers little attraction, except by its bold cliffs, so dreaded by mariners. The few trees a traveller from Haverfordwest to Menevia meets on his road are stunted and bent to the east, and the branches to the west are stopped in their growth, an evident sign that strong winds from the Atlantic often rage on these shores. Great difficulties had to be surmounted to erect such stately buildings in the remotest corner of Wales; yet the college, if restored and transported to Oxford, would stand pre-eminent by the side of the stately halls of the first university of Britain. The cathedral has often been described. Bangor and Llandaff Cathedrals stand in deep hollows, showing the predilection of Welshmen in choosing valleys for their churches; St. David's Church, in Menevia, is, in like manner, built between two hills, and is not seen till you come close to it.

The writer visited it in August, 1876, and, like most visitors, was struck by the grandeur of the place. Here, as everywhere else in England, the work of restoration is carried on with activity and skill. Money is not spared, and the best architectural talent is employed. As a Catholic priest, he could not but regret to see two altar-slabs—one with five crosses, the other with only three or four—used as paving-stones. It was on such an altar that St. David, on the last Sunday of his life, celebrated the sacred mysteries of the body and blood of our Lord. Some time after the Reformation, the Protestant bishops sent orders to their clergy to take down the altar-stones and have them trampled upon. In our days of the revival of Catholic ideas, several clergymen, who begin to realise the holy Sacrifice of the Mass, and the sacredness of an altar on which the Saviour of the world condescends to be offered as a victim, have taken away these stones, thinking it is not proper that they should be trodden upon.

CHAPTER XV.

SAINT SAMSON, ARCHBISHOP OF DÔL, BRITTANY.[1]

The family of St. Samson.

BETWEEN the years 461 and 468, when Pope Hilary ruled the Church, and Leo I. the Empire, Dubricius being Archbishop, and Illtyd Abbot of Lantwit-Major, there lived in Britain two noble families formed by the intermarriage of two brothers with two sisters, whose history is interesting, not only for giving illustrious saints to the Church, but also for the remarkable occurrence that, having first knelt before the altar and vowed to share together the blessings and the trials of married life, they, later on, again presented themselves at the sacred shrine, when the two husbands received the habit and tonsure of religion, whilst the two wives took the veil as nuns. They did this at the suggestion of a son, or nephew, named Samson, who was a young ecclesiastic, then residing at Barry Island. The two brothers, Amon and Umbrafel, were probably of Armorican descent; but the sisters, Anna and Affrella, were pure Cambrians, being daughters of Meurig, King of Glamorgan.

(1) This Life is compiled from the "Liber Landavensis," from the work of Albert le Grand, "Vies des Saints de la Bretagne-Armorique," and from Lobineau's "Vies des Saints de Bretagne."

Amon married the elder sister, Anna, and his brother Affella, the younger. The last-named pair were blessed with offspring, whilst the others were for a long time childless, which was a great grief to both. They longed for little ones to play around them, and inherit their name and their possessions. Being endowed with strong faith, they earnestly implored of God to bestow upon them the much-desired gift, and they entreated Dubricius and Illtyd to unite with them in praying for the same intention. They also gave abundant alms to the poor, and contributed largely to the building of churches, with the hope of moving God to grant their petition; they even promised that, in the event of a child being born to them, they would consecrate him, like the young Samuel, to the service of the Lord.

Samson a child of prayer.

We read that both husband and wife undertook a long journey northward, to visit a hermit who was looked upon as a saint, being confident that such holy prayers would storm heaven in their behalf. Nor were they disappointed.[1] The hermit had a vision, in which he beheld a knight and a lady toiling as pilgrims over hills and through valleys, until at last they reached his cell. The saint inquired who they were, and what was their object in seeking his solitude, and was told, in answer, that the pilgrims were a husband and wife whose marriage had not yet

---

(1) "Liber Landavensis."

been blessed by children, though for years they had importuned heaven to grant them this favour; and that now they had journeyed to his cell to solicit his intercession. The hermit was commanded to inform his pious visitors that heaven had made known to him the purport of their visit, and that they were to return home and give thanks to God, for their request was granted.

When the saint had delivered this message, the pilgrims retraced their steps, greatly consoled. Anna herself was also favoured with a vision, which confirmed that of the hermit; and she was distinctly told that the child she had prayed for and obtained was destined to be a powerful instrument in the hands of God for the propagation of the Gospel.

In the following year Anna brought forth a child, who was baptised by St. Illtyd, receiving at the font the name of Samson. This event took place either in 490 or 496.[1]

The chieftain and his wife were subsequently blessed with several other children, most of whom were remarkable for exemplary lives. One daughter, however, proved an exception to this rule, and was the cause of grievous trouble to father, mother, and relatives, through a dissoluteness of life from which she could not be reclaimed either by religion or duty.

The young Samson arrives at Lantwit-Major.

It was the custom of the British nobility to

---

(1) "Britaunia Sancta." Butler's "Lives of the Saints."

send their children at an early age to a monastic school. Amongst the numerous scholastic institutions of South Wales, that of Lantwit-Major was held in the highest estimation; for Illtyd, the principal, had not his equal in Britain in the science of education. He was also a particular friend of the family, and to him, therefore, was the early training of Samson entrusted.

On the arrival of the child with his parents at Lantwit-Major, Illtyd seems to have been inspired, like Simeon of old, in the Temple of Jerusalem. "Let us return thanks to heaven," he said, "for the great mercy which has been vouchsafed to our country. This child, born within our shores, is destined to become a great light, whose rays will illumine many people, both in this island and beyond the seas. He will open heaven to thousands of souls. You see before you the future doctor of many nations, the spiritual father of many saints, the glory of the Church and of Britain."

Chroniclers have handed down to us a few circumstances connected with the early life of Samson, when at the college of Illtyd, which afford us an insight into the customs of that monastic seminary, and supply us with evidence that the course of education followed there in those old times was as complete as it is at present in the best managed of our modern colleges.

Classics, rhetoric, mathematics, and natural

history were taught by the most competent masters; but preference was given to the study of Holy Scripture. Manual labour is discarded in our day; then, far from being disdained, it seems to have formed a part of the education. The teachers were all monks, and spent a part of the day in the fields or in the workshops. The scholars, therefore, naturally looked upon physical labour as a noble occupation. When they saw a Doctor of Science equally expert with the spade or axe as with the pen, they felt no shame in engaging in similar works; therefore, all scholars, whether rich or poor, the sons of the Kings of Glamorgan, of Gwent, or of any other chieftain, were ordered to take their turn in the fields, to weed barley, oats, or wheat, to drive away deer or birds, or to tend sheep or cows on the high cliffs which border the Bristol Channel at Lantwit.

The old Welsh legends, delighting as they do in the marvellous, take particular pleasure in depicting the boy Samson in the fields at Lantwit-Major, with a sling in his hand and some stones in his pocket, driving away sparrows and other birds. The little winged creatures were no sooner driven off than they again returned, thus testing the patience of the young guardian, until, worn out, he calls upon the birds, in the name of God, to gather round him; then, when they have obeyed, he shuts them up in a barn, and, lying down upon the ground, falls asleep.

On one summer day, in harvest-time, most of the community of Lantwit-Major were in the fields, either cutting corn or binding sheaves. A serpent, being disturbed, suddenly glided from a bush and bit one of the brethren. The poison in a short time took effect, and all hope of his recovery was given up. Samson sought the Abbot, and asked his permission to cure the dying brother.

Strong faith of Samson.

"I know," he said, " of an infallible remedy, which I learnt from my Father. It is simple, and consists but of a few ingredients and a few words."

The Abbot replied, somewhat abruptly, "Do you say you learnt it from your father? Was he a magician? Did he teach you sorcery?"

"The father I spoke of," replied the youth, "is He of whom the Scripture says, 'Thy hands have made me, and have compassed me on all sides.'"

The Abbot, struck by the lively faith of the student, bade him go to the suffering brother, saying, "May your Father and mine restore him to health."

When Samson came to the dying man, he made the sign of the Cross on the wound, and washed it with water mingled with oil, in the name of the Holy Trinity, and the man immediately recovered. On beholding this miracle, Samson blushed, and retired as fast as possible.

We consider it due to truth not to omit mention of this miracle attributed to St. Samson, and recorded in three different Lives of the saint.

Faith is strong enough to move mountains, and, as a missionary priest for twenty years, both in and out of Europe, the writer of this biography feels bound to bear witness of having several times received convincing evidence of the benefit resulting from confidence in the sign of the Cross.

Frequently a poor working-man will visit his priest, entreating him, in the name of God, to make the sign of the Cross over some hideous wound. He cares not if the world smiles at the simplicity of his faith, but trusts that the invocation of the Holy Trinity may benefit him both in soul and body. The power of faith is the same in the nineteenth century as in the first.[1]

Our forefathers were eminently men of faith, and experienced the benefits thereof. It is related that whenever St. Samson met with any obscure passages of Holy Scripture, he always betook himself to prayer, and found it the best

(1) The sign of the Cross is an outward expression of our deep confidence in the Holy Trinity, and in the power of redemption. In the hands of Christians, it became a great instrument for performing miracles, as fully evidenced by hagiographers. Thus, St. Macrina the younger, when eaten up by cancer, was cured by the sign of the Cross. St. Edward the Confessor, King of England, by the sole use of the sign of the Cross healed wounds otherwise incurable. By the same holy sign Pope St. Leo IV. extinguished a fire which threatened the ruin of the Church of St. Peter. It was by the virtue of the sign of the Cross that the first Christians—the hermits—delivered those possessed by the devil. "In the name of God crucified," said St. Anthony, the great hermit of the East, "we put the devils to flight." Where the sign of the Cross is made, magical art becomes powerless, and poisonous draughts cannot hurt.—MIGNE's "La Mystique Chretienne."

of teachers, whereby he was enabled to elucidate the verses which were most abstruse.

When Samson had completed his studies, and attained the age of twenty-one or twenty-two, his father wished him to return home. The chieftain was, naturally, proud of his son, who was now an accomplished youth, endowed with great physical strength, and highly cultivated in mind. Amon pictured for him a glorious career, as a valiant commander in the battle-field and wise governor of his subjects; and, indeed, he seemed to have quite forgotten that he had devoted this child of prayer, so long desired, to the service of the Church even before his birth. Far different were the views regarding him which were now entertained by the chieftain.

Samson, however, soon dispelled these dreams, by informing his father that he felt himself called upon to embrace the religious state, and had, consequently, made up his mind to do so without delay.

Samson embraces the religious life.

This communication was at first far from pleasing to his parents; but they could not help remembering the time—now upwards of twenty years gone by—when, in praying to be blessed with a son, they had promised to consecrate the child to God if he himself felt called to that Divine service. They also recalled to mind the prediction of Iltyd concerning their son—that he would become a luminary of the Church—and, feeling convinced that the step he was about to take was the inauguration of the future career which had been foretold, they could no longer resist the force of circumstances, and, withdrawing their opposition, they blessed Samson, and consented to his following his vocation.

The young man at once returned to Lantwit-Major, where he received the religious habit, and was gradually promoted to holy orders.

All the biographers of Samson concur in stating that whilst he was being ordained deacon, Dubricius, the Bishop, and the Abbot, Illtyd, beheld a heavenly dove hovering above him during the whole time of Mass, and when the Bishop lifted up his hand over him the dove alighted upon his shoulder; and, later on, when the young deacon was promoted to the priesthood, the same vision re-appeared. This miraculous dove thus present at the ordination was a clear indication to Dubricius and to Illtyd that the young ecclesiastic was pure of heart, undefiled in conscience, and a friend of God.

We are told that at Lantwit-Major the new religious proved an example to his brethren. It would seem to have been a custom of the house that when any aspirant was about to be promoted to holy orders, the opinion of the community was consulted. In the case of Samson, the monks were unanimous in declaring him to be a model to them all. Indeed, we are informed that, not satisfied with observing the ordinary rules, he imposed upon himself penances, such as fasting, long prayers, and watches during the night. He slept upon the bare ground, and his diet consisted of vegetables, discarding altogether the use of animal food. His fasts were so extraordinary as to attract the attention of Illtyd, who at times deemed himself bound to restrain the young monk in his mortifications.[1]

We regret to be forced to chronicle the criminal conduct pursued by two nephews of Illtyd towards the saintly religious. These young men did not possess a spark of monastic spirit. Under the mask of humility, they concealed within their breasts unbounded ambition. At Lantwit-Major a general opinion prevailed that Samson would probably be the successor of Illtyd. His two nephews thought, as they were near relatives of the Abbot, one of them should succeed him in the direction of the monastery. *Hatred borne to Samson by two nephews of Illtyd.*

Samson stood in their way, and they allowed envy and hatred to gain such mastery over them that, instigated by these dreadful passions, they went so far as to make an attempt to get rid of him by poison. The saint was warned of their designs by an inward inspiration, and, through a miracle, escaped their machinations. One of these enemies he won over to repentance; the other was visited by the judgment of God, and

---

(1) Sectione litterarum totam noctem ducebut insomnem ; et si quando quiescere opus esset seipsum parieti aut alicujus rei firmamento inclinans nunquam inlecto dormitabat nunquam alicujus animalis carnem in tota vita gustavit.

became possessed by the devil after partaking of the body and blood of our Lord at Holy Communion.

<small>Samson at Barry Island.</small>
Shortly after his ordination as priest, Samson left Lantwit-Major, and settled in Barry Island,[1] which lies about midway between Lantwit-Major and Cardiff, and is separated from the mainland by a narrow channel, dry at ebb tide. The little island contains three or four hundred acres of land, and is guarded by cliffs both on the east and west, which give it a picturesque appearance. On the highest point of ground there is a spring, or rather a holy well, said to possess curative properties. An hydrologist will at once conclude that its water comes from the mainland, under the sea. It is now a dreary and uncultivated spot, but in former times produced corn, grass, and timber.

By the ancient hagiographers this place is sometimes called Enes Peiro (the Island of Peiro), and at others the island near Lantwit.

The following circumstances, which are mentioned in the "Life of St. Cadoc," were the occasion of giving to it the definitive name which it retains to this day:—

The founder of Llancarvan Monastery, during one of his annual visits to the island of the Bristol Channel, for the purpose of making a

---

(1) The writer thinks that the island *near* Lantwit, as it is called, is Barry Island. There is no other in the Bristol Channel capable of affording shelter to a religious community of any importance. Flat Holms, it is true, is reported to have been inhabited by some few monks and hermits, but not by a regular community; and it could not be called *the island near* Lantwit.

spiritual retreat, found on landing at Barry Island that he had forgotten his Enchiridion, or Breviary, at Flat Holms. Two of the brethren sailed back for the book, so indispensable in the recital of the Divine office. On their return they were caught in a gale, their boat capsized, and the two brethren drowned. The body of one, whose name was Baroc, was washed ashore on the little island, where it was honourably buried, and the place ever afterwards bore his name.

Peiro was Abbot at the time Samson joined this religious colony. Shortly after his arrival at his new home, he was called away for a time, under the following circumstances:—

Amon, his father, had an illness, which was considered so dangerous that he was strongly advised to lose no time in making his confession and receiving Holy Communion and Extreme Unction, for the purpose of preparing his soul for eternity. "No," exclaimed the sick man, as if inspired. "I shall not die yet, and there is no need at present to fortify my soul with the last Sacraments. I want to see my son, Samson; send for him. He is a true servant of God; his heart is as pure as running water, and the Holy Ghost dwells within him. I know that when he comes he will cure both my soul and my body, for I have received assurance of it in a vision."

Samson visits his sick father. He induces two families to embrace the religious life.

Messengers were, in consequence, despatched to Barry Island to request the immediate attendance of Samson. At first he declined, on the plea that he could be of no use, and that he had left father and mother for ever in this world, to meet them hereafter in heaven.

Peiro, the Abbot, however, represented to him that filial duty was a virtue, and, if ever its practice was necessary, it was so in the present instance.

Samson obeyed, and set out, accompanied by a deacon, it being probably the rule that no monk should travel alone. Great was the joy of his whole family on his arrival at the paternal mansion. Amon soon recovered his health, and felt that a great change was taking place in his mind.

The young priest exercised a fascinating influence over all by his holy life and by his eloquence. He so forcibly set forth the immeasurable advantage which the service of God possessed over that of the world as to produce the deepest impression on all. He assured them that his own life as a monk was infinitely preferable to that which *they* had followed up to the present. *Chieftains*, as a rule, trifled away their existence in follies, hunting deer or wolves, or, more criminally, in useless wars, where hundreds of lives were sacrificed on the most flimsy pretexts. *The religious*, on the contrary, passed their lives in prayer and labour, fed the poor, and consecrated their time to the conversion of Christian sinners or unbaptised Pagans.

It is related of Amon that he was not alone sick in body, but in soul as well. Guilty of some grievous sin, he could not summon up courage enough to confess it, and in consequence his conscience was disturbed by the most bitter reproaches. An inward voice ever whispered, "Amon, thou didst not fear to commit sin, but now thou art too great a coward to acknowledge thy fault." The arrival of his son, Samson, however, set all to right, for, with a contrite heart, he made a sincere confession.

Nothing under the sun can be more useless, in many instances, than the lives of the rich. In the Day of Judgment, how many will mourn that theirs had not been the lot of Lazarus rather than that of Dives. God, in His mercy, bestowed this grace of light on the two brothers who had wedded the two sisters, and also on their wives. They all became impressed with the necessity of changing their lives, and, finally, all came to the resolution of following their son and nephew along the path traced out by the Evangelical Counsels. Father and mother, uncle and aunt, by mutual consent determined to separate, and lead henceforth a life of continency. Having made a settlement of their temporal affairs, they retired from the world; the men accompanied Samson to Barry Island, and the ladies entered a convent; and so, on the return of the saintly young priest and the deacon to their monastery, the boat which bore them to their sea-girt home contained also two more aspirants to religious perfection.

Dubricius happened at that time to be on the island, and when Bishop, Abbot, and community learnt that the two strangers who had arrived were not only noblemen, but also the father and uncle of Samson, and that they had come, not as visitors, but with the fixed purpose of sharing the monastic life, joining the sacred psalmody, and assisting in the cultivation of their farm, so great was the admiration excited by this self-devotion that it instilled fresh fervour into the whole community.

We next find Samson occupying the position of Procurator to the Monastery, very much to the benefit of the surrounding poor. Every religious house, in those days, was a public hospital for the indigent, and a free hotel for the traveller.

The new Procurator seems to have expended a larger amount in alms than his predecessor in the office, for complaints were made to Dubricius that Samson's extravagance in this respect had the effect of bringing all the vagabonds of South Wales to Barry Island. His saintly superior, however, instead of checking, entirely approved of his conduct.

On the death of the Abbot, our saint was unanimously chosen to be his successor,[1] and,

---

(1) The account given by Lobineau of Peiro is not very flattering. According to this author, the Abbot possessed more external than real and solid virtue. He understood how to rule a religious community, but could not govern himself; and however regular his conduct in public might be, in private he was not to be admired.

according to the "Liber Landavensis," ruled that community for three years and a half.

During the interval he sailed for Ireland, in company of some Irish monks, who, as they were returning from a pilgrimage to Rome, visited Barry Island. Finding that they were, comparatively, better versed in Holy Scripture and theology than his brethren at home, he sought improvement by spending some time in their society. His stay in Ireland, however, was of short duration. Whilst waiting at a certain seaport for a vessel to carry him back to Britain, he became a guest at a monastery on the shore, the Abbot of which was tormented by the devil. He commanded the evil spirit to depart and leave in peace a servant of God, a soul consecrated to Him not only by baptism, but also by religious profession. The devil obeyed, and the Abbot became so much attached to his deliverer that he determined to live under him for the rest of his days. Accordingly, he resigned his dignity, and followed Samson to Barry Island.

The Irish community were not slow in appreciating the great merit of the Cambrian saint. They regarded him as a master of spiritual life, and thought that those over whom he ruled would be wisely governed. They would have made him their Superior had it been possible; but as he could not comply with this request, they begged him, on his return to

Britain, to send one of his brethren to be their abbot, so entirely did they rely on his prudence and wisdom.

On his arrival in Wales, Samson had the satisfaction of finding that his religious brethren lived up to the spirit of their profession. His father and uncle gave general edification by their regularity in following the path of monastic perfection, in which the *latter* excelled all others, and had in consequence been ordained priest by St. Dubricius.

When Samson, mindful of his promise to the Irish monks, looked about for some religious qualified to become their ruler, he could find none more adapted for the position than Umbrafel, his uncle, and, accordingly, directed him to lose no time in proceeding to Ireland for the purpose of undertaking the direction of the monastery, and exhorted him to prove himself, by his wisdom and conduct, deserving of the trust.

Samson himself then followed the inclination which always impelled him to seek solitude, and left Barry Island, in company with his father, Amon, the late Irish Abbot, and another priest.[1] They followed the banks of the Bristol Channel eastward, in the direction of Gloucester, until they came to a hut, built in the vicinity of a clear fountain. Some lover of solitude had, no doubt, once tenanted it. There Samson left his

---

(1) "Liber Landavensis." Lobineau says that Amon followed his brother, Umbrafel, to Ireland. He may have done so, and after a while returned to Wales.

three companions, and, urged by the spirit of the Eastern hermits, pursued his way until he discovered a secret cavern, where he decided to fix his abode, for he looked upon it as a spot prepared for him by the hand of God. He felt happy; for here worldly pre-occupations could no longer intrude or interfere with his soul in its upward flight into the regions of heavenly contemplation, and his only companions would be God and His angels. Every Sunday, however, he left his solitude and proceeded to the hut beside the well, to join his brethren for the celebration of the holy Sacrifice of the Mass, after which he spent with them some part of the day, and then returned to his hermitage for the remainder of the week.

If Samson fled from the world, the world pursued him; for we find his solitude broken in upon, and the saint forced to abandon it. At a synod held in the neighbourhood, probably at Caerleon, the leading members of the clergy made earnest inquiries about him, and a deputation was appointed to wait upon and request his attendance at the synod. His brothers of the priesthood gave it as their opinion that, although the mode of life he had adopted was undoubtedly edifying, still it was not fitting that such a light should be hidden under a bushel, and that God having gifted him with a variety of talents, they must be turned to account for the benefit of the Church. He was, therefore, ordered to give up the solitude which was beneficial to himself alone, and resume his community life, where he would be useful to others also; and, to hasten matters, he was at once placed at the head of a monastery, said to have been founded by St. Germanus.

The Synod also decreed that Samson should give a course of spiritual instruction for their edification before adjourning, a duty which the saint discharged to the satisfaction of all present.

Let us now proceed to examine the episcopal career of St. Samson. The hand of God again becomes apparent in the election of His servant to this dignity.

An ancient custom which existed in the Cambrian Church was never to consecrate less than three bishops at once. According to the canon law, three prelates were to assist at any consecration, and on three priests the British bishops conferred the plenitude of the priesthood, but on no lesser number without grave reasons.[1]

Samson consecrated Bishop Dubricius was in want of bishops to fill up episcopal vacancies. Two priests, already elected, had arrived at Caerleon, and were lodged in Samson's monastery, along with the consecrating prelates. A third was still required, the choice of whom was to be decided upon at the episcopal meeting.

We do not read that the Archbishop and his colleagues had ever thought of Samson, or, at

---

(1) Lobineau. "Liber Landavensis."

least, arrived at any conclusion as to his election.

The appearance of an angel relieved them from all anxiety on the subject. The heavenly messenger intimated to Dubricius that it was the will of his Divine Master that Samson should be consecrated. When the Archbishop communicated this vision to his colleagues, they at once replied: "Heaven has spoken; we have nothing to do but obey."

The designs of God were made clearly manifest to Samson also; for during the night, when at prayer, the supernatural world had been opened to him, and he beheld himself surrounded by a great number of persons clothed in white, and saw amongst them three bishops, radiant with sanctity. He inquired who they were, and for what purpose they visited his cell. The leader replied: "I am Peter, the Prince of the Apostles, and these are James and John the Evangelists. We were sent to consecrate thee." Having said this, the vision disappeared.[1]

During the ceremony of consecration God was pleased to again glorify His servant. A dove, the symbol of the Holy Ghost, hovered above his head; and afterwards, when he celebrated the holy Sacrifice of the Mass, streams of light were seen to proceed from his mouth.

A certain amount of obscurity veils the earlier part of the episcopal life of our saint. Some of his biographers incline to the belief that he

(1) "Liber Landavensis."

became Archbishop of York. In the Breton Manuscripts he is mentioned as such, and the invasion of York by the Saxons is the reason assigned for his emigration to Brittany.

Other authors, on the contrary, hold to the opinion that Samson remained in his monastery and acted as coadjutor to St. Dubricius, who was far advanced in years, until he felt himself called upon to consecrate the remainder of his life to evangelising the Armoricans.

In the designs of God a new field awaited the zeal and intelligence of Samson on the western shores of Gaul. As he knelt before the altar, one Saturday in Holy Week, his guardian angel again appeared, and said: " Servant of God, depart from thy country and cross the sea to the shores of Armorica. There thou shalt labour to evangelise the people of thy race, who speak thy native language."

Samson's departure for Brittany.

Samson consulted St. Dubricius, and, having obtained his approval and consent, at once prepared for his departure. The Easter solemnities being over, he left his monastery to pay a parting visit to his old master, St. Illtyd, to his religious brethren at Barry Island, and to his mother. His relatives, as we have seen, were scattered. His father led an obscure life as a monk, his uncle ruled a religious community in Ireland, and his mother and aunt were secluded in convents. He visited the latter, and had great consolation in finding both ladies fervent in the practice of the Evangelical Counsels. His mother had built a church, and on seeing her son, now a bishop, she reminded him of a conversation which had passed between them years before, when, acting on his advice, she had resolved, together with her husband, to enter religion.

"You remember," she said, "how, at that time, you exhorted me to erect a church. I promised to follow your counsel, and said that a day would come when, as a consecrated bishop, you would bless my work. Now the church is finished and ready to be opened for Divine service. Now, too, my son, you, by the grace of God, are a bishop, and will consecrate my church before you embark for Brittany. My words at that time were uttered without much reflection, and I did not count on their being literally realised. It seems I was a prophet without knowing it."

During this visit Samson learnt, with great satisfaction, that his brothers and cousins led Christian lives and kept the commandments of God. The conduct of his younger sister, however, saddened his heart. She had none of the piety of her relatives, but was vain, and light in her conduct. She was, in fact, a scandal to the country; and, to have greater freedom for her sinful pursuits, she lived alone; indeed, no virtuous mother would allow her to associate with her daughters. In vain had her own mother, her aunt, brothers, and cousins, endeavoured to reform her. Even Samson, who thought his position as bishop might exercise a beneficial influence over her, failed to make any impression. Thus, in the most carefully tended flock we sometimes find a black sheep.

Delayed in his voyage. Having paid these visits, Samson departed for Armorica, accompanied by many religious, who were willing to share his future lot. Being short of provisions and water, the expedition landed on some part of the coast of Britain, where they were hospitably received in a monastery called Dochori.[1] The Prior, on being informed of Samson's destination, inquired into the motives which induced him to leave his country. The Bishop answered that his purpose was to preach the Gospel to his neglected countrymen in Armorica. The Prior then said, "If, as I believe, you seek sincerely the service of the Church, you need not travel as far as Brittany. In this country there is an extensive field for the exercise of your zeal. This province is still far from being cleansed from idolatry; thousands within it retain pagan customs, mingled with a weak mixture of Christianity, to this day. Before you extends a vast, uncultivated vineyard, if you be willing to labour in it."

This communication, which appealed to his zeal for souls, induced Samson to delay the completion of his voyage. He dismissed his

(1) Lobineau

ships, and he and his companions devoted themselves to the evangelising of that province, half Christian and half pagan.

One day, when passing through a certain town or village, he found the inhabitants celebrating a pagan festival. They carried in procession a hideous idol, singing and dancing around it. The chieftain of the place presided over these ceremonies. The Bishop remonstrated, and strongly denounced the sinful and foolish act of worshipping a dumb idol. The chieftain replied that he and his people were deeply attached to the customs of their forefathers; that the god whom *he*, a stranger, denounced, was the god worshipped by their ancestors, and they would adore no other divinity.

This short speech was loudly applauded, and Samson saw that at that moment further argument would be of no avail. The games were carried on with greater enthusiasm than ever. A young boy, who attracted general attention from the spirited manner in which he rode round the idol, was thrown from his horse, broke his neck, and died on the spot. This accident saddened the people, and put a stop to their mirth. Samson then made his way through the crowd, and thus addressed the multitude:—

"This young man is, unfortunately, dead. Can your god restore him to life? Destroy that idol, and worship the only true God; for by calling on His sacred Name I will cause the dead to arise."

The people agreed to this proposal, and the Bishop, kneeling down before the corpse, remained for two hours in prayer. At the expiration of that time the young man again returned to life.

This miracle produced the desired effect. The idol appeared in its real colours to the people—a dumb and useless piece of clay—which they rushed upon and broke into fragments.

From that moment the instructions of the Bishop were attended to, and pagan customs were discarded and replaced by those sacred to Christianity.

To give permanence to his work, the saint built a monastery, in which he left some of his brethren, under the guidance of his father, Amon, whom he exhorted to spend the remainder of his life in working for the conversion of that district. Then, having received the blessing of his aged parent, he engaged a vessel and set sail for Brittany, where the providence of God had already prepared a new home for him and his companions.

Privatus, a rich nobleman of Armorica, was, as we have already mentioned, much afflicted in his family, his wife and daughter both suffering from disease pronounced incurable. The prayers of the husband and father had been offered up a thousand times to obtain from God the favour of a cure for those so dear to him, and for whom all human skill was unavailing. In the end, his prayers were heard, and he was favoured with a vision, in which he was told that within three days they would be restored to health by a stranger from beyond the sea. Privatus passed these three days walking along the sea-shore, and anxiously watching every sail as it was wafted past. At last a boat drew near the place where he was standing, and a party of monks landed. On hearing they came from Britain, he accosted their leader, Samson, and related to him his tale of sorrow. The bishop followed the chieftain to his house, and by his prayers restored health to both the sufferers.

Samson and his brethren passed their first night in Brittany under the roof of this family. Privatus, in gratitude to his benefactor, begged him to remain on his territory, and offered to place at his disposal any land he might choose for the formation of a settlement. Samson accepted this offer, and spent part of the night in prayer and thanksgiving to Almighty God for His provident care of him and his brethren.

On the following day the British monks set out to explore the country, and on coming to an old pit, situated in the midst of a level and swampy plain, selected that as a site whereon to erect their monastery. Being unwilling to cause any inconvenience to their kind entertainers, they at once set to work, and, as a temporary shelter, constructed a hut, which they covered with reeds and rushes; and under this humble roof they passed their second night, bundles of straw serving them as beds. Here they were satisfied to remain until, by the work of their hands, they had provided themselves with a better habitation. Such, in a few words, was the humble foundation of the Archbishopric of Dôl.

The British colonists spent some years in constructing their church and monastery. Agricultural labour, however, was not neglected, for, according to an invariable rule of monastic life, the necessaries of life must be produced from the ground belonging to each foundation. Meanwhile, the spiritual wants of the surrounding district were attended to by the clerical members of the community.

The next event of importance mentioned in connection with the life of our saint is his journey to Paris, and his relations with Childebert. Brittany was not altogether independent of the King of the Franks, and, living on the frontiers of a powerful neighbour, the Bretons naturally felt the influence of a stronger nation over a weaker.

In visiting the French Court, St. Samson was influenced by two motives. The first was to secure, by a clearly-defined charter, the territory granted to him by Privatus on the plains of Dôl; the second, to claim protection for the son of Hoel II., King of Armorica, who had been his fellow-student at Lantwit-Major, Glamorganshire.

Comorre, Count of Cornouaille, an ambitious and unprincipled man, had treacherously assassinated his king, Hoel II., whilst hunting. Not feeling safe as long as Judwal, Hoel's son, was alive, the murderer of the father thirsted for the blood of the son. The young prince sought shelter in the monastery of Eleonor, his uncle, where he was willingly received; but the Abbot, being aware that the tyrant had no respect for the laws either of God or man, judged it prudent, after a time, to place his nephew on board ship and recommend him to make his way to Paris and claim the protection of Childebert. In Brittany, meanwhile, Comorre was imprisoning the nobles, plundering the peasantry, and perpetrating every kind of wickedness.

At the Court of Childebert St. Samson denounced the crimes of Comorre, and asked the Frank King to help the country against an usurper.

Childebert gave ear to the appeal of Samson, and, furnishing the injured prince with men and money, advised him to levy an army and attack the usurper. The Bretons, rejoicing at the prospect of escaping being murdered and plundered by Comorre, flocked to the standard of their lawful king, and the tyrant was driven from the country, together with the Danes and Normans by whose assistance he had maintained

St. Samson and the King.

his usurpation. The power of God continued to follow St. Samson during the whole period of his residence amongst the Franks.

Gaul had produced wonderful saints, venerated all over the world, such as St. Martin of Tours and St. Germanus, the great champion of orthodoxy. These holy men had wrought miracles—cured the sick, summoned the dead from their graves, stilled tempests at sea and calmed the storm-tossed waves. Devils, also, had trembled and fled before them.

In the person of Samson, God gave convincing proofs to the Franks that the island of Britain could also boast of having given birth to men endowed with supernatural powers, for, during his journey through Gaul, the British Bishop gave sight to a man who had been born blind, by making the sign of the Cross over his eyes.

One of the chief officers of Childebert, who was possessed by a devil, implored Samson to deliver him from this infernal obsession. The saint, in the name of God, commanded the demon to depart and leave in peace a soul stamped with Divine grace by the Sacrament of baptism. In obedience to this command, the devil vanished.

All these events caused the name and fame of Samson to be celebrated throughout Gaul, and he was regarded by all as a man of eminent sanctity. Childebert appreciated his talents and virtues, became his protector, and bestowed upon him the islands of Jersey and Guernsey.

Albert le Grand states that the Bishops of Armorica, who, with the bulk of their flocks, were of British origin, urged Childebert and Judwal to exert their influence for obtaining the dignity of Archbishop for Samson. They represented that in Britain he held that position, and insisted that no less was due to him in Armorica. In order to form a See worthy of this title, they agreed that a part of their respective dioceses should be ceded to the future Archbishop. To further the final settlement of this affair, an embassy was despatched to Pope Pelagius, at Rome.

The messengers were successful in their mission; the Pope acceded to the request of the Armorican Church, and Dôl was erected not only into an episcopal but a metropolitan See, in the year of our Lord 555.

The installation of Samson, consequent on this decree, took place in the Abbey Church, in the presence of the suffragan bishops and of King Judwal. The crowd assembled to witness the ceremony were struck with amazement at the humble appearance of the saint; for the new Archbishop, dispensing with the pomp usual on such occasions, walked barefoot to the church, and on approaching the altar devoutly prostrated himself on the pavement of the sanctuary.

This new creation caused some disagreement between the Metropolitan See of Tours and the Bretons, the former claiming jurisdiction over

Dôl and Tours.

the Armorican dioceses. About ten years later, in 566 or 567, we find a canon forbidding the consecration of any bishop in Armorica, whether he be Gaul or Breton, without the previous consent of the Metropolitan of Tours and his suffragans.[1]

On the other side, the Bretons, forming a different nationality from the Gauls and Franks in civil administration, and being governed by a king of their own race, claimed to be ruled in ecclesiastical matters also by a prelate of the same stock and speaking their native tongue, as only fair and appropriate. This controversy occupied the attention of several Popes—Innocent III. and Alexander VI. amongst others. In our days (1877) Brittany prides herself on possessing an Archbishop and Cardinal.

We all know that the difference between the native country of St. Samson and St. Augustine arose chiefly from a similar question, the Britons being unwilling to yield submission to the Metropolitan of the Saxons.

When Divine Providence had thus opened to our saint a field whereon to exercise his zeal, he began the work at once and in earnest. He made visitations through his diocese with regularity, and carefully studied its needs.

(1) L'Archevôihé de Dôl date du regne de Judual. "Les Bretons voulurent alors se donner un Archevêque, comme ils venaient de se donner un nouveau roi ; cequi fit á l'Eglise de Dôl s'elever contre celle de Tours, à cause du bienheureux Samson Archevêque d'York, qui pendant qu'il était exilé en Bretagne, avait gouverné l'Eglise de Dôl avec les Marques de la dignité Archiepiscopale." Ce sont les termes de l'Eglise de Tours dans son fameux procès contre celle de Dôl.—*Notes in Albert le Grand.*

Several churches had been burnt down during the war; these he rebuilt, and founded at Dôl a seminary for the education of young men designed for the priesthood.[1] Once a year—according to the canon laws—he met his suffragans, to discuss with them a plan of union for the spiritual working of the province. These conferences were generally opened on the first of November.

We also find St. Samson assisting at Councils which were not within his own province, and appending his name in the following terms to one of those held at Paris:—" Ego Samso, peccutor adscripsi "—(I, Samson, a sinner, have signed).

In the Channel Islands ceded by Childebert to the holy Bishop, Paganism was not yet extinct, and many idolatrous customs were still retained by the people, which were the more cherished because they pandered to the sensual pleasures of corrupt nature. St. Samson visited these islands for the purpose of evangelising their half-pagan half-Christian inhabitants; and to accomplish this he spared neither fatigue nor expense. He began with the children, and in

---

(1) A hymn to St. Samson thus alludes to this subject :—

"Barbaro late populata ferro
Templa consurgunt, reparantur aræ
Quas furor stravit, pietas vicissim,
     Eregit œdes.

"Erudit, vitâ prœeunte, Clerum.
Legitus sacris populum coercet;
Quas deus dotes dedit ad salubrem
     Applicat usum.

order to attract them, presented each with a gold medal.

Before returning to the mainland he erected parishes, over which he appointed rectors, and left several priests to assist them in carrying on the good work.

Samson ended his life at Dôl, on the twenty-eighth of July, probably in the year 565. Before his death he exhorted his numerous religious brethren to keep up to the spirit of the monastic rule of life.

God, who glorified his servant during life, shed additional lustre over his grave, which testified to his sanctity in a variety of ways. Several of his brethren were favoured with supernatural visions, in which they beheld the soul of their Bishop borne upwards to the Throne of God.

His body was interred in the sanctuary of his cathedral, at the Gospel side of the altar. When the remains were placed in the vault, a heavenly melody was heard in the air, which rose above the voices of the clergy who were chanting the funeral service, and after the grave had closed over the saint the tomb was for a time surrounded by supernatural light, and the air perfumed with the sweetest odours.

St. Samson holds a conspicuous place amongst the British saints of the sixth century, and was regarded with great veneration both in his native island and in the western provinces of France.

ST. SAMSON.

Hagiographers vied with each other in recording his life, for one of them—Lobineau—tells us that in his days *fourteen* different biographies of Samson were preserved in the Royal Library of Paris.

Crowds of pilgrims from Gaul and Britain visited his tomb, confident that their afflictions of body or of mind would be relieved through the holy bishop's intercession with God.

Glancing over the life of St. Samson, we cannot but remark the especial care with which his Divine Master watched over his whole career. An angel guarded his footsteps, as Raphael did those of the young Tobias. His birth was an answer to repeated prayers, and announced by an angel to his parents. And we may in this place observe, that when this same child of prayer grew up to be a priest and a bishop, married persons who were childless used to visit and entreat him to obtain for them by his prayers the blessing of offspring.

In the earlier period of his monastic life, when a conspiracy, the result of jealousy, threatened his life, he was warned of the danger by his guardian angel; and in a heavenly vision he was commanded to be in readiness for his consecration as bishop, and it was again an angel who directed him to cross over to Brittany.

At whatever place he fixed his dwelling, whether in Britain, Armorica, or at the Court of the Frank Kings, the power of working miracles followed him. Some of these we have placed before the reader; others may be found in the works of Albert le Grand, the "Liber Landavensis," &c.

In two or three instances we find the name of Samson in connection with dragons. The narrative of conflicts between saints and such monsters are often mentioned in the lives of these holy men, and are occasionally coloured with fiction and exaggeration.

During his visit to Childebert, that prince informed Samson that a certain place on the banks of the Seine was frequented by a huge dragon, which was the terror of the neighbourhood, and carried away to his cavern both men and beasts. No one dared to do battle with this monster. Knights and warriors were powerless for such a conquest. It was a feat reserved for the servants of God. The King, therefore, begged of St. Samson, in the name of his Divine Master, to deliver the country from the ravages of this horrid reptile. The Bishop complied with the King's request, and approached the lair of the savage with the greatest confidence, and in the name of the King of kings and Master of heaven and earth, commanded the dragon to depart from the land and never again to appear. The serpent obeyed, and was seen no more.

This episode in the life of our saint is not to be regarded as a pious narrative of the legendary form, which delights in marvellous events, whether authenticated or otherwise; for Childebert, in order to testify to the expulsion of the dragon, ordered a monastery to be built on the spot, as a commemoration of what had there taken place. This monastery was called Pentall, and was a kind of priory, a dependence of Dôl.

It would be no easy task to count the disciples of the Archbishop of Dôl. Few saints ever possessed a more fascinating influence over souls. St. Bernard, in the twelfth century, left the world at the age of twenty-two, and persuaded his father, his uncle, and his many brothers to follow him to the cloister. Samson also, as we have seen, instilled into the souls of his numerous relatives—father, mother, uncle, aunt, brothers, and cousins the love of the monastic life which was so deeply rooted in his own. He possessed the gift of imparting to others the religious enthusiasm that filled his own soul. Amongst his disciples, besides Amon, his father, and Umbrafel, his uncle, we may mention Maglorius, his cousin; St. Similian, Abbot of Tourai; St. Ethben, St. Guennole the younger, and St. Meen, Abbot of Gael.

In the ancient English Litanies the name of Samson is the first invoked amongst the British saints.

His feast is kept on the twenty-eighth of July, and also his Office in the Breviaries of Dôl, Leon, and St. Brieuc, which contained nine lessons, whilst that of St. Meen included twelve.

The memory of St. Samson is celebrated also in the Breviaries of the dioceses of Nantes, Quimper, Rennes, Treguier, and Orleans.[1]

(1) Lobineau.

CHAPTER XVI.

Saint Paulus Aurelianus;
or,
St. Paul de Leon.[1]

PAULUS AURELIANUS (in Breton, Pôl de Leon), son of Porphirius Aurelianus, as indicated by his own name and that of his father, was descended —at least on the paternal side—from a Roman family which had settled in Britain. We cannot discover any mention of his mother's name, but as it is stated that he was cousin to St. Samson, this lady must have been of purely Celtic blood, and a daughter of Western Britain.

Paul, according to general opinion, was born in the year of our Lord 492, at a place called Pen O'chen. Whether this was situated in Cornwall or in Cambria we have not sufficient evidence to certify.[2]

It is related by his biographers that Paul was the favourite child—in fact, the Benjamin of his father's house—where he was more beloved than his brothers and sisters.

(1) Compiled from the Breton MSS., as found in the works of Albert le Grand and Lobineau.

(2) The ancient name of Cowbridge, near Cardiff, was Penohen, but other localities may have been similarly called.

The first rudiments of education were imparted to him, not at Lantwit-Major, but at some other school. It seemed as if Porphirius had dreaded the well-known magical influence exercised by St. Illtyd in infusing into the minds of his young students a hatred of the world and a love for the religious life. His parents wished the boy to receive an education such as would fit him for a worldly career, and his masters were strongly urged to practise him, as far as his age allowed, in the use of arms and in all such exercises as would tend to develope physical strength.

<small>Early tendency to ascetic life.</small>

The boy, however, used candidly to declare that these accomplishments would be of no avail to him. A day would, indeed, come when he would enlist as a soldier, but the standard under which he meant to fight would be that of the King of kings. With the simplicity peculiar to children, he often communicated his inward feelings to his parents.

Such sentiments as these being frequently repeated by the child, caused everyone to remark that he would one day enter religion, because the grace of God was working within his soul in that direction. This at last induced his father and mother to alter their views with regard to Lantwit-Major, and they determined to confide the education of Paul to the well-known zeal and piety of St. Illtyd.

During his residence at this celebrated seminary, the young Aurelianus became thoroughly enamoured with the ascetic life. He communicated to his saintly preceptor the strong attraction he felt for solitude. What he had heard and read of St. Paul the Hermit, St. Anthony, and other Fathers of the Egyptian deserts, and also of solitaries in his own land, so deeply impressed his mind that his only desire was to retire to some lonely spot and there give himself up solely to heavenly contemplation.

The Abbot at first thought that such a form of life was not suitable for a youth at the early age of sixteen. It was not without danger, nor altogether screened from the temptations of the devil. However, on reflection, he came to the conclusion that this inclination on the part of his pupil was the result of Divine grace, and, blessing Paul, consented to his wishes. The young lover of solitude left Lantwit-Major, and, returning to the place of his birth, chose as his retreat a secluded spot on the estates of his father.

To this solitude he was followed, if not immediately, at least some time after, by twelve companions. These young recluses, according to monastic custom, built an oratory, and erected around it twelve separate huts, in which each dwelt in solitude, meeting only in the church for the purpose of singing the Divine Office. In fact, they followed very much the same mode of life as was afterwards adopted by the Carthusians.

On the Sundays of each week, however, and

also on the great festivals of the Church, the thirteen hermits sat down at the same table, and on these occasions the severity of the diet was somewhat relaxed.

At these general meals Paul took some fish, but never touched animal food. His ordinary diet was limited to bread and salt, and water from the spring was his only drink.

The British Saints models of temperance. In reviewing the lives of the British saints, we cannot fail to be struck with the great example of temperance they present to us. Gildas was surnamed Aquarius (the water drinker); David, in his rule, permits no other drink. Yet these men hardly knew what sickness was, worked in the fields, and often lived to be centenarians, or not far from it. In the present day intemperance is the sin of Britain. It invades the palaces of the great and the homes of the working classes. It ensnares victims in every stage of life. The young and the old, the matron and the maiden, are often drawn to destruction by this degrading vice.

During the fifth and sixth centuries this country was, as we learn from Gildas, by no means free from the sin of drunkenness, and this fact, no doubt, greatly influenced the British saints in their total abstinence from intoxicating stimulants. Though they acknowledged them to be gifts of God, which might be used in moderation, yet, partly in the spirit of penance, partly to give good example to a race addicted to intemperance, they restricted themselves solely to the use of water.

When Paul had attained the canonical age—having already received the various minor orders—he was ordained priest, as were also the young companions of his solitude, who, like himself, were highly educated.

The members of the little community were now in a position to be useful in the service of the Church, and, on an appeal being made to their zeal for the salvation of souls, they quitted their solitude.

A certain Prince named Mark, the place of whose abode is not indicated, invited Paul and his companions to visit his territory, for the purpose of preaching the Gospel to his people. The young priests consulted together, and unanimously agreed to accept the vineyard offered for their cultivation, and started at once for their new mission. *Beginning of missionary life.*

They commenced their work at the court of the Prince, where they succeeded in evangelising him and all his household. They then spread themselves over the country, leaving everywhere permanent traces of their zeal and labour.

Paul endeared himself to all wherever he went, and the people, fearing to lose their apostle, petitioned the King to take measures to secure his being consecrated bishop, as such a step, they thought, would bind him to the country.

It was very difficult to overcome the determined opposition with which Paul met this proposal. He declared that he would rather stem the roughest waves and winds, and spend his life in navigating stormy seas, than be loaded with the heavy burden of the episcopacy.

On reflection, however, his mind became disturbed with the fear of resisting the will of God. The well-known motto, "*Vox populi vox Dei,*" resounded in his ears. In this perplexity, he betook himself to prayer to obtain light to direct him in the fulfilment of the Divine decrees.

<small>First appearance of the angel bidding him to Armorica.</small> One day, whilst thus engaged, an angel appeared to him, and said, "Paul, this country is not to be the field of thy labours. Depart from hence, and in due course God will lead thee to the land thou art to evangelise."

Having communicated this vision to his brethren, he visited Mark, in order to inform him of what had taken place. The Prince used every argument to induce the missionaries to remain in his kingdom. Paul replied that no choice rested with him in the matter; he must obey the will of God, which had been manifested to him by the angel; and this being unanswerable, the Prince was forced to yield.

Abraham was commanded to leave his country and his kindred in the following words:—" And the Lord said to Abraham, Go forth out of thy country and from thy kindred and out of thy father's house, and come into the land which I shall show thee."[1] The country appointed to be his future abode was not named. Whether the Patriarch formed any idea of the land which was to be his new abode, or whether he was in perfect ignorance on the subject, is not stated. Commentators are divided in their opinions.

After this heavenly visitation Paul found himself for a second time in a state of perplexity. That he was to leave his native shores he could have no doubt, but his future destination had not been distinctly revealed to him. However, he set forth from the territories of Mark, confident that all obscurity would soon disappear and the path he was to follow be clearly indicated.

He commenced preparations for his departure by visiting his sister, who, like himself, had entered religion, and been elected by the sisterhood abbess of the community. The convent seems to have been situated on the English Channel, probably in Cornwall. Paul and his companions remained in the neighbourhood for some time, exhorting the nuns to live up to the spirit of Jesus Christ, whom they had chosen for their spouse.

Preparations were meanwhile being made for a sea voyage. Vessels were engaged, sailors secured, and ordered to be ready as soon as possible. The night before his departure was spent by Paul in prayer and communion with heaven. There

---

[1] Genesis.

is no record of what passed, or whether another angelic manifestation was vouchsafed to him; but in the morning the little community set sail.

The sailors wondered at the eccentricity of their passengers, for, on inquiring in which direction they were to steer, they were told simply to unfurl the sails and allow the ship to be guided by the winds and by the providence of God, who would be their pilot.

The arrival at Ouessant Island.

The first land they approached happened to be the island of Ouessant, not far from the entrance to the Bay of Brest. This is a spot unfortunately but too well known to seafaring men, for scarcely a year passes but some ships are wrecked on its shores. At the present time it contains a population of about two thousand three hundred souls, but what number of human beings dwelt upon its soil in the days of Paul cannot now be ascertained.

Ouessant and the neighbouring little islands scattered here and there in its vicinity were even then celebrated in Celtic tradition. According to the general Pagan opinion, they were peopled by phantoms.

Saturn was still worshipped in these lonely isles, and vestals consecrated by vow, like those of Rome, to perpetual virginity, were believed to be endowed with power to raise a tempest or bid the waves be still. They professed to be able to foretell future events, and delivered their oracles to such as were bold enough to row over to their almost inaccessible abode.

As Montalembert observes, along these coasts wander the skeletons of the shipwrecked, seeking a shroud and a grave. This is a tradition which lasted until the end of the sixth century. Even during the reigns of Clovis and his successors, the fishermen who frequented the shores of these islands were exempted from the service of war and from the payment of tribute, because they were obliged to convey to Great Britain the souls of the departed.

"Towards midnight," says Procopius, "a knock is heard at the doors of the fishermen, and a low voice calls upon them. They arise and hasten to the shore; there they find strange boats awaiting them. These they must row across the sea, and though no one is to be seen, the boats are so full of invisible passengers that they seem in danger of sinking, and are scarcely a finger's breadth above the level of the water. The journey is accomplished in less than an hour, although with their own boats it would be difficult to complete it in a night. On arriving at their destination, the vessels are so entirely emptied that their keels can be seen. Nothing is visible, but the sailors hear a voice which calls the spiritual voyagers one by one, addressing them by the same titles they bore during life. To this is added the father's name in the case of a man, the husband's in that of a woman."

This small British colony was destined, even in the lifetime of its first founders, to win over these fishermen to the faith of Christ Indeed, the day was not far distant when a Frank King was to bestow the island of Ouessant on Paul and his diocese in perpetuity.

The following description of the fishermen of Ouessant was written a few centuries back:—
"The island converted by St. Paul was called by him *Doue Sant*, in French *Dieu Saint*. He destroyed the pagan temples, or converted them into Catholic churches. From that time the golden era seems to have reigned over this small corner of the earth. Religion had created a brotherly union amongst its inhabitants. Honesty in business and purity of life prevailed throughout the island, and any person who did not possess these two virtues was immediately expelled. A lawsuit or a lie were equally repudiated. If any contention arose it was settled at the door of the church, after Mass, by the first man of position who came out, and his judgment was never appealed against." [1]

For what period of time the British monks remained in the island is not stated. They seem to have resumed their monastic life, and built temporary huts around an oratory; but they do not appear to have regarded this as their land of promise, although its seclusion was admirably adapted to their love of solitude.

[1] Albert le Grand.

Paul, as usual, sought to know the will of Heaven as to his future course, and the angel again appeared to him and pointed to the continent whose shores were visible from the island, to indicate that there lay the field of their future labours. They at once set forth, and, passing by the small island of Molene, at the entrance of the port of Brest, they landed, and encamped for a time; then, crossing to the continent, disembarked on the shore between Brest and Morlaix. *Landing in Brittany.*

The district where they first settled is called to this day by the name of our saint, Lampaul (Llanpaul). There, as was their wont, they constructed an oratory and temporary huts, and there, for the fourth time since their departure from the territory of King Mark, they fixed a new abode. It is likely they did so without reference to the ownership of the ground, and expected to be called to account by its possessor; so they did not yet look upon it as the spot chosen for them by Heaven, but resolved patiently to await the course of events. Although Lampaul did become the head-quarters of the colony, many of its members scattered themselves here and there, each choosing for himself such place as best suited his love of retirement and solitude.

The legend relates that whilst in this locality one of the brethren, who had built his hut beside a clear fountain in the vicinity, came to

Paul and complained of the annoyance he received from a wild buffalo. This animal showed his displeasure at the intrusion of a stranger into his favourite haunts by one day driving his horns through the walls of the hut, throwing it down, and breaking it to pieces.

Paul visited the scene of devastation, and on the buffalo making his appearance, commanded him, in the name of God, never again to disturb the abode of a Christian, or pass beyond the limits of the surrounding forests to disturb the peace of a servant of Jesus Christ. The animal at once turned, disappeared into the woods, and was seen no more.

Montalembert justly observes that by none of the apostles of Brittany, was Paul of Leon surpassed in the power which he possessed over wild beasts. On another occasion he tamed and reduced to a state of domesticity a ferocious she-bear and her cubs, whose race was long marked and preserved by the country people. Then, again, an enormous bear drew back before him until she fell into a ditch and broke her neck.

As we have remarked, the missionaries did not feel that Lampaul was a secure settlement. The land was not their own, and they could be disturbed at any moment, as they did not know whether its owner was a Christian or a Pagan—a man disposed to favour monks, or their deadly enemy. It was, therefore, out of the question to think of erecting a monastery whilst in this uncertainty. Once more they betook themselves to prayer to ascertain the Divine will; once more an angel appeared to St. Paul, and directed him to seek an interview with the Prince of the country, who would provide for them a permanent home.

Rejoicing in the idea that they had at last come to the end of their wanderings, they again took to their boats, sailing from west to east, and keeping as near to the shore as possible. Their supply of water being exhausted, they landed, but could find no spring. Then Paul, with the confidence of Moses, called upon the Lord, and forthwith a miraculous fountain burst forth.

Whilst resting beside these waters, they descried in the distance a large herd of cattle, which was being driven by a shepherd. They approached, and made inquiries about the Prince of the country and his place of residence, and requested the peasant to direct them to some inhabited spot whereon they could settle.

Visit to Prince Withur. The shepherd informed them that the Prince was his own master, and offered to conduct the strangers to his place of abode. As they travelled along, he told them that his lord was very kind-hearted, and at his court they would surely obtain the grant of a district suitable to their purpose, as the Prince never refused hospitality to strangers or emigrants. Following the shepherd, they came at last to Roscoff, and from that place were obliged to cross over three miles of sea in order to reach the island of Batz, where Withur resided.

This Prince possessed many accomplishments. He was, in the first place, a good Christian, was highly educated, and fond of religious study, and was also a man of business, to which he attended with the greatest regularity.

The strangers from Britain found him, on their introduction, in the act of copying, with his own hands, the four Gospels.

It is said that he recognised Paul at once, having met him in Britain during his residence there, either as a traveller or as a student. The country he ruled over had been bestowed upon him by the Frank King, whose wise policy it was to encourage colonists to settle in a district very thinly populated.

Aurelianus made Withur acquainted with the place whence he came, the object he had in view, and the circumstances connected with it. He said that his wish was to obey the Divine will; that an angel had appeared to him in the island of Britain, at Ouessant, and again when he landed on these shores, and had commanded him to seek out the sovereign of the country, because near him he would find a permanent home; that it was obedience to a Divine voice which led him to his presence. Withur listened with wonder to these details, which were narrated with all the conviction of truth.

In consequence of the Armorican Prince's

charity to the poor, there was a constant coming and going of persons in distress from the mainland to the island, for seldom did anyone in misery return unrelieved. God at this time glorified his servant Paul in sight of all the people. Amongst the poor travellers he met on the road he restored sight to three blind men, the faculty of speech to two who were deprived of it, and the use of his limbs to a paralysed man.

Withur, recognising the providence of God in sending him such a Thaumaturgas, resolved to make the most of his services. The inhabitants of the country had been terrified, and great devastations committed, by a huge serpent or crocodile, and the Prince besought Paul to deliver the land from this monster. The saint, in the name and power of God, acceded to this request, and the reptile was seen no more.

The Armorican Prince was rich, and naturally generous. The candid narrative of his visitors, and the wonders he had witnessed, pre-occupied his mind. An inward voice whispered to him that he had been chosen as an instrument to secure for his country the services of these servants of God and provide for them a home. Without hesitation, therefore, he presented Paul and his companions with his own house, together with all he possessed in the island of Batz, *Settlement in the island of Batz.*

including the Books of the Gospel which he had written out with his own hand.[1]

This donation was thankfully accepted by the little community, and all recognised the kind providence of God in what had taken place, and now, indeed, felt they had gained the promised land to which the angel had directed them.

They lost no time in making such changes in their new abode as were suitable to the monastic life, and as soon as possible laid the foundations of a large church.

The saintly lives led by the monks who had lately arrived from Britain edified the Armoricans, many of whom presented themselves as novices.

Paul, in particular, attracted the admiration of all, and the people manifested a desire that he should be consecrated bishop; but even this general wish could not overcome the opposition of our saint. In his native Britain he had determinedly declined the episcopal dignity, and he saw no reason to deviate from his former resolution in Armorica. In his humility, he considered that his elevation to the episcopacy could neither benefit his own soul nor the souls of others.

Stratagem used to make him Bishop.

Withur, however, backed as he was by public opinion, strongly expressed, was determined not

(1) The island of Batz contains at present a population of 1167 inhabitants, who are under the spiritual care of two priests. The old church is dedicated to St. Paul. On an eminence facing the cemetery stands a cross, the base of which is fixed in a Druidical stone—the Celtic dolmen, or stone table. The Gospel of Prince Withur was preserved in the Cathedral of Leon down to the last century.

to be beaten, and, after many plans, at last resorted to the following stratagem:—

He visited Paul, and, in confidence, informed him that he besought a particular favour from him.

"I am," he said, "greatly indebted to Childebert, King of the Franks. From him I received the large territory over which I reign. I am sorry to say, I never properly recognised the kindness of the King; for since my settlement in this country I even neglected to send ambassadors to my benefactor, as I was bound to do, both by custom and gratitude.

Besides this duty of etiquette, I have business of the greatest importance to transact with the Frank King, and my request is, that you will go to Paris and represent my interests at Court. You will, at the same time, be able to obtain the signature of Childebert to the charters by which I have granted you land for the service of religion; because in this country we are not altogether independent of the Franks. On being presented to the King, you will hand him these letters. They are stamped with the seal he presented to me at our last meeting, and which he will at once recognise. Then attentively consider what he says, and report it to me."

As it was impossible to refuse a service asked of him by his benefactor, Paul accepted the mission, and prepared for immediate departure.

On arriving at the Court of Childebert, the

British monk presented the letters which had been committed to his charge. One of these was worded as follows:—

"On receiving this, my epistle, my Lord and King, be it known unto you that I, your servant Withur, forward it by the hands of the man of God called Paul, whose consecration as bishop we earnestly entreat you to procure, notwithstanding his own strong opposition. He is most worthy, and admirably suited to the dignity, but, when more than once strongly urged to accept it, he has invariably declined. I can certify that there does not live in our country a priest more highly qualified than he for the episcopal charge, both by exemplary life and depth of learning."

Childebert, on reading this letter, entered heart and soul into the stratagem. He communicated it to Judwal, the exiled King of Brittany, and requested his assistance in carrying out the wishes of Withur and his people.

In his frequent interviews with Paul, the Frank King dwelt on the duty which devolved upon a priest of giving his services where they would tend to most advantage in the vineyard of the Lord, and represented that a man who had been endowed with so many gifts and accomplishments as he possessed, should not confine them within the seclusion of a monastery, and the King enforced his opinion by instancing the Gospel parable of the servants to whom talents were entrusted being required to expend them in that manner which would ensure the greatest amount of interest, and begged the Abbot to reflect whether he might not draw down upon himself the reproaches addressed to the servant who had hidden the treasure committed to his charge.

These last words cut Paul to the heart. He threw himself on his knees before Childebert, and professed himself an unprofitable servant. The King raised him, and, borrowing an ivory crosier from a bishop who was present, he handed it to Paul, saying, "Receive, then, Father, the episcopal dignity, and thus extend the sphere of your usefulness." Three bishops visited the Frank Court to officiate at the consecration of Paulus Aurelianus.

Childebert was thus the means of giving a saintly bishop to Brittany. The Frank Kings were, however, in the habit of unduly interfering in the election of the Armorican bishops, and were, in consequence, publicly censured by the Metropolitan of Tours in a provincial Council.

The admiration of Childebert for the noble soul of Paul continually increased as he became more intimately acquainted with him, and on his taking leave, the King not only ratified the charters of Prince Withur in connection with his donations to the British monk, but, with royal munificence, himself bestowed on the new bishop the island of Ouessant and all other territories in his possession in the country of Occismor.

The new prelate was received on his arrival in his diocese with general rejoicing, which took the form of a national demonstration. His people were not only triumphant at seeing Paul return as their bishop, but were also proud of the honourable reception accorded to him at the Frank Court as their ambassador.

Prince Withur met Paul at Morlaix, several miles beyond his capital, and as they proceeded thither in company, the procession, already imposing, was increased by the numerous parties who continually joined in as it passed along. Indeed, the whole scene recalled to mind the triumphal march of a Roman general on his way to the Capitol after the conquest of distant regions.

The Bishop was installed in the cathedral church of Occismor, instead of at Batz.

The former town was chosen by Conan Meriadec, the founder of the British settlement in Armorica, at the end of the fourth century (384-385), as the capital of his new dominions. Previous to that event it was a flourishing town, built by the Roman colonists, and is believed to have contained a community of Christians in all the religious fervour of early times. This place, the cradle of the British race in Armorica, no longer exists; even its position cannot now be traced with certainty. In God's providence it was destined to be supplanted by another capital —St. Paul de Leon—which was to last for centuries.

The Britons who settled in that part of Armorica were Christians—at least in name—and were followed to their new country by their own priests. Hence the first bishops and monks were, almost without exception, of British or Irish birth. The land was not, however, altogether free from Paganism. Heathen superstitions, rites, customs, and ideas, condemned by the Christian religion, prevailed in certain localities. Satanic rites and bloody sacrifices upon the Celtic Dolmen were not entirely forgotten, and even in those times Pagan temples and sacred groves were to be seen.

The new bishop commenced his work with all the earnestness of an apostle. He erected parishes throughout his diocese, both on the mainland and the adjacent islands. Ouessant, the largest amongst them, was endeared to Paul and his companions as their first resting-place after their exodus from Britain, and was not forgotten.

The bishop divided his diocese into three archdeaconries—Leon, Ock, and Kimilidily. Besides his monastery at Batz, he founded several others—Kerlouan (named Kerpaul), at Plougar, and Lanpaul. Nor had he much difficulty in filling these religious houses with aspirants to the cloister. Novices from all parts of the country sought admittance into these holy institutions, which became the nursery of a well-trained clergy. Amongst these we may specially notice Gwevrod, Tanguy, and Jouva.

St. Paul and the hermit Gwevrod.

On one of his episcopal visitations, when passing through the present parish of Ploudaniel, St. Paul was told that a holy hermit, a native of Britain, like himself, led an edifying life in a wood not far distant. On visiting him, the hermit related that he had come over from Britain with Tugdual (most likely from the west of Britain), that he had been elected Abbot of Loc-Kirec Monastery, but had resigned that dignity in order to follow his inclination for solitude. Paul, recognising in the solitary great talents for missionary work, advised him to leave his retreat and labour for the conversion of souls in his diocese. He told the hermit how he himself had so much loved solitude that at the age of sixteen he had left Lantwit-Major, with the consent of St. Illtyd, to follow this vocation; but when summoned by Mark to preach the Gospel to his subjects, he had regarded it as a call from heaven; and had, later on, at the bidding of an angel, forsaken his native land and come to Armorica to work for the conversion of souls in that land; and that, being constrained to accept episcopacy, he consecrated his life to the welfare of his flock, although at all times much preferring solitude. "Now, as your Bishop," added the saint, "I invite you to help in gaining souls to Jesus Christ. You cannot decline my request. You are a priest of the Church of God; assist me, therefore, to extend her doctrines and her practices throughout this land."

The hermit at last yielded, followed his bishop to Occismor, was appointed Vicar-General, and became very useful.

It is related of Gwevrod that, on a certain Sunday, as he was passing through the country, he met a man who was cutting thorns with which to fill up a gap in the fence of a corn-field. The Vicar-General remonstrated with him for breaking the law of the Christians by thus working on a Sunday. The man only laughed, and went on with his work, and the priest continued his journey. The man found, shortly afterwards, that the axe was fastened to his hand. He tried in vain to wrench it off, but all his efforts were without avail. Terrified and repentant, he hastened to Occismor, and, in presence of St. Paul and his Vicar-General, confessed his sin before the altar, and, prostrate upon its steps, received absolution.

On another occasion a similar transgression was also punished. The *Alter Ego* of St. Paul, whilst passing through Occismor one day, observed a young woman busy washing at the door of a house. It was a Feast of our Lady, and the priest stopped to remonstrate against this violation of the law of the Church. The young woman said people must eat whether it be Sunday or Festival day, and she could not see any reason why she should not earn her bread on these days as well as on others. Not long after she was struck with paralysis both in her hands and in her feet, and at once recognised in this the hand of God. She fasted for a week, and entreated Gwevrod to make the sign of the Cross upon her. He did so, and she was cured. The church of Creiz-Caer, the spire of which is the finest in Brittany, was built and dedicated to our blessed Lady, to commemorate this miracle, on the very spot where it took place.

St. Paul and Gurguy.

On a certain day, a young nobleman, with remorse and affliction stamped upon his countenance, came to St. Paul to seek his advice as to the best way of making satisfaction for a terrible crime he had committed—the murder of his own sister.

"I am the son of Galonus and Florence of Tremazan," said the unhappy young man. "My mother died young, leaving two children —my sister Haude and myself. My name is Gurguy. Shortly after our mother's death, our father—to our great grief—married a British lady, who was richly dowered, but infected with the Pelagian heresy. She soon acquired unlimited influence over our father, and reigned supreme in the house. The day she entered under our roof was the dawn of a life of trial and misery to us children. Like most stepmothers, she did not love either the son or daughter of her husband's first wife, but, on the contrary, manifested her hatred of them both by word and action.

Having grown to manhood, after eight years

of long and intense suffering, I could no longer brook this tyranny and ill-treatment, and thought of leaving home to try my fortune at the Court of Childebert; but for love of my sister I delayed my departure for some time, feeling certain that the persecution would increase in my absence. When I communicated my plans to Haude, she wept and entreated of me not to leave her unprotected. However, on a certain day, having been grossly insulted by my step-mother, I could endure it no longer, and left my father's house."

It appeared that Haude had reason to oppose the departure of her brother, for soon after she was subjected to additional cruelties. The poor young lady was treated like a servant, deprived of her companions, shut out from the chapel at whose altar she was wont to seek consolation, and at last turned away from her father's home and sent to live in a farm-house. There she felt happy, and lived like a nun in a convent.

Several years elapsed, during which the young nobleman made his way at the Court of Paris; but neither distance nor the dissipations of a royal city could make him forget his dear sister, though all correspondence between them was prevented by their step-mother. But some persons from his country, who were visiting Paris, gave him details of the cruel treatment which Haude was undergoing. This determined him to see with his own eyes what foundation there was for these reports. With this purpose he left Paris, and presented himself, in disguise, at the castle of his father. The illustrious guest from the Frank Court inquired after the Lady Haude, whose praises, he said, were on the lips of everyone who came to Paris from Brittany, and he expressed a great desire to make her acquaintance.

The cunning step-mother took him aside, and, affecting deep interest in the stranger, informed him, in the strictest confidence, as she stated, that her husband's daughter, of whom he had heard so favourable a report, was, she grieved to say, a hypocrite, and a girl of such light behaviour that, for the honour of the family, they had been forced to remove her to a farmhouse.

Haude's brother, unfortunately, allowed himself to be deceived by this calumny, and became indignant at the supposed shameful conduct of his sister. He went to the farm, where he was informed that Haude was washing linen in the brook. He proceeded thither, and found her busily occupied at this work. On hearing her name called aloud, the young maiden looked up, and, not recognising her brother, fled away in alarm. This, unfortunately, seemed to him a confirmation of his step-mother's calumny, as he attributed her flight to the consciousness of guilt, which rendered her unable to bear the shame of meeting him. Acting under this false conclusion, and inflamed with rage, the unfortunate young man drew his sword and pursued the fugitive, with the determination of washing away the stain she had brought upon the family in her blood. He soon overtook her, and, terrible to relate, ran his sword through her body and afterwards cut off her head.

No sooner was the crime effected than a sense of its enormity rushed upon the mind of the fratricide. He burst into tears, groaned like a man in despair, and fell on his knees beside the lifeless body of his once dearly-loved sister.

The people of the neighbourhood hastened to the spot, and, as they reverently removed the remains of Haude, loudly lamented the sad end of this long-persecuted angel.

As soon as the unhappy brother recovered from the swoon into which he had fallen, he learned, with terrible anguish, the shameful conduct of his step-mother, and the innocence of the victim of her malice and of his own unrestrained passion.

Gurguy, having poured forth his tale of horror and remorse into the compassionate heart of the holy priest, added, "Life has become a burden to me. Ever freshly to my mind recurs the remembrance of that murder, because if any one deserved to fall under my sword it was my wicked, crafty step-mother, and not my innocent sister, who was as pure as an angel. I refrained from vengeance, however, and God's judgment has overtaken our persecutor, who suddenly dropped dead. To you, father, do I now appeal. Tell me, I implore you, how I can make satisfaction for the murder of my sister?"

The Bishop was deeply grieved as he listened to this narrative and saw before him the noble-hearted young man who had been deluded into committing a most abominable crime.

"My son," he said, "family pride, a worldly spirit, which could not leave vengeance to the Lord, and an uncontrolled temper which robs the soul of reason and reflection, were the causes of this crime. May God forgive your hastiness and anger! You travelled from Paris to protect your sister from your step-mother, and yet believed her calumnies against this persecuted angel, and did not even give your victim a chance of explanation. Go now for forty days into solitude. Pray and weep for your sister, and implore the forgiveness of heaven. After that time return to me.

After the expiration of the alloted time, the young nobleman presented himself before the bishop, as he had been commanded, told him that he had performed his penance, and begged admittance into one of his monasteries; for in the solitude of the woods God had visited his soul, enlightened him with new ideas, and turned his heart altogether against the world. St. Paul, and several priests who were conferring with him on ecclesiastical business, were startled when, on the entrance of Gurguy, they beheld a sort of halo surrounding the head of the penitent murderer, in the form of a supernatural crown. The young knight, perceiving surprise depicted on every countenance, attributed it to the horror which guiltless men must experience at the sight of an assassin. From that day his baptismal name of Gurguy was changed for that of Tanguy, or the wreath of fire.

Having assured St. Paul of his irrevocable determination to leave the world, Tanguy begged of him the favour of admission into his monastery of Batz. His request being granted, he edified the brotherhood by a most exemplary life. Later on, St. Paul sent him to found a monastery at Relec, nine miles from Morlaix, and another at St. Matthew, at the entrance of the roads of Brest, where he had inherited from his father a large tract of land, which the town of Brest and its environs now nearly covers.

The greatest friendship existed between St. Paul and Tanguy. On a certain day, long after the events we have mentioned, when they had met to converse on spiritual matters, and to ensure solitude had retired into a forest, an angel appeared, and said, " Be of good heart, for in a short time both of you will be taken from this valley of tears to your home in heaven." The scene of this apparition has ever since been called "Coat-eles," or the Forest of the Angelic Vision. The prophecy was realised, for Tanguy and his

Bishop departed this life on the same day, being the twelfth of March.

St. Paul and his nephew Jovin.

Jovin, the nephew of St. Paul, enlightens us as regards the power of performing miracles granted by heaven to his uncle. Jovin, or Jaoua, was born in Ireland, his mother being sister of Paulus Aurelianus. He was educated in England, where he learned to appreciate the virtues and talents of his uncle, and even entertained ideas of embracing the religious life.

His family having, probably, some notion of his designs, recalled him to Ireland, where they supplied him with horses and hounds and everything else deemed suitable for the position of a young nobleman.

To satisfy his parents, he entered into their views, and joined in all the national sports, not losing, however, his desire for entering religion.

Letters from Great Britain announced that Paul and twelve other priests had sailed for Armorica and landed safely at Ouessant. Jovin suddenly resolved to join his uncle, and, to prevent opposition, decided on leaving home secretly. Having procured a ship, he directed the sailors to steer for Ouessant, but contrary winds drove them into the Bay of Brest.

After remaining for some time in the Monastery of Landevennec, the young aspirant succeeded in joining his uncle, was ordained priest, and sent to evangelise the inhabitants of Braspars and its neighbourhood, in the district of

Cornouailles, which is only divided from Leon by a ridge of mountains. There he began to preach the Gospel, a part of the people being still plunged in the darkness of Paganism. He, like every other apostle, met with friends and enemies; some who listened to the precepts of Jesus Christ, and others opposed to Christian morality.

Amongst the latter was a nobleman who hated the preacher of the Gospel, for the simple reason that many of his dissolute companions were won by him to abandon their sinful way of life. This wicked man heartily cursed those priests from beyond the sea who, according to his report, disturbed the country and interfered with old customs and modes of life. More than once he was heard to say it was a pity the ocean had not swallowed them on their voyage.

On a certain day an ecclesiastical conference was held not far from the residence of this impious man, who looked upon this as a favourable opportunity of getting rid of the men of Christ. He collected a band of ruffians, and, placing himself at their head, approached the place of conference. Finding the door of the church closed, he burst it open, put the congregation to flight, and, rushing to the altar, slew the priest who was celebrating Mass, and had reached that part of the Canon where *Nobis peccatoribus* is said. Jovin and the Abbot of Landevennec escaped. The latter, however, was overtaken and put to the sword by the sacrilegious assassin.

Divine vengeance soon overtook this murderer of monks. He became possessed by the devil, and there was much difficulty in restraining him from doing violence on himself and others, and the country was also visited by a scourge in the shape of a huge dragon, which spread terror and devastation all around.

The people laid their grievances before St. Paul, and implored him to come to Faou and deliver them from the terrible visitations of the devil and the dragon.

The Bishop promised to comply with their wishes, and dismissed the messengers, reccommending the performance of penance, in order to obtain the mercy of God, who is ever ready to forgive those who repent.

When on his way to fulfil his promise, in company with some of his brethren, they stopped at a place called Mousterpaol, to recite the Divine Office. Whilst thus engaged an angel appeared to Paul, and consoled him with the assurance that God would bless his mission.

On arriving at the village, the saint soon collected the scattered inhabitants around him, and at once commenced instructing them in the Christian doctrine. One day he thus addressed them:—

"In order to convince you of the truth of the Gospel, and on the formal promise that you will renounce all your superstitions and do penance, I will deliver you from the dragon, in the name of our Lord Jesus Christ."

The people with one voice promised to do all that was required of them. Then the Bishop directed Jovin to prepare the altar for the holy Sacrifice of the Mass, and after its celebration he left the church, in procession, and commanded the serpent to come forth from wherever he might be, without doing harm to anyone. The monster obeyed, slowly advanced towards the saint, and lay down at his feet. The Bishop bound his stole round his neck, and, plunging a stick into the ground, tied the serpent to it, ordering him not to move from that spot until desired to do so.[1]

This being done, Paul visited the residence of the murderer of the two abbots, and, by the sign of the Cross, drove away the evil spirit. Then he instructed him in the Christian religion, and administered the sacrament of baptism, bestowing upon him the name of Paul.

(1) L'Abbe Gaume, in his learned treatise, "Du St. Esprit," shows at length how Satan, in his relations with mankind, evinces a great partiality to the serpent. Clothed in the body of that reptile, he tempted our first parents in the terrestrial paradise. In Holy Scriptures the king of the City of Evil is often called the dragon—"*Draco Magnus*," the serpent. At all times, everywhere, in Egypt, amongst the Babylonians, he wished to be worshipped amongst the Pagans under the form of a serpent. The supreme god of the Persians, Medes, Phœnicians, and others was the serpent, with a hawk's head ; so much so, that the temples of many nations went by the general name of *Dracontia*. Amongst the refined Greeks, the only irrational animal admitted into the ranks of the gods was the serpent. The duties of the Roman vestals consisted not only in keeping alive the sacred fire, but also in feeding the serpent associated to the numerous gods of that Pagan empire. In China they worship to this day the great dragon ; the seal of the Celestial Empire is a dragon. In India this reptile is publicly worshipped. The Indian women and children wear silver serpents round their ankles and wrists. In Africa,

The people followed the example of their ruler, and were received into the Church.

Like most of the Welsh saints whom we have introduced to our readers, Paul, as he advanced in life, seemed to yearn after the solitude of his early years, and relied in a great measure on his disciples for carrying on the work of his diocese. He particularly esteemed Jovin, whose consecration as bishop he is believed to have obtained from St. Samson, Archbishop of Dôl. After this event he retired to his monastery of Batz.

The newly-consecrated bishop died on the second of March, and was succeeded by Tiernomallus, who also, after a short period, departed this life.

Paul came to Occismor to assist at the funeral of the late prelate, and at a conference of the clergy which took place on the occasion, the necessity of his again undertaking the administration of the diocese was so strongly urged that he was compelled to yield to the general wish,

---

temples are erected to this hideous reptile, a priesthood do duty in the said temples, and feed its divine tenant. Amongst the ancient Pagan nations of Europe we also notice the same false notions. We are not, then, to wonder that the zealous British missionaries, founders of Christian churches amongst the Pagans, should have met in the serpent or dragon a sworn enemy. The struggles of St. Armel, Tugdual, Efflam, and Paul of Leon with the dragon are explained in the light of faith. It is a battle of principles between Christianity and Paganism. It is the Christian man not surrendering himself, like our first parents, to Satan disguised into a serpent, but battling, in the name of the Redeemer, against the seducer of his race. The description given of these dragons, their wonderful size, agility, strength, and horrid appearance, is somewhat extraordinary. But modern science, represented by such men as Cuvier, in France, and Buckland, in England, who have carefully studied the fossils brought to light by excavations, leave no doubt that huge animals, of the most extraordinary size, have existed. We find these fossils embedded in the bowels of the earth, and such as have been disinterred may be seen in our public museums.—(*Vide* Abbé Gaume, "Traité du St. Esprit." Vol. I.).

and once more resumed the pastoral duties; but after a few months, feeling that his age and infirmities rendered him unequal to the task, he entrusted the diocese to the charge of one of his monks, called Cetomerinus, whom he consecrated bishop A.D. 556, in the presence of Judwal, Prince of Brittany.

During the ceremony, a voice from the crowd was heard imploring the venerable bishop to pity his misery and pray to God on his behalf. It was a blind man who thus interrupted the sacred function. St. Paul touched his eyes, and he at once recovered his sight. Judwal was so much impressed by this miracle that, to testify his admiration of it, he conceded a large tract of land for the service of religion. The place was ever afterwards called *Menesty*, or Menishty, the House of the Monk—that is to say, the Refuge of St. Paul.

Once more could the saint return without scruple to his dear solitude, confident that the spiritual wants of his flock would be attended to. In his little island he gave himself up unreservedly to contemplation, and lived for many years in great austerity, and, though worn out by penance and by age, always presented to his brethren the example of monastic perfection. When in prayer, he seemed to hold commune with the angels, and, like Daniel, was favoured with the gift of prophecy. He foretold that, in times to come, his monastery would be entirely destroyed by the Normans, and that war, with all its train of misery, would for a long period spread devastation through the country. He also foretold that after his death great contention would arise between the inhabitants of Batz and his brethren and the clergy and people of Occismor as to the possession of his body. In order, if possible, to avoid this dissension, he expressed a wish to be interred in his cathedral church ; but this proved of no avail in averting what he dreaded.

We have already mentioned that St. Paul and Tanguy, whilst praying together, had received intimation that their departure from this world would be proximate.

But towards the end of his career the saint received a further warning on the same subject. In order not to inconvenience his brethren, he lived in a small house which he had constructed close to the monastery. On a certain night, the greater part of which he had spent in prayer, he was about to fall asleep when he felt himself gently shaken ; he beheld the room illuminated, and an angel standing beside him. "Paul," said the heavenly messenger, "thou hast fought valiantly, and run thy career nobly. It is now meet that the Just Judge give thee thy reward. Prepare thyself for thy departure from this world on next Sunday, for on that day thou shalt enter into the glory of thy Lord." The angel having spoken these words, disappeared, but the heavenly radiance still continued to illume the apartment.

On the following morning the saint celebrated the holy Sacrifice of the Mass with extraordinary devotion. It was, perhaps, for the last time. Then he called together his monastic brethren, and communicated to them the celestial vision with which he had been favoured on the preceding night. His countenance gleamed with a supernatural light. The faithful servant was at last about to be united to his heavenly Master, never again to be separated from Him. After urging his brethren to act up to the spirit of the religious life, he assured them that the Pastor of the vineyard would give to them a holy bishop who would carry on the work of the Church with zeal and discretion.

Having spoken thus, he was obliged to rest upon his bed, which he never again was able to rise from. On the following Sunday he requested Bishop Cetomerinus to administer to him the Sacraments of Holy Communion and Extreme Unction. Shortly after he spoke a few encouraging words to those around him, and concluded by blessing them in the following words:—

"My children, may the blessing of God, whom we adore, Father, Son, and Holy Ghost, descend upon you, and ever remain with you." Whilst the recipients of this benediction were in the act of answering "Amen," the saint gave up his soul to his Creator, without the least struggle. According to Albert le Grand, he was then one hundred and two years of age.[1]

As the holy bishop had foretold, a great dispute arose amongst the people as to his place of burial. The body lay in state in the church of the Monastery of Batz, and was visited by crowds from all parts of the country. The sea was literally covered with the fleets of boats which were employed conveying people to and from the island.

On the day appointed for the funeral, the Bishop arrived to remove the body to Occismor, but the islanders opposed his being transferred from Batz. As in the case of St. Teilo, second Bishop of Llandaff, each party looked upon its own claim as undeniable.

The islanders urged that it was upon their island he had first settled on his arrival from Britain, that he had passed a great part of his time amongst them, and had there died; and sought thus to prove themselves entitled to the possession of his remains. The canons of his cathedral, together with the rest of the inhabitants of his diocese, maintained that a bishop should be buried in his metropolitan church, and that such was the wish of the deceased prelate, as plainly stated in his last moments. Neither party would yield, and the

---

[1] The exact date of St. Paul's death cannot be clearly ascertained. Some place it in the year 573, and others in 597. The new Breviary of Quimper assigns 570, and M. de Freminville 594.—LOBINEAU.

altercation became so warm as to degenerate into a general contention.

Bishop Cetomerinus at last proposed a plan of settlement which was accepted by all. He ordered bullocks to be yoked to two carts, with their heads turned respectively towards the monastery and towards Occismor; the body was so placed as to rest half on one cart and half on the other; the bullocks were then started, and the cart on which the coffin remained was to decide the place of burial. The cart directed towards Occismor was the favoured one, and the departed bishop was accordingly buried in his own cathedral.

If at the present day a Breton, dwelling on the shores of Armorica, between Brest and Morlaix, were asked to point out Occismor, he would answer that no such town existed in the *Departement*, and in making this statement he would neither tell an untruth nor indicate ignorance. The name of the capital of Conan Meriadec has long since disappeared. But any native of Brittany will be quite ready to inform the traveller of the position of St. Pol de Leon, or Castel Pol. In such veneration did the inhabitants of his diocese hold their first bishop, that they called his episcopal see by his name, and that of Occismor became merged into Castel Paul, or St. Pol de Leon, which place is well known wherever the Breton language is spoken.

The diocese has been united to that of Quimper, but it is proposed to restore it to its original dignity. The cathedral erected over the grave of St. Paulus Aurelianus is one of the finest in Armorica, and the spire of the Church of Creisker, in the same town, is unsurpassed by any other in France.

Visitors to Coventry admire its lofty and beautiful towers, but those who have seen the spire of St. Paul de Leon incline to give it the preference. The Bretons are so proud of this *Clocher* that it holds a distinctive place in the national songs of the country. It is a bold and highly-finished tower, which stands on four pillars, nine feet in diameter, and is altogether disconnected from the walls of the church. One would almost imagine it to be a magical construction, so airily is it poised.

The Bretons have reason to be proud of their churches and spires. The Departement of Finistere is neither rich nor poor; it contains a population of more than six hundred thousand inhabitants; but one would have to travel far to find churches and towers so beautiful. The spire and sculptured Calvary are special to the diocese of Quimper, and draws the particular attention of architectural travellers through Lower Brittany. From the chain of mountains which divides Leon from Cornouailles scores of magnificent spires are visible, which seem to rise in the air like gigantic needles. These fanes constructed by our ancestors might be kept in better order.

What heaven-inspired architects our forefathers were, as they manifested through these magnificent erections their faith and their zeal for the glory of the house of God! St. Paul de Leon is the first of these remarkable churches, but Landivisian, St. Thegonnec, Lanpaul, and many others may be instanced as fine specimens of Gothic architecture.

Modern towns, such as Brest, have arisen in the diocese of St. Paul and neighbourhood; but how inferior are the churches, even in a naval town numbering eighty thousand inhabitants, when compared with the noble old temples in the surrounding villages. The peasant of Brittany, when he visits Brest, may be struck with the appearance of the stately fleet of men-of-war, but when he returns to his own hamlet will remark, with a feeling of pride, that the large town does not possess a single steeple the spire of which approaches in beauty that of his village church; and this is perfectly correct, for no churches in Brest, Lorient, etc., can match those of Hennebon, Pont Croix, Quimper, or Locronan. As the order of faith has waned, the art of erecting befitting temples to Almighty God seems also to have decreased.

Mary Stuart, Queen of Scotland, caught in a storm on those shores, made a vow that, if saved from wreck, she would erect a church on or near the spot she should reach, in thanksgiving for her safety. Her vessel was driven into Roscoff, a few miles from St. Paul de Leon. The walls and other portions of the church erected in fulfilment of her vow are still in their position.

CHAPTER XVII.

St. Gildas, Abbot.[1]

GILDAS—surnamed the *Wise*, by some, the Historian, or Badonicus, by others—was one of the celebrated scholars trained by St. Illtyd at Lantwit-Major. Of his collaborators in the vineyard of the Lord—than most of whom he was somewhat younger—we have already spoken in the preceding chapters.

Britain, Scotland, and Brittany each claim to this day the honour of being the birth-place of St. Patrick; Dumbarton, on the Clyde, in Scotland, and Bath, in Somersetshire, assert alike the privilege of numbering Gildas amongst their most illustrious sons.

The surname of Badonicus, which succeeding generations superadded to his own, indicates the fact stated by Gildas himself, that he was born during that year of our Lord in which King Arthur inflicted a crushing blow upon the Saxons

---

(1) Compiled from the "Britannia Sancta," Albert le Grand, "Vierdes Saints de Bretagne-Armorique," Lobineau. The "Britannia Sancta" states that the life of Gildas is compiled from John of Basco, and derived from an ancient manuscript in the library of Fleury, and collated with that of Caradocus of Llancarvan and his Acts in Capgrave. The Breton writers availed themselves of the MSS. of their own country, and consider Mabbillon's Life more correct than any other.

by defeating them on Mount Badon, in the vicinity of Bath. This memorable event, according to the general opinion of historians, took place in the year 493.

Like St. Cadoc of Llancarvan, St. David, and St. Teilo, Gildas was of illustrious birth, and descended from a family not only Christian in name, but distinguished for strict observance of the laws of God and of the Church. Several of his relatives had forsaken the world and its vanities and devoted themselves to the service of God in the cloister.[1]

Amongst the students of Lantwit-Major a custom existed which is not uncommon in our modern colleges, of affixing an adjective to the names of scholars, which served to denote some striking peculiarity either in their physical appearance, temperament, or habits. In accordance with this custom, Gildas was surnamed " Aquarius," or the Water-drinker (in Welsh, Dwr Ifur),[2] because he never drank any kind of fermented beverage, and during his whole life sacredly observed this total abstinence.

As soon as he had attained a sufficient age, his parents committed Gildas to the care of St. Illtyd, and at Lantwit-Major his capacity for learning was soon discovered. As he advanced

(1) Armorican writers, in the notes appended to Albert le Grand, observe :—" We must not confound Gildas the Abbot of Rhuys with Gildas the Albanian monk of Glastonbury. The latter was son of Conan Meriadec, the founder of the British colony in Armorica, who married Dererea, sister of St. Patrick.

(2) In Breton, Dour ever.

in years the Holy Scriptures became his favourite study, and those who read his writings will at once perceive there was scarcely a verse of sacred writ which was not stamped upon his memory. Early meditations on such subjects enlightened his faith and kindled within his heart the fire of Divine love, and decided him on withdrawing altogether from the empty world to consecrate his life to the service of God.

When his studies at Lantwit-Major were completed he crossed over to Ireland, there to perfect his education and learn from the disciples of St. Patrick that ascetic science in which the Irish were so proficient. In that country Gildas sought instruction in Divine and human knowledge from the most celebrated masters, and, like an industrious bee, gathered from every flower, for his own benefit and that of his neighbours, the honey of virtue and science.[1]

When ordained priest, we find our saint actively engaged in missionary works, both in Britain and Ireland. He preached the Gospel to pagans and heretics, for in his time many Christians were still infected by the Pelagian heresy.

God bestowed a wonderful blessing on the labours of the young priest, for great was the number of unbelievers whom he converted to Christ. He was endowed with the power of

---

(1) Tanquam apis prudentissima diversorum florum succos collegit atqua in alvea matris Ecclesiæ reconditit ut intempore opportuno mellifiua evangelii verba in populo effunderet.—"Acta" Gildas.

working miracles, which added weight to his preaching.

Crowds gathered around him, and through his teaching Pagans embraced Christianity and were baptised, and those who were separated from the Church by Pelagianism hastened to seek reconciliation with that loving mother. His fame as an orator and a saint was echoed across the Irish sea, and at the repeated request of one of her kings he returned to that island. He there continued the same work—built churches and monasteries, regulated the Liturgy, and taught for some time in the famous school of Armagh.[1]

It is remarked that the young apostle, though indulgent to others, was severe towards himself. He failed not to chastise his own body, so as to bring his passions under subjection, lest, with all his learning and his teaching of others, he should himself become a castaway. It is stated that from the age of fifteen to the end of his life he took nourishment but on three days of the week. Perhaps, like St. Samson, his physical strength was miraculously sustained by the holy Eucharist. A hair shirt covered his body, the bare ground was his bed, a stone his pillow. So great were his mortifications that his existence under them was looked upon as a miracle. Perhaps strong natural passions, which he was determined to subdue, demanded this austerity of life.

(1) "Britannia Sancta."

Between the years 527 and 530 Gildas left Britain, and passed over to Armorica. It is recorded in his Acts that this step was taken *Jussû Dei*, or by the order of God, which, no doubt, implies that he, like St. Samson, had been visited by an angel, who, in the name of his Master, commanded him to spend the remainder of his life amongst his brethren and countrymen in Armorica.

Gildas was at that time in the prime of life—between thirty and forty years of age. But, though still young, he had great experience of mankind, and of affairs of all sorts, having from the time of his ordination been actively engaged in missionary life, both in Britain and Ireland.

However, on crossing to Armorica, his mind seems to have been made up to change his busy life for one of solitude, for he selected as his abode one of those small islands which lie between Belle Isle and the southern part of Morbihan. This little island of Houat sheltered Gildas from the world for a few years, for in that narrow home he had no other companions but God and his angels, and a few poor fishermen, whom he instructed in the Christian religion.

But these mariners, who daily sailed to the mainland to dispose of their fish, revealed the retreat of the hermit, and told wonderful things concerning his way of life. His solitude was soon disturbed by crowds of visitors, some prompted by curiosity, others desirous of advice from a master of the spiritual life.

Many, indeed, remained in the island to share his mode of living, and their number gradually increasing, the saint was forced to look out for a more spacious retreat on the opposite shores.

A neighbouring prince, who had probably been his fellow-student at Lantwit-Major, together with his two brothers, Tugdual and Eleanor, presented him with a castle on the seashore. Gildas changed this into a regular monastery, which was soon filled with a great number of disciples.

The sick and the afflicted of the neighbouring counties flocked to the peninsula of Rhuys, confident of being cured by the servant of God. The crowds became so great that Gildas quitted the monastery, and hid himself in a neighbouring cavern. He thought no one could discover him, for on the banks of the river Blavæt he found a natural cave, and in its hollow he erected an oratory, digging here and there to suit his plan.

But the people were determined to find the saint, and at last succeeded in discovering his retreat, and then an almost unbroken procession of the infirm made their way to it; for God glorified His servant by the performance of several miracles. On this spot also another monastery soon arose.

Gildas and Triphina.—Amongst the numerous events connected with the life of our saint, none is more interesting than that which relates to St. Triphina. This episode is to this day narrated by the story-teller in the Breton homes, coloured, of course, by the imagination of the bards. The facts are as follow:—

Varoch, Count of Vannes, son of Hoel I. and St. Pompeia, had a daughter, both virtuous and beautiful. Her father, naturally, doted upon this child, and, as the legend states, would have preferred the loss of his horses, manors, or the whole of his estates rather than see a single cloud upon the brow of his daughter.

The day of misfortune was, however, at hand. Commore, Count of Cornouailles, fell in love with the young Triphina, and sought her hand in marriage. But his proposal was not agreeable either to father or daughter, for this nobleman bore the worst reputation in the country, and was considered by the people to be the most wicked man upon the face of the earth, since the days of the first murderer, Cain. Whilst yet a youth, he delighted in vice, and the pleasure he took in tormenting his fellow-creatures was so well known that his mother caused the alarm-bell to be tolled whenever he left the castle, in order to warn people to keep out of his way. When he became his own master, his propensity to cruelty seemed to increase, instances of which were whispered about that were calculated to strike the most courageous hearts with terror. Amongst other reports, it was said that when he returned from the chase without having killed any game, he made up for his loss of sport by setting his dogs to attack persons in the fields and tear them to pieces. One fact was specially terrible. He had married several times, and his wives had successively disappeared, without even having received the last Sacraments of the Church, and he was suspected of having murdered them either with his hunting knife, by fire, water, or poison.[1]

Varoch and Triphina were justified in feeling averse to such a union; but Commore was powerful, and had always a large army at hand; so the Count of Vannes was greatly embarrassed. His mind, however, was firmly made up never to give his daughter to such a monster; but he coloured his refusal as well as he could, to avoid as much as possible irritating the dangerous suitor.

Commore repeated his proposal, and even sent messengers to Gildas, of whose influence over father and daughter he was aware, requesting his good services in the matter, and assuring the saint that, whatever his life heretofore might have been, he was now determined to change altogether for the better. The Abbot was not to be deceived by such specious promises, and informed the envoys of Commore that he would never advise a marriage which would probably result in the murder of Triphina, and be the

(1) Legend of Prince Commore, Emile Souvestre. Lobineau.

occasion of her father pining away with grief; he could not in conscience become an accomplice in risking such an eventuality.

Unrebuked by this answer, the prince requested an interview with the father of his intended wife, and this could not be refused by one nobleman to another.

Both father and daughter solicited the presence of Gildas on this occasion, and he complied with their wish. The Count of Vannes, much perplexed, thus addressed the saint: "My dear Abbot, Commore persists in his demand to marry Triphina, but I swear that he shall never receive her hand from me. I entrust my daughter to you, Gildas, and leave the affair entirely in your hands."

Gildas was greatly perplexed, and Triphina, with tears and sobs, exclaimed, "Would to God I had been the daughter of a beggar, for then I could, at least, have married a beggar I liked. You may as well cover me with a pall and commence singing my funeral service."

On the other side, a refusal was equivalent to an immediate declaration of war; for Commore, being disappointed in his love, would look upon his dismissal as a personal injury, and demand satisfaction on the battle-field.

However the saint, as if under inspiration from above, replied: "Well, Prince Varoch, in the name of God I accept your daughter, and make myself answerable for her safety."

Having spoken thus, the saint visited Commore, and obliged him to promise, in the most solemn manner, on his knees before the altar, that he would treat Triphina with the greatest respect. "Bear in mind," said the holy Abbot, "that you receive her, not from me, but from God. Treat her with respect, not as the daughter of man, but of the King of kings."

The marriage was solemnised shortly after, with great pomp. Gildas, however, declined being present at the ceremony, but retired to his monastery to pray to the Almighty for blessings on the union.

Triphina and her husband spent some months together happily, and the young bride, with the simplicity of an innocent heart, trusted unreservedly in the thorough conversion of her spouse; but persons of more experience shook their heads, and said, "It is difficult to change a wolf into a lamb."

When there was expectation of a child being born of this marriage, Commore, instead of hailing the event with joy, seemed rather to resent it. He became cool in his manner to his wife, then rough, and finally unbearable, and hatred took the place of love.

Triphina was alarmed, and trembled for her own life and that of her child. She feared that at any moment she might fall a victim to his brutality. Her terror was increased by the reports of her servants, who advised her to seek safety in flight; and she felt that by remaining any longer with her husband she would surely share the fate of his former wives, and expose her infant to the danger of dying without the sacrament of baptism.

With a few trusty servants she planned her escape, and, when every preparation was completed, secretly left the castle and took the road to Vannes.

Her husband was furious when he became aware of her flight, and swore to be revenged in her blood. He mounted the fleetest horse in his stables, and, taking with him two hounds, started in pursuit.

Discovering her where she lay concealed amongst leaves, at the outskirts of a forest, he dismounted, and, if we may believe the "Acts" of Gildas and Tremewr, cut off her head.

The servants escaped, and brought the sad tidings to the father of the poor victim at Vannes. The bereaved parent at once despatched messengers to inform Gildas of what had occurred, the whole blame of which, in his grief, he threw upon the saint. "My daughter is dead," he said. "I entrusted her to you, and in the name of God you made yourself answerable for her. In the name of the same God, restore her to me."

The "Acts" of Gildas assert that when the holy Abbot arrived at Vannes, he knelt beside the body of Triphina and restored her to life, and that in due time she gave birth to her child. At the baptismal font the infant received the name of Gildas, but the people surnamed him Trec'hmeur, or, more correctly, Trec'hmaro— "the Conqueror of Death"—on account of his life having been preserved under such terrific circumstances.

It is related that this child lived to become a young man, when, being met by his cruel father, as he was returning from church, the monster, uninfluenced by the sentiments of paternity or the innocence of youth, cut off his head.

The great collegiate church of Carhaix, in Finistere, was dedicated to this pious youth and his mother, Triphina, who entered a monastery, where she ended her days in the odour of sanctity.

After these events Gildas continued to lead a retired life, devoting his time to the administration of his monasteries of Rhuys and Blavet, as also to that of St. Demetrius. Periodically he revisited the small island of Houat, his first habitation on his arrival in Brittany. Every place he went he was favoured with the gift of supernatural power, which drew hundreds to follow him.

During his last days on earth, Gildas received extraordinary personal lights from God. One night, in the island of Houat, as he was sighing after the beatitude of heaven, and lamenting to his Divine Master the weariness of this temporal life, an angel stood before him, and intimated that his prayers had been heard, and within eight days he would enjoy in heaven the vision of his God. Next morning he despatched a message to his brethren at Rhuys, requesting them to come to Houat to receive his last will. His injunctions were chiefly directed to the recommendation of mutual charity and humility, as the foundation of Christian life.

On the eighth day after the vision, Gildas caused himself to be carried to the Oratory, where he made his confession to the Abbot of Rhuys, and received the Viaticum and Extreme Unction.

Foreseeing that probably contention on the point might arise amongst his monastic brethren, he left the following instructions as to his funeral:—" My children," he said " when I am gone, do not allow any disputes to arise amongst you concerning my body. A decayed corpse is not worth taking notice of. After my death, let my mortal remains be placed in a boat, together with the stone which I used as my pillow. Launch the boat, and let the tide and the wind waft it whithersoever Almighty God pleases. He will defray the expense of my burial. It matters little in what place the body awaiteth the general resurrection—whether it be in the bowels of the earth or in the depths of the sea."

His orders were obeyed, and his body placed in a boat, which was sent adrift.

Some monks from Cornouailles, who had travelled by sea to assist at the funeral of the saint, on hearing of what had been done, rowed after the boat to secure its contents, but it at once sank beneath the waves.

The monks of Rhuys, however, three months later on found the body of Gildas, cast up on the dry beach, as fresh and in as good preservation as on the day he departed from this world.

Lobineau observes that what is here related means, perhaps, nothing more than the translation of the body from the island of Houat to the Chapel of the Holy Cross, on the mainland. However, Lobineau seems at times inclined to forget that God is wonderful in his saints.

Gildas is considered by some as the most ancient writer in Britain, although British literature possesses a work by Fastidius, Bishop of London—"*De vita Christiana, de mediis ad Conservandam Viduitatem*"—which is anterior to any of the Abbot of Rhuys.

Lobineau observes that anyone who studies the writings of Gildas must be struck with the burning zeal, divine science, prophetic vision, and intrepidity which are the characteristics of an apostle. The refinement of a polished writer and the prolixity of a rhetorician may be absent, but the words of the holy abbot are burning with faith and charity, and produce the conviction that they proceed from the pen of a saint.

Gildas as a writer. The works of Gildas may be found in the

"*Cursus Completus Patrum,*" edited by the Abbé Migne, Paris. They were composed in the retirement of Brittany, probably about the year 543. A desire to serve mankind, and the repeated entreaties of his monastic brethren, induced him, as he mentions in his Preface, to undertake his difficult task.[1] "Wherefore, in zeal for the house of God and for His holy law, and constrained by the reasonings of my own thoughts and the entreaties of my brethren, I now discharge the debt so long demanded of me; humble, indeed, in style, but faithful, as I think, and friendly to all Christ's youthful soldiers, though severe and insupportable to foolish apostates. The former, if I am not mistaken, will receive the same with tears, flowing from the love of God; but the latter will receive them with such sorrow as is extorted from the indignation and pusillanimity of a convicted conscience."

After a touching Preface, in which Gildas, like Jeremias, weeps over the ruin of his country, the destruction of the Church, and the slaughter and captivity of his countrymen, he gives a synopsis of the history of Britain, in twenty-six chapters. Then we find letters of rebuke to several British chieftains, and, last of all, the "*Increpatio ad Clerum.*"

The severe reproaches to the clergy were, as Butler observes, addressed to the ministers of the

---

[1] "Gildas." Translated by J. Giles, D.C.L., Oxford.

Church in North Britain. Wales, especially the South, was governed by saintly bishops and priests, whom Gildas would have looked upon as his exemplars. This period was a continuation of the time of Dubricius, Illtyd, Cadoc, David, Teilo, Samson, Padarn, Daniel of Bangor, and Oudoceus.

More glorious days than these had never dawned for the Church of Wales. Never had she produced such a number of saints as during the life of Gildas; although his vocation seems to have been more the condemnation of crime than the illustration of the beauty of virtue.

Extracts from the works of Gildas. In case any of our readers may wish for an example of the style of Gildas, we copy the following passage of his "Epistle to the Chieftains":—[1]

"Britain has kings, but they are tyrants. She has judges, but unrighteous ones, generally engaged in plunder and rapine, but who always prey upon the innocent. Whenever they exert themselves to avenge or to protect, it is sure to be in the favour of robbers and criminals. They abound in wives, and yet are addicted to fornication and adultery. They are ready to take oaths, and as often perjure themselves; they make a vow, and almost immediately falsify it. They engage in wars, but their wars are unjust, and waged against their own countrymen. They rigorously prosecute thieves throughout the

---

(1) Translation by J. A. Giles, Oxford.

country, but entertain at their own table those who are truly robbers, whom they not only cherish but reward. They are bountiful in alms, but nullify them by the multiplicity of their crimes. They occupy the seat of justice, but rarely attend to the right rule of judgment; they despise the innocent, if humble, but seize every occasion of exalting the evil-minded, the proud, murderers, adulterers, and enemies of God, who deserve to be destroyed and their names forgotten. Many prisoners are confined within their gaols, loaded with irons, but this is the result of treachery rather than of just punishment of crime. And when they have taken an oath before the altar, in the name of God, they depart, and think no more of the holy altar than if it were merely a heap of stones."

Having rebuked Constantine, Prince of Cornwall, for his many sins, which may be summed up in the murder of two royal youths and their attendants, which murder was committed before the altar; of casting off his lawful wife; of violating several oaths, sworn at the foot of the altar, whilst calling on God and on the blessed Virgin to witness his sincerity, Gildas invites this Prince to repentance in the following touching manner:— *Constantine rebuked.*

"Why do you remain insensible whilst you murder your own soul? Why do you wilfully kindle for yourself the eternal fires of hell? Why, like a bitter enemy, do you stab yourself with your own sword, and pierce yourself with your own javelin? When will your appetite be satisfied with those cups of poison? Look backwards, I beseech you, for you are labouring and bowed down by a heavy burden, and God, as He has promised, will give you ease. All who desire can come to him. *He does not will the death of the sinner, but rather that he be converted and live.* *Unloose,* as the Prophet says, O, captive son of Sion, the *bonds from off thy neck.* Return, I pray you, from the regions of sin to your most loving Father, who, when his son rejects the food of swine and dreads the danger of dying from famine, kills the fatted calf and brings forth the festal robe and royal ring to honour the penitent. Then you shall begin to taste of heavenly hope, and feel *how sweet is the Lord.* But if you despise this advice, know for certain that in a short time you will find yourself engulphed and burning in the darksome floods of hell, out of which there is no redemption."

In order to understand Gildas fully—to appreciate his nature, his temper, his love, his justice, the manner, somewhat rude, yet stamped with Divine charity, in which he expresses his thoughts—we must read his reprimand to Maelgwn.

Epistle to Maglocune Maelgwyn, King of North Wales.

It commences in the following forcible language:—" Oh, thou dragon of the island, who hast deprived many kings of their dominions and of their lives, though thou occupiest the last place in my writings, thou art first in mischief. Thou exceedest many in power, as also in malice. Thou art more liberal in gifts than others, and also more licentious in sin. Thou art strong in arms, but still stronger in accomplishing the destruction of thine own soul. Maglocune, why art thou (as though inflamed with wine of the grapes of Sodom) revelling in the black pool of thine offences? Why dost thou wilfully heap a mountain of sins upon thy royal shoulders? Why dost thou show thyself to the King of kings, who has bestowed upon thee both power and physical strength beyond almost every other king in Britain, not equally superior in virtue than the others, but rather the contrary, for thy sins are much worse."[1]

Then the holy monk proceeds to enumerate such as were public and known of the evil deeds of this prince. "Didst thou not, even in thine early youth, oppress the king, thine uncle, and his soldiers with sword, spear, and fire, having no regard to the words of the Prophet, which say, 'The blood-thirsty and deceitful man shall not live out half his days. . . . Woe be to thee who spoilest, and shalt not thou thyself be spoiled?'"

Gildas then goes on to describe how Maelgwn, being torn by remorse, entered the cloister, meditated on the Ritual of the Lord and on the *rules of the monks*, and finally took the vows of

[1] "Gildas," translated by J. A. Giles, Oxford.

religion, with a firm intention of observing them faithfully, giving joy to the Church and benefitting his own soul.

Maelgwn did not persevere in the religious life, but, giving ear to the devil, *the father of all castaways*, he threw off the habit of the cloister. His conversion had given joy to heaven and earth, and his return to evil ways was the cause of grief and lamentation.

Gildas then contrasts the two phases of the life of this prince. Instead of listening to the praises of God, sweetly chanted by the soldiers of the Lord, or sounded forth by instruments of ecclesiastical melody, he now hearkens with pleasure to his own praise, issuing from the mouths of the drunken votaries of Bacchus. If, whilst residing in the cloister, this unfortunate prince put a check on his passions, the moment he left it he cast all restraint aside and perpetrated every imaginable crime. Violating his religious vow of continence, he seduced the wife of his own nephew, and finally murdered his own lawful wife and his nephew also, whose widow he afterwards married publicly, to the great scandal of every honest man in Wales.

In reference to this event, Gildas writes:—
" What holy person is there who would not weep and lament at hearing such a history? What priest whose heart lieth open before God would not, whilst listening to it, exclaim with the Prophet, ' Who shall give water to my head and

to my eyes a fountain of tears, that day and night I may bewail my people who are destroyed?'"

The objurgation is carried on by showing to the guilty prince how, in the Old Testament, God punished such sins, as in the cases of Saul, David, Solomon, etc.

There is some analogy between St. Jerome and Gildas, both in turn of mind and mode of expressing thoughts. They inveigh in equally strong terms against the vices of the society of their day. St. Jerome did not spare the upper classes of Rome any more than Gildas the aristocracy of Britain. These two monks, in their independence of heart, did not shrink from the duty, no matter how unpleasant, of exposing the disorders of mankind. *Certain resemblance between St. Jerome and Gildas as writers.*

St. Jerome's style of writing was more elegant than that of Gildas, but both were perfect masters of the science of God and knowledge of Scripture, which is evident from the happy quotations that illustrate every page of their writings.

It must not be inferred from the works of St. Jerome that everyone in Rome was unworthy; many of the most illustrious inhabitants of that city followed him to the cloister, and placed all their earthly possessions at his disposal.

The same assertion may be made with regard to Britain in the days of Gildas. Never was Wales more fruitful in saints, whose lives are recorded in our hagiographies, and whose memories are commemorated in the Breviaries and Missals of the Catholic Church.

We cannot deny the statement of the saint as regards the murders and immoralities of certain princes, and perhaps of many other persons; but in every society there exists two classes of men—the good and the bad. This division commenced with the two first children born of Adam—Cain and Abel. In this world two cities have always existed—Jerusalem and Babylon—the city of God, and that of Satan.

In our own lifetime we have over and over again heard that the British race had degenerated far beyond any other nation. More than once we felt shocked at this assertion, and could not help remarking that those who judge so hastily have never thoroughly studied the ancient history of this country.

As compared with other races, such as Gauls, Italians, and Spaniards, who, like them, were converted to Christ, we cannot see why the Britons of the fifth and sixth centuries should be considered extraordinarily wicked and exceeding in crime their brethren in other parts of Christendom.

If we read the description given by Montalembert of the first Merovingians in France, of the Visigoths in Spain, and of the social state of Italy, and then turn to Britain, we shall not find her so much behind other countries which also had been overrun by new races.

British Princes, like many of their compeers in our own times, exhibited in their conduct a strange mixture of virtue and abominable vice. Thus, Constantine the First, who was rebuked by Gildas, is said to have become a monk and apostle; Maelgwyn, notwithstanding his vices, granted land to churches, was the friend of St. Cadoc, his confessor, and, though he persecuted St. Kentigern, gave assistance to his monastic brethren. Pebiau, of Herefordshire, the grandfather of St. Dubricius, could not control his passion of anger, but repented, and helped in the good works of his grandchild, St. Dubricius. Gwynlyw, father of St. Cadoc, carried off his wife, Gwladys, by force from the home of her parents, and yet ended his days as a hermit on Stowe Hill, Newport.

These chieftains were more expert in handling the sword than in controlling their passions; being Christians, however, by baptism, the grace of the Sacrament, sooner or later, brought them to repentance; and, though the early Princes of Glamorgan were not exempt from crime, yet their children and grandchildren led exemplary lives in the cloister, such as we observe in Samson, Maglorius, and others.

Morgan, who was excommunicated by Bishop Oudoceus for the crime of murder and perjury, bestowed a code of wise laws upon his country.

Gildas and the political state of Britain.

Gildas was perfectly correct in his description of the vices of his countrymen. When left to themselves, after the departure of the Romans, the British chieftains did not exhibit those patriotic virtues so necessary to the safety of a country, and, consequently, deserved the following reproaches which issued from the pen of the Abbot of Rhuys:—

"It has been, and still is, the custom of our nation to be powerless in repelling foreign foes, but active and bold in kindling and carrying on civil war.

"Patriotism and union are the life of a nation. A city divided against itself cannot stand."

It is beyond doubt that the ancient chieftains of Britain allowed their ambition and private disputes to interfere with their national spirit.

Having studied the writings of Gildas, let the reader peruse those of Geoffrey of Monmouth. Though a Briton in sympathy, the events narrated by this author tell the same unfortunate tale. Thus, Vortigern induces Constans, a monk of Royal blood, to throw aside the monastic habit in order to undertake the government of the island, as he considered that the weak prince would be a tool in his hands. Later on, he caused him to be assassinated, and assuming the royal power himself, called in the aid of the Saxons to enable him to consolidate his throne. Becoming enamoured of a Saxon princess, he, through her wiles, was persuaded to throw open the country to foreign adventurers.

When Germanus, in his crusade against

Pelagianism, visited Britain, the conduct of some of the British princes grieved him to the *heart;* and the holy Bishop could point to painful facts when desirous of proving the necessity of grace to enable mankind to curb their wild passions.

Well could he say, "Look around and behold the state of man when unassisted by Divine grace. When left to himself there can be no greater slave to carnal passions, ambition, deceit, and treachery; murder, immorality in all its varieties, cunning, avarice, exaction, and intemperance are his masters."

When religion and the love of God dies out in the heart of a man, it is vain to expect either patriotism or love of country. Love of self then becomes the dominant sentiment, and to that idol he will basely sacrifice all that is noble and loyal.

However unpolished some persons may consider the writings of St. Gildas, a lover of truth and uprightness overlooks all deficiencies in admiration for the saint, whose every word evinces his love for God and sorrow at seeing the Divine laws despised and trampled under foot.

Gildas was a priest after the Lord's own heart, one who, like Moses, Elias, and St. Paul, bore the brunt of every battle in the interest of his Master.

A true priest is expected to excel in love and fortitude. His duty is to stand sentinel on the walls of the city of God, and defend it against His enemies. Were he to witness their advance without sounding the alarm, he would not be a soldier worthy of Christ.

"*Clama, necesses; quasi tuba exalta vocem tuam, et annuntia populo meo scelera eorum et domui Jacob peccata eorum,*" says Isaias the Prophet. (Isa. lviii.)[1] When surrounded with iniquity we must denounce it. No matter what opposition we may meet with, we must not allow ourselves to be put to silence. The more stubborn our enemy, the more resolute must be the front we oppose to his attacks.

Woe to the priest who, either directly or indirectly, connives at the sins of the people. Did St. John the Baptist hold his peace and look calmly on the vices of Herod?

St. Gildas had imbibed the spirit of the saints, and, like them, did not shrink from denouncing the sins of his brethren and countrymen.

The Church of God is not surrendered to her enemies as long as she possesses souls enkindled with the love and devotion which burned in the heart of the saintly Abbot of Rhuys.

The feast of St. Gildas is celebrated on the eleventh of May, and was also kept on January twenty-ninth. His name is invoked in the English Litanies.

(1) Cry, cease not; lift up thy voice like a trumpet, and show my people their wicked doings, and the house of Jacob their sins.

www.ingramcontent.com/pod-product-compliance
Lightning Source LLC
Chambersburg PA
CBHW021227300426
44111CB00007B/450